EVERYMAN'S LIBRARY
EDITED BY ERNEST RHYS

POETRY
& DRAMA

THE POEMS OF KEATS

THE PUBLISHERS OF *EVERYMAN'S LIBRARY* WILL BE PLEASED TO SEND FREELY TO ALL APPLICANTS A LIST OF THE PUBLISHED AND PROJECTED VOLUMES TO BE COMPRISED UNDER THE FOLLOWING THIRTEEN HEADINGS:

TRAVEL ❧ SCIENCE ❧ FICTION
THEOLOGY & PHILOSOPHY
HISTORY ❧ CLASSICAL
FOR YOUNG PEOPLE
ESSAYS ❧ ORATORY
POETRY & DRAMA
BIOGRAPHY
REFERENCE
ROMANCE

IN FOUR STYLES OF BINDING: CLOTH, FLAT BACK, COLOURED TOP; LEATHER, ROUND CORNERS, GILT TOP; LIBRARY BINDING IN CLOTH, & QUARTER PIGSKIN

LONDON: J. M. DENT & SONS, LTD.
NEW YORK: E. P. DUTTON & CO.

POETS ARE THE TRUMPETS WHICH SING TO BATTLE. POETS ARE THE UNACKNOWLEDGED LEGISLATORS OF THE WORLD. SHELLEY

The POEMS OF JOHN KEATS

EVERY MAN I WILL GO WITH THEE & BE THY GVIDE

IN THY MOST NEED TO GO BY THY SIDE

LONDON: PUBLISHED by J·M·DENT & SONS·L^{TD} AND IN NEW YORK BY E·P·DUTTON & CO

FIRST ISSUE OF THIS EDITION . *April* 1906
REPRINTED . . . . *October* 1906; *July* 1909
January 1911 .

CONTENTS

SHORTER POEMS PUBLISHED IN 1817

	PAGE
DEDICATION. To LEIGH HUNT, Esq.	xxiii
"I stood tip-toe upon a little hill"	1
Specimen of an Induction to a Poem	7
Calidore. A Fragment	9
To some Ladies	13
On Receiving a Curious Shell and a Copy of Verses from the same Ladies	14
To Georgiana Augusta Wylie. "Hadst thou liv'd in the days of old"	15
To Hope	17
Imitation of Spenser	18
Three Sonnets on Woman. "Woman! when I behold thee flippant, vain"	19

EPISTLES

To George Felton Mathew	21
To my Brother George	23
To Charles Cowden Clarke	27

SONNETS

To my Brother George	31
To ****** "Had I a man's fair form"	31
Written on the Day Mr Leigh Hunt left Prison	32
"How many bards gild the lapses of time!"	32
To a Friend who sent me some Roses	32
To G. A. W. [Georgiana Augusta Wylie]	33
"O Solitude! if I must with thee dwell"	33
To my Brothers	34
Keen Fitful Gusts are Whispering Here and There	34
To One Who has been Long in City Pent	35
On First Looking into Chapman's Homer	35
On Leaving some Friends at an Early Hour	36

PAGE
Addressed to Haydon 36
Addressed to the Same 36
On the Grasshopper and Cricket 37
To Kosciusko 37
Happy is England 38
Sleep and Poetry 38

POEMS PUBLISHED IN 1820

Ode to a Nightingale 49
Ode on a Grecian Urn 51
Ode to Psyche 52
To Fancy 54
To the Poets. "Bards of Passion and of Mirth" . . 57
Lines on the Mermaid Tavern 58
Robin Hood. To a Friend 58
To Autumn 60
Ode on Melancholy 61
Sonnet to Byron 62
Sonnet to Chatterton 62
Sonnet to Spenser 63
Ode to Apollo 63
Sonnet to a Young Lady who sent me a Laurel Crown . 65
Hymn to Apollo 65
Sonnet. "As from the darkening gloom" . . 66
Sonnet. "Oh! how I love, on a fair summer's eve" . 67
Sonnet. "After dark vapours have oppress'd our plains" . 67
Sonnet. Written on the blank space of a leaf at the end of
    Chaucer's Tale of The Flowre and the Lefe . . 67
Sonnet on Seeing the Elgin Marbles for the First Time . 68
Sonnet to Haydon (with the above) 68
Sonnet on a Picture of Leander 69
Lines to —— "Think not of it, sweet one, so; —" . 69
Lines. "Unfelt, unheard, unseen" 70
Sonnet on the Sea 70
Sonnet on Leigh Hunt's Poem, The "Story of Rimini" . 71

FRAGMENTS

To Reynolds. "Where's the Poet? show him! show him!" . 72
Modern Love 72
Fragment of "The Castle Builder" 73

Contents

	PAGE
Welcome joy, and welcome sorrow	74
Sonnet to a Cat	75
Lines on a Lock of Milton's Hair	75
Sonnet written before re-reading " King Lear "	77
"When I have Fears that I may cease to be"	77
Playful Lines. " Hence Burgundy, Claret and Port"	78
Sonnet to the Nile	79
Sonnet to a Lady seen for a Few Moments at Vauxhall	79
Answer to a Sonnet by J. H. Reynolds. " Blue ! 'Tis the life of Heaven "	80
Sonnet to J. H. Reynolds	80
To Reynolds. "O Thou whose face hath felt the Winter's wind"	81
Sonnet. The Human Seasons	81
Extracts from an Opera :—	
"O ! were I one of the Olympian Twelve	82
Daisy's Song	82
Folly's Song	82
Song. " The stranger lighted from his steed "	83
"Asleep ! O sleep a little while, white pearl !"	84
Faery Song. "Shed no tear ! oh shed no tear !"	84
Faery Song. "Ah ! woe is me ! poor silver-wing !"	85
Sonnet to Homer	85
Song. "Spirit here that reignest !"	86

POEMS WRITTEN AT TEIGNMOUTH

In a Letter to Haydon	87
Where be You Going, you Devon Maid ?	88
Teignmouth Epistle to John Hamilton Reynolds	88
Dawlish Fair	91
Fragment of an Ode to Reynolds, May 1818	92
Acrostic. Georgiana Augusta Keats	92
Sonnet on Visiting the Tomb of Burns	93
Meg Merrilies	93
Sonnet on Ailsa Rock	94
Sonnet Written in Burns' Cottage	95
Walking in Scotland	95
Staffa	97
Sonnet Written upon the Top of Ben Nevis	98
Fragment of a Sonnet from Ronsard	99
A Prophecy—To his Brother George in America	99

Contents

	PAGE
"In a drear-nighted December"	101
Stanza written at the close of Canto 2, Book 5, of Spenser's *Faerie Queen*	102
The Eve of Saint Mark	102
Ode to Fanny	105
Sonnet to Sleep	107
Song. "Hush, hush ! Tread softly !"	107
Song. "I had a dove, and the sweet dove died"	108
Ode on Indolence	108
Sonnet. "Why did I laugh to-night?"	110
Sonnet on a Dream	110
Spenserian Stanzas on Charles Armitage Brown	111
Ballad. La Belle Dame sans Merci	112
Song of Four Fairies	113
Two Sonnets on Fame. "Fame like a wayward girl"	116
"How fevered is the man"	116
Sonnet on the Sonnet. "If by dull rhymes"	117
A Party of Lovers	117
Sonnet. "The day is gone"	118
Lines to Fanny	118
Sonnet to Fanny. "I cry your mercy"	120
Sonnet Written on a Summer Evening	120
Keats' last Sonnet. "Bright Star ! would I were stedfast as thou art—"	121
The Eve of St. Agnes	122
Lamia	133
Isabella, or the Pot of Basil	151
Endymion	164
Hyperion	264
Hyperion, a Vision	286
Otho the Great	299
The Cap and Bells, or the Jealousies	356
King Stephen	377

INTRODUCTION

AT the beginning of the few brief years of extraordinary happiness which Keats enjoyed, before his fatal illness declared itself, he wrote from Carisbrooke (18th April 1817): "I find I cannot exist without poetry—without eternal poetry—half the day will not do. . . ." Here is the clue to the whole artistic career—some five or six years long—of the most wholly and completely obsessed English poet in the whole calendar. Even Shelley, whom one ranks with him by a natural association in time and poetry, thought first of liberty and liberty's revolt; while Coleridge looked to philosophy, and Wordsworth loved Nature and himself her votary, more than that spirit of poetry which for Keats was a breathing, embodied creature and wore a visible garment. This devotion of his it was that helped him to triumph as he did over gross circumstance—the rank habits of the Georgian middle-class, the familiarity of Mr Charles Brown (who wished to play family-doctor to the muse), and all the mixed sentimentalism and brutality of the years succeeding Waterloo. It brought him safe through his adventures of youth, subdued the taunts of the evil-speakers, and procured him his claim to nobility before he died ; much as the knight in the romance turned by force of chivalry the damsel Maledisant into the damsel Bienpensant and gained a castle. It almost redeems the things in his history that we would rather have never known, and that the painful economy of his editors has insisted on our knowing. It even casts a glamour over the weaker side of his poetry—its conceits, lovesick anguish, borrowed finery, and the rest.

The reality of the service and experience in the art with which he followed his genius, can be tested in various ways. The greatest sign of all is to be seen in the amazing intellectual and imaginative advance from "Endymion" to "Hyperion." In the one, almost every trick of egregious fancy and the ornamental art of rhyme is employed in its extravagance along with the real and imaginative faculties of the mind. Traces of the friend of Brown and the disciple of Leigh Hunt, traces of the true poet and the true Keats, are to be found side by side in this passage of "Endymion," the invocation to Arethusa :—

> "Dear maiden, steal
> Blushing into my soul, and let us fly
> These dreary caverns for the open sky.
> I will delight thee all my winding course,
> From the green sea up to my hidden source
> About Arcadian forests ; and will show
> The channels where my coolest waters flow
> Through mossy rocks ; where 'mid exuberant green
> I roam in pleasant darkness, more unseen
> Than Saturn in his exile ; where I brim
> Round flowery islands, and take thence a skim
> Of mealy sweets, which myriads of bees
> Buzz from their honey'd wings : and thou shouldst please
> Thyself to choose the richest, where we might
> Be incense-pillow'd every summer night.
> Doff all sad fears, thou white deliciousness,
> And let us be thus comforted ; unless
> Thou couldst rejoice to see my hopeless stream
> Hurry distracted from Sol's temperate beam,
> And pour to death along some hungry sands."

Turn on, then, to a classic passage in the same poem, where Keats really finds himself, and grows equal to his argument :—

> "Wherever beauty dwells,
> In gulf or aerie, mountains or deep dells,
> In light, in gloom, in star or blazing sun,
> Thou pointest out the way, and straight 'tis won.
> Amid his toil thou gavest Leander breath ;
> Thou leddest Orpheus through the gleams of death ;

Thou madest Pluto bear thin element :
And now, O winged Chieftain ! thou hast sent
A moonbeam to the deep, deep water-world,
To find Endymion."

Or to the Bacchantic interlude in Book IV., where you have so simple and choice an echo of the "merry-melancholy" note, heard in some old English country songs :—

"To sorrow
        I bade good-morrow
And thought to leave her far away behind ;
        But cheerly, cheerly,
            She loves me dearly ;
She is so constant to me, and so kind.
        I would deceive her,
        And so leave her,
But ah ! she is so constant and so kind."

In "Endymion," Keats is trying his hand ; it is his young experiment, full of delights and crudities, both of idea and style. In "Hyperion" he has mastered his instrument : in its greater passages his music and thought ring true, as they do in his high compeers and in Milton, his master, making one realise the discipline that he put himself through and that made him say : "The Genius of Poetry must work out its own salvation in a man. It cannot be matured by law and precept, but by sensation and watchfulness in itself." He had the courage of his errors too ; he knew "Endymion's" defect:—"In 'Endymion' I leaped headlong into the sea," he said afterwards, "and thereby have become better acquainted with the Soundings, the quicksands, and the rocks, than if I had stayed upon the green shore and piped a silly pipe." What Soundings, and what avoiding of rocks and sands there had been, one perceives, as reading in "Hyperion," one comes upon a speech like that of Cœlus, speaking, clear and sonorous, out of universal space :—

"Art thou, too, near such doom ? vague fear there is :
For I have seen my sons most unlike Gods.

Divine ye were created, and divine
In sad demeanour, solemn, undisturb'd.
Unruffled, like high Gods, ye lived and ruled :
Now I behold in you fear, hope, and wrath ;
Actions of rage and passion ; even as
I see them, on the mortal world beneath,
In men who die.—This is the grief, O Son !
Sad sign of ruin, sudden dismay, and fall !
Yet do thou strive ; as thou art capable,
As thou canst move about, an evident God,
And canst oppose to each malignant hour
Ethereal presence :—I am but a voice ;
My life is but the life of winds and tides,—
No more than winds and tides can I avail :—
But thou canst.—Be thou therefore in the van
Of circumstance ; yea, seize the arrow's barb
Before the tense string murmur."

There is surely the greatest writing in that kind which
a poet of Keats' years has ever given us. The poetry that
is re-born out of old poetry and that brings new blood into
the literary antiquity never rose to a more majestic harmony.
But if this is in too august a mode, try " The Eve of St.
Mark," which he left unfinished at his death, and which one
of the most accomplished and original women I have known
has termed " Pre-Raphaelitism in a nutshell."

"Upon a Sabbath-day it fell ;
Twice holy was the Sabbath-bell,
That call'd the folk to evening prayer,
The city streets were clean and fair
From wholesome drench of April rains,
And, on the western window panes,
The chilly sunset faintly told
Of unmatured green, valleys cold,
Of the green thorny bloomless hedge,
Of rivers new with spring-tide sedge,
Of primroses by shelter'd rills,
And daisies on the aguish hills." . . .

There is no consolation in thinking that the poet who
was capable of writing in the two different but equally
authentic modes of "Hyperion" and "The Eve of St.

Mark," when he died had written his best. He was developing, advancing by great strides in his art, up to the very eve of his death. He had left behind his early masters, even those who, like Leigh Hunt, had largely aided him both for good and evil; he had thrown away the mistaken guitar that Leigh Hunt lent him, and turned to other instruments. So we read that on finishing "Endymion" in November 1817, Keats had taken up expressly the study of Shakespeare's Sonnets.

"One of the three books I have with me is 'Shakespeare's Poems,'" he wrote on one occasion to Reynolds. "I never found so many beauties in the Sonnets; they seem to be full of fine things said unintentionally—in the intensity of working out conceits. Is this to be borne? Hark ye!—

> 'When lofty trees I see barren of leaves,
> Which erst from heat did canopy the herd,
> And Summer's green all girded up in sheaves,
> Borne on the bier with white and bristly beard.'

". . . He overwhelms a genuine lover of poetry with all manner of abuse, talking about—

> 'A poet's rage
> And stretched metre of an antique song,'

which, by the by, will be a capital motto for my poem, won't it? He speaks too of 'Time's antique pen,' and 'April's first-born flowers,' and 'Death's eternal cold.'—By the Whim-King! I'll give you a stanza, because it is not material in connection, and when I wrote it I wanted you to give your vote, pro or con

> "Chrystalline Brother of the belt of Heaven,
> Aquarius! to whom King Jove hath given
> Two liquid pulse-streams, 'stead of feather'd wings—
> Two fan-like fountains—thine illuminings
> For Dian-play:
> Dissolve the frozen purity of air;
> Let thy white shoulders, silvery and bare,
> Show cold through wat'ry pinions : make more bright
> The Star-Queen's crescent on her marriage-night ;
> Haste, haste away!"

In the following winter, Keats was able to make study, too, of Shakespeare on the stage; he even acted as dramatic critic in *The Champion* on one or two occasions, during his friend Reynolds' absence. Criticising *Retribution: or, the Chieftain's Daughter*, a forgotten and a very poor play, in which Macready acted at Covent Garden Theatre, in January 1818, Keats breaks into this most unaccustomed dramatic-critic's vein:—

"What exquisite names did our old dramatists christen their plays withal! The title of an old play gives us a direct taste and surmise of its inwards, as the first lines of the *Paradise Lost* smack of the great Poem. The names of old plays are Dantean inscriptions over the gates of hell, heaven or purgatory. Some of such enduring pathos that in these days we may not for decency utter them, 'honor dishonorable'! In these days we may but think of passion's seventh heaven, and but just mention how crystalline the third is. The old dramatists and their title-pages are old Britain kings and their provinces. The fore page of a love play was ever 'to Cupid's service bowed,' as *The Mad Lover, The Broken Heart*—or spake its neighbourhood to the 'shores of old romance,' as *The Winter's Tale, The Two Noble Kinsmen*."

One sees from this that Keats could never have become a mere formal, exemplary critic and reviewer. One is driven by it to speculate, too, about his future service as a dramatic poet, had he only lived. For the poor plays he wrote with Brown looking on, are no index to the range of his dramatic powers; and that he was potential on this side, too, no one who reads his poetry can doubt.

The fact is, if you will re-read his poems, in the light of his biography and his letters, the immensity of the reserve fund of powers casually indicated or half revealed, which he carried to his grave with him, must impress itself on you at point after point. He began by a fashion of verse which depends on an ornamentation in words and fanciful ideas. Compare him with that austere Cumbrian, Leigh Hunt's opposite, to whom at first he felt antipathetic, and you see his early disposition. He brought splendid clothes to poetry; while Wordsworth worked with the very bones of language, with organic simplicity, and sometimes then thought an old coat good enough for the lyric muse. But Keats was content, like Wordsworth, to turn to Milton; and you realise his latent strength in that discipleship. You realise it too in his confession, as he stands at the feet of Homer:—

> " Standing aloof in giant ignorance,
>   Of thee I hear and of the Cyclades,
> As one who sits ashore and longs perchance
>   To visit dolphin-coral in deep seas.
> So thou wast blind!—but then the veil was rent;
>   For Jove uncurtain'd Heaven to let thee live,
> And Neptune made for thee a spermy tent,
>   And Pan made sing for thee his forest-hive;
> Aye, on the shores of darkness there is light,
>   And precipices show untrodden green;
> There is a budding morrow in midnight;
>   There is a triple sight in blindness keen;
> Such seeing hadst thou, as it once befel,
> To Dian, Queen of Earth, and Heaven, and Hell."

You realise it too by this boyish confession of faith, uttered in all the simplicity of his heart, in one of his letters to Reynolds:—

" I am certain of nothing but of the holiness of the heart's affections, and the truth of Imagination. What the Imagination seizes as Beauty must be Truth, whether it existed before or not;—for I have the same idea of all our passions as of Love: they are all, in their sublime, creative of essential Beauty. In a word, you may know my favourite speculation by my first book, and the little song I sent in my last, which is a representation from the fancy of the probable mode of operating in these matters. The

Imagination may be compared to Adam's dream : he awoke and found it truth. I am more zealous in this affair, because I have never yet been able to perceive how anything can be known for truth by consecutive reasoning—and yet [so] it must be. Can it be that even the greatest philosopher ever arrived at his goal without putting aside numerous objections? However it may be, O for a life of sensations rather than of thoughts! It is "a Vision in the form of Youth," a shadow of reality to come—and this consideration has further convinced me—for it has come as auxiliary to another favourite speculation of mine—that we shall enjoy ourselves hereafter by having what we called happiness on earth repeated in a finer tone. And yet such a fate can only befall those who delight in sensation, rather than hunger, as you do, after Truth. Adam's dream will do here, and seems to be a conviction that Imagination and its empyreal reflection is the same as human life and its spiritual repetition. But, as I was saying, the simple imaginative mind may have its rewards in the repetition of its own silent working coming continually on the spirit with a fine suddenness.

"To compare great things with small, have you never, by being surprised with an old melody, in a delicious place, by a delicious voice, *felt* over again your very speculations and surmises at the time it first operated on your soul? Do you not remember forming to yourself the singer's face—more beautiful than it was possible, and yet, with the elevation of the moment, you did not think so? Even then you were mounted on the wings of Imagination, so high that the prototype must be hereafter—that delicious face you will see. Sure this cannot be exactly the case with a complex mind—one that is imaginative, and at the same time careful of its fruits,—who would exist partly on sensation, partly on thought—to whom it is necessary that 'years should bring the philosophic mind?' Such a one I consider yours, and therefore it is necessary to your eternal happiness that you not only drink this old wine of Heaven, which I shall call the redigestion of our most ethereal musings upon earth, but also increase in knowledge, and know all things."

The young poet who wrote this was as much a philosopher as any that ever tried to state his belief, human and divine, but he was too fine an artist to let his philosophy over-ride his poetry. By his poetry, and that only half or a quarter fulfilled, we see him to have been potentially great,—great in intellect as well as fantasy; and count his death as one of the irreparable darkest calamities of literature, to be ranked with the death of Marlowe and the drowning of Shelley.

In a companion volume to this it is intended to give presently Lord Houghton's *Life and Letters*, with certain additions; and as his biography in full will appear there, it is unnecessary to summarise it here. The following table gives his complete published works :—

Sonnets : "To Solitude "; "On First Looking into Chapman's Homer "; "To Kosciusko"; "After Dark Vapors have Oppress'd Our Plains "; "To Haydon"; "On Seeing the Elgin Marbles"; "Written on a Blank Space at the End of Chaucer's Tale of The Flowre and the Lefe"; "On the Grass-hopper and Cricket," *Examiner*, 1816-1817. Poems, 1817. Sonnet : "On the Sea" "Articles on Kean as a Shakespearian Actor, and in Richard III.," *Champion*, 1817. "Endymion," 1818; "Ode to a Nightingale," *Annals of the Fine Arts*, 1819. Sonnets : "To Ailsa Rock"; "The Human Seasons," Leigh Hunt's *Literary Pocket-Book*, 1819. "Lamia, Isabella, The Eve of St. Agnes, and Other Poems" (including "Hyperion"), 1820. Sonnet : "A Dream after reading Dante's 'Paolo and Francesca'"; "La Belle Dame sans Merci," *Indicator*, 1820. "Ode on a Grecian Urn," *Annals of the Fine Arts*, 1820. Another version of Keats' "Hyperion," Ed. R. M. Milnes, vol. iii., *Philobiblion Society*, 1856-7. Hyperion : a facsimile of Keats' autograph, with MS. of "The Fall of Hyperion : a Dream," Ed. E. de Selincourt, *Clarendon Press*, 1905.

Other poems by Keats have appeared for the first time posthumously in *The Gem*, 1829; Hood's *Comic Annual*, 1830; Hood's *Magazine*, 1844; *Athenæum*, June 1873.

COLLECTED EDITIONS : The Poetical Works of Coleridge, Shelley and Keats, 1829. Poetical Works, Standard Library, 1840. Poetical Works with

Memoir by R. M. Milnes (Lord Houghton). 1854, 1871, 1876 (Aldine Ed.), 1883, with Memoir by W. M. Rossetti. 1872, 1880. The Poetical Works and Other Writings of John Keats, now first brought together, including poems and numerous letters not before published. Ed. H. B. Forman, 4 vols. 1883. By same Editor, Poetry and Prose (containing new matter), 1890. Complete Works, 1900-1.

Life, Letters, and Literary Remains, including most of the poems unpublished in Keats' lifetime : "Otho the Great," a tragedy ; "King Stephen," a fragment; "The Cap and Bells, or the Jealousies," a faëry tale, unfinished; "Some Miscellaneous Poems" (1815-1819), and his last Sonnet, Ed. R. M. Milnes, 1848. 1867. (without the *Literary Remains*, but with variant of "Hyperion.") Letters to Fanny Brawne, Ed. H. B. Forman, 1878, 1889. Letters to his Family and Friends, Ed. S. Colvin, 1891. Life of Keats, by W. M. Rossetti, 1887 ; Life, by Sidney Colvin (Eng. Men of Letters), 1887.

1906.

DEDICATION.

TO LEIGH HUNT, ESQ.

GLORY and Loveliness have pass'd away;
   For if we wander out in early morn,
   No wreathed incense do we see upborne
Into the east to meet the smiling day:
No crowd of nymphs soft-voiced and young and gay,
   In woven baskets bringing ears of corn,
   Roses, and pinks, and violets, to adorn
The shrine of Flora in her early May.
But there are left delights as high as these.
   And I shall ever bless my destiny,
That in a time when under pleasant trees
   Pan is no longer sought, I feel a free,
A leafy luxury, seeing I could please,
   With these poor offerings, a man like thee.

KEATS' POEMS

SHORTER POEMS
PUBLISHED IN 1817.

"I STOOD TIP-TOE UPON A LITTLE HILL."

" Places of nestling green for poets made."
—Story of Rimini.

I STOOD tip-toe upon a little hill,
The air was cooling, and so very still,
That the sweet buds which with a modest pride
Pull droopingly, in slanting curve aside,
Their scantly-leaved, and finely-tapering stems,
Had not yet lost their starry diadems
Caught from the early sobbing of the morn.
The clouds were pure and white as flocks new-shorn,
And fresh from the clear brook; sweetly they slept
On the blue fields of heaven, and then there crept
A little noiseless noise among the leaves,
Born of the very sigh that silence heaves:
For not the faintest motion could be seen
Of all the shades that slanted o'er the green.
There was wide wand'ring for the greediest eye,
To peer about upon variety;
Far round the horizon's crystal air to skim,
And trace the dwindled edgings of its brim;
To picture out the quaint, and curious bending
Of the fresh woodland alley never-ending;
Or by the bowery clefts, and leafy shelves,
Guess where the jaunty streams refresh themselves.
I gazed awhile, and felt as light and free
As though the fanning wings of Mercury
Had play'd upon my heels: I was light-hearted,
And many pleasures to my vision started;
So I straightway began to pluck a posey
Of luxuries bright, milky, soft, and rosy.
A bush of May-flowers with the bees about them;

A

Ah, sure no tasteful nook would be without them;
And let a lush laburnum oversweep them,
And let long grass grow round the roots, to keep them
Moist, cool, and green ; and shade the violets,
That they may bind the moss in leafy nets.

A filbert hedge with wildbriar overtwined,
And clumps of woodbine taking the soft wind
Upon their summer thrones ; there too should be
The frequent chequer of a youngling tree,
That with a score of light green brethren shoots
From the quaint mossiness of aged roots :
Round which is heard a spring-head of clear waters,
Babbling so wildly of its lovely daughters,
The spreading blue-bells : it may haply mourn
That such fair clusters should be rudely torn
From their fresh beds, and scatter'd thoughtlessly
By infant hands, left on the path to die.

Open afresh your round of starry folds,
Ye ardent marigolds !
Dry up the moisture from your golden lids,
For great Apollo bids
That in these days your praises should be sung
On many harps, which he has lately strung ;
And when again your dewiness he kisses,
Tell him, I have you in my world of blisses :
So haply when I rove in some far vale,
His mighty voice may come upon the gale.

Here are sweet peas, on tip-toe for a flight
With wings of gentle flush o'er delicate white,
And taper fingers catching at all things,
To bind them all about with tiny rings.
Linger awhile upon some bending planks
That lean against a streamlet's rushy banks,
And watch intently Nature's gentle doings:
They will be found softer than ringdoves' cooings.
How silent comes the water round that bend !
Not the minutest whisper does it send
To the o'erhanging sallows : blades of grass
Slowly across the chequer'd shadows pass.

Why, you might read two sonnets, ere they reach
To where the hurrying freshnesses aye preach
A natural sermon o'er their pebbly beds ;
Where swarms of minnows show their little heads,
Staying their wavy bodies 'gainst the streams,
To taste the luxury of sunny beams
Temper'd with coolness. How they ever wrestle
With their own sweet delight, and ever nestle
Their silver bellies on the pebbly sand !
If you but scantily hold out the hand,
That very instant not one will remain ;
But turn your eye, and they are there again.
The ripples seem right glad to reach those cresses,
And cool themselves among the em'rald tresses;
The while they cool themselves, they freshness give,
And moisture, that the bowery green may live :
So keeping up an interchange of favours,
Like good men in the truth of their behaviours.
Sometimes goldfinches one by one will drop
From low-hung branches : little space they stop.
But sip, and twitter, and their feathers sleek ;
Then off at once, as in a wanton freak :
Or perhaps, to show their black and golden wings,
Pausing upon their yellow flutterings.
Were I in such a place, I sure should pray
That nought less sweet might call my thoughts away,
Than the soft rustle of a maiden's gown
Fanning away the dandelion's down ;
Than the light music of her nimble toes
Patting against the sorrel as she goes.
How she would start, and blush, thus to be caught
Playing in all her innocence of thought !
O let me lead her gently o'er the brook,
Watch her half-smiling lips and downward look ;
O let me for one moment touch her wrist ;
Let me one moment to her breathing list ;
And as she leaves me, may she often turn
Her fair eyes looking through her locks auburne.
What next ? a tuft of evening primroses,
O'er which the mind may hover till it dozes ;
O'er which it well might take a pleasant sleep,
But that 'tis ever startled by the leap

Of buds into ripe flowers ; or by the flitting
Of divers moths, that aye their rest are quitting ;
Or by the moon lifting her silver rim
Above a cloud, and with a gradual swim
Coming into the blue with all her light.
O Maker of sweet poets ! dear delight
Of this fair world and all its gentle livers ;
Spangler of clouds, halo of crystal rivers,
Mingler with leaves, and dew and tumbling streams,
Closer of lovely eyes to lovely dreams,
Lover of loneliness, and wandering,
Of upcast eye, and tender pondering !
Thee must I praise above all other glories
That smile us on to tell delightful stories.
For what has made the sage or poet write
But the fair paradise of Nature's light ?
In the calm grandeur of a sober line,
We see the waving of the mountain pine ;
And when a tale is beautifully staid,
We feel the safety of a hawthorn glade :
When it is moving on luxurious wings,
The soul is lost in pleasant smotherings :
Fairy dewy roses brush against our faces,
And flowering laurels spring from diamond vases ;
O'erhead we see the jasmine and sweetbriar,
And bloomy grapes laughing from green attire,
While at our feet, the voice of crystal bubbles
Charms us at once away from all our troubles :
So that we feel uplifted from the world,
Walking upon the white clouds wreath'd and curl'd.
So felt he, who first told how Psyche went
On the smooth wind to realms of wonderment ;
What Psyche felt, and Love, when their full lips
First touch'd ; what amorous and fondling nips
They gave each other's cheeks ; with all their sighs,
And how they kist each other's tremulous eyes :
The silver lamp,—the ravishment—the wonder—
The darkness—loneliness—the fearful thunder ;
Their woes gone by, and both to heaven upflown,
To bow for gratitude before Jove's throne.
So did he feel, who pull'd the boughs aside,
That we might look into a forest wide,

To catch a glimpse of Fauns, and Dryades
Coming with softest rustle through the trees;
And garlands woven of flowers wild, and sweet,
Upheld on ivory wrists, or sporting feet:
Telling us how fair, trembling Syrinx fled
Arcadian Pan, with such a fearful dread.
Poor nymph,—poor Pan,—how he did weep to find
Naught but a lovely sighing of the wind
Along the reedy stream! a half-heard strain,
Full of sweet desolation—balmy pain.

What first inspir'd a bard of old to sing
Narcissus pining o'er the untainted spring
In some delicious ramble, he had found
A little space, with boughs all woven round;
And in the midst of all, a clearer pool
Than e'er reflected in its pleasant cool
The blue sky, here and there serenely peeping,
Through tendril wreaths fantastically creeping.
And on the bank a lonely flower he spied,
A meek and forlorn flower, with nought of pride,
Drooping its beauty o'er the watery clearness,
To woo its own sad image into nearness:
Deaf to light Zephyrus, it would not move;
But still would seem to droop, to pine, to love.
So while the poet stood in this sweet spot,
Some fainter gleamings o'er his fancy shot;
Nor was it long ere he had told the tale
Of young Narcissus, and sad Echo's bale.

Where had he been, from whose warm head outflew
That sweetest of all songs, that ever new,
That aye refreshing, pure deliciousness,
Coming ever to bless
The wanderer by moonlight? to him bringing
Shapes from the invisible world, unearthly singing
From out the middle air, from flowery nests,
And from the pillowy silkiness that rests
Full in the speculation of the stars.
Ah! surely he had burst our mortal bars:
Into some wond'rous region he had gone,
To search for thee, divine Endymion!

He was a Poet, sure a lover too,
Who stood on Latmus' top, what time there blew
Soft breezes from the myrtle vale below :
And brought, in faintness solemn, sweet and slow,
A hymn from Dian's temple ; while upswelling,
The incense went to her own starry dwelling.
But though her face was clear as infant's eyes,
Though she stood smiling o'er the sacrifice,
The Poet wept at her so piteous fate,
Wept that such beauty should be desolate :
So in fine wrath some golden sounds he won,
And gave meek Cynthia her Endymion.

Queen of the wide air ; thou most lovely queen
Of all the brightness that mine eyes have seen !
As thou exceedest all things in thy shine,
So every tale, does this sweet tale of thine.
O for three words of honey, that I might
Tell but one wonder of thy bridal night !

Where distant ships do seem to show their keels,
Phœbus awhile delay'd his mighty wheels,
And turn'd to smile upon thy bashful eyes,
Ere he his unseen pomp would solemnise.
The evening weather was so bright, and clear,
That men of health were of unusual cheer ;
Stepping like Homer at the trumpet's call,
Or young Apollo on the pedestal :
And lovely women were as fair and warm
As Venus looking sideways in alarm.
The breezes were ethereal, and pure,
And crept through half-closed lattices to cure
The languid sick ; it cool'd their fever'd sleep,
And soothed them into slumbers full and deep.
Soon they awoke clear-eyed : nor burned with thirsting,
Nor with hot fingers, nor with temples bursting :
And springing up, they met the wond'ring sight
Of their dear friends, nigh foolish with delight ;
Who feel their arms, and breasts, and kiss, and stare,
And on their placid foreheads part the hair.
Young men and maidens at each other gazed,
With hands held back, and motionless, amazed

To see the brightness in each other's eyes;
And so they stood, fill'd with a sweet surprise,
Until their tongues were loosed in poesy.
Therefore no lover did of anguish die:
But the soft numbers, in that moment spoken,
Made silken ties, that never may be broken.
Cynthia! I cannot tell the greater blisses
That follow'd thine, and thy dear shepherd's kisses:
Was there a poet born?—but now no more—
My wand'ring spirit must no farther soar.

SPECIMEN OF AN INDUCTION TO A POEM

Lo! I must tell a tale of chivalry;
For large white plumes are dancing in mine eye.
Not like the formal crest of latter days,
But bending in a thousand graceful ways;
So graceful, that it seems no mortal hand,
Or e'en the touch of Archimago's wand,
Could charm them into such an attitude.
We must think rather, that in playful mood
Some mountain breeze had turn'd its chief delight
To show this wonder of its gentle might.
Lo! I must tell a tale of chivalry;
For while I muse, the lance points slantingly
Athwart the morning air: some lady sweet,
Who cannot feel for cold her tender feet,
From the worn top of some old battlement
Hails it with tears, her stout defender sent;
And from her own pure self no joy dissembling,
Wraps round her ample robe with happy trembling.
Sometimes, when the good knight his rest could take,
It is reflected, clearly, in a lake,
With the young ashen boughs, 'gainst which it rests,
And th' half-seen mossiness of linnets' nests.
Ah! shall I ever tell its cruelty,
When the fire flashes from a warrior's eye,
And his tremendous hand is grasping it,
And his dark brow for very wrath is knit?
Or when his spirit, with more calm intent,

Leaps to the honours of a tournament,
And makes the gazers round about the ring
Stare at the grandeur of the balancing !
No, no ! this is far off :—then how shall I
Revive the dying tones of minstrelsy,
Which linger yet about lone gothic arches,
In dark green ivy, and among wild larches ?
How sing the splendour of the revelries,
When butts of wine are drank off to the lees ?
And that bright lance, against the fretted wall,
Beneath the shade of stately banneral,
Is slung with shining cuirass, sword, and shield ?
Where ye may see a spur in bloody field.
Light-footed damsels move with gentle paces
Round the wide hall, and show their happy faces ;
Or stand in courtly talk by fives and sevens :
Like those fair stars that twinkle in the heavens.
Yet must I tell a tale of chivalry :
Or wherefore comes that steed so proudly by ?
Wherefore more proudly does the gentle knight
Rein in the swelling of his ample might ?
Spenser ! thy brows are arched, open, kind,
And come like a clear sunrise to my mind ;
And always does my heart with pleasure dance,
When I think on thy noble countenance :
Where never yet was aught more earthly seen
Than the pure freshness of thy laurels green.
Therefore, great bard, I not so fearfully
Call on thy gentle spirit to hover nigh
My daring steps : or if thy tender care,
Thus startled unaware,
Be jealous that the foot of other wight
Should madly follow that bright path of light
Traced by thy lov'd Libertas ; he will speak,
And tell thee that my prayer is very meek ;
That I will follow with due reverence,
And start with awe at mine own strange pretence.
Him thou wilt hear ; so I will rest in hope
To see wide plains, fair trees, and lawny slope ;
The morn, the eve, the light, the shade, the flowers ;
Clear streams, smooth lakes, and overlooking towers.

CALIDORE

A FRAGMENT

YOUNG Calidore is paddling o'er the lake;
His healthful spirit eager and awake
To feel the beauty of a silent eve,
Which seem'd full loth this happy world to leave,
The light dwelt o'er the scene so lingeringly.
He bares his forehead to the cool blue sky,
And smiles at the far clearness all around,
Until his heart is well-nigh overwound,
And turns for calmness to the pleasant green
Of easy slopes, and shadowy trees that lean
So elegantly o'er the waters' brim
And show their blossoms trim.
Scarce can his clear and nimble eyesight follow
The freaks and dartings of the black-wing'd swallow,
Delighting much to see it, half at rest,
Dip so refreshingly its wings and breast
'Gainst the smooth surface, and to mark anon
The widening circles into nothing gone.

And now the sharp keel of his little boat
Comes up with ripple, and with easy float,
And glides into a bed of water-lilies:
Broad-leaved are they, and their white canopies
Are upward turn'd to catch the heavens' dew
Near to a little island's point they grew;
Whence Calidore might have the goodliest view
Of this sweet spot of earth. The bowery shore
Went off in gentle windings to the hoar
And light blue mountains: but no breathing man,
With a warm heart, and eye prepared to scan
Nature's clear beauty, could pass lightly by
Objects that look'd out so invitingly
On either side. These gentle Calidore
Greeted, as he had known them long before.

The sidelong view of swelling leafiness,
Which the glad setting sun in gold doth dress,
Whence, ever and anon, the jay outsprings,
And scales upon the beauty of its wings.

The lonely turret, shatter'd and outworn,
Stands venerably proud ; too proud to mourn
Its long-lost grandeur : fir-trees grow around,
Aye dropping their hard fruit upon the ground.
The little chapel, with the cross above,
Upholding wreaths of ivy ; the white dove,
That on the windows spreads his feathers light,
And seems from purple clouds to wing its flight.

Green tufted islands casting their soft shades
Across the lake ; sequester'd leafy glades,
That through the dimness of their twilight show
Large dock-leaves, spiral foxgloves, or the glow
Of the wild cat's-eyes, or the silvery stems
Of delicate birch-trees, or long grass which hems
A little brook.   The youth had long been viewing
These pleasant things, and heaven was bedewing
The mountain flowers, when his glad senses caught
A trumpet's silver voice.   Ah ! it was fraught
With many joys for him : the warder's ken
Had found white coursers prancing in the glen :
Friends very dear to him he soon will see ;
So pushes off his boat most eagerly.
And soon upon the lake he skims along,
Deaf to the nightingale's first under-song ;
Nor minds he the white swans that dream so sweetly,
His spirit flies before him so completely.
And now he turns a jutting point of land,
Whence may be seen the castle gloomy and grand :
Nor will a bee buzz round two swelling peaches,
Before the point of his light shallop reaches
Those marble steps that through the water dip :
Now over them he goes with hasty trip,
And scarcely stays to ope the folding doors ;
Anon he leaps along the oaken floors
Of halls and corridors.

Delicious sounds ! those little bright-eyed things
That float about the air on azure wings,
Had been less heartfelt by him than the clang
Of clattering hoofs : into the court he sprang,
Just as two noble steeds, and palfreys twain,

Were slanting out their necks with loosen'd rein;
While from beneath the threat'ning portcullis
They brought their happy burthens. What a kiss,
What gentle squeeze he gave each lady's hand!
How tremblingly their delicate ankles spann'd!
Into how sweet a trance his soul was gone,
While whisperings of affection
Made him delay to let their tender feet
Come to the earth; with an incline so sweet
From their low palfreys o'er his neck they bent:
And whether there were tears of languishment,
Or that the evening dew had pearl'd their tresses,
He feels a moisture on his cheek, and blesses,
With lips that tremble, and with glistening eye,
All the soft luxury
That nestled in his arms. A dimpled hand,
Fair as some wonder out of Fairyland,
Hung from his shoulder like the drooping flowers
Of whitest cassia, fresh from summer showers:
And this he fondled with his happy cheek,
As if for joy he would no further seek:
When the kind voice of good Sir Clerimond
Came to his ear, like something from beyond
His present being: so he gently drew
His warm arms, thrilling now with pulses new,
From their sweet thrall, and forward gently bending,
Thank'd Heaven that his joy was never-ending;
While 'gainst his forehead he devoutly press'd
A hand Heaven made to succour the distress'd
A hand that from the world's bleak promontory
Had lifted Calidore for deeds of glory.

Amid the pages, and the torches' glare,
There stood a knight, patting the flowing hair
Of his proud horse's mane: he was withal
A man of elegance, and stature tall:
So that the waving of his plumes would be
High as the berries of a wild ash tree,
Or as the winged cap of Mercury.
His armour was so dexterously wrought
In shape, that sure no living man had thought
It hard, and heavy steel: but that indeed

It was some glorious form, some splendid weed,
In which a spirit new come from the skies
Might live, and show itself to human eyes.
'Tis the far-famed, the brave Sir Gondibert,
Said the good man to Calidore alert ;
While the young warrior with a step of grace
Came up,—a courtly smile upon his face,
And mailed hand held out, ready to greet
The large-eyed wonder and ambitious heat
Of the aspiring boy ; who as he led
Those smiling ladies, often turn'd his head
To admire the visor arch'd so gracefully
Over a knightly brow ; while they went by,
The lamps that from the high roof'd hall were pendent,
And gave the steel a shining quite transcendent.

Soon in a pleasant chamber they are seated,
The sweet-lipp'd ladies have already greeted
All the green leaves that round the window clamber,
To show their purple stars, and bells of amber.
Sir Gondibert has doff'd his shining steel,
Gladdening in the free and airy feel
Of a light mantle ; and while Clerimond
Is looking round about him with a fond
And placid eye, young Calidore is burning
To hear of knightly deeds, and gallant spurning
Of all unworthiness ; and how the strong of arm
Kept off dismay, and terror, and alarm
From lovely woman : while brimful of this,
He gave each damsel's hand so warm a kiss,
And had such manly ardour in his eye,
That each at other look'd half-staringly :
And then their features started into smiles,
Sweet as blue heavens o'er enchanted isles.
Softly the breezes from the forest came,
Softly they blew aside the taper's flame ;
Clear was the song from Philomel's far bower ;
Grateful the incense from the lime-tree flower ;
Mysterious, wild, the far-heard trumpet's tone ;
Lovely the moon in ether, all alone :
Sweet too the converse of these happy mortals,
As that of busy spirits when the portals

Are closing in the West; or that soft humming
We hear around when Hesperus is coming.
Sweet be their sleep.   *   *   *   *

TO SOME LADIES

WHAT though, while the wonders of nature exploring,
　　I cannot your light, mazy footsteps attend;
Nor listen to accents, that almost adoring,
　　Bless Cynthia's face, the enthusiast's friend?

Yet over the steep, whence the mountain-stream rushes,
　　With you, kindest friends, in idea I rove;
Mark the clear tumbling crystal, its passionate gushes,
　　Its spray, that the wild flower kindly bedews.

Why linger ye so, the wild labyrinth strolling?
　　Why breathless, unable your bliss to declare?
Ah! you list to the nightingale's tender condoling,
　　Responsive to sylphs, in the moonbeamy air.

'Tis morn, and the flowers with dew are yet drooping,
　　I see you are treading the verge of the sea:
And now! ah, I see it—you just now are stooping
　　To pick up the keepsake intended for me.

If a cherub, on pinions of silver descending,
　　Had brought me a gem from the fretwork of Heaven;
And, smiles with his star-cheering voice sweetly blending,
　　The blessings of Tighe had melodiously given.

It had not created a warmer emotion
　　Than the present, fair nymphs, I was blest with from
　　　　you;
Than the shell, from the bright golden sands of the ocean,
　　Which the emerald waves at your feet gladly threw.

For, indeed, 'tis a sweet and peculiar pleasure
　　(And blissful is he who such happiness finds),
To possess but a span of the hour of leisure
　　In elegant, pure, and aerial minds.

ON RECEIVING A CURIOUS SHELL AND A COPY
OF VERSES FROM THE SAME LADIES

Hast thou from the caves of Golconda, a gem
    Pure as the ice-drop that froze on the mountain?
Bright as the humming-bird's green diadem,
    When it flutters in sunbeams that shine through a
        fountain?

Hast thou a goblet for dark sparkling wine;
    That goblet right heavy, and massy, and gold?
And splendidly mark'd with the story divine
    Of Armida the fair, and Rinaldo the bold?

Hast thou a steed with a mane richly flowing?
    Hast thou a sword that thine enemy's smart is?
Hast thou a trumpet rich melodies blowing?
    And wear'st thou the shield of the famed Britomartis?

What is it that hangs from thy shoulder so brave,
    Embroider'd with many a spring-peering flower?
Is it a scarf that thy fair lady gave?
    And hastest thou now to that fair lady's bower?

Ah! courteous Sir Knight, with large joy thou art crown'd;
    Full many the glories that brighten thy youth!
I will tell thee my blisses, which richly abound
    In magical powers to bless and to soothe.

On this scroll thou seest written in characters fair
    A sunbeaming tale of a wreath, and a chain:
And, warrior, it nurtures the property rare
    Of charming my mind from the trammels of pain.

This canopy mark: 'tis the work of a fay;
    Beneath its rich shade did King Oberon languish,
When lovely Titania was far, far away,
    And cruelly left him to sorrow and anguish.

There, oft would he bring from his soft-sighing lute
 Wild strains to which, spell-bound, the nightingales
  listen'd!
The wondering spirits of Heaven were mute,
 And tears 'mong the dewdrops of morning oft glisten'd.

In this little dome, all those melodies strange,
 Soft, plaintive, and melting, for ever will sigh;
Nor e'er will the notes from their tenderness change,
 Nor e'er will the music of Oberon die.

So when I am in a voluptuous vein,
 I pillow my head on the sweets of the rose,
And list to the tale of the wreath, and the chain,
 Till its echoes depart; then I sink to repose.

Adieu! valiant Eric! with joy thou art crown'd,
 Full many the glories that brighten thy youth,
I too have my blisses, which richly abound
 In magical powers to bless and to soothe.

TO GEORGIANA AUGUSTA WYLIE

HADST thou lived in days of old,
O what wonders had been told
Of thy lively countenance,
And thy humid eyes, that dance
In the midst of their own brightness,
In the very fane of lightness;
Over which thine eyebrows, leaning,
Picture out each lovely meaning:
In a dainty bend they lie,
Like the streaks across the sky,
Or the feathers from a crow
Fallen on a bed of snow:
Of thy dark hair, that extends
Into many graceful bends;
As the leaves of hellebore
Turn to whence they sprung before;
And behind each ample curl
Peeps the richness of a pearl.

Downward too flows many a tress
With a glossy waviness,
Full, and round like globes that rise
From the censer to the skies
Through sunny air.   Add too the sweetness
Of thy honied voice; the neatness
Of thine ankle lightly turn'd :
With those beauties scarce discern'd,
Kept with such sweet privacy,
That they seldom meet the eye
Of the little Loves that fly
Round about with eager pry.
Saving when with freshening lave,
Thou dipp'st them in the taintless wave;
Like twin water-lilies, born
In the coolness of the morn.
O, if thou hadst breathed then,
Now the Muses had been ten.
Couldst thou wish for lineage higher
Than twin-sister of Thalia?
At least for ever, evermore
Will I call the Graces four.
Hadst thou lived when chivalry
Lifted up her lance on high,
Tell me what thou wouldst have been?
Ah ! I see the silver sheen
Of thy broider'd floating vest
Cov'ring half thine ivory breast :
Which, O Heavens ! I should see,
But that cruel Destiny
Has placed a golden cuirass there,
Keeping secret what is fair.
Like sunbeams in a cloudlet nested,
Thy locks in knightly casque are rested :
O'er which bend four milky plumes
Like the gentle lily's blooms
Springing from a costly vase.
See with what a stately pace
Comes thine alabaster steed ;
Servant of heroic deed !
O'er his loins, his trappings glow
Like the northern lights on snow.

Mount his back! thy sword unsheath!
Sign of the enchanter's death;
Bane of every wicked spell;
Silencer of dragon's yell.
Alas! thou this wilt never do,
Thou art an enchantress too,
And wilt never surely spill
Blood of those whose eyes can kill.

TO HOPE

WHEN by my solitary hearth I sit,
   And hateful thoughts enwrap my soul in gloom;
When no fair dreams before my "mind's eye" flit,
   And the bare heath of life presents no bloom;
Sweet Hope! ethereal balm upon me shed,
And wave thy silver pinions o'er my head.

Whene'er I wander, at the fall of night,
   Where woven boughs shut out the moon's bright ray,
Should sad Despondency my musings fright,
   And frown, to drive fair Cheerfulness away,
Peep with the moonbeams through the leafy roof,
And keep that fiend Despondence far aloof.

Should Disappointment, parent of Despair,
   Strive for her son to seize my careless heart
When, like a cloud, he sits upon the air,
   Preparing on his spell-bound prey to dart:
Chase him away, sweet Hope, with visage bright,
And fright him, as the morning frightens night.

Whene'er the fate of those I hold most dear
   Tells to my fearful breast a tale of sorrow,
O bright-eyed Hope, my morbid fancy cheer;
   Let me awhile thy sweetest comforts borrow:
Thy heaven-born radiance around me shed,
And wave thy silver pinions o'er my head!

Should e'er unhappy love my bosom pain,
   From cruel parents, or relentless fair,

O let me think it is not quite in vain
   To sigh out sonnets to the midnight air !
Sweet Hope ! ethereal balm upon me shed,
And wave thy silver pinions o'er my head.

In the long vista of the years to roll,
   Let me not see our country's honour fade ;
O let me see our land retain her soul !
   Her pride, her freedom ; and not freedom's shade.
From thy bright eyes unusual brightness shed—
Beneath thy pinions canopy my head !

Let me not see the patriot's high bequest,
   Great liberty ! how great in plain attire !
With the base purple of a court oppress'd,
   Bowing her head, and ready to expire :
But let me see thee stoop from Heaven on wings
That fill the skies with silver glitterings !

And as, in sparkling majesty, a star
   Gilds the bright summit of some gloomy cloud :
Brightening the half-veil'd face of Heaven afar :
   So, when dark thoughts my boding spirit shroud,
Sweet Hope ! celestial influence round me shed,
Waving thy silver pinions o'er my head.

   February, 1815.

IMITATION OF SPENSER

Now Morning from her orient chamber came,
And her first footsteps touch'd a verdant hill :
Crowning its lawny crest with amber flame,
Silvering the untainted gushes of its rill ;
Which, pure from mossy beds, did down distil,
And after parting beds of simple flowers,
By many streams a little lake did fill,
Which round its marge reflected woven bowers,
And, in its middle space, a sky that never lowers.

There the kingfisher saw his plumage bright,
Vying with fish of brilliant dye below;
Whose silken fins' and golden scales' light
Cast upward, through the waves, a ruby glow:
There saw the swan his neck of arched snow,
And oar'd himself along with majesty:
Sparkled his jetty eyes; his feet did show
Beneath the waves like Afric's ebony,
And on his back a fay reclined voluptuously.

Ah! could I tell the wonders of an isle
That in that fairest lake had placed been,
I could e'en Dido of her grief beguile;
Or rob from aged Lear his bitter teen:
For sure so fair a place was never seen
Of all that ever charm'd romantic eye:
It seem'd an emerald in the silver sheen
Of the bright waters; or as when on high,
Through clouds of fleecy white, laughs the cærulean sky.

And all around it dipp'd luxuriously
Slopings of verdure through the glossy tide,
Which, as it were in gentle amity,
Rippled delighted up the flowery side;
As if to glean the ruddy tears it tried,
Which fell profusely from the rose-tree stem!
Haply it was the workings of its pride,
In strife to throw upon the shore a gem
Outvying all the buds in Flora's diadem,

.   .   .   .   .   .

1812.

THREE SONNETS ON WOMAN

WOMAN! when I behold thee flippant, vain,
    Inconstant, childish, proud, and full of fancies;
    Without that modest softening that enhances
The downcast eye, repentant of the pain
That its mild light creates to heal again;
    E'en then, elate, my spirit leaps and prances,
    E'en then my soul with exultation dances,

For that to love, so long, I've dormant lain:
But when I see thee meek, and kind, and tender,
  Heavens! how desperately do I adore
Thy winning graces;—to be thy defender
  I hotly burn—to be a Calidore—
A very Red Cross Knight—a stout Leander—
  Might I be loved by thee like these of yore.

Light feet, dark violet eyes, and parted hair;
  Soft dimpled hands, white neck and creamy breast;
  Are things on which the dazzled senses rest
Till the fond, fixed eyes forget they stare.
From such fine pictures, Heavens! I cannot dare
  To turn my admiration, though unpossess'd
  They be of what is worthy,—though not drest
In lovely modesty, and virtues rare.
Yet these I leave as thoughtless as a lark:
  These lures I straight forget,—e'en ere I dine,
Or thrice my palate moisten: but when I mark
  Such charms with mild intelligences shine,
My ear is open like a greedy shark,
  To catch the tunings of a voice divine.

Ah! who can e'er forget so fair a being?
  Who can forget her half-retiring sweets?
  God! she is like a milk-white lamb that bleats
For man's protection. Surely the All-seeing,
Who joys to see us with his gifts agreeing,
  Will never give him pinions, who intreats
  Such innocence to ruin,—who vilely cheats
A dove-like bosom. In truth there is no freeing
One's thoughts from such a beauty; when I hear
  A lay that once I saw her hand awake,
Her form seems floating palpable, and near:
  Had I e'er seen her from an arbour take
A dewy flower, oft would that hand appear,
  And o'er my eyes the trembling moisture shake.

EPISTLES

TO GEORGE FELTON MATHEW

" Among the rest a shepherd (though but young
Yet hartned to his pipe) with all the skill
His few yeeres could, began to fill his quill."
Britannia's Pastorals.—BROWNE.

SWEET are the pleasures that to verse belong,
And doubly sweet a brotherhood in song ;
Nor can remembrance, Mathew ! bring to view
A fate more pleasing, a delight more true
Than that in which the brother poets joy'd,
Who, with combined powers, their wit employed
To raise a trophy to the drama's muses.
The thought of this great partnership diffuses
Over the genius-loving heart, a feeling
Of all that's high, and great, and good, and healing.
Too partial friend ! fain would I follow thee
Past each horizon of fine poesy ;
Fain would I echo back each pleasant note,
As o'er Sicilian seas clear anthems float
'Mong the light skimming gondolas far parted,
Just when the sun his farewell beam has darted :
But 'tis impossible ; far different cares
Beckon me sternly from soft " Lydian airs,"
And hold my faculties so long in thrall,
That I am oft in doubt whether at all
I shall again see Phœbus in the morning :
Or flush'd Aurora in the roseate dawning !
Or a white Naiad in a rippling stream ;
Or a rapt seraph in a moonlight beam ;
Or again witness what with thee I've seen,
The dew by fairy feet swept from the green,
After a night of some quaint jubilee
Which every elf and fay had come to see :
When bright processions took their airy march
Beneath the curved moon's triumphal arch.

But might I now each passing moment give
To the coy muse, with me she would not live
In this dark city, nor would condescend
'Mid contradictions her delights to lend.
Should e'er the fine-eyed maid to me be kind,
Ah! surely it must be whene'er I find
Some flowery spot, sequester'd, wild, romantic,
That often must have seen a poet frantic;
Where oaks, that erst the Druid knew, are growing,
And flowers, the glory of one day, are blowing;
Where the dark-leaved laburnum's drooping clusters
Reflect athwart the stream their yellow lustres,
And intertwined the cassia's arms unite,
With its own drooping buds, but very white.
Where on one side are covert branches hung,
'Mong which the nightingales have always sung
In leafy quiet; where to pry, aloof
Atween the pillars of the sylvan roof,
Would be to find where violet beds were nestling,
And where the bee with cowslip bells was wrestling.
There must be too a ruin dark and gloomy,
To say, "Joy not too much in all that's bloomy."

Yet that is vain—O Mathew! lend thy aid
To find a place where I may greet the maid—
Where we may soft humanity put on,
And sit, and rhyme, and think on Chatterton;
And that warm-hearted Shakspeare sent to meet him
Four laurell'd spirits, heavenward to entreat him.
With reverence would we speak of all the sages
Who have left streaks of light athwart their ages:
And thou shouldst moralise on Milton's blindness,
And mourn the fearful dearth of human kindness
To those who strove with the bright golden wing
Of genius, to flap away each sting
Thrown by the pitiless world. We next could tell
Of those who in the cause of freedom fell;
Of our own Alfred, of Helvetian Tell;
Of him whose name to ev'ry heart's a solace,
High-minded and unbending William Wallace.
While to the rugged north our musing turns,
We well might drop a tear for him and Burns.

Felton ! without incitements such as these,
How vain for me the niggard muse to tease !
For thee, she will thy every dwelling grace,
And make "a sunshine in a shady place" :
For thou wast once a flow'ret blooming wild,
Close to the source, bright, pure, and undefiled,
Whence gush the streams of song: in happy hour
Came chaste Diana from her shady bower,
Just as the sun was from the east uprising ;
And, as for him some gift she was devising,
Beheld thee, pluck'd thee, cast thee in the stream
To meet her glorious brother's greeting beam.
I marvel much that thou hast never told
How, from a flower, into a fish of gold
Apollo changed thee : how thou next didst seem
A black-eyed swan upon the widening stream ;
And when thou first didst in that mirror trace
The placid features of a human face ;
That thou hast never told thy travels strange,
And all the wonders of the mazy range
O'er pebbly crystal, and o'er golden sands ;
Kissing thy daily food from Naiads' pearly hands.

November, 1815.

TO MY BROTHER GEORGE

FULL many a dreary hour have I past
My brain bewilder'd, and my mind o'ercast
With heaviness; in seasons when I've thought
No sphery strains by me could e'er be caught
From the blue dome, though I to dimness gaze
On the far depth where sheeted lightning plays ;
Or, on the wavy grass outstretch'd supinely,
Pry 'mong the stars, to strive to think divinely :
That I should never hear Apollo's song,
Though feathery clouds were floating all along
The purple west, and, two bright streaks between,
The golden lyre itself were dimly seen :
That the still murmur of the honey-bee
Would never teach a rural song to me :

That the bright glance from beauty's eyelids slanting
Would never make a lay of mine enchanting,
Or warm my breast with ardour to unfold
Some tale of love and arms in time of old.

But there are times, when those that love the bay,
Fly from all sorrowing far, far away ;
A sudden glow comes on them, nought they see
In water, earth, or air, but poesy.
It has been said, dear George, and true I hold it,
(For knightly Spenser to Libertas told it)
That when a poet is in such a trance,
In air he sees white coursers paw and prance,
Bestridden of gay knights, in gay apparel,
Who at each other tilt in playful quarrel ;
And what we, ignorantly, sheet-lightning call,
Is the swift opening of their wide portal,
When the bright warder blows his trumpet clear,
Whose tones reach nought on earth but poet's ear,
When these enchanted portals open wide,
And through the light the horsemen swiftly glide,
The Poet's eye can reach those golden halls,
And view the glory of their festivals :
Their ladies fair, that in the distance seem
Fit for the silvering of a seraph's dream ;
Their rich brimmed goblets, that incessant run,
Like the bright spots that move about the sun ;
And when upheld, the wine from each bright jar
Pours with the lustre of a falling star.
Yet further off are dimly seen their bowers,
Of which no mortal eye can reach the flowers ;
And 'tis right just, for well Apollo knows
'Twould make the Poet quarrel with the rose.
All that's reveal'd from that far seat of blisses,
Is, the clear fountains' interchanging kisses,
As gracefully descending, light and thin,
Like silver streaks across a dolphin's fin,
When he upswimmeth from the coral caves,
And sports with half his tail above the waves.

These wonders strange he sees, and many more,
Whose head is pregnant with poetic lore :

Should he upon an evening ramble fare
With forehead to the soothing breezes bare,
Would he nought see but the dark, silent blue,
With all its diamonds trembling through and through?
Or the coy moon, when in the waviness
Of whitest clouds she does her beauty dress,
And staidly paces higher up, and higher,
Like a sweet nun in holiday attire?
Ah, yes! much more would start into his sight—
The revelries and mysteries of night:
And should I ever see them, I will tell you
Such tales as needs must with amazement spell you.

These are the living pleasures of the bard:
But richer far posterity's award.
What does he murmur with his latest breath,
While his proud eye looks through the film of death?
"What though I leave this dull and earthly mould,
Yet shall my spirit lofty converse hold
With after times.—The patriot shall feel
My stern alarum, and unsheath his steel;
Or in the senate thunder out my numbers,
To startle princes from their easy slumbers.
The sage will mingle with each moral theme
My happy thoughts sententious: he will teem
With lofty periods when my verses fire him,
And then I'll stoop from heaven to inspire him.
Lays have I left of such a dear delight
That maids will sing them on their bridal-night;
Gay villagers, upon a morn of May,
When they have tired their gentle limbs with play,
And form'd a snowy circle on the grass,
And plac'd in midst of all that lovely lass
Who chosen is their queen,—with her fine head
Crowned with flowers purple, white and red:
For there the lily and the musk-rose sighing,
Are emblems true of hapless lovers dying:
Between her breasts, that never yet felt trouble,
A bunch of violets full blown, and double,
Serenely sleep:—she from a casket takes
A little book,—and then a joy awakes
About each youthful heart,—with stifled cries,

And rubbing of white hands, and sparkling eyes :
For she's to read a tale of hopes and fears :
One that I foster'd in my youthful years :
The pearls, that on each glistening circlet sleep,
Gush ever and anon with silent creep,
Lured by the innocent dimples. To sweet rest
Shall the dear babe, upon its mother's breast,
Be lull'd with songs of mine. Fair world, adieu !
Thy dales and hills are fading from my view :
Swiftly I mount, upon wide-spreading pinions,
Far from the narrow bounds of thy dominions.
Full joy I feel, while thus I cleave the air,
That my soft verse will charm thy daughters fair,
And warm thy sons !" Ah, my dear friend and brother,
Could I, at once, my mad ambition smother,
For tasting joys like these, sure I should be
Happier, and dearer to society.
At times, 'tis true, I've felt relief from pain
When some bright thought has darted through my brain :
Through all that day I've felt a greater pleasure
Than if I'd brought to light a hidden treasure.
As to my sonnets, though none else should heed them,
I feel delighted, still, that you should read them.
Of late, too, I have had much calm enjoyment,
Stretch'd on the grass at my best-loved employment
Of scribbling lines for you. These things I thought
While, in my face, the freshest breeze I caught.
E'en now I am pillow'd on a bed of flowers
That crowns a lofty cliff, which proudly towers
Above the ocean waves. The stalks and blades
Chequer my tablet with their quivering shades.
On one side is a field of drooping oats,
Through which the poppies show their scarlet coats
So pert and useless, that they bring to mind
The scarlet-coats that pester humankind.
And on the other side, outspread, is seen
Ocean's blue mantle, streak'd with purple and green !
Now, 'tis I see a canvass'd ship, and now
Mark the bright silver curling round her prow ;
I see the lark down-dropping to his nest,
And the broad-wing'd sea-gull never at rest ;
For when no more he spreads his feathers free,

His breast is dancing on the restless sea.
Now I direct my eyes into the west,
Which at this moment is in sunbeams drest:
Why westward turn?   'Twas but to say adieu!
'Twas but to kiss my hand, dear George, to you!

August, 1816.

TO CHARLES COWDEN CLARKE

OFT have you seen a swan superbly frowning,
And with proud breast his own white shadow crowning;
He slants his neck beneath the waters bright
So silently, it seems a beam of light
Come from the galaxy: anon he sports,—
With outspread wings the Naiad Zephyr courts,
Or ruffles all the surface of the lake
In striving from its crystal face to take
Some diamond water-drops, and them to treasure
In milky nest, and sip them off at leisure.
But not a moment can he there ensure them,
Nor to such downy rest can he allure them;
For down they rush as though they would be free,
And drop like hours into eternity.
Just like that bird am I in loss of time,
Whene'er I venture on the stream of rhyme;
With shatter'd boat, oar snapt, and canvas rent,
I slowly sail, scarce knowing my intent;
Still scooping up the water with my fingers,
In which a trembling diamond never lingers.

By this, friend Charles, you may full plainly see
Why I have never penn'd a line to thee:
Because my thoughts were never free and clear,
And little fit to please a classic ear;
Because my wine was of too poor a savour
For one whose palate gladdens in the flavour
Of sparkling Helicon:—small good it were
To take him to a desert rude and bare,
Who had on Baiæ's shore reclined at ease,
While Tasso's page was floating in a breeze

That gave soft music from Armida's bowers,
Mingled with fragrance from her rarest flowers :
Small good to one who had by Mulla's stream
Fondled the maidens with the breasts of cream ;
Who had beheld Belphœbe in a brook,
And lovely Una in a leafy nook,
And Archimago leaning o'er his book :
Who had of all that's sweet tasted, and seen,
From silvery ripple, up to beauty's queen ;
From the sequester'd haunts of gay Titania,
To the blue dwelling of divine Urania :
One who of late had ta'en sweet forest walks
With him who elegantly chats and talks—
The wrong'd Libertas—who has told you stories
Of laurel chaplets, and Apollo's glories ;
Of troops chivalrous prancing through a city,
And tearful ladies, made for love and pity :
With many else which I have never known.
Thus have I thought ; and days on days have flown
Slowly, or rapidly—unwilling still
For you to try my dull, unlearned quill.
Nor should I now, but that I've known you long ;
That you first taught me all the sweets of song :
The grand, the sweet, the terse, the free, the fine :
What swell'd with pathos, and what right divine :
Spenserian vowels that elope with ease,
And float along like birds o'er summer seas :
Miltonian storms, and more, Miltonian tenderness,
Michael in arms, and more, meek Eve's fair slenderness.
Who read for me the sonnet swelling loudly
Up to its climax, and then dying proudly ?
Who found for me the grandeur of the ode,
Growing, like Atlas, stronger from its load ?
Who let me taste that more than cordial dram,
The sharp, the rapier-pointed epigram ?
Show'd me that epic was of all the king,
Round, vast, and spanning all, like Saturn's ring ?
You too upheld the veil from Clio's beauty,
And pointed out the patriot's stern duty ;
The might of Alfred, and the shaft of Tell ;
The hand of Brutus, that so grandly fell
Upon a tyrant's head.   Ah ! had I never seen

Or known your kindness, what might I have been?
What my enjoyments in my youthful years,
Bereft of all that now my life endears?
And can I e'er these benefits forget?
And can I e'er repay the friendly debt?
No, doubly no;—yet should these rhymings please,
I shall roll on the grass with twofold ease;
For I have long time been my fancy feeding
With hopes that you would one day think the reading
Of my rough verses not an hour misspent;
Should it e'er be so, what a rich content!
Some weeks have pass'd since last I saw the spires
In lucent Thames reflected:—warm desires
To see the sun o'erpeep the eastern dimness.
And morning-shadows streaking into slimness
Across the lawny fields, and pebbly water;
To mark the time as they grow broad and shorter;
To feel the air that plays about the hills,
And sips its freshness from the little rills;
To see high, golden corn wave in the light
When Cynthia smiles upon a summer's night,
And peers among the cloudlets, jet and white,
As though she were reclining in a bed
Of bean-blossoms, in heaven freshly shed.
No sooner had I stepp'd into these pleasures,
Than I began to think of rhymes and measures:
The air that floated by me seem'd to say,
"Write! thou wilt never have a better day."
And so I did. When many lines I'd written,
Though with their grace I was not oversmitten,
Yet, as my hand was warm, I thought I'd better
Trust to my feelings, and write you a letter.
Such an attempt required an inspiration
Of a peculiar sort,—a consummation;—
Which, had I felt, these scribblings might have been
Verses from which the soul would never wean;
But many days have passed since last my heart
Was warm'd luxuriously by divine Mozart;
By Arne delighted, or by Handel madden'd;
Or by the song of Erin pierced and sadden'd:
What time you were before the music sitting,
And the rich notes to each sensation fitting.

Since I have walk'd with you through shady lanes
That freshly terminate in open plains,
And revell'd in a chat that ceased not,
When, at night-fall, among your books we got :
No, nor when supper came, nor after that,—
Nor when reluctantly I took my hat ;
No, nor till cordially you shook my hand
Mid-way between our homes :—your accents bland
Still sounded in my ears, when I no more
Could hear your footsteps touch the gravelly floor.
Sometimes I lost them, and then found again ;
You changed the footpath for the grassy plain.
In those still moments I have wish'd you joys
That well you know to honour :—" Life's very toys,
With him," said I, " will take a pleasant charm ;
It cannot be that aught will work him harm."
These thoughts now come o'er me with all their might :—
Again I shake your hand,—friend Charles, good-night.

September, 1816.

SONNETS

TO MY BROTHER GEORGE

MANY the wonders I this day have seen:
  The sun, when first he kist away the tears
  That fill'd the eyes of Morn ;—the laurell'd peers
Who from the feathery gold of evening lean ;—
The Ocean with its vastness, its blue green,
  Its ships, its rocks, its caves, its hopes, its fears,
  Its voice mysterious, which whoso hears
Must think on what will be, and what has been.
E'en now, dear George, while this for you I write,
  Cynthia is from her silken curtains peeping
So scantly, that it seems her bridal night,
  And she her half-discover'd revels keeping.
But what, without the social thought of thee,
Would be the wonders of the sky and sea ?

TO * * * * *
HAD I A MAN'S FAIR FORM

HAD I a man's fair form, then might my sighs
  Be echoed swiftly through that ivory shell,
  Thine ear, and find thy gentle heart ; so well
Would passion arm me for the enterprise :
But ah ! I am no knight whose foeman dies ;
  No cuirass glistens on my bosom's swell ;
  I am no happy shepherd of the dell
Whose lips have trembled with a maiden's eyes.
Yet must I doat upon thee,—call thee sweet,
  Sweeter by far than Hybla's honey'd roses
  When steep'd in dew rich to intoxication.
Ah ! I will taste that dew, for me 'tis meet,
  And when the moon her pallid face discloses,
  I'll gather some by spells, and incantation.

WRITTEN ON THE DAY THAT MR LEIGH HUNT LEFT PRISON

WHAT though, for showing truth to flatter'd state,
    Kind Hunt was shut in prison, yet has he,
    In his immortal spirit, been as free
As the sky-searching lark, and as elate.
Minion of grandeur! think you he did wait?
    Think you he nought but prison-walls did see,
    Till, so unwilling, thou unturn'dst the key?
Ah, no! far happier, nobler was his fate!
In Spenser's halls he stray'd, and bowers fair,
    Culling enchanted flowers; and he flew
With daring Milton through the fields of air:
    To regions of his own his genius true
Took happy flights.   Who shall his fame impair
    When thou art dead, and all thy wretched crew?

HOW MANY BARDS

How many bards gild the lapses of time!
    A few of them have ever been the food
    Of my delighted fancy,—I could brood
Over their beauties, earthly, or sublime:
And often, when I sit me down to rhyme,
    These will in throngs before my mind intrude:
    But no confusion, no disturbance rude
Do they occasion; 'tis a pleasing chime.
So the unnumber'd sounds that evening store;
    The songs of birds—the whispering of the leaves—
    The voice of waters—the great bell that heaves
With solemn sound,—and thousand others more,
    That distance of recognisance bereaves,
Make pleasing music, and not wild uproar.

TO A FRIEND WHO SENT ME SOME ROSES

As late I rambled in the happy fields,
    What time the skylark shakes the tremulous dew
    From his lush clover covert;—when anew

Adventurous knights take up their dinted shields ;
I saw the sweetest flower wild nature yields,
  A fresh-blown musk-rose ; 'twas the first that threw
  Its sweets upon the summer : graceful it grew
As is the wand that queen Titania wields.
And, as I feasted on its fragrancy,
  I thought the garden-rose it far excell'd ;
But when, O Wells ! thy roses came to me,
  My sense with their deliciousness was spell'd :
Soft voices had they, that with tender plea
  Whisper'd of peace, and truth, and friendliness unquell'd.

TO G. A. W.

NYMPH of the downward smile and sidelong glance !
  In what diviner moments of the day
  Art thou most lovely ? when gone far astray
Into the labyrinths of sweet utterance ?
Or when serenely wandering in a trance
  Of sober thought ? Or when starting away,
  With careless robe to meet the morning ray,
Thou sparest the flowers in thy mazy dance ?
Haply 'tis when thy ruby lips part sweetly,
  And so remain, because thou listenest :
But thou to please were nurtured so completely
  That I can never tell what mood is best,
I shall as soon pronounce which Grace more neatly
  Trips it before Apollo than the rest.

O SOLITUDE ! IF I MUST WITH THEE DWELL

O SOLITUDE ! if I must with thee dwell,
  Let it not be among the jumbled heap
  Of murky buildings : climb with me the steep,—
Nature's observatory—whence the dell,
In flowery slopes, its river's crystal swell,
  May seem a span ; let me thy vigils keep
  'Mongst boughs pavilion'd, where the deer's swift leap
Startles the wild bee from the foxglove bell.

B

But though I'll gladly trace these scenes with thee,
Yet the sweet converse of an innocent mind,
Whose words are images of thoughts refined,
Is my soul's pleasure; and it sure must be
Almost the highest bliss of human-kind,
When to thy haunts two kindred spirits flee.

TO MY BROTHERS

SMALL, busy flames play through the fresh-laid coals,
    And their faint cracklings o'er our silence creep
    Like whispers of the household gods that keep
A gentle empire o'er fraternal souls,
And while, for rhymes, I search around the poles,
    Your eyes are fix'd, as in poetic sleep,
    Upon the lore so voluble and deep,
That aye at fall of night our care condoles.
This is your birth-day, Tom, and I rejoice
    That thus it passes smoothly, quietly:
Many such eves of gently whispering noise
    May we together pass, and calmly try
What are this world's true joys,—ere the great Voice
    From its fair face shall bid our spirits fly.

November 18, 1816.

KEEN FITFUL GUSTS ARE WHISPERING
HERE AND THERE

KEEN fitful gusts are whispering here and there
    Among the bushes, half leafless and dry;
    The stars look very cold about the sky,
And I have many miles on foot to fare;
Yet feel I little of the cold bleak air,
    Or of the dead leaves rustling drearily,
    Or of those silver lamps that burn on high,
Or of the distance from home's pleasant lair:
For I am brimful of the friendliness
    That in a little cottage I have found;

Of fair-haired Milton's eloquent distress,
  And all his love for gentle Lycid' drown'd,
Of lovely Laura in her light green dress,
  And faithful Petrarch gloriously crown'd.

TO ONE WHO HAS BEEN LONG IN
CITY PENT

To one who has been long in city pent,
  'Tis very sweet to look into the fair
  And open face of heaven,—to breathe a prayer
Full in the smile of the blue firmament.
Who is more happy, when, with heart's content,
  Fatigued he sinks into some pleasant lair
  Of wavy grass, and reads a debonair
And gentle tale of love and languishment?
Returning home at evening, with an ear
  Catching the notes of Philomel,—an eye
Watching the sailing cloudlet's bright career,
  He mourns that day so soon has glided by,
E'en like the passage of an angel's tear
  That falls through the clear ether silently.

ON FIRST LOOKING INTO CHAPMAN'S
HOMER

Much have I travell'd in the realms of gold,
  And many goodly states and kingdoms seen;
  Round many western islands have I been
Which bards in fealty to Apollo hold.
Oft of one wide expanse had I been told,
  That deep-brow'd Homer ruled as his demesne:
  Yet did I never breathe its pure serene
Till I heard Chapman speak out loud and bold:
Then felt I like some watcher of the skies
  When a new planet swims into his ken;
Or like stout Cortez when with eagle eyes
  He stared at the Pacific—and all his men
Look'd at each other with a wild surmise—
  Silent, upon a peak in Darien.

ON LEAVING SOME FRIENDS AT AN EARLY HOUR

GIVE me a golden pen, and let me lean
    On heap'd-up flowers, in regions clear, and far ;
    Bring me a tablet whiter than a star,
Or hand of hymning angel, when 'tis seen
The silver strings of heavenly harp atween :
    And let there glide by many a pearly car,
    Pink robes, and wavy hair, and diamond jar
And half-discover'd wings, and glances keen.
The while let music wander round my ears,
    And as it reaches each delicious ending,
    Let me write down a line of glorious tone,
And full of many wonders of the spheres :
    For what a height my spirit is contending !
    'Tis not content so soon to be alone.

ADDRESSED TO HAYDON

HIGH-MINDEDNESS, a jealousy for good,
    A loving-kindness for the great man's fame,
    Dwells here and there with people of no name,
In noisome alley, and in pathless wood :
And where we think the truth least understood,
    Oft may be found a " singleness of aim,"
    That ought to frighten into hooded shame
A money-mongering, pitiable brood.
How glorious this affection for the cause
    Of steadfast genius, toiling gallantly !
What when a stout unbending champion awes
    Envy and malice to their native sty ?
Unnumber'd souls breathe out a still applause,
    Proud to behold him in his country's eye.

ADDRESSED TO THE SAME

GREAT spirits now on earth are sojourning :
    He of the cloud, the cataract, the lake,
    Who on Helvellyn's summit, wide awake

Catches his freshness from Archangel's wing :
He of the rose, the violet, the spring,
   The social smile, the chain for Freedom's sake :
   And lo ! whose steadfastness would never take
A meaner sound than Raphael's whispering.
And other spirits there are standing apart
   Upon the forehead of the age to come ;
These, these will give the world another heart,
   And other pulses.   Hear ye not the hum
Of mighty workings?——
   Listen awhile, ye nations, and be dumb.

ON THE GRASSHOPPER AND CRICKET

THE poetry of earth is never dead :
   When all the birds are faint with the hot sun,
   And hide in cooling trees, a voice will run
From hedge to hedge about the new-mown mead.
That is the grasshopper's—he takes the lead
   In summer luxury,—he has never done
   With his delights, for when tired out with fun,
He rests at ease beneath some pleasant weed.
The poetry of earth is ceasing never :
   On a lone winter evening, when the frost
Has wrought a silence, from the stove there shrills
The Cricket's song, in warmth increasing ever,
   And seems to one in drowsiness half-lost,
The Grasshopper's among some grassy hills.

December 30, 1816

TO KOSCIUSKO

GOOD Kosciusko ! thy great name alone
   Is a full harvest whence to reap high feeling ;
   It comes upon us like the glorious pealing
Of the wide spheres—an everlasting tone.
And now it tells me, that in worlds unknown,
   The names of heroes, burst from clouds concealing,
   Are changed to harmonies, for ever stealing
Through cloudless blue, and round each silver throne,

It tells me too, that on a happy day,
    When some good spirit walks upon the earth,
Thy name with Alfred's, and the great of yore,
    Gently commingling, gives tremendous birth
To a loud hymn, that sounds far, far away
To where the great God lives for evermore.

HAPPY IS ENGLAND

HAPPY is England! I could be content
    To see no other verdure than its own ;
    To feel no other breezes than are blown
Through its tall woods with high romances blent ;
Yet do I sometimes feel a languishment
    For skies Italian, and an inward groan
    To sit upon an Alp as on a throne,
And half forget what world or worldling meant.
Happy is England, sweet her artless daughters :
    Enough their simple loveliness for me,
Enough their whitest arms in silence clinging :
    Yet do I often warmly burn to see
Beauties of deeper glance, and hear their singing,
And float with them about the summer waters.

SLEEP AND POETRY

"As I lay in my bed slepe full unmete
Was unto me, but why that I ne might
Rest I ne wist, for there n' as erthly wight
(As I suppose) had more of hertis ese
Than I, for I n' ad sicknesse nor disese."
—CHAUCER.

WHAT is more gentle than a wind in summer ?
What is more soothing than the pretty hummer
That stays one moment in an open flower,
And buzzes cheerily from bower to bower ?
What is more tranquil than a musk-rose blowing
In a green island, far from all men's knowing ?

More healthful than the leafiness of dales?
More secret than a nest of nightingales?
More serene than Cordelia's countenance?
More full of visions than a high romance?
What, but thee, Sleep? Soft closer of our eyes!
Low murmurer of tender lullabies!
Light hoverer around our happy pillows!
Wreather of poppy buds, and weeping willows!
Silent entangler of a beauty's tresses!
Most happy listener! when the morning blesses
Thee for enlivening all the cheerful eyes
That glance so brightly at the new sun-rise.

But what is higher beyond thought than thee?
Fresher than berries of a mountain-tree?
More strange, more beautiful, more smooth, more regal,
Than wings of swans, than doves, than dim-seen eagle?
What is it? And to what shall I compare it?
It has a glory, and nought else can share it:
The thought thereof is awful, sweet, and holy,
Chasing away all worldliness and folly:
Coming sometimes like fearful claps of thunder;
Or the low rumblings earth's regions under;
And sometimes like a gentle whispering
Of all the secrets of some wondrous thing
That breathes about us in the vacant air;
So that we look around with prying stare,
Perhaps to see shapes of light, aërial limning;
And catch soft floatings from a faint-heard hymning;
To see the laurel-wreath, on high suspended,
That is to crown our name when life is ended.
Sometimes it gives a glory to the voice,
And from the heart up-springs, rejoice! rejoice!
Sounds which will reach the Framer of all things,
And die away in ardent mutterings.

No one who once the glorious sun has seen,
And all the clouds, and felt his bosom clean
For his great Maker's presence, but must know
What 'tis I mean, and feel his being glow:
Therefore no insult will I give his spirit,
By telling what he sees from native merit.

O Poesy ! for thee I hold my pen,
That am not yet a glorious denizen
Of thy wide heaven—should I rather kneel
Upon some mountain-top until I feel
A glowing splendour round about me hung,
And echo back the voice of thine own tongue?
O Poesy ! for thee I grasp my pen,
That am not yet a glorious denizen
Of thy wide heaven ; yet, to my ardent prayer,
Yield from thy sanctuary some clear air,
Smoothed for intoxication by the breath
Of flowering bays, that I may die a death
Of luxury, and my young spirit follow
The morning sunbeams to the great Apollo,
Like a fresh sacrifice ; or, if I can bear
The o'erwhelming sweets, 'twill bring me to the fair
Visions of all places : a bowery nook
Will be elysium—an eternal book
Whence I may copy many a lovely saying
About the leaves, and flowers—about the playing
Of nymphs in woods and fountains ; and the shade
Keeping a silence round a sleeping maid ;
And many a verse from so strange influence
That we must ever wonder how, and whence
It came.   Also imaginings will hover
Round my fire-side, and haply there discover
Vistas of solemn beauty, where I'd wander
In happy silence, like the clear Meander
Through its lone vales ; and where I found a spot
Of awfuller shade, or an enchanted grot,
Or a green hill o'erspread with chequer'd dress
Of flowers, and fearful from its loveliness,
Write on my tablets all that was permitted,
All that was for our human senses fitted.
Then the events of this wide world I'd seize
Like a strong giant, and my spirit tease,
Till at his shoulders it should proudly see
Wings to find out an immortality.

Stop and consider ! life is but a day ;
A fragile dewdrop on its perilous way
From a tree's summit ; a poor Indian's sleep

While his boat hastens to the monstrous steep
Of Montmorenci.   Why so sad a moan?
Life is the rose's hope while yet unblown;
The reading of an ever-changing tale;
The light uplifting of a maiden's veil;
A pigeon tumbling in clear summer air;
A laughing schoolboy, without grief or care,
Riding the springy branches of an elm.

O for ten years, that I may overwhelm
Myself in poesy! so I may do the deed
That my own soul has to itself decreed.
Then I will pass the countries that I see
In long perspective, and continually
Taste their pure fountains.   First the realm I'll pass
Of Flora, and old Pan, sleep in the grass,
Feed upon apples red, and strawberries,
And choose each pleasure that my fancy sees;
Catch the white-handed nymphs in shady places,
To woo sweet kisses from averted faces,—
Play with their fingers, touch their shoulders white
Into a pretty shrinking with a bite
As hard as lips can make it; till agreed,
A lovely tale of human life we'll read.
And one will teach a tame dove how it best
May fan the cool air gently o'er my rest;
Another, bending o'er her nimble thread,
Will set a green robe floating round her head,
And still will dance with ever-varied ease,
Smiling upon the flowers and the trees;
Another will entice me on, and on,
Through almond blossoms and rich cinnamon;
Till in the bosom of a leafy world
We rest in silence, like two gems upcurl'd
In the recesses of a pearly shell.

And can I ever bid these joys farewell?
Yes, I must pass them for a nobler life,
Where I may find the agonies, the strife
Of human hearts: for lo! I see afar,
O'er-sailing the blue cragginess, a car
And steeds with streamy manes—the charioteer

Looks out upon the winds with glorious fear;
And now the numerous tramplings quiver lightly
Along a huge cloud's ridge; and now with sprightly
Wheel downward come they into fresher skies,
Tipt round with silver from the sun's bright eyes.
Still downward with capacious whirl they glide;
And now I see them on a green hill-side
In breezy rest among the nodding stalks.
The charioteer with wondrous gesture talks
To the trees and mountains; and there soon appear
Shapes of delight, of mystery, and fear,
Passing along before a dusky space
Made by some mighty oaks—as they would chase
Some ever-fleeting music, on they sweep.
Lo! how they murmur, laugh, and smile, and weep:
Some with upholden hand and mouth severe;
Some with their faces muffled to the ear
Between their arms; some clear in youthful bloom,
Go glad and smilingly athwart the gloom;
Some looking back, and some with upward gaze;
Yes, thousands in a thousand different ways
Flit onward—now a lovely wreath of girls
Dancing their sleek hair into tangled curls;
And now broad wings. Most awfully intent
The driver of those steeds is forward bent,
And seems to listen: O that I might know
All that he writes with such a hurrying glow!

The visions all are fled—the car is fled
Into the light of heaven, and in their stead
A sense of real things comes doubly strong,
And, like a muddy stream, would bear along,
My soul to nothingness: but I will strive
Against all doubtings, and will keep alive
The thought of that same chariot, and the strange
Journey it went.

Is there so small a range
In the present strength of manhood, that the high
Imagination cannot freely fly
As she was wont of old? prepare her steeds,
Paw up against the light, and do strange deeds
Upon the clouds? Has she not shown us all?

From the clear space of ether, to the small
Breath of new buds unfolding? From the meaning
Of Jove's large eyebrow, to the tender greening
Of April meadows? here her altar shone,
E'en in this isle; and who could paragon
The fervid choir that lifted up a noise
Of harmony, to where it aye will poise
Its mighty self of convoluting sound,
Huge as a planet, and like that roll round,
Eternally around a dizzy void?
Aye, in those days the Muses were nigh cloy'd
With honours: nor had any other care
Than to sing out and soothe their wavy hair.

Could all this be forgotten? Yes, a schism
Nurtured by foppery and barbarism
Made great Apollo blush for this his land.
Men were thought wise who could not understand
His glories; with a puling infant's force
They sway'd about upon a rocking-horse,
And thought it Pegasus. Ah, dismal-soul'd!
The winds of heaven blew, the ocean roll'd
Its gathering waves—ye felt it not. The blue
Bared its eternal bosom, and the dew
Of summer night collected still to make
The morning precious: Beauty was awake!
Why were ye not awake? But ye were dead
To things ye knew not of,—were closely wed
To musty laws lined out with wretched rule
And compass vile; so that ye taught a school
Of dolts to smooth, inlay, and clip, and fit,
Till, like the certain wands of Jacob's wit,
Their verses tallied. Easy was the task:
A thousand handicraftsmen wore the mask
Of Poesy. Ill-fated, impious race!
That blasphemed the bright Lyrist to his face,
And did not know it,—no, they went about,
Holding a poor, decrepit standard out,
Mark'd with most flimsy mottoes, and in large
The name of one Boileau!

                 O ye whose charge
It is to hover round our pleasant hills!

Whose congregated majesty so fills
My boundly reverence, that I cannot trace
Your hallow'd names, in this unholy place,
So near those common folk; did not their shames
Affright you?   Did our old lamenting Thames
Delight you? did ye never cluster round
Delicious Avon, with a mournful sound,
And weep?   Or did ye wholly bid adieu
To regions where no more the laurel grew?
Or did ye stay to give a welcoming
To some lone spirits who could proudly sing
Their youth away, and die?   'Twas even so.
But let me think away those times of woe:
Now 'tis a fairer season; ye have breathed
Rich benedictions o'er us; ye have wreathed
Fresh garlands: for sweet music has been heard
In many places; some has been upstirr'd
From out its crystal dwelling in a lake,
By a swan's ebon bill; from a thick brake,
Nested and quiet in a valley mild,
Bubbles a pipe; fine sounds are floating wild
About the earth: happy are ye and glad.
These things are, doubtless; yet in truth we've had
Strange thunders from the potency of song;
Mingled indeed with what is sweet and strong,
From majesty: but in clear truth the themes
Are ugly cubs, the poets' Polyphemes
Disturbing the grand sea.   A drainless shower
Of light is poesy; 'tis the supreme of power;
'Tis might half slumbering on its own right arm:
The very archings of her eyelids charm
A thousand willing agents to obey,
And still she governs with the mildest sway:
But strength alone, though of the Muses born,
Is like a fallen angel: trees uptorn,
Darkness, and worms, and shrouds, and sepulchres
Delight it; for it feeds upon the burrs
And thorns of life; forgetting the great end
Of poesy, that it should be a friend
To soothe the cares, and lift the thoughts of man.

    Yet I rejoice: a myrtle fairer than
E'er grew in Paphos, from the bitter weeds

Lifts its sweet head into the air, and feeds
A silent space with ever-sprouting green.
All tenderest birds there find a pleasant screen,
Creep through the shade with jaunty fluttering,
Nibble the little cupped flowers and sing.
Then let us clear away the choking thorns
From round its gentle stem ; let the young fawns,
Yeaned in after-times, when we are flown,
Find a fresh sward beneath it, overgrown
With simple flowers : let there nothing be
More boisterous than a lover's bended knee ;
Nought more ungentle than the placid look
Of one who leans upon a closed book ;
Nought more untranquil than the grassy slopes
Between two hills.   All hail, delightful hopes !
As she was wont, th' imagination
Into most lovely labyrinths will be gone,
And they shall be accounted poet kings
Who simply tell the most heart-easing things.
Oh may these joys be ripe before I die !

Will not some say that I presumptuously
Have spoken ? that from hastening disgrace
'Twere better far to hide my foolish face ?
That whining boyhood should with reverence bow
Ere the dread thunderbolt could reach me ?   How !
If I do hide myself, it sure shall be
In the very fane, the light of Poesy
If I do fall, at least I will be laid
Beneath the silence of a poplar shade ;
And over me the grass shall be smooth shaven ;
And there shall be a kind memorial graven.
But off, Despondence ! miserable bane !
They should not know thee, who athirst to gain
A noble end, are thirsty every hour.
What though I am not wealthy in the dower
Of spanning wisdom ; though I do not know
The shiftings of the mighty winds that blow
Hither and thither all the changing thoughts
Of man : though no great ministering reason sorts
Out the dark mysteries of human souls
To clear conceiving : yet there ever rolls

A vast idea before me, and I glean
Therefrom my liberty; thence too I've seen
The end and aim of Poesy.   'Tis clear
As anything most true; as that the year
Is made of the four seasons—manifest
As a large cross, some old cathedral's crest,
Lifted to the white clouds.   Therefore should I
Be but the essence of deformity,
A coward, did my very eyelids wink
At speaking out what I have dared to think.
Ah! rather let me like a madman run
Over some precipice; let the hot sun
Melt my Dedalian wings, and drive me down
Convulsed and headlong!   Stay! an inward frown
Of conscience bids me be more calm awhile.
An ocean dim, sprinkled with many an isle,
Spreads awfully before me.   How much toil!
How many days! what desperate turmoil!
Ere I can have explored its widenesses.
Ah, what a task! upon my bended knees,
I could unsay those—no, impossible;
Impossible!

                    For sweet relief I'll dwell
On humbler thoughts, and let this strange assay
Begun in gentleness die so away.
E'en now all tumult from my bosom fades:
I turn full-hearted to the friendly aids
That smooth the path of honour; brotherhood,
And friendliness, the nurse of mutual good.
The hearty grasp that sends a pleasant sonnet
Into the brain ere one can think upon it;
The silence when some rhymes are coming out;
And when they're come, the very pleasant rout:
The message certain to be done to-morrow.
'Tis perhaps as well that it should be to borrow
Some precious book from out its snug retreat,
To cluster round it when we next shall meet.
Scarce can I scribble on: for lovely airs
Are fluttering round the room like doves in pairs;
Many delights of that glad day recalling,
When first my senses caught their tender falling.

And with these airs come forms of elegance
Stooping their shoulders o'er a horse's prance,
Careless, and grand—fingers soft and round
Parting luxuriant curls; and the swift bound
Of Bacchus from his chariot, when his eye
Made Ariadne's cheek look blushingly.
Thus I remember all the pleasant flow
Of words at opening a portfolio.

    Things such as these are harbingers
To trains of peaceful images: the stirs
Of a swan's neck unseen among the rushes;
A linnet starting all about the bushes:
A butterfly, with golden wings broad-parted,
Nestling a rose, convulsed as though it smarted
With over-pleasure—many, many more,
Might I indulge at large in all my store
Of luxuries: yet I must not forget
Sleep, quiet with his poppy coronet:
For what there may be worthy in these rhymes
I partly owe to him: and thus, the chimes
Of friendly voices had just given place
To as sweet a silence, when I 'gan retrace
The pleasant day, upon a couch at ease.
It was a poet's house who keeps the keys
Of Pleasure's temple—round about were hung
The glorious features of the bards who sung
In other ages—cold and sacred busts
Smiled at each other.   Happy he who trusts
To clear Futurity his darling fame!
Then there were fauns and satyrs taking aim
At swelling apples with a frisky leap
And reaching fingers 'mid a luscious heap
Of vine-leaves.   Then there rose to view a fane
Of liney marble, and thereto a train
Of nymphs approaching fairly o'er the sward:
One, loveliest, holding her white hand toward
The dazzling sun-rise; two sisters sweet
Bending their graceful figures till they meet
Over the trippings of a little child:
And some are hearing, eagerly, the wild
Thrilling liquidity of dewy piping.

See, in another picture, nymphs are wiping
Cherishingly Diana's timorous limbs;
A fold of lawny mantle dabbling swims
At the bath's edge, and keeps a gentle motion
With the subsiding crystal: as when ocean
Heaves calmly its broad swelling smoothness o'er
Its rocky marge, and balances once more
The patient weeds, that now unshent by foam
Feel all about their undulating home.
Sappho's meek head was there half smiling down
At nothing; just as though the earnest frown
Of over-thinking had that moment gone
From off her brow, and left her all alone.

Great Alfred's too, with anxious, pitying eyes,
As if he always listen'd to the sighs
Of the goaded world; and Kosciusko's, worn
By horrid suff'rance—mightily forlorn.

Petrarch, outstepping from the shady green,
Starts at the sight of Laura; nor can wean
His eyes from her sweet face.   Most happy they
For over them was seen a free display
Of outspread wings, and from between them shone
The face of Poesy: from off her throne
She overlook'd things that I scarce could tell,
The very sense of where I was might well
Keep sleep aloof: but more than that there came
Thought after thought to nourish up the flame
Within my breast; so that the morning light
Surprised me even from a sleepless night;
And up I rose refresh'd, and glad, and gay,
Resolving to begin that very day
These lines; and howsoever they be done,
I leave them as a father does his son.

POEMS PUBLISHED IN 1820

TO A NIGHTINGALE

My heart aches, and a drowsy numbness pains
  My sense, as though of hemlock I had drunk,
Or emptied some dull opiate to the drains
  One minute past, and Lethe-wards had sunk :
'Tis not through envy of thy happy lot,
  But being too happy in thy happiness,—
    That thou, light-winged Dryad of the trees,
      In some melodious plot
  Of beechen green, and shadows numberless,
    Singest of summer in full-throated ease.

O for a draught of vintage, that hath been
  Cool'd a long age in the deep-delved earth,
Tasting of Flora and the country-green,
  Dance, and Provençal song, and sun-burnt mirth !
O for a beaker full of the warm South,
  Full of the true, the blushful Hippocrene,
    With beaded bubbles winking at the brim,
      And purple-stained mouth ;
  That I might drink and leave the world unseen,
    And with thee fade away into the forest dim :

Fade far away, dissolve, and quite forget
  What thou among the leaves hast never known,
The weariness, the fever, and the fret
  Here, where men sit and hear each other groan ;
Where palsy shakes a few, sad, last grey hairs,
  Where youth grows pale, and spectre-thin, and dies ;
    Where but to think is to be full of sorrow
      And leaden-eyed despairs ;
  Where beauty cannot keep her lustrous eyes,
    Or new Love pine at them beyond to-morrow.

Away! away! for I will fly to thee,
  Not charioted by Bacchus and his pards,
But on the viewless wings of Poesy,
  Though the dull brain perplexes and retards:
Already with thee! tender is the night,
    And haply the Queen-Moon is on her throne,
      Cluster'd around by all her starry Fays;
        But here there is no light,
    Save what from heaven is with the breezes blown
      Through verdurous glooms and winding mossy ways.

I cannot see what flowers are at my feet,
  Nor what soft incense hangs upon the boughs,
But, in embalmed darkness, guess each sweet
  Wherewith the seasonable month endows
The grass, the thicket, and the fruit-tree wild;
    White hawthorn, and the pastoral eglantine;
      Fast-fading violets cover'd up in leaves;
        And mid-May's eldest child,
    The coming musk-rose, full of dewy wine,
      The murmurous haunt of flies on summer eves.

Darkling I listen; and for many a time
  I have been half in love with easeful Death,
Call'd him soft names in many a mused rhyme,
  To take into the air my quiet breath;
Now more than ever seems it rich to die,
    To cease upon the midnight with no pain,
      While thou art pouring forth thy soul abroad
        In such an ecstasy!
    Still wouldst thou sing, and I have ears in vain—
      To thy high requiem become a sod.

Thou wast not born for death, immortal Bird!
  No hungry generations tread thee down;
The voice I hear this passing night was heard
  In ancient days by emperor and clown:
Perhaps the self-same song that found a path
    Through the sad heart of Ruth, when sick for home,
      She stood in tears amid the alien corn;
        The same that oft-times hath
    Charm'd magic casements, opening on the foam
      Of perilous seas, in faery lands forlorn.

Forlorn! the very word is like a bell
  To toll me back from thee to my sole self.
Adieu! the fancy cannot cheat so well
  As she is famed to do, deceiving elf,
Adieu! adieu! thy plaintive anthem fades
  Past the near meadows, over the still stream,
    Up the hill-side; and now 'tis buried deep
      In the next valley-glades:
  Was it a vision, or a waking dream?
    Fled is that music:—do I wake or sleep?

ON A GRECIAN URN

THOU still unravish'd bride of quietness!
  Thou foster-child of Silence and slow Time,
Sylvan historian, who canst thus express
  A flowery tale more sweetly than our rhyme:
What leaf-fringed legend haunts about thy shape
  Of deities or mortals, or of both,
    In Tempe or the dales of Arcady?
  What men or gods are these?   What maidens loath?
What mad pursuit?   What struggle to escape?
  What pipes and timbrels?   What wild ecstasy?

Heard melodies are sweet, but those unheard
  Are sweeter; therefore, ye soft pipes, play on;
Not to the sensual ear, but, more endear'd,
  Pipe to the spirit ditties of no tone:
Fair youth, beneath the trees, thou canst not leave
  Thy song, nor ever can those trees be bare;
    Bold Lover, never, never canst thou kiss,
Though winning near the goal—yet, do not grieve;
    She cannot fade, though thou hast not thy bliss,
  For ever wilt thou love, and she be fair!

Ah, happy, happy boughs! that cannot shed
  Your leaves, nor ever bid the Spring adieu;
And, happy melodist, unwearied,
  For ever piping songs for ever new;
More happy love! more happy, happy love!
  For ever warm and still to be enjoy'd,
    For ever panting and for ever young;

All breathing human passion far above,
  That leaves a heart high sorrowful and cloy'd,
    A burning forehead, and a parching tongue.

Who are these coming to the sacrifice?
  To what green altar, O mysterious priest,
Lead'st thou that heifer lowing at the skies,
  And all her silken flanks with garlands drest?
What little town by river or sea-shore,
  Or mountain-built with peaceful citadel,
    Is emptied of its folk, this pious morn?
And, little town, thy streets for evermore
  Will silent be; and not a soul to tell
    Why thou art desolate, can e'er return.

O Attic shape! Fair attitude! with brede
  Of marble men and maidens overwrought,
With forest branches and the trodden weed;
  Thou, silent form! dost tease us out of thought
As doth eternity: Cold Pastoral!
  When old age shall this generation waste,
    Thou shalt remain, in midst of other woe
Than ours, a friend to man, to whom thou say'st,
"Beauty is truth, truth beauty,"—that is all
  Ye know on earth, and all ye need to know.

TO PSYCHE

TO HIS BROTHER AND SISTER

"The following poem, the last I have written, is the first and only one with which I have taken even moderate pains; I have, for the most part, dashed off my lines in a hurry; this one I have done leisurely; I think it reads the more richly for it, and it will I hope encourage me to write other things in even a more peaceable and healthy spirit. You must recollect that Psyche was not embodied as a goddess before the time of Apuleius the Platonist, who lived after the Augustan age, and consequently the goddess was never worshipped or sacrificed to with any of the ancient fervour, and perhaps never thought of in the old religion: I am more orthodox than to let a heathen goddess be so neglected."—*Feb.*, 1819.

O GODDESS! hear these tuneless numbers, wrung
  By sweet enforcement and remembrance dear,

And pardon that thy secrets should be sung,
    Even into thine own soft-conchèd ear:
Surely I dreamt to-day, or did I see
    The wingèd Psyche with awaken'd eyes?
I wander'd in a forest thoughtlessly,
    And, on the sudden, fainting with surprise,
Saw two fair creatures, couchèd side by side
    In deepest grass, beneath the whispering roof
    Of leaves and trembled blossoms, where there ran
        A brooklet, scarce espied:
'Mid hush'd, cool-rooted flowers fragrant-eyed,
    Blue, silver-white, and budded Tyrian,
They lay calm-breathing on the bedded grass;
    Their arms embracèd, and their pinions too;
    Their lips touch'd not, but had not bade adieu
As if disjoinèd by soft-handed slumber,
And ready still past kisses to outnumber
    At tender eye-dawn of aurorean love:
        The wingèd boy I knew;
    But who wast thou, O happy, happy dove?
        His Psyche true!

O latest-born and loveliest vision far
    Of all Olympus' faded hierarchy!
Fairer than Phœbe's sapphire-region'd star,
    Or Vesper, amorous glow-worm of the sky;
Fairer than these, though temple thou hast none,
    Nor altar heap'd with flowers;
Nor Virgin-choir to make delicious moan
    Upon the midnight hours;
No voice, no lute, no pipe, no incense sweet
    From chain-swung censer teeming;
No shrine, no grove, no oracle, no heat
    Of pale-mouth'd prophet dreaming.
O brightest! though too late for antique vows,
    Too, too late for the fond believing lyre,
When holy were the haunted forest boughs,
    Holy the air, the water, and the fire;
Yet even in these days so far retired
    From happy pieties, thy lucent fans,
    Fluttering among the faint Olympians,
I see, and sing, by my own eyes inspired.

So let me be thy choir, and make a moan
    Upon the midnight hours!
Thy voice, thy lute, thy pipe, thy incense sweet
    From swinged censer teeming:
Thy shrine, thy grove, thy oracle, thy heat
    Of pale-mouth'd prophet dreaming.

Yes, I will be thy priest, and build a fane
    In some untrodden region of my mind,
Where branched thoughts, new-grown with pleasant pain,
    Instead of pines shall murmur in the wind:
Far, far around shall those dark-cluster'd trees
    Fledge the wild-ridged mountains steep by steep;
And there by zephyrs, streams, and birds, and bees,
    The moss-lain Dryads shall be lull'd to sleep;
And in the midst of this wide quietness
    A rosy sanctuary will I dress
With the wreath'd trellis of a working brain,
    With buds, and bells, and stars without a name.
With all the gardener Fancy e'er could feign,
    Who breeding flowers, will never breed the same:
And there shall be for thee all soft delight
    That shadowy thought can win,
A bright torch, and a casement ope at night,
    To let the warm Love in!

TO FANCY

Ever let the Fancy roam,
Pleasure never is at home:
At a touch sweet Pleasure melteth,
Like to bubbles when rain pelteth;
Then let winged Fancy wander
Through the thought still spread beyond her:
Open wide the mind's cage door,
She'll dart forth, and cloudward soar,
O sweet Fancy! let her loose;
Summer's joys are spoilt by use,
And the enjoying of the Spring

Fades as does its blossoming :
Autumn's red-lipp'd fruitage too,
Blushing through the mist and dew
Cloys with tasting :   What do then?
Sit thee by the ingle, when
The sear faggot blazes bright,
Spirit of a winter's night ;
When the soundless earth is muffled,
And the caked snow is shuffled
From the ploughboy's heavy shoon ;
When the Night doth meet the Noon
In a dark conspiracy
To banish Even from her sky.
Sit thee there, and send abroad,
With a mind self-overawed,
Fancy, high-commission'd :—send her ;
She has vassals to attend her :
She will bring, in spite of frost,
Beauties that the earth hath lost ;
She will bring thee, all together,
All delights of summer weather ;
All the buds and bells of May,
From dewy sward or thorny spray ;
All the heaped Autumn's wealth,
With a still, mysterious stealth
She will mix these pleasures up
Like three fit wines in a cup,
And thou shalt quaff it :—thou shalt hear
Distant harvest-carols clear ;
Rustle of the reaped corn ;
Sweet birds antheming the morn :
And, in the same moment—hark !
'Tis the early April lark,
Or the rooks, with busy caw,
Foraging for sticks and straw.
Thou shalt, at one glance, behold
The daisy and the marigold ;
White-plumed lilies, and the first
Hedge-grown primrose that hath burst ;
Shaded hyacinth, alway
Sapphire queen of the mid-May ;
And every leaf, and every flower

Pearled with the self-same shower.
Thou shalt see the field-mouse peep
Meagre from its celled sleep ;
And the snake all winter-thin
Cast on sunny bank its skin !
Freckled nest eggs thou shalt see
Hatching in the hawthorn-tree,
When the hen-bird's wing doth rest
Quiet on her mossy nest ;
Then the hurry and alarm
When the bee-hive casts its swarm ;
Acorns ripe down-pattering
While the autumn breezes sing.

Oh, sweet Fancy ! let her loose ;
Everything is spoilt by use :
Where's the cheek that doth not fade,
Too much gazed at ?   Where's the maid
Whose lip mature is ever new ?
Where's the eye, however blue,
Doth not weary ?   Where's the face
One would meet in every place ?
Where's the voice, however soft,
One would hear so very oft ?
At a touch sweet Pleasure melteth
Like to bubbles when rain pelteth.
Let, then, winged Fancy find
Thee a mistress to thy mind :
Dulcet-eyed as Ceres' daughter,
Ere the God of Torment taught her
How to frown and how to chide ;
With a waist and with a side
White as Hebe's, when her zone
Slipt its golden clasp, and down
Fell her kirtle to her feet,
While she held the goblet sweet,
And Jove grew languid.—Break the mesh
Of the Fancy's silken leash ;
Quickly break her prison-string,
And such joys as these she'll bring.—
Let the winged Fancy roam,
Pleasure never is at home

TO THE POETS

BARDS of Passion and of Mirth,
Ye have left your souls on earth !
Have ye souls in heaven too,
Double-lived in regions new ?
Yes, and those of heaven commune
With the spheres of sun and moon ;
With the noise of fountains wondrous,
And the parle of voices thund'rous ;
With the whisper of heaven's trees
And one another, in soft ease
Seated on Elysian lawns
Browsed by none but Dian's fawns ;
Underneath large blue-bells tented,
Where the daisies are rose-scented,
And the rose herself has got
Perfume which on earth is not ;
Where the nightingale doth sing
Not a senseless, tranced thing,
But divine, melodious truth,
Philosophic numbers smooth ;
Tales and golden histories
Of heaven and its mysteries.

Thus ye live on high, and then
On the earth ye live again ;
And the souls ye left behind you
Teach us, here, the way to find you,
Where your other souls are joying
Never slumber'd, never cloying.
Here, you earth-born souls still speak
To mortals, of their little week ;
Of their sorrows and delights ;
Of their passions and their spites ;
Of their glory and their shame ;
What does strengthen, and what maim.
Thus ye teach us, every day,
Wisdom, though fled far away.

Bards of Passion and of Mirth,
Ye have left your souls on earth !
Ye have souls in heaven too,
Double-lived in regions new !

LINES ON THE MERMAID TAVERN

Souls of poets dead and gone,
What Elysium have ye known,
Happy field or mossy cavern,
Choicer than the Mermaid Tavern ?
Have ye tippled drink more fine
Than mine host's Canary wine ?
Or are fruits of Paradise
Sweeter than those dainty pies
Of venison ?   O generous food !
Drest as though bold Robin Hood
Would, with his maid Marian,
Sup and bowse from horn and can.

I have heard that on a day
Mine host's sign-board flew away,
Nobody knew whither, till
An Astrologer's old quill
To a sheepskin gave the story,—
Said he saw you in your glory,
Underneath a new old-sign
Sipping beverage divine,
And pledging with contented smack
The Mermaid in the Zodiac.

Souls of poets dead and gone,
What Elysium have ye known,
Happy field or mossy cavern,
Choicer than the Mermaid Tavern ?

ROBIN HOOD

TO A FRIEND

No ! those days are gone away,
And their hours are old and gray,

And their minutes buried all
Under the down-trodden pall
Of the leaves of many years :
Many times have Winter's shears,
Frozen North, and Chilling East,
Sounded tempests to the feast
Of the forest's whispering fleeces,
Since men knew nor rent nor leases.

No, the bugle sounds no more,
And the twanging bow no more ;
Silent is the ivory shrill
Past the heath and up the hill ;
There is no mid-forest laugh,
Where lone Echo gives the half
To some wight, amazed to hear
Jesting, deep in forest drear.

On the fairest time of June
You may go, with sun or moon,
Or the seven stars to light you,
Or the polar ray to right you ;
But you never may behold
Little John, or Robin bold :
Never one, of all the clan,
Thrumming on an empty can
Some old hunting ditty, while
He doth his green way beguile
To fair hostess Merriment,
Down beside the pasture Trent ;
For he left the merry tale,
Messenger for spicy ale.

Gone, the merry morris din ;
Gone, the song of Gamelyn ;
Gone, the tough-belted outlaw
Idling in the " grené shawe " ;
All are gone away and past !
And if Robin should be cast
Sudden from his tufted grave,
And if Marian should have
Once again her forest days,
She would weep, and he would craze ;

He would swear, for all his oaks,
Fall'n beneath the dock-yard strokes,
Have rotted on the briny seas ;
She would weep that her wild bees
Sang not to her—strange ! that honey
Can't be got without hard money !

      So it is ; yet let us sing
Honour to the old bow-string !
Honour to the bugle-horn !
Honour to the woods unshorn !
Honour to the Lincoln green !
Honour to the archer keen !
Honour to tight little John,
And the horse he rode upon !
Honour to bold Robin Hood,
Sleeping in the underwood :
Honour to Maid Marian,
And to all the Sherwood clan !
Though their days have hurried by
Let us two a burden try.

TO AUTUMN

SEASON of mists and mellow fruitfulness !
    Close bosom-friend of the maturing sun ;
Conspiring with him how to load and bless
    With fruit the vines that round the thatch-eaves run ;
To bend with apples the moss'd cottage-trees,
    And fill all fruit with ripeness to the core ;
      To swell the gourd, and plump the hazel shells
With a sweet kernel ; to set budding more,
And still more, later flowers for the bees,
Until they think warm days will never cease,
      For Summer has o'er-brimm'd their clammy cells.

Who hath not seen thee oft amid thy store ?
    Sometimes whoever seeks abroad may find
Thee sitting careless on a granary floor,
    Thy hair soft-lifted by the winnowing wind ;

Or on a half-reap'd furrow sound asleep,
  Drowsed with the fumes of poppies, while thy hook
    Spares the next swath and all its twined flowers ;
And sometime like a gleaner thou dost keep
  Steady thy laden head across a brook ;
  Or by a cider-press, with patient look,
    Thou watchest the last oozings, hours by hours.

Where are the songs of Spring ? Ay, where are they ?
  Think not of them, thou hast thy music too,
    While barred clouds bloom the soft-dying day,
And touch the stubble-plains with rosy hue ;
  Then in a wailful choir, the small gnats mourn
  Among the river sallows, borne aloft
    Or sinking as the light wind lives or dies ;
And full-grown lambs loud bleat from hilly bourn ;
  Hedge-crickets sing ; and now with treble soft
  The redbreast whistles from a garden-croft,
    And gathering swallows twitter in the skies.

ON MELANCHOLY

No, no ! go not to Lethe, neither twist
  Wolf's-bane, tight-rooted, for its poisonous wine ;
Nor suffer thy pale forehead to be kiss'd
  By nightshade, ruby grape of Proserpine ;
Make not your rosary of yew-berries,
  Nor let the beetle nor the death-moth be
    Your mournful Psyche, nor the downy owl
A partner in your sorrow's mysteries ;
  For shade to shade will come too drowsily,
    And drown the wakeful anguish of the soul.

But when the melancholy fit shall fall
  Sudden from heaven like a weeping cloud,
That fosters the droop-headed flowers all,
  And hides the green hill in an April shroud ;
Then glut thy sorrow on a morning rose,
  Or on the rainbow of the salt sand-wave,
    Or on the wealth of globed peonies ;

Or if thy mistress some rich anger shows,
    Emprison her soft hand, and let her rave,
      And feed deep, deep upon her peerless eyes.

She dwells with Beauty—Beauty that must die;
    And Joy, whose hand is ever at his lips
Bidding adieu; and aching Pleasure nigh,
    Turning to poison while the bee-mouth sips:
Ay, in the very temple of Delight
    Veil'd Melancholy has her sovran shrine,
      Though seen of none save him whose strenuous tongue
Can burst Joy's grape against his palate fine:
His soul shall taste the sadness of her might,
    And be among her cloudy trophies hung.

TO BYRON

BYRON! how sweetly sad thy melody!
    Attuning still the soul to tenderness,
    As if soft Pity, with unusual stress,
Had touch'd her plaintive lute, and thou being by,
Hadst caught the tones, nor suffer'd them to die.
    O'ershadowing sorrow doth not make thee less
    Delightful: thou thy griefs dost dress
With a bright halo, shining beamily,
As when a cloud the golden moon doth veil,
    Its sides are tinged with a resplendent glow,
Through the dark robe oft amber rays prevail,
    And like fair veins in sable marble flow.
Still warble, dying swan! still tell the tale,
    The enchanting tale, the tale of pleasing woe.

TO CHATTERTON

O CHATTERTON! how very sad thy fate!
    Dear child of sorrow—son of misery!
    How soon the film of death obscured that eye,

Whence **Genius** mildly flash'd, and high debate.
How soon that voice, majestic and elate,
   Melted in dying numbers! Oh! how nigh
   Was night to thy fair morning. Thou didst die
A half-blown flow'ret which cold blasts amate.
But this is past: thou art among the stars
   Of highest heaven: to the rolling spheres
Thou sweetest singest: nought thy hymning mars,
   Above the ingrate world and human fears.
On earth the good man base detraction bars
   From thy fair name, and waters it with tears.

TO SPENSER

SPENSER! a jealous honourer of thine,
   A forester deep in thy midmost trees,
Did, last eve, ask my promise to refine
   Some English, that might strive thine ear to please.
   But, Elfin-poet! 'tis impossible
For an inhabitant of wintry earth
   To rise, like Phœbus, with a golden quill,
Fire-wing'd, and make a morning in his mirth.
   It is impossible to 'scape from toil
O' the sudden, and receive thy spiriting:
   The flower must drink the nature of the soil
Before it can put forth its blossoming:
   Be with me in the summer days, and I
   Will for thine honour and his pleasure try.

ODE TO APOLLO

IN thy western halls of gold,
   When thou sittest in thy state,
Bards, that erst sublimely told
   Heroic deeds, and sang of fate,
With fervour seize their adamantine lyres,
Whose chords are solid rays, and twinkle radiant fires

Here Homer with his nervous arms
   Strikes the twanging harp of war,

And even the western splendour warms,
    While the trumpets sound afar :
But, what creates the most intense surprise,
His soul looks out through renovated eyes.

Then, through thy Temple wide, melodious swells
    The sweet majestic tone of Maro's lyre :
The soul delighted on each accent dwells,—
    Enraptured dwells,—not daring to respire,
The while he tells of grief around a funeral pyre.

'Tis awful silence then again ;
    Expectant stand the spheres ;
    Breathless the laurell'd peers,
Nor move, till ends the lofty strain,
Nor move till Milton's tuneful thunders cease,
And leave once more the ravish'd heavens in peace.

Thou biddest Shakspeare wave his hand,
    And quickly forward spring
The Passions—a terrific band—
    And each vibrates the string
That with its tyrant temper best accords,
While from their Master's lips pour forth the inspiring
    words.

A silver trumpet Spenser blows,
    And, as its martial notes to silence flee,
From a virgin chorus flows
    A hymn in praise of spotless Chastity.
'Tis still ! Wild warblings from the Æolian lyre
Enchantment softly breathe, and tremblingly expire.

Next thy Tasso's ardent numbers
    Float along the pleased air,
Calling youth from idle slumbers,
    Rousing them from Pleasure's lair :
Then o'er the strings his fingers gently move,
And melt the soul to pity and to love.

But when *Thou* joinest with the Nine,
And all the powers of song combine,
    We listen here on earth :

The dying tones that fill the air,
    And charm the ear of evening fair,
From thee, great God of Bards, receive their heavenly birth.
    February, 1815.

TO A YOUNG LADY WHO SENT ME A
LAUREL CROWN

FRESH morning gusts have blown away all fear
    From my glad bosom,—now from gloominess
    I mount for ever—not an atom less
Than the proud laurel shall content my bier.
No! by the eternal stars! or why sit here
    In the Sun's eye, and 'gainst my temples press
    Apollo's very leaves, woven to bless
By thy white fingers and thy spirit clear.
Lo! who dares say, "Do this"? Who dares call down
    My will from its high purpose? Who say, "Stand,"
Or "Go"? This mighty moment I would frown
    On abject Cæsars—not the stoutest band
Of mailed heroes should tear off my crown:
    Yet would I kneel and kiss thy gentle hand!

HYMN TO APOLLO

        GOD of the golden bow,
            And of the golden lyre,
        And of the golden hair,
            And of the golden fire,
                Charioteer
                Round the patient year,
        Where—where slept thine ire,
    When like a blank idiot I put on thy wreath.
            Thy laurel, thy glory,
            The light of thy story,
    Or was I a worm—too low creeping for death?
            O Delphic Apollo!

    The Thunderer grasp'd and grasp'd,
        The Thunderer frown'd and frown'd;
C

The eagle's feathery mane
    For wrath became stiffen'd—the sound
        Of breeding thunder
        Went drowsily under,
    Muttering to be unbound.
O why didst thou pity, and beg for a worm?
        Why touch thy soft lute
        Till the thunder was mute,
Why was I not crush'd—such a pitiful germ?
        O Delphic Apollo!

The Pleiades were up,
    Watching the silent air;
The seeds and roots in Earth
    Were swelling for summer fare;
        The Ocean, its neighbour,
        Was at his old labour,
    When, who—who did dare
To tie for a moment thy plant round his brow,
        And grin and look proudly,
        And blaspheme so loudly,
And live for that honour, to stoop to thee now?
        O Delphic Apollo!

AS FROM THE DARKENING GLOOM

As from the darkening gloom a silver dove
    Upsoars, and darts into the eastern light,
    On pinions that nought moves but pure delight,
So fled thy soul into the realms above,
Regions of peace and everlasting love;
    Where happy spirits, crown'd with circlets bright
    Of starry beam, and gloriously bedight,
Taste the high joy none but the blest can prove.
There thou or joinest the immortal quire
    In melodies that even heaven fair
Fill with superior bliss, or, at desire
    O' the omnipotent Father, cleav'st the air
On holy message sent.—What pleasure's higher?
    Wherefore does any grief our joy impair?

    1816.

SUMMER'S EVE

OH ! how I love, on a fair summer's eve,
    When streams of light pour down the golden west,
    And on the balmy zephyrs tranquil rest
The silver clouds, far—far away to leave
All meaner thoughts, and take a sweet reprieve
    From little cares ; to find, with easy quest,
    A fragrant wild, with Nature's beauty drest,
And there into delight my soul deceive,
There warm my breast with patriotic lore,
    Musing on Milton's fate—on Sydney's bier—
Till their stern forms before my mind arise :
Perhaps on wing of Poesy upsoar,
    Full often dropping a delicious tear,
When some melodious sorrow spells mine eyes.

AFTER DARK VAPOURS

AFTER dark vapours have oppress'd our plains
    For a long dreary season, comes a day
    Born of the gentle South, and clears away
From the sick heavens all unseemly stains.
The anxious month, relieved from its pains,
    Takes as a long-lost right the feel of May,
    The eye-lids with the passing coolness play,
Like rose-leaves with the drip of summer rains.
And calmest thoughts come round us—as of leaves
    Budding—fruit ripening in stillness—autumn suns
Smiling at eve upon the quiet sheaves,—
Sweet Sappho's cheek,—a sleeping infant's breath,—
    The gradual sand that through an hour-glass runs,—
A woodland rivulet,—a Poet's death.

    Jan., 1817.

WRITTEN ON THE BLANK SPACE OF A LEAF AT THE END OF CHAUCER'S TALE OF "THE FLOWRE AND THE LEFE"

THIS pleasant tale is like a little copse;
    The honied lines so freshly interlace,
    To keep the reader in so sweet a place,

So that he here and there full-hearted stops ;
And oftentimes he feels the dewy drops
   Come cool and suddenly against his face,
   And, by the wandering melody, may trace
Which way the tender-legged linnet hops.
Oh ! what a power has white simplicity !
   What mighty power has this gentle story !
   I, that do ever feel athirst for glory,
Could at this moment be content to lie
   Meekly upon the grass, as those whose sobbings
   Were heard of none beside the mournful robins.

     1817.

ON SEEING THE ELGIN MARBLES FOR
THE FIRST TIME

My spirit is too weak ; mortality
   Weighs heavily on me like unwilling sleep,
   And each imagined pinnacle and steep
Of godlike hardship tells me I must die
Like a sick eagle looking at the sky.
   Yet 'tis a gentle luxury to weep,
   That I have not the cloudy winds to keep
Fresh for the opening of the morning's eye.
Such dim-conceived glories of the brain
   Bring round the heart an indescribable feud ;
So do these wonders a most dizzy pain,
   That mingles Grecian grandeur with the rude
Wasting of old Time—with a billowy main,
   A sun, a shadow of a magnitude.

TO HAYDON

(WITH THE ABOVE)

Haydon ! forgive me that I cannot speak
   Definitely of these mighty things ;
   Forgive me, that I have not eagle's wings,
That what I want I know not where to seek.

And think that I would not be over-meek,
   In rolling out upfollow'd thunderings,
   Even to the steep of Heliconian springs,
Were I of ample strength for such a freak.
Think, too, that all these numbers should be thine;
   Whose else?   In this who touch thy vesture's hem?
For, when men stared at what was most divine
   With brainless idiotism and o'erwise phlegm,
Thou hadst beheld the full Hesperian shine
   Of their star in the east, and gone to worship them!

ON A PICTURE OF LEANDER

COME hither, all sweet maidens soberly,
   Down-looking aye, and with a chasten'd light
   Hid in the fringes of your eyelids white,
And meekly let your fair hands joined be,
As if so gentle that ye could not see,
   Untouch'd, a victim of your beauty bright,
   Sinking away to his young spirit's night,
Sinking bewilder'd 'mid the dreary sea:
'Tis young Leander toiling to his death;
   Nigh swooning, he doth purse his weary lips
For Hero's cheek, and smiles against her smile.
   O horrid dream! see how his body dips,
Dead-heavy; arms and shoulders gleam a while:
He's gone; up bubbles all his amorous breath!

LINES TO ———

   THINK not of it, sweet one, so;—
      Give it not a tear;
   Sigh thou mayst, and bid it go
      Any—anywhere.

   Do not look so sad, sweet one,—
      Sad and fadingly;
   Shed one drop then—it is gone—
      Oh! 'twas born to die!

Still so pale? then, dearest, weep;
  Weep, I'll count the tears,
And each one shall be a bliss
  For thee in after years.

Brighter has it left thine eyes
  Than a sunny rill;
And thy whispering melodies
  Are tenderer still.

Yet—as all things mourn a while
  At fleeting blisses;
Let us too; but be our dirge
  A dirge of kisses.

1817.

LINES

Unfelt, unheard, unseen,
  I've left my little queen,
Her languid arms in silver slumber lying:
  Ah! through their nestling touch,
  Who—who could tell how much
There is for madness—cruel, or complying?

Those faery lids how sleek!
  Those lips how moist!—they speak,
In ripest quiet, shadows of sweet sounds:
  Into my fancy's ear
  Melting a burden dear,
How "Love doth know no fulness, nor no bounds."

True!—tender monitors!
  I bend unto your laws:
This sweetest day for dalliance was born!
  So, without more ado,
  I'll feel my heaven anew,
For all the blushing of the hasty morn.

1817.

ON THE SEA

It keeps eternal whisperings around
　Desolate shores, and with its mighty swell
　Gluts twice ten thousand caverns, till the spell
Of Hecate leaves them their old shadowy sound.
Often 'tis in such gentle temper found,
　That scarcely will the very smallest shell
　Be moved for days from whence it sometime fell,
When last the winds of heaven were unbound.
Oh ye! who have your eye-balls vex'd and tired,
　Feast them upon the wideness of the Sea;
Oh ye! whose ears are dinn'd with uproar rude,
　Or fed too much with cloying melody,—
Sit ye near some old cavern's mouth, and brood
Until ye start, as if the sea-nymphs quired!

　Aug., 1817.

ON LEIGH HUNT'S POEM, THE "STORY OF RIMINI"

Who loves to peer up at the morning sun,
　With half-shut eyes and comfortable cheek,
　Let him, with this sweet tale, full often seek
For meadows where the little rivers run;
Who loves to linger with that brightest one
　Of heaven—Hesperus—let him lowly speak
　These numbers to the night, and starlight meek,
Or moon, if that her hunting be begun.
He who knows these delights, and too is prone
　To moralise upon a smile or tear,
Will find at once a region of his own,
　A bower for his spirit, and will steer
To alleys, where the fir-tree drops its cone,
　Where robins hop, and fallen leaves are sear.

　1817.

FRAGMENTS

TO REYNOLDS

WHERE'S the Poet? show him! show him,
Muses nine! that I may know him.
'Tis the man who with a man
Is an equal, be he King,
Or poorest of the beggar-clan,
Or any other wondrous thing
A man may be 'twixt ape and Plato;
'Tis the man who with a bird,
Wren, or Eagle, finds his way to
All its instincts; he hath heard
The Lion's roaring, and can tell
What his horny throat expresseth,
And to him the Tiger's yell
Comes articulate and presseth
On his ear like mother-tongue.

MODERN LOVE

AND what is love? It is a doll, dress'd up,
For idleness to cosset, nurse and dandle;
A thing of soft misnomers, so divine
That silly youth doth think to make itself
Divine by loving, and so goes on
Yawning and doting a whole summer long,
Till Miss's comb is made a pearl tiara,
And common Wellingtons turn Romeo boots;
Then Cleopatra lives at number seven,
And Antony resides in Brunswick Square.
Fools! if some passions high have warm'd the world,
If Queens and Soldiers have play'd deep for hearts,
It is no reason why such agonies

Should be more common than the growth of weeds.
Fools! make me whole again that weighty pearl
The Queen of Egypt melted, and I'll say
That ye may love in spite of beaver hats.

FRAGMENT OF "THE CASTLE BUILDER"

. . . .

TO-NIGHT I'll have my friar—let me think
About my room,—I'll have it in the pink;
It should be rich and sombre, and the moon,
Just in its mid-life in the midst of June,
Should look thro' four large windows, and display
Clear, but for gold-fish vases in the way,
Their glassy diamonding on Turkish floor;
The tapers keep aside, an hour or more,
To see what else the moon alone can show;
While the night-breeze doth softly let us know
My terrace is well-bower'd with oranges.
Upon the floor the dullest spirit sees
A guitar-ribbon and a lady's glove
Beside a crumple-leaved tale of love;
A tambour-frame, with Venus sleeping there
All finish'd but some ringlets of her hair;
A viol, bow-strings torn, cross-wise upon
A glorious folio of Anacreon;
A skull upon a mat of roses lying,
Ink'd purple with a song concerning dying;
An hour-glass on the turn, amid the trails
Of passion-flower;—just in time there sails
A cloud across the moon,—the lights bring in,
And see what more my phantasy can win.
It is a gorgeous room, but somewhat sad;
The draperies are so, as tho' they had
Been made for Cleopatra's winding-sheet:
And opposite the steadfast eye doth meet
A spacious looking-glass, upon whose face,
In letters raven-sombre, you may trace
Old "Mene, Mene, Tekel, Upharsin."
Greek busts and statuary have ever been

C2

Held, by the finest spirits, fitter far
Than vase grotesque and Siamesian jar ;
Therefore 'tis sure a want of Attic taste
That I should rather love a Gothic waste
Of eyesight on cinque-coloured potter's clay,
Than on the marble fairness of old Greece.
My table-coverlets of Jason's fleece
And black Numidian sheep-wool should be wrought,
Gold, black, and heavy, from the Lama brought.
My ebon sofas should delicious be
With down from Leda's cygnet progeny.
My pictures all Salvator's, save a few
Of Titian's portraiture, and one, though new,
Of Haydon's in its fresh magnificence.
My wine—oh good ! 'tis here at my desire,
And I must sit to supper with my friar.

.   .   .   .

WELCOME JOY, AND WELCOME SORROW

"Under the flag
Of each his faction, they to battle bring
Their embryo atoms."—MILTON.

WELCOME joy, and welcome sorrow,
    Lethe's weed and Hermes' feather ;
Come to-day and come to-morrow,
    I do love you both together !
    I love to mark sad faces in fair weather ;
And hear a merry laugh amid the thunder;
    Fair and foul I love together :
Meadows sweet where flames are under,
And a giggle at a wonder ;
Visage sage at pantomime ;
Funeral, and steeple-chime ;
Infant playing with a skull ;
Morning fair, and shipwreck'd hull ;
Nightshade with the woodbine kissing ;
Serpents in red roses hissing ;
Cleopatra regal-dress'd
With the aspic at her breast ;
Dancing music, music sad,
Both together, sane and mad ;

Muses bright and muses pale;
Sombre Saturn, Momus hale;—
Laugh and sigh, and laugh again;
Oh! the sweetness of the pain!
Muses bright and muses pale,
Bare your faces of the veil;
Let me see; and let me write
Of the day and of the night—
Both together:—let me slake
All my thirst for sweet heart-ache;
Let my bower be of yew,
Interwreath'd with myrtles new;
Pines and lime-trees full in bloom
And my couch a low grass-tomb.

TO A CAT

Cat! who hast pass'd thy grand climacteric,
 How many mice and rats hast in thy days
 Destroy'd?—How many tit bits stolen? Gaze
With those bright languid segments green, and prick
Those velvet ears—but pr'ythee do not stick
 Thy latent talons in me—and upraise
 Thy gentle mew—and tell me all thy frays
Of fish and mice, and rats and tender chick.
Nay, look not down, nor lick thy dainty wrists—
 For all the wheezy asthma,—and for all
Thy tail's tip is nick'd off—and though the fists
 Of many a maid have given thee many a maul,
Still is that fur as soft as when the lists
 In youth thou enter'dst on glass-bottled wall.

ON A LOCK OF MILTON'S HAIR

"I was at Hunt's the other day, and he surprised me with a real authenticated lock of Milton's hair. I know you would like what I wrote thereon, so here it is—as they say of a Sheep in a Nursery Book." —*Jan.*, 1818.

Chief of organic numbers!
Old Scholar of the Spheres
Thy spirit never slumbers,
But rolls about our ears

For ever and for ever!
O what a mad endeavour
      Worketh He,
Who to thy sacred and ennobled hearse
Would offer a burnt sacrifice of verse
      And melody.

How heavenward thou soundest!
Live Temple of sweet noise.
And Discord unconfoundest,
Giving Delight new joys,
And Pleasure nobler pinions:
O where are thy dominions?

      Lend thine ear
To a young Delian oath—ay, by thy soul,
By all that from thy mortal lips did roll,
And by the kernel of thy earthly love,
Beauty in things on earth and things above,
      I swear!

    When every childish fashion
    Has vanished from my rhyme,
    Will I, grey gone in passion,
    Leave to an after-time
    Hymning and Harmony
Of thee and of thy works, and of thy life;
But vain is now the burning and the strife;
Pangs are in vain, until I grow high-rife
      With old Philosophy,
And mad with glimpses of futurity.

For many years my offerings must be hush'd;
When I do speak, I'll think upon this hour,
Because I feel my forehead hot and flushed,
Even at the simplest vassal of thy power,
      A lock of thy bright hair,—
      Sudden it came,
And I was startled when I caught thy name
      Coupled so unaware;
Yet at the moment temperate was my blood—
I thought I had beheld it from the flood!

WRITTEN BEFORE RE-READING
"KING LEAR"

O GOLDEN-TONGUED Romance with serene lute!
  Fair plumed Syren! Queen! if far away!
  Leave melodizing on this wintry day,
Shut up thine olden volume, and be mute.
Adieu! for once again the fierce dispute,
  Betwixt Hell torment and impassion'd clay
  Must I burn through; once more assay
The bitter sweet of this Shakespearian fruit.
Chief Poet! and ye clouds of Albion,
  Begetters of our deep eternal theme,
When I am through the old oak forest gone,
  Let me not wander in a barren dream,
But when I am consumed with the Fire,
Give me new Phœnix-wings to fly at my desire,

Jan., 1818.

WHEN I HAVE FEARS

WHEN I have fears that I may cease to be
  Before my pen has glean'd my teeming brain,
Before high-piled books, in charact'ry,
  Hold like full garners the full-ripen'd grain;
When I behold, upon the night's starr'd face,
  Huge cloudy symbols of a high romance,
And feel that I may never live to trace
  Their shadows, with the magic hand of chance;
And when I feel, fair creature of an hour!
  That I shall never look upon thee more,
Never have relish in the faery power
  Of unreflecting love!—then on the shore
Of the wide world I stand alone, and think,
Till Love and Fame to nothingness do sink.

1817.

PLAYFUL LINES

From a Letter to Reynolds, July 31, 1818

HENCE Burgundy, Claret and Port;
 Away with old Hock and Madeira,
Too earthly ye are for my sport;
 There's a beverage brighter and clearer.
Instead of a pitiful rummer,
My wine overbrims a whole summer;
  My bowl is the sky,
  And I drink at my eye,
  Till I feel in brain
  A Delphian pain.——
Then follow, my Caius, then follow;
  On the green of the hill
  We will drink our fill
  Of golden sunshine,
  Till our brains intertwine
With the glory and grace of Apollo!
  God of the meridian,
   And of the east and west,
  To thee my soul is flown,
   And my body is earthward pressed.——
  It is an awful mission,
  A terrible division;
  And leaves a gulph austere
  To be filled with worldly fear.
  Aye, when the soul's fled
  To high above our head,
  Affrighted do we gaze
  After its airy maze,
  As doth a mother wild,
  When her young infant child
  Is in an eagle's claws.——
  And is not this the cause
  Of madness?—God of song,
  Thou bearest me along
  Through sights I scarce can bear;
  O let me, let me share

With the hot lyre and thee,
The staid Philosophy ;
Temper my lonely hours,
And let me see thy bowers
More unalarmed !

TO THE NILE

Son of the old Moon-mountains African !
Stream of the Pyramid and Crocodile !
We call thee fruitful, and that very while
A desert fills our seeing's inward span :
Nurse of swart nations since the world began,
Art thou so fruitful ? or dost thou beguile
Those men to honour thee, who, worn with toil,
Rest them a space 'twixt Cairo and Decan ?
O may dark fancies err ! They surely do ;
'Tis ignorance that makes a barren waste
Of all beyond itself. Thou dost bedew
Green rushes like our rivers, and dost taste
The pleasant sun-rise. Green isles hast thou too,
And to the sea as happily dost haste.

TO A LADY SEEN FOR A FEW MOMENTS
AT VAUXHALL

Time's sea hath been five years at its slow ebb ;
    Long hours have to and fro let creep the sand ;
Since I was tangled in thy beauty's web,
    And snared by the ungloving of thine hand.
And yet I never look on midnight sky,
    But I behold thine eyes' well memoried light ;
I cannot look upon the rose's dye,
    But to thy cheek my soul doth take its flight ;
I cannot look on any budding flower,
    But my fond ear, in fancy at thy lips,
And hearkening for a love-sound, doth devour
    Its sweets in the wrong sense :—Thou dost eclipse
Every delight with sweet remembering,
And grief unto my darling joys dost bring.

ANSWER TO A SONNET BY J. H. REYNOLDS, ENDING—

" Dark eyes are dearer far
Than those that mock the hyacinthine bell."

BLUE ! 'Tis the life of heaven,—the domain
   Of Cynthia,—the wide palace of the sun,—
The tent of Hesperus, and all his train,—
   The bosomer of clouds, gold, grey, and dun.
Blue ! 'Tis the life of waters—ocean
   And all its vassal streams : pools numberless
May rage, and foam, and fret, but never can
   Subside, if not to dark-blue nativeness.
Blue ! gentle cousin of the forest-green,
   Married to green in all the sweetest flowers—
Forget-me-not,—the blue-bell,—and, that queen
   Of secrecy, the violet : what strange powers
Hast thou, as a mere shadow !   But how great,
When in an Eye thou art alive with fate !

Feb., 1818.

TO J. H. REYNOLDS

O THAT a week could be an age, and we
   Felt parting and warm meeting every week,
Then one poor year a thousand years would be,
   The flush of welcome ever on the cheek :
So could we live long life in little space,
   So time itself would be annihilate,
So a day's journey in oblivious haze
   To serve our joys would lengthen and dilate.
O to arrive each Monday morn from Ind !
   To land each Tuesday from the rich Levant !
In little time a host of joys to bind,
   And keep our souls in one eternal pant !
This morn, my friend, and yester-evening taught
Me how to harbour such a happy thought.

TO REYNOLDS

"I was led into these thoughts, my dear Reynolds, by the beauty of the morning operating on a sense of idleness. I have not read any books—the morning said I was right. I had no idea but of the morning, and the Thrush said I was right, seeming to say—" (*Letter to Reynolds, Feb.,* 1818.)

O THOU whose face hath felt the Winter's wind,
Whose eye has seen the snow-clouds hung in mist,
And the black elm tops 'mong the freezing stars!
To thee the spring will be a harvest time.
O thou whose only book has been the light
Of supreme darkness, which thou feddest on
Night after night, when Phœbus was away!
To thee the spring shall be a triple morn.
O fret not after knowledge. I have none,
And yet my song comes native with the warmth.
O fret not after knowledge! I have none,
And yet the evening listens. He who saddens
At thought of idleness cannot be idle,
And he's awake who thinks himself asleep.

THE HUMAN SEASONS

FOUR Seasons fill the measure of the year;
    There are four seasons in the mind of man:
He has his lusty Spring, when fancy clear
    Takes in all beauty with an easy span:
He has his Summer, when luxuriously
    Spring's honey'd cud of youthful thought he loves
To ruminate, and by such dreaming high
    Is nearest unto Heaven: quiet coves
His soul has in its Autumn, when his wings
    He furleth close; contented so to look
On mists in idleness—to let fair things
    Pass by unheeded as a threshold brook.
He has his Winter too of pale misfeature,
Or else he would forego his mortal nature.

EXTRACTS FROM AN OPERA

O ! WERE I one of the Olympian twelve
Their godships should pass this into a law,—
That when a man doth set himself in toil
After some beauty veiled far away,
Each step he took should make his lady's hand
More soft, more white, and her fair cheek more fair,
And for each briar-berry he might eat
A kiss should bud upon the tree of love,
And pulp and ripen richer every hour,
To melt away upon the traveller's lips.

   .   .   .   .   .   .

DAISY'S SONG

The sun, with his great eye,
Sees not so much as I ;
And the moon, all silver, proud,
Might as well be in a cloud.

And O the spring—the spring !
I lead the life of a king !
Couch'd in the teeming grass,
I spy each pretty lass.

I look where no one dares,
And I stare where no one stares ;
And when the night is nigh,
Lambs bleat my lullaby.

   .   .   .   .   .   .

FOLLY'S SONG

When wedding fiddles are a-playing,
               Huzza for folly O !
And when maidens go a-Maying,
               Huzza, &c.
When a milk-pail is upset,
               Huzza, &c.
And the clothes left in the wet,
               Huzza, &c.

When the barrel's set abroach,
    Huzza, &c.
When Kate Eyebrow keeps a coach,
    Huzza, &c.
When the pig is over-roasted,
    Huzza, &c.
And the cheese is over-toasted,
    Huzza, &c.
When Sir Snap is with his lawyer,
    Huzza, &c.
And Miss Chip has kiss'd the sawyer,
    Huzza, &c.

.   .   .   .   .

Oh, I am frighten'd with most hateful thoughts!
Perhaps her voice is not a nightingale's,
Perhaps her teeth are not the fairest pearl;
Her eye-lashes may be, for aught I know,
Not longer than the May-fly's small fan-horns;
There may not be one dimple on her hand,
And freckles many! Ah! a careless nurse,
In haste to teach the little thing to walk,
May have crumpt up a pair of Dian's legs,
And warpt the ivory of a Juno's neck.

.   .   .   .   :

SONG

The stranger lighted from his steed,
  And ere he spake a word
He seized my lady's lily hand,
  And kiss'd it all unheard.

The stranger walk'd into the hall,
  And ere he spake a word
He kiss'd my lady's cherry lips,
  And kiss'd 'em all unheard.

The stranger walk'd into the bower.—
  But my lady first did go,—
Aye hand in hand into the bower
  Where my lord's roses blow.

My lady's maid had a silken scarf,
    And a golden ring had she,
And a kiss from the stranger, as off he went
    Again on his fair palfrey.

      .   .   .   .   .   .

Asleep!   O sleep a little while, white pearl!
And let me kneel, and let me pray to thee,
And let me call Heaven's blessing on thine eyes,
And let me breathe into the happy air,
That doth enfold and touch thee all about,
Vows of my slavery, my giving up,
My sudden adoration, my great love!

     1818.

FAERY SONG

SHED no tear! oh shed no tear!
The flower will bloom another year.
Weep no more! oh weep no more!
Young buds sleep in the root's white core.
Dry your eyes! oh dry your eyes!
For I was taught in Paradise
To ease my breast of melodies—
             Shed no tear.

Overhead! look overhead!
'Mong the blossoms white and red—
Look up, look up.   I flutter now
On this flush pomegranate bough.
See me! 'tis this silvery bill
Ever cures the good man's ill.
Shed no tear!   Oh shed no tear!
The flower will bloom another year.
Adieu, adieu!—I fly, adieu!
I vanish in the heaven's blue—
             Adieu!   Adieu!

FAERY SONG

AH! woe is me! poor Silver-wing!
　That I must chant thy lady's dirge,
And death to this fair haunt of spring,
Of melody, and streams of flowery verge,—
　　　Poor Silver-wing! ah! woe is me!
　　　That I must see
These blossoms snow upon thy lady's pall!
　Go, pretty page, and in her ear
　Whisper that the hour is near.
　Softly tell her not to fear
Such calm favonian burial!
　Go, pretty page! and soothly tell,—
　The blossoms hang by a melting spell,
And fall they must ere a star wink thrice
　　　Upon her closed eyes,
That now in vain are weeping their last tears
　At sweet life leaving, and these arbours green,—
Rich dowry from the Spirit of the Spheres,—
　　　Alas! poor Queen!

TO HOMER

STANDING aloof in giant ignorance,
　Of thee I hear and of the Cyclades,
As one who sits ashore and longs perchance
　To visit dolphin-coral in deep seas.
So thou wast blind!—but then the veil was rent;
　For Jove uncurtain'd Heaven to let thee live,
And Neptune made for thee a spermy tent,
　And Pan made sing for thee his forest-hive;
Ay, on shores of darkness there is light,
　And precipices show untrodden green;
There is a budding morrow in midnight;
　There is a triple sight in blindness keen;
Such seeing hadst thou, as it once befel,
To Dian, Queen of Earth, and Heaven, and Hell.

　　1818.

FAERY SONG

Spirit here that reignest !
Spirit here that painest !
Spirit here that burnest !
Spirit here that mournest !
    Spirit ! I bow
    My forehead low,
  Enshaded with thy pinions !
    Spirit ! I look,
    All passion-struck,
  Into thy pale dominions !

Spirit here that laughest !
Spirit here that quaffest !
Spirit here that dancest !
Noble soul that prancest !
    Spirit ! with thee
    I join in the glee,
  While nudging the elbow of Momus !
    Spirit ! I flush
    With a Bacchanal blush,
  Just fresh from the banquet of Comus !

POEMS WRITTEN AT TEIGNMOUTH

IN A LETTER TO HAYDON

"I have enjoyed the most delightful walks these three fine days, beautiful enough to make me content."

HERE all the summer could I stay,
  For there's a Bishop's Teign,
  And King's Teign,
And Coomb at the clear Teign's head;
  Where, close by the stream,
  You may have your cream,
All spread upon barley bread.

  There's Arch Brook,
  And there's Larch Brook,—
Both turning many a mill;
  And cooling the drouth
  Of the salmon's mouth,
And fattening his silver gill.

  There's a wild wood,
  A mild hood,
To the sheep on the lea o' the down,
  Where the golden furze,
  With its green, thin spurs,
Doth catch at the maiden's gown.

  There's Newton Marsh,
  With its spear-grass harsh,—
A pleasant summer level;
  Where the maidens sweet
  Of the Market street,
Do meet in the dark to revel.

  There's Barton rich
  With dyke and ditch,
And hedge for the thrush to live in.
  And the hollow tree
  For the buzzing bee,
And a bank for the wasp to hive in.

And O and O
The daisies blow,
And the primroses are waken'd ;
And the violets white
Sit in silver light,
And the green buds are long in the spike end.

Then who would go
Into dark Soho,
And chatter with dank-hair'd critics,
When he can stay
For the new-mown hay,
And startle the dappled crickets ?

WHERE BE YOU GOING, YOU DEVON MAID?

" There's a bit of doggerel ; you would like a bit of botheral."

WHERE be you going, you Devon maid ?
And what have ye there in the basket ?
Ye tight little fairy, just fresh from the dairy,
Will ye give me some cream if I ask it ?

I love your hills and I love your dales,
And I love your flocks a-bleating ;
But oh, on the heather to lie together,
With both our hearts a-beating !

I'll put your basket all safe in a nook ;
Your shawl I'll hang on a willow ;
And we will sigh in the daisy's eye,
And kiss on a grass-green pillow.

TEIGNMOUTH

EPISTLE TO JOHN HAMILTON REYNOLDS

" In hopes of cheering you through a minute or two, I was deter-
mined, will he nill he, to send you some lines, so you will excuse the
unconnected subject and careless verse. You know, I am sure, Claude's
'Enchanted Castle,' and I wish you may be pleased with my remembrance of it.'— *March*, 1818.

DEAR Reynolds ! as last night I lay in bed,
There came before my eyes that wonted thread

Of shapes, and shadows, and remembrances,
That every other minute vex and please :
Things all disjointed come from north and south,—
Two Witch's eyes above a Cherub's mouth,
Voltaire with casque and shield and habergeon,
And Alexander with his nightcap on ;
Old Socrates a-tying his cravat,
And Hazlitt playing with Miss Edgeworth's cat ;
And Junius Brutus, pretty well, so so,
Making the best of 's way towards Soho.

Few are there who escape these visitings,—
Perhaps one or two whose lives have patent wings,
And thro' whose curtains peeps no hellish nose,
No wild-boar tushes, and no Mermaid's toes ;
But flowers bursting out with lusty pride,
And young Æolian harps personified ;
Some Titian colours touch'd into real life,—
The sacrifice goes on ; the pontiff knife
Gleams in the Sun, the milk-white heifer lows,
The pipes go shrilly, the libation flows :
A white sail shows above the green-head cliff,
Moves round the point, and throws her anchor stiff ;
The mariners join hymn with those on land.

You know the " Enchanted Castle,"—it doth stand
Upon a rock, on the border of a Lake,
Nested in trees, which all do seem to shake
From some old magic-like Urganda's Sword.
O Phœbus ! that I had thy sacred word
To show this Castle, in fair dreaming wise,
Unto my friend, while sick and ill he lies !

You know it well enough, where it doth seem
A mossy place, a Merlin's Hall, a dream ;
You know the clear Lake, and the little Isles,
The mountains blue, and cold near neighbour rills,
All which elsewhere are but half animate ;
There do they look alive to love and hate,
To smiles and frowns ; they seem a lifted mound
Above some giant, pulsing underground.

Part of the Building was a chosen See,
Built by a banished Santon of Chaldee :
The other part, two thousand years from him,
Was built by Cuthbert de Saint Aldebrim ;
Then there's a little wing, far from the Sun,
Built by a Lapland Witch turn'd maudlin Nun ;
And many other juts of aged stone
Founded with many a mason-devil's groan.

The doors all look as if they oped themselves,
The windows as if latch'd by Fays and Elves,
And from them comes a silver flash of light,
As from the westward of a Summer's night ;
Or like a beauteous woman's large blue eyes
Gone mad thro' olden songs and poesies.

See ! what is coming from the distance dim !
A golden Galley all in silken trim !
Three rows of oars are lightening, moment whiles
Into the verd'rous bosoms of those isles ;
Towards the shade, under the Castle wall,
It comes in silence,—now 'tis hidden all.
The Clarion sounds, and from a Postern-gate
An echo of sweet music doth create
A fear in the poor Herdsman, who doth bring
His beasts to trouble the enchanted spring—
He tells of the sweet music, and the spot,
To all his friends, and they believe him not.

O, that our dreamings all, of sleep or wake,
Would all their colours from the sunset take :
From something of material sublime,
Rather than shadow our own soul's day-time
In the dark void of night.   For in the world
We jostle,—but my flag is not unfurl'd
On the Admiral-staff,—and to philosophise
I dare not yet !   Oh, never will the prize
High reason, and the love of good and ill,
Be my award !   Things cannot to the will
Be settled, but they tease us out of thought ;
Or is it that imagination brought

Beyond its proper bound, yet still confin'd,
Lost in a sort of Purgatory blind,
Cannot refer to any standard law
Of either earth or heaven? It is a flaw
In happiness, to see beyond our bourn,—
It forces us in summer skies to mourn,
It spoils the singing of the Nightingale.

Dear Reynolds? I have a mysterious tale,
And cannot speak it: the first page I read
Upon a Lampit rock of green sea-weed
Among the breakers; 'twas a quiet eve,
The rocks were silent, the wide sea did weave
An untumultuous fringe of silver foam
Along the flat brown sand; I was at home
And should have been most happy,—but I saw
Too far into the sea, where every maw
The greater on the less feeds evermore.—
But I saw too distinct into the core
Of an eternal fierce destruction,
And so from happiness I far was gone.
Still am I sick of it, and though, to-day,
I've gather'd young spring-leaves, and flowers gay
Of periwinkle and wild strawberry,
Still do I that most fierce destruction see,—
The Shark at savage prey,—the Hawk at pounce,—
The gentle Robin, like a Pard or Ounce,
Ravening a Worm,—Away, ye horrid moods!
Moods of one's mind! You know I hate them well.
You know I'd sooner be a clapping Bell
To some Kamschatkan Missionary Church,
Than with these horrid moods be left i' the lurch.

DAWLISH FAIR

OVER the hill and over the dale,
    And over the Bourne to Dawlish,
Where ginger-bread wives have a scanty sale,
    And ginger-bread nuts are smallish.

FRAGMENT

To Reynolds, May, 1818

"It is impossible to know how far knowledge will console us for the death of a friend and the 'ill that flesh is heir to.' With respect to the affections and poetry, you must know by a sympathy my thoughts that way, and I dare say these few lines will be but a ratification. I wrote them on May-day, and intend to finish the ode all in good time."

Mother of Hermes! and still youthful Maia!
       May I sing to thee
As thou wast hymned on the shores of Baiæ?
       Or may I woo thee
In earlier Sicilian? or thy smiles
Seek as they once were sought, in Grecian isles,
By bards who died content on pleasant sward,
Leaving great verse unto a little clan?
O, give me their old vigour, and unheard
Save of the quiet primrose, and the span
       Of heaven and few ears,
Rounded by thee, my song should die away
       Content as theirs,
Rich in the simple worship of a day.

ACROSTIC

Georgiana Augusta Keats

G ive me your patience, sister, while I frame
E xact in capitals your golden name;
O r sue the fair Apollo and he will
R ouse from his heavy slumber and instil
G reat love in me for thee and Poesy.
I magine not that greatest mastery
A nd kingdom over all the realms of verse,
N ears more to heaven in aught, than when we nurse
A nd surety give to love and brotherhood.

A nthropophagi in Othello's mood ;
U lysses stormed, and his enchanted belt
G low with the Muse, but they are never felt
U nbosomed so and so eternal made,
S uch tender incense in their laurel shade
T o all the regent sisters of the time
A s this poor offering to you, sister mine.

K ind sister ! aye, this third name says you are ;
E nchanted has it been the Lord knows when ;
A nd may it taste to you like good old wine,
T ake you to real happiness and give
S ons, daughters, and a home like honeyed hive.

ON VISITING THE TOMB OF BURNS

THE town, the churchyard, and the setting sun,
The clouds, the trees, the rounded hills all seem,
Though beautiful, cold—strange—as in a dream,
I dreamed long ago, now new begun.
The short-lived paly Summer is but won
From Winter's ague, for one hour's gleam ;
Though sapphire-warm, their stars do never beam !
All is cold Beauty ; pain is never done :
For who has mind to relish, Minos-wise,
The Real of Beauty, free from that dead hue
Sickly imagination and sick pride
Cast wan upon it ! Burns ! with honour due
I oft have honour'd thee. Great shadow ! hide
Thy face ; I sin against thy native skies.

MEG MERRILIES

OLD MEG she was a gipsy ;
  And lived upon the moors :
Her bed it was the brown heath turf,
  And her house was out of doors.

Her apples were swart blackberries,
    Her currants, pods o' broom ;
Her wine was dew of the wild white rose,
    Her book a church-yard tomb.

Her brothers were the craggy hills,
    Her sisters larchen trees ;
Alone with her great family
    She lived as she did please.
No breakfast had she many a morn,
    No dinner many a noon,
And, 'stead of supper, she would stare
    Full hard against the moon.

But every morn, of woodbine fresh
    She made her garlanding,
And, every night, the dark glen yew
    She wove, and she would sing.
And with her fingers, old and brown,
    She plaited mats of rushes,
And gave them to the cottagers
    She met among the bushes.

Old Meg was brave as Margaret Queen,
    And tall as Amazon ;
An old red blanket cloak she wore,
    A ship-hat had she on :
God rest her aged bones somewhere !
    She died full long agone !

SONNET ON AILSA ROCK

HEARKEN, thou craggy ocean-pyramid,
    Give answer by thy voice—the sea-fowl's screams !
    When were thy shoulders mantled in huge streams ?
When from the sun was thy broad forehead hid ?
How long is't since the mighty Power bid
    Thee heave to airy sleep from fathom dreams—
    Sleep in the lap of thunder or sunbeams—

Or when grey clouds are thy cold coverlid!
Thou answer'st not; for thou art dead asleep.
  Thy life is but two dead eternities,
The last in air, the former in the deep!
  First with the whales, last with the eagle-skies
Drown'd wast thou till an earthquake made thee steep,
  Another cannot wake thy giant-size!

WRITTEN IN BURNS' COTTAGE

THIS mortal body of a thousand days
Now fills, O Burns, a space in thine own room,
Where thou didst dream alone on budded bays,
Happy and thoughtless of thy day of doom!
My pulse is warm with thine own Barley-bree,
My head is light with pledging a great soul,
My eyes are wandering, and I cannot see,
Fancy is dead and drunken at its goal;
Yet can I stamp my foot upon thy floor,
Yet can I ope thy window-sash to find
The meadow thou hast tramped o'er and o'er,—
Yet can I think of thee till thought is blind,—
Yet can I gulp a bumper to thy name,—
O smile among the shades, for this is fame!

WALKING IN SCOTLAND

THERE is a charm in footing slow across a silent plain,
Where patriot battle has been fought, where glory had the
    gain;
There is a pleasure on the heath, where Druids old have
    been,
Where mantles grey have rustled by, and swept the nettled
    green;
There is a joy in every spot made known in times of old,
New to the feet although each tale a hundred times be told;
There is a deeper joy than all, more solemn in the heart,
More parching to the tongue than all, of more divine a
    smart,

When weary steps forget themselves upon a pleasant turf,
Upon hot sand, or flinty road, or sea-shore iron surf,
Toward the castle or the cot, where long ago was born
One who was great through mortal days, and died of fame
    unshorn.

Light heather-bells may tremble then,—but they are far
    away ;
Wood-lark may sing from sandy fern,—the Sun may hear
    his lay ;
Runnels may kiss the grass on shelves and shallows clear,—
But their low voices are not heard, tho' come on travels
    drear ;
Blood-red the sun may set behind black mountain peaks,
Blue tides may sluice and drench their time in caves and
    weedy creeks,
Eagles may seem to sleep wing-wide upon the air,
Ring-doves may fly convulsed across to some high cedared
    lair,—
But the forgotten eye is still fast lidded to the ground,
As palmer's that with weariness mid-desert shrine hath
    found.

At such a time the soul's a child, in childhood is the brain,
Forgotten is the worldly heart,—alone it beats in vain !
Ay, if a madman could have leave to pass a healthful day,
To tell his forehead's swoon and faint, when first began
    decay,
He might make tremble many a one, whose spirit had gone
    forth
To find a Bard's low cradle-place about the silent north !
Scanty the hour, and few the steps, beyond the bourn of
    care !
Beyond the sweet and bitter world,—beyond it unaware !
Scanty the hour, and few the steps,—because a longer stay
Would bar return and make a man forget his mortal way !
O horrible ! to lose the sight of well-remember'd face,
Of Brother's eyes, of Sister's brow,—constant to every place,
Filling the air as on we move with portraiture intense,
More warm than those heroic tints that pain a painter's
    sense,

When shapes of old come striding by, and visages of old,
Locks shining black, hair scanty grey, and passions manifold!

No, no,—that horror cannot be! for at the cable's length
Man feels the gentle anchor pull, and gladdens in its strength:
One hour, half idiot, he stands by mossy waterfall,
But in the very next he reads his soul's memorial;
He reads it on the mountain's height, where chance he may sit down,
Upon rough marble diadem, that hill's eternal crown.
Yet be his anchor e'er so fast, room is there for a prayer,
That man may never lose his mind in mountains black and bare;
That he may stray, league after league, some great birthplace to find,
And keep his vision clear from speck, his inward sight unblind.

STAFFA

Not Aladdin magian
Ever such a work began;
Not the wizard of the Dee
Ever such a dream could see;
Not St John, in Patmos' Isle,
In the passion of his toil,
When he saw the churches seven,
Golden-aisled, built up in heaven,
Gazed at such a rugged wonder,
As I stood its roofing under.
Lo! I saw one sleeping there,
On the marble cold and bare;
While the surges wash'd his feet,
And his garments white did beat
Drench'd about the sombre rocks;
On his neck his well-grown locks,
Lifted dry above the main,
Were upon the curl again.

D

"What is this? and what art thou?"
Whisper'd I, and touch'd his brow;
"What art thou? and what is this?"
Whisper'd I, and strove to kiss
The spirit's hand, to wake his eyes;
Up he started in a trice:
"I am Lycidas," said he,
"Fam'd in funeral minstrelsy!
This was architectured thus
By the great Oceanus!—
Here his mighty waters play
Hollow organs all the day;
Here, by turns, his dolphins all,
Finny palmers, great and small,
Come to pay devotion due,—
Each a mouth of pearls must strew!
Many a mortal of these days,
Dares to pass our sacred ways;
Dares to touch, audaciously,
This cathedral of the sea!
I have been the pontiff-priest,
Where the waters never rest,
Where a fledgy sea-bird choir
Soars for ever!   Holy fire
I have hid from mortal man;
Proteus is my Sacristan!
But the dulled eye of mortal
Hath pass'd beyond the rocky portal:
So for ever will I leave
Such a taint, and soon unweave
All the magic of the place."
So saying, with a Spirit's glance
He dived!

BEN NEVIS

READ me a lesson, Muse, and speak it loud
Upon the top of Nevis, blind in mist!
I look into the chasms, and a shroud
Vaporous doth hide them,—just so much I wist

Mankind do know of hell; I look o'erhead,
And there is sullen mist,—even so much
Mankind can tell of heaven; mist is spread
Before the earth, beneath me,—even such,
Even so vague is man's sight of himself!
Here are the craggy stones beneath my feet,—
Thus much I know that, a poor witless elf,
I tread on them,—that all my eye doth meet
Is mist and crag, not only on this height,
But in the world of thought and mental might!

FRAGMENT OF A SONNET

FROM RONSARD

NATURE withheld Cassandra in the skies
  For more adornment, a full thousand years;
She took their cream of Beauty, fairest dies,
  And shaped and tinted her above all peers:
Meanwhile Love kept her dearly with his wings,
  And underneath their shadow fill'd her eyes
With such a richness that the cloudy Kings
  Of high Olympus utter'd slavish sighs.
When from the Heavens I saw her first descend,
  My heart took fire, and only burning pains—
They were my pleasures—they my Life's sad end:
  Love pour'd her beauty into my warm veins.

A PROPHECY

TO HIS BROTHER GEORGE IN AMERICA

"If I had a prayer to make for any great good, next to Tom's recovery, it should be that one of your children should be the first American poet. I have a great mind to make a prophecy; and they say that prophecies work out their own fulfilment."—*Oct.* 29, 1818.

'TIS the witching hour of night,
Orbed is the moon and bright,
And the stars they glisten, glisten,
Seeming with bright eyes to listen—
    For what listen they?

For a song and for a charm.
See they glisten in alarm,
And the moon is waxing warm
    To hear what I shall say.
Moon ! keep wide thy golden ears—
Hearken, stars ! and hearken, spheres !—
Hearken, thou eternal sky !
I sing an Infant's lullaby,
    A pretty lullaby.
Listen, listen, listen, listen,
Glisten, glisten, glisten, glisten,
    And hear my lullaby !
Though the rushes that will make
Its cradle still are in the lake—
Though the linen that will be
Its swathe, is on the cotton tree—
Though the woollen that will keep
It warm, is on the silly sheep—
Listen, starlight, listen, listen,
Glisten, glisten, glisten, glisten,
    And hear my lullaby :
Child, I see thee ! Child, I've found thee
Midst of the quiet all around thee !
Child, I see thee ! Child, I spy thee !
And thy mother sweet is nigh thee !
Child, I know thee ! Child no more,
But a Poet evermore !
See, see, the lyre, the lyre,
In a flame of fire,
Upon the little cradle's top
Flaring, flaring, flaring,
Past the eyesight's bearing.
Awake it from its sleep,
And see if it can keep
Its eyes upon the blaze—
    Amaze, amaze !
It stares, it stares, it stares,
It dares what no one dares !
It lifts its little hand into the flame
Unharm'd, and on the strings
Paddles a little tune, and sings,
With dumb endeavour sweetly—

Bard art thou completely !
          Little child
            O' th' western wild,
Bard art thou completely !
Sweetly with dumb endeavour
A Poet now or never,
          Little child
            O' th' western wild,
A Poet now or never !

IN A DREAR-NIGHTED DECEMBER

In a drear-nighted December,
Too happy, happy tree,
Thy branches ne'er remember
Their green felicity :
The north cannot undo them
With a sleety whistle through them ;
Nor frozen thawings glue them
From budding at the prime.

In a drear-nighted December,
Too happy, happy brook,
Thy bubblings ne'er remember
Apollo's summer look ;
But with a sweet forgetting,
They stay their crystal fretting,
Never, never petting
About the frozen time.

Ah ! would 'twere so with many
A gentle girl and boy !
But were there ever any
Writhed not at passèd joy ?
To know the change and feel it.
When there is none to heal it
Nor numbed sense to steal it,
Was never said in rhyme.

STANZA

*Written at the end of Canto 2, Book 5, of Spenser's
"Faerie Queene."*

IN after time a sage of mickle lore,
   Ycleped Typographus, the giant, took
And did refit his limbs as heretofore,
   And made him read in many a learnèd book,
And into many a lively legend look ;
   Thereby in goodly themes so training him,
That all his brutishness he quite forsook,
   When, meeting Artegall and Talus grim,
   The one he struck stone blind, the other's eyes
     woxe dim.

THE EVE OF SAINT MARK

(UNFINISHED)

UPON a Sabbath-day it fell ;
Twice holy was the Sabbath-bell,
That call'd the folk to evening prayer ;
The city streets were clean and fair
From wholesome drench of April rains ;
And, on the western window panes,
The chilly sunset faintly told
Of unmatured green, vallies cold,
Of the green thorny bloomless hedge,
Of rivers new with spring-tide sedge,
Of primroses by shelter'd rills,
And daisies on the aguish hills.
Twice holy was the Sabbath-bell :
The silent streets were crowded well
With staid and pious companies,
Warm from their fire-side orat'ries ;
And moving, with demurest air,
To even-song, and vesper prayer,
Each arched porch, and entry low,
Was fill'd with patient folk and slow,

With whispers hush, and shuffling feet,
While play'd the organ loud and sweet.
The bells had ceased, the prayers begun,
And Bertha had not yet half done
A curious volume, patch'd and torn,
That all day long, from earliest morn,
Had taken captive her two eyes,
Among its golden broideries ;
Perplex'd her with a thousand things,—
The stars of heaven, and angels' wings,
Martyrs in a fiery blaze,
Azure saints and silver rays,
Moses' breastplate, and the seven
Candlesticks John saw in heaven,
The winged Lion of Saint Mark,
And the Covenantal Ark,
With its many mysteries
Cherubim and golden mice.

Bertha was a maiden fair,
Dwelling in th' old minster-square ;
From her fire-side she could see,
Sidelong, its rich antiquity,
Far as the Bishop's garden-wall ;
Where sycamores and elm-trees tall,
Full-leaved, the forest had outstript,
By no sharp north-wind ever nipt,
So shelter'd by the mighty pile.
Bertha arose, and read awhile,
With forehead 'gainst the window-pane.
Again she tried, and then again,
Until the dusk eve left her dark
Upon the legend of St. Mark.
From plaited lawn-frill, fine and thin,
She lifted up her soft warm chin,
With aching neck and swimming eyes,
And dazed with saintly imag'ries.

All was gloom, and silent all,
Save now and then the still foot-fall
Of one returning homewards late,
Past the echoing minster-gate.

The clamorous daws, that all the day
Above tree-tops and towers play,
Pair by pair had gone to rest,
Each in its ancient belfry-nest,
Where asleep they fall betimes,
To music and the drowsy chimes.
All was silent, all was gloom,
Abroad and in the homely room:
Down she sat, poor cheated soul!
And struck a lamp from the dismal coal;
Lean'd forward, with bright drooping hair
And slant book, full against the glare.
Her shadow, in uneasy guise,
Hover'd about, a giant size,
On ceiling-beam and old oak chair,
The parrot's cage, and panel square;
And the warm angled winter-screen,
On which were many monsters seen,
Call'd doves of Siam, Lima mice,
And legless birds of Paradise,
Macaw, and tender Av'davat,
And silken-furr'd Angora cat.
Untired she read, her shadow still
Glower'd about, as it would fill
The room with wildest forms and shades,
As though some ghostly queen of spades
Had come to mock behind her back,
And dance, and ruffle her garments black.
Untired she read the legend page,
Of holy Mark, from youth to age,
On land, on sea, in pagan chains,
Rejoicing for his many pains.
Sometimes the learned eremite,
With golden star, or dagger bright,
Referr'd to pious poesies
Written in smallest crow-quill size
Beneath the text; and thus the rhyme
Was parcell'd out from time to time:
——" Als writith he of swevenis,
Men han beforne they wake in bliss,
Whanne that hir friendes thinke him bound
In crimped shroude farre under grounde;

And how a litling child mote be
A saint er its nativitie,
Gif that the modre (God her blesse!)
Kepen in solitarinesse,
And kissen devoute the holy croce.
Of Goddes love, and Sathan's force,—
He writith; and thinges many mo
Of swiche thinges I may not shew.
Bot I must tellen verilie
Somdel of Saintè Cicilie,
And chieflie what he auctorethe
Of Saintè Markis life and dethe:"

At length her constant eyelids come
Upon the fervent martyrdom;
Then lastly to his holy shrine,
Exalt amid the tapers' shine
At Venice,—

1819.

TO FANNY

PHYSICIAN Nature! let my spirit blood!
O ease my heart of verse and let me rest;
Throw me upon thy Tripod, till the flood
Of stifling numbers ebbs from my full breast.
A theme! a theme! great nature! give a theme;
      Let me begin my dream.
I come—I see thee, as thou standest there,
Beckon me not into the wintry air.

Ah! dearest love, sweet home of all my fears,
And hopes, and joys, and panting miseries,—
To-night, if I may guess, thy beauty wears
      A smile of such delight,
      As brilliant and as bright,
As when with ravish'd, aching, vassal eyes,
      Lost in soft amaze,
         I gaze, I gaze!

Who now, with greedy looks, eats up my feast?
What stare outfaces now my silver moon?
Ah! keep that hand unravish'd at the least;
      Let, let, the amorous burn—
      But, pr'ythee, do not turn
The current of your heart from me so soon.
      O! save, in charity,
      The quickest pulse for me.

Save it for me, sweet love! though music breathe
Voluptuous visions into the warm air,
Though swimming through the dance's dangerous wreath;
      Be like an April day,
      Smiling and cold and gay,
A temperate lily, temperate as fair;
      Then, Heaven! there will be
      A warmer June for me.

Why, this—you'll say, my Fanny! is not true:
Put your soft hand upon your snowy side,
Where the heart beats: confess—'tis nothing new—
      Must not a woman be
      A feather on the sea,
Sway'd to and fro by every wind and tide?
      Of as uncertain speed
      As blow-ball from the mead?

I know it—and to know it is despair
To one who loves you as I love, sweet Fanny!
Whose heart goes flutt'ring for you everywhere,
      Nor, when away you roam,
      Dare keep its wretched home,
Love, love alone, his pains severe and many:
      Then, loveliest! keep me free,
      From torturing jealousy.

Ah! if you prize my subdued soul above
The poor, the fading, brief pride of an hour;
Let none profane my Holy See of love,
      Or with a rude hand break
      The sacramental cake:
Let none else touch the just new-budded flower.
      If not—may my eyes close,
      Love! on their last repose.

TO SLEEP

O soft embalmer of the still midnight !
  Shutting, with careful fingers and benign,
Our gloom-pleased eyes, embower'd from the light,
  Enshaded in forgetfulness divine ;
O soothest Sleep ! if so it please thee, close,
  In midst of this thine hymn, my willing eyes,
Or wait the amen, ere thy poppy throws
  Around my bed its lulling charities ;
  Then save me, or the passed day will shine
Upon my pillow, breeding many woes ;
  Save me from curious conscience, that still lords
Its strength, for darkness burrowing like a mole ;
  Turn the key deftly in the oiled wards,
And seal the hushed casket of my soul.

1819.

HUSH, HUSH !

Hush, hush ! Tread softly ! hush, hush, my dear !
  All the house is asleep, but we know very well
That the jealous, the jealous old bald-pate may hear,
  Tho' you've padded his nightcap—O sweet Isabel !
    Tho' your feet are more light than a Faery's feet,
    Who dances on bubbles where brooklets meet,—
Hush, hush ! soft tiptoe ! hush, hush, my dear !
For less than a nothing the jealous can hear.

No leaf doth tremble, no ripple is there
  On the river,—all's still, and the night's sleepy eye
Closes up, and forgets all its Lethean care,
  Charm'd to death by the drone of the humming May-fly ;
    And the moon, whether prudish or complaisant,
    Has fled to her bower, well knowing I want
No light in the dusk, no torch in the gloom,
But my Isabel's eyes and her lips pulp'd with bloom.

Lift the latch! ah gently! ah tenderly—sweet!
  We are dead if that latchet gives one little chink.
Well done!—now those lips, and a flowery seat—
  The old man may sleep, and the planets may wink;
    The shut rose shall dream of our loves and awake
    Full-blown, and such warmth for the morning take,
The stock-dove shall hatch his soft twin-eggs and coo,
While I kiss to the melody, aching all through!
1818.

THE DOVE

I HAD a dove, and the sweet dove died;
  And I have thought it died of grieving;
O, what could it grieve for? its feet were tied
  With a single thread of my own hand's weaving;

Sweet little red feet, why should you die?
Why should you leave me, sweet bird, why?
You lived alone in the forest tree,
Why, pretty thing! would you not live with me?
I kissed you oft and gave you white peas;
Why not live sweetly, as in the green trees?

ON INDOLENCE

"They toil not, neither do they spin."

ONE morn before me were three figures seen,
  With bowed necks, and joined hands, side-faced;
And one behind the other stepp'd serene,
  In placid sandals, and in white robes graced;
    They pass'd, like figures on a marble urn,
    When shifted round to see the other side;
They came again; as when the urn once more
    Is shifted round, the first green shades return;
    And they were strange to me, as may betide
With vases, to one deep in Phidian lore.

How is it, Shadows! that I knew ye not?
  How came ye muffled in so hush a mask?
Was it a silent deep-disguised plot
  To steal away, and leave without a task
    My idle days?   Ripe was the drowsy hour;
  The blissful cloud of summer-indolence
Benumb'd my eyes; my pulse grew less and less;
    Pain had no sting, and pleasure's wreath no flower:
  O, why did ye not melt, and leave my sense
Unhaunted quite of all but—nothingness?

A third time pass'd they by, and, passing, turn'd
  Each one the face a moment whiles to me;
Then faded, and to follow them I burn'd
  And ached for wings, because I knew the three;
    The first was a fair Maid, and Love her name;
  The second was Ambition, pale of cheek,
And ever watchful with fatigued eye;
    The last, whom I love more, the more of blame
  Is heap'd upon her, maiden most unmeek,—
I knew to be my demon Poesy.

They faded, and, forsooth! I wanted wings:
  O folly!   What is Love? and where is it?
And for that poor Ambition! it springs
  From a man's little heart's short fever-fit;
    For Poesy!—no,—she has not a joy,—
At least for me,—so sweet as drowsy noons,
And evenings steep'd in honied indolence;
    O, for an age so shelter'd from annoy,
  That I may never know how change the moons,
Or hear the voice of busy common-sense!

And once more came they by;—alas! wherefore?
  My sleep had been embroider'd with dim dreams;
My soul had been a lawn besprinkled o'er
  With flowers, and stirring shades, and baffled beams:
    The morn was clouded, but no shower fell,
  Tho' in her lids hung the sweet tears of May;
The open casement press'd a new-leaved vine,
    Let in the budding warmth and throstle's lay;
  O Shadows! 'twas a time to bid farewell!
Upon your skirts had fallen no tears of mine.

So, ye three Ghosts, adieu! Ye cannot raise
   My head cool-bedded in the flowery grass;
For I would not be dieted with praise,
   A pet-lamb in a sentimental farce!
     Fade softly from my eyes, and be once more
In masque-like figures on the dreamy urn;
Farewell! I yet have visions for the night,
    And for the day faint visions there is store;
Vanish, ye Phantoms! from my idle spright,
   Into the clouds, and never more return!

WHY DID I LAUGH TO-NIGHT?

Why did I laugh to-night? No voice will tell:
   No God, no Demon of severe response,
Deigns to reply from Heaven or from Hell.
   Then to my human heart I turn at once.
Heart! Thou and I are here, sad and alone;
   I say, why did I laugh? O mortal pain!
O Darkness! Darkness! ever must I moan,
   To question Heaven and Hell and Heart in vain.
Why did I laugh? I know this Being's lease,
   My fancy to its utmost blisses spreads;
Yet would I on this very midnight cease,
   And the world's gaudy ensigns see in shreds;
Verse, Fame, and Beauty are intense indeed,
But Death intenser—Death is Life's high meed.

   1819.

ON A DREAM

As Hermes once took to his feathers light,
   When lulled Argus, baffled, swoon'd and slept,
So on a Delphic reed, my idle spright,
   So play'd, so charm'd, so conquer'd, so bereft
The dragon-world of all its hundred eyes,
   And seeing it asleep, so fled away,
Not to pure Ida with its snow-cold skies,
   Nor unto Tempe, where Jove grieved a day;

But to that second circle of sad Hell,
    Where in the gust, the whirlwind, and the flaw
Of rain and hail-stones, lovers need not tell
    Their sorrows,—pale were the sweet lips I saw,
Pale were the lips I kiss'd, and fair the form
I floated with, about that melancholy storm.

1819.

ON CHARLES ARMITAGE BROWN

Three Spenserian Stanzas

1

He is to weet a melancholy carle :
Thin in the waist, with bushy head of hair,
As hath the seeded thistle when a parle
It holds with Zephyr, ere it sendeth fair
Its light balloons into the summer air ;
Therto his beard had not begun to bloom,
No brush had touch'd his chin or razor sheer ;
No care had touch'd his cheek with mortal doom,
But new he was and bright as scarf from Persian loom.

2

Ne cared he for wine, or half-and-half
Ne cared he for fish or flesh or fowl,
And sauces held he worthless as the chaff ;
He 'sdeigned the swine-head at the wassail-bowl ;
Ne with lewd ribbalds sat he cheek by jowl ;
Ne with sly Lemans in the scorner's chair ;
But after water-brooks this Pilgrim's soul
Panted, and all his food was woodland air
Though he would oft-times feast on gilliflowers rare.

3

The slang of cities in no wise he knew,
Tipping the wink to him was heathen Greek ;
He sipp'd no olden Tom or ruin blue,
Or nantz or cherry-brandy drank full meek
By many a damsel brave and rouge of cheek ;

Nor did he know each aged watchman's beat,
Nor in obscured purlieus would he seek
For curled Jewesses, with ankles neat,
Who as they walk abroad make tinkling with their feet.

BALLAD

LA BELLE DAME SANS MERCI

O WHAT can ail thee, knight-at-arms,
    Alone and palely loitering?
The sedge has wither'd from the lake,
    And no birds sing.

O what can ail thee, knight-at-arms,
    So haggard and so woe-begone?
The squirrel's granary is full,
    And the harvest's done.

I see a lily on thy brow
    With anguish moist and fever dew,
And on thy cheeks a fading rose
    Fast withereth too.

I met a lady in the meads,
    Full beautiful—a faery's child,
Her hair was long, her foot was light,
    And her eyes were wild.

I made a garland for her head,
    And bracelets too, and fragrant zone;
She look'd at me as she did love,
    And made sweet moan.

I set her on my pacing steed,
    And nothing else saw all day long,
For sidelong would she bend, and sing
    A faery's song.

She found me roots of relish sweet,
    And honey wild, and manna dew,
And sure in language strange she said—
    " I love thee true ! "

She took me to her elfin grot,
    And there she wept and sigh'd full sore,
And there I shut her wild, wild eyes
    With kisses four.

And there she lulled me asleep,
    And there I dream'd—ah! woe betide!
The latest dream I ever dream'd
    On the cold hill's side.

I saw pale kings and princes too,
    Pale warriors, death-pale were they all;
They cried—"La Belle Dame sans Merci
    Hath thee in thrall!"

I saw their starved lips in the gloam,
    With horrid warning gaped wide,
And I awoke and found me here,
    On the cold hill's side.

And this is why I sojourn here,
    Alone and palely loitering,
Though the sedge is wither'd from the lake,
    And no birds sing.

SONG OF FOUR FAIRIES

FIRE, AIR, EARTH, AND WATER,

SALAMANDER, ZEPHYR, DUSKETHA, AND BREAMA.

Sal. Happy, happy, glowing fire!
Zep. Fragrant air! delicious light!
Dus. Let me to my glooms retire!
Bre. I to green-weed rivers bright!
Sal. Happy, happy glowing fire!
Dazzling bowers of soft retire,
Ever let my nourish'd wing,
Like a bat's, still wandering,
Faintly fan your fiery spaces,
Spirit sole in deadly places.

In unhaunted roar and blaze,
Open eyes that never daze,
Let me see the myriad shapes
Of men, and beasts, and fish, and apes,
Portray'd in many a fiery den,
And wrought by spumy bitumen
On the deep intenser roof,
Arched every way aloof.
Let me breathe upon their skies,
And anger their live tapestries ;
Free from cold, and every care
Of chilly rain and shivering air.

   Zep. Spirit of Fire ! away ! away !
Or your very roundelay
Will sear my plumage newly budded
From its quilled sheath, all studded
With the self-same dews that fell
On the May-grown Asphodel.
Spirit of Fire—away ! away !

   Bre. Spirit of Fire—away ! away !
Zephyr, blue-eyed fairy, turn,
And see my cool sedge-buried urn,
Where it rests its mossy brim
'Mid water-mint and cresses dim ;
And the flowers, in sweet troubles,
Lift their eyes above the bubbles,
Like our Queen, when she would please
To sleep and Oberon *will* tease—
Love me, blue-eyed Fairy ! true.
Soothly I am sick for you.

   Zep. Gentle Breama ! by the first
Violet young nature nurst,
I will bathe myself with thee,
So you sometimes follow me
To my home, far, far in west,
Beyond the nimble-wheeled quest
of the golden-browed sun.
Come with me, o'er tops of trees,
To my fragrant palaces,
Where they ever floating are
Beneath the cherish of a star
Call'd Vesper, who with silver veil

Ever hides his brilliance pale,
Ever gently-drowsed doth keep
Twilight for the Fayes to sleep.
Fear not that your watery hair
Will thirst in drouthy ringlets there ;
Clouds of stored summer rains
Thou shalt taste, before the stains
Of the mountain soil they take,
And too unlucent for thee make.
I love thee, crystal Fairy, true !
Sooth I am as sick for you !

   Sal. Out, ye aguish Fairies, out !
Chilly lovers, what a rout
Keep ye with your frozen breath,
Colder than the mortal death !
Adder-eyed Dusketha, speak !
Shall we leave these, and go seek
In the earth's wide entrails old
Couches warm as theirs are cold ?
O for a fiery gloom and thee,
Dusketha, so enchantingly
Freckle-wing'd and lizard-sided !

   Dus. By thee, Sprite, will I be guided !
I care not for cold or heat :
Frost and flame, or sparks, or sleet,
To my essence are the same ;—
But I honour more the flame.
Sprite of Fire, I follow thee
Wheresoever it may be,—
To the torrid spouts and fountains,
Underneath earth-quaked mountains ;
Or, at thy supreme desire,
Touch the very pulse of fire
With my bare unlidded eyes.

   Sal. Sweet Dusketha ! paradise !
Off, ye icy Spirits, fly !
Frosty creatures of the sky.

   Dus. Breathe upon them, fiery sprite !

   Zep. }
   Bre. } Away ! away to our delight !

   Sal. Go, feed on icicles, while we
Bedded in tongue-flames will be.

Dus. Lead me to those feverous glooms,
Sprite of Fire!
    Bre.   Me to the blooms,
Blue-eyed Zephyr, of those flowers
Far in the west where the May-cloud lowers;
And the beams of still Vesper, when winds are all wist,
Are shed through the rain and the milder mist,
And twilight your floating bowers.

    1819.

ON FAME

FAME, like a wayward girl, will still be coy
    To those who woo her with too slavish knees,
But makes surrender to some thoughtless boy,
    And dotes the more upon a heart at ease;
She is a Gipsy,—will not speak to those
    Who have not learnt to be content without her;
A Jilt, whose ear was never whisper'd close,
    Who thinks they scandal her who talk about her;
A very Gipsy is she, Nilus-born,
    Sister-in-law to jealous Potiphar;
Ye love-sick Bards! repay her scorn for scorn;
    Ye Artists lovelorn! madmen that ye are!
Make your best bow to her and bid adieu,
Then, if she likes it, she will follow you.

    1819.

ON FAME

"You cannot eat your cake and have it too."—*Proverb.*

How fever'd is the man, who cannot look
    Upon his mortal days with temperate blood,
Who vexes all the leaves of his life's book,
    And robs his fair name of its maidenhood;
It is as if the rose should pluck herself,
    Or the ripe plum finger its misty bloom,
As if a Naiad, like a meddling elf,
    Should darken her pure grot with muddy gloom;

But the rose leaves herself upon the briar,
  For winds to kiss and grateful bees to feed,
And the ripe plum still wears its dim attire;
  The undisturbed lake has crystal space;
  Why then should man, teasing the world for grace,
Spoil his salvation for a fierce miscreed?

1819.

ON THE SONNET

If by dull rhymes our English must be chain'd,
And, like Andromeda, the Sonnet sweet
Fetter'd, in spite of pained loveliness;
Let us find out, if we must be constrain'd,
  Sandals more interwoven and complete
To fit the naked foot of poesy;
Let us inspect the lyre, and weigh the stress
Of every chord, and see what may be gain'd
  By ear industrious, and attention meet;
Misers of sound and syllable, no less
Than Midas of his coinage, let us be
  Jealous of dead leaves in the bay wreath crown;
So, if we may not let the Muse be free,
  She will be bound with garlands of her own.

1819.

A PARTY OF LOVERS

Pensive they sit, and roll their languid eyes,
Nibble their toast and cool their tea with sighs;
Or else forget the purpose of the night,
Forget their tea, forget their appetite.
See, with cross'd arms they sit—Ah! happy crew,
The fire is going out and no one rings
For coals, and therefore no coals Betty brings.
A fly is in the milk-pot.   Must he die
Circled by a humane society?
No, no; there, Mr Werter takes his spoon,
Inserts it, dips the handle, and lo! soon

The little straggler, sav'd from perils dark,
Across the teaboard draws a long wet mark.

Romeo!   Arise, take snuffers by the handle,
There's a large cauliflower in each candle.
A winding sheet—ah, me! I must away
To No. 7, just beyond the circus gay.
Alas, my friend, your coat sits very well;
Where may your Tailor live?   I may not tell
O pardon me.   I'm absent now and then
Where *might* my Tailor live?   I say again
I cannot tell, let me no more be teazed;
He lives in Wapping, might live where he pleased.

THE DAY IS GONE

THE day is gone, and all its sweets are gone!
  Sweet voice, sweet lips, soft hand, and softer breast,
Warm breath, light whisper, tender semi-tone,
  Bright eyes, accomplish'd shape, and lang'rous waist!
Faded the flower and all its budded charms,
  Faded the sight of beauty from my eyes,
Faded the shape of beauty from my arms,
  Faded the voice, warmth, whiteness, paradise—
Vanish'd unseasonably at shut of eve,
  When the dusk holiday—or holinight
Of fragrant-curtain'd love begins to weave
  The woof of darkness thick, for hid delight;
But, as I've read love's missal through to-day,
He'll let me sleep, seeing I fast and pray.

  1819.

LINES TO FANNY

WHAT can I do to drive away
Remembrance from my eyes? for they have seen,
Ay, an hour ago, my brilliant Queen!
Touch has a memory.   O say, love, say,
What can I do to kill it and be free
In my old liberty?

When every fair one that I saw was fair
Enough to catch me in but half a snare,
Not keep me there:
When, howe'er poor or particolour'd things,
My muse had wings,
And ever ready was to take her course
Whither I bent her force,
Unintellectual, yet divine to me ;—
Divine, I say !—What sea-bird o'er the sea
Is a philosopher the while he goes
Winging along where the great water throes ?
How shall I do
To get anew
Those moulted feathers, and so mount once more
Above, above
The reach of fluttering Love,
And make him cower lowly while I soar ?
Shall I gulp wine ?   No, that is vulgarism,
A heresy and schism,
Foisted into the canon-law of love ;—
No,—wine is only sweet to happy men ;
More dismal cares
Seize on me unawares,—
Where shall I learn to get my peace again ?
To banish thoughts of that most hateful land,
Dungeoner of my friends, that wicked strand
Where they were wreck'd and live a wreck'd life ;
That monstrous region, whose dull rivers pour,
Ever from their sordid urns unto the shore,
Unown'd of any weedy-haired gods ;
Whose winds, all zephyrless, hold scourging rods,
Iced in the great lakes, to afflict mankind ;
Whose rank-grown forests, frosted, black, and blind,
Would fright a Dryad ; whose harsh herbaged meads
Make lean and lank the starv'd ox while he feeds ;
There bad flowers have no scent, birds no sweet song,
And great unerring Nature once seems wrong.

O, for some sunny spell
To dissipate the shadows of this hell !
Say they are gone,—with the new dawning light
Steps forth my lady bright !

O, let me once more rest
My soul upon that dazzling breast !
Let once again these aching arms be placed,
The tender gaolers of thy waist !
And let me feel that warm breath here and there
To spread a rapture in my very hair,—
O, the sweetness of the pain !
Give me those lips again !
Enough ! Enough ! it is enough for me
To dream of thee !

     Oct., 1819.

TO FANNY

I CRY your mercy—pity—love !—ay, love !
    Merciful love that tantalises not,
One-thoughted, never-wandering, guileless love,
    Unmask'd, and being seen—without a blot !
O ! let me have thee whole,—all—all—be mine !
    That shape, that fairness, that sweet minor zest
Of love, your kiss,—those hands, those eyes divine,
    That warm, white, lucent, million-pleasured breast,—
Yourself—your soul—in pity give me all,
    Withhold no atom's atom or I die,
Or living on, perhaps, your wretched thrall,
    Forget, in the midst of idle misery,
Life's purposes,—the palate of my mind
Losing its gust, and my ambition blind !

    1819.

WRITTEN ON A SUMMER EVENING

THE church bells toll'd a melancholy round,
    Calling the people to some other prayers,
    Some other gloominess, more dreadful cares,
More hearkening to the sermon's horrid sound.
Surely the mind of man is closely bound
    To some blind spell : seeing that each one tears
    Himself from fireside joys and Lydian airs,
Fond converse high of those with glory crown'd.

Still, still they toll, and I should feel a damp,
  A chill as from a tomb, did I not know
That they are dying like an outburnt lamp,—
  That 'tis their sighing, wailing, as they go
  Into oblivion—that fresh flowers will grow,
And many glories of immortal stamp.

1816.

HIS LAST SONNET

BRIGHT star! would I were steadfast as thou art—
  Not in lone splendour hung aloft the night,
And watching, with eternal lids apart,
  Like Nature's patient, sleepless Eremite,
The moving waters at their priestlike task
  Of pure ablution round earth's human shores,
Or gazing on the new soft fallen mask
  Of snow upon the mountains and the moors—
No—yet still steadfast, still unchangeable,
  Pillow'd upon my fair love's ripening breast,
To feel for ever its soft fall and swell,
  Awake for ever in a sweet unrest,
Still, still to hear her tender-taken breath,
And so live ever—or else swoon to death.

THE EVE OF ST. AGNES

St. Agnes' Eve—ah, bitter chill it was!
The owl, for all his feathers, was a-cold;
The hare limp'd trembling through the frozen grass,
And silent was the flock in woolly fold:
Numb were the Beadsman's fingers while he told
His rosary, and while his frosted breath,
Like pious incense from a censer old,
Seem'd taking flight for heaven without a death,
Past the sweet Virgin's picture, while his prayer he saith.

His prayer he saith, this patient, holy man;
Then takes his lamp, and riseth from his knees,
And back returneth, meagre, barefoot, wan,
Along the chapel aisle by slow degrees:
The sculptured dead, on each side seem to freeze,
Emprison'd in black, purgatorial rails:
Knights, ladies, praying in dumb orat'ries,
He passeth by, and his weak spirit fails
To think how they may ache in icy hoods and mails.

Northward he turneth through a little door,
And scarce three steps, ere Music's golden tongue
Flatter'd to tears this aged man and poor.
But no—already had his death-bell rung;
The joys of all his life were said and sung;
His was harsh penance on St. Agnes' Eve:
Another way he went, and soon among
Rough ashes sat he for his soul's reprieve,
And all night kept awake, for sinner's sake to grieve.

That ancient Beadsman heard the prelude soft;
And so it chanced, for many a door was wide,
From hurry to and fro.   Soon, up aloft,
The silver, snarling trumpets 'gan to chide:
The level chambers, ready with their pride,

Were glowing to receive a thousand guests :
The carved angels, ever eager-eyed,
Stared, where upon their heads the cornice rests,
With hair blown back, and wings put crosswise on their
    breasts.

At length burst in the argent revelry,
With plume, tiara, and all rich array,
Numerous as shadows haunting fairily
The brain new-stuff'd, in youth, with triumphs gay
Of old romance.   These let us wish away,
And turn, sole-thoughted, to one Lady there,
Whose heart had brooded, all that wintry day,
On love, and wing'd St. Agnes' saintly care,
As she had heard old dames full many times declare.

They told her how, upon St. Agnes' Eve,
Young virgins might have visions of delight,
And soft adorings from their loves receive
Upon the honey'd middle of the night,
If ceremonies due they did aright ;
As, supperless to bed they must retire,
And couch supine their beauties, lily white ;
Nor look behind, nor sideways, but require
Of Heaven with upward eyes for all that they desire.

Full of this whim was thoughtful Madeline :
The music, yearning like a God in pain,
She scarcely heard : her maiden eyes divine,
Fix'd on the floor, saw many a sweeping train
Pass by—she heeded not at all : in vain
Came many a tiptoe, amorous cavalier,
And back retired ; not cool'd by high disdain,
But she saw not : her heart was otherwhere ;
She sigh'd for Agnes' dreams, the sweetest of the year.

She danced along with vague, regardless eyes,
Anxious her lips, her breathing quick and short :
The hallow'd hour was near at hand, she sighs :
Amid the timbrels, and the throng'd resort
Of whisperers in anger or in sport ;

'Mid looks of love, defiance, hate, and scorn,
  Hoodwink'd with faery fancy; all amort,
  Save to St. Agnes and her lambs unshorn,
And all the bliss to be before to-morrow morn.

So, purposing each moment to retire,
  She linger'd still.   Meantime, across the moors,
Had come young Porphyro, with heart on fire
  For Madeline.   Beside the portal doors,
Buttress'd from moonlight, stands he, and implores
  All saints to give him sight of Madeline,
  But for one moment in the tedious hours,
  That he might gaze and worship all unseen;
Perchance speak, kneel, touch, kiss—in sooth such things
      have been.

He ventures in: let no buzz'd whisper tell,
  All eyes be muffled, or a hundred swords
Will storm his heart, Love's feverous citadel:
  For him, those chambers held barbarian hordes,
Hyena foemen, and hot-blooded lords,
  Whose very dogs would execration howl
  Against his lineage; not one breast affords
  Him any mercy in that mansion foul,
Save one old beldame, weak in body and in soul.

Ah, happy chance! the aged creature came,
  Shuffling along with ivory-headed wand,
To where he stood, hid from the torch's flame,
  Behind a broad hall pillar, far beyond
The sound of merriment and chorus bland.
  He startled her: but soon she knew his face,
  And grasp'd his fingers in her pisied hand,
  Saying, "Mercy Porphyro! hie thee from this place;
They are all here to-night, the whole blood-thirsty race!

"Get hence! get hence! there's dwarfish Hildebrand:
  He had a fever late, and in the fit
He cursed thee and thine, both house and land:
  Then there's that old Lord Maurice, not a whit
More tame for his grey hairs—Alas me! flit!

Flit like a ghost away."—"Ah, Gossip dear,
We're safe enough; here in this arm-chair sit,
And tell me how"—"Good saints! not here, not here;
Follow me, child, or else these stones will be thy bier.'

He follow'd through a lowly arched way,
Brushing the cobwebs with his lofty plume;
And as she mutter'd "Well-a—well-a-day!"
He found him in a little moonlight room,
Pale, latticed, chill, and silent as a tomb.
"Now tell me where is Madeline," said he,
"O tell me, Angela, by the holy loom
Which none but secret sisterhood may see,
When they St. Agnes' wool are weaving piously."

"St. Agnes! Ah! it is St. Agnes' Eve—
Yet men will murder upon holy days.
Thou must hold water in a witch's sieve,
And be liege-lord of all the Elves and Fays
To venture so: it fills me with amaze
To see thee, Porphyro!—St. Agnes' Eve!
God's help! my lady fair the conjurer plays
This very night: good angels her deceive!
But let me laugh awhile,—I've mickle time to grieve."

Feebly she laugheth in the languid moon,
While Porphyro upon her face doth look,
Like puzzled urchin on an aged crone
Who keepeth closed a wondrous riddle-book,
As spectacled she sits in chimney nook.
But soon his eyes grew brilliant, when she told
His lady's purpose; and he scarce could brook
Tears, at the thought of those enchantments cold,
And Madeline asleep in lap of legends old.

Sudden a thought came like a full-blown rose,
Flushing his brow, and in his pained heart
Made purple riot: then doth he propose
A stratagem, that makes the beldame start:
"A cruel man and impious thou art!
Sweet lady! let her pray, and sleep and dream
Alone with her good angels, far apart
From wicked men like thee. Go, go! I deem
Thou canst not surely be the same that thou didst seem."

"I will not harm her, by all saints I swear!"
Quoth Porphyro: "O may I ne'er find grace
When my weak voice shall whisper its last prayer,
If one of her soft ringlets I displace,
Or look with ruffian passion in her face.
Good Angela, believe me, by these tears;
Or I will, even in a moment's space,
Awake, with horrid shout, my foemen's ears,
And beard them, though they be more fang'd than wolves
    and bears."

"Ah! why wilt thou affright a feeble soul?
A poor, weak, palsy-stricken, churchyard thing,
Whose passing-bell may ere the midnight toll;
Whose prayers for thee, each morn and evening,
Were never miss'd." Thus plaining, doth she bring
A gentler speech from burning Porphyro;
So woeful, and of such deep sorrowing,
That Angela gives promise she will do
Whatever he shall wish, betide her weal or woe.

Which was, to lead him, in close secrecy,
Even to Madeline's chamber, and there hide
Him in a closet, of such privacy
That he might see her beauty unespied,
And win perhaps that night a peerless bride,
While legion'd fairies paced the coverlet,
And pale enchantment held her sleepy-eyed.
Never on such a night have lovers met,
Since Merlin paid his Demon all the monstrous debt.

"It shall be as thou wishest," said the Dame:
"All cates and dainties shall be stored there
Quickly on this feast-night: by the tambour frame
Her own lute thou wilt see: no time to spare,
For I am slow and feeble, and scarce dare
On such a catering trust my dizzy head.
Wait here, my child, with patience kneel in prayer
The while. Ah! thou must needs the lady wed,
Or may I never leave my grave among the dead."

So saying she hobbled off with busy fear.
The lover's endless minutes slowly pass'd ;
The dame return'd, and whisper'd in his ear
To follow her ; with aged eyes aghast
From fright of dim espial.   Safe at last
Through many a dusky gallery, they gain
The maiden's chamber, silken, hush'd and chaste ;
Where Porphyro took covert, pleased amain.
His poor guide hurried back with agues in her brain.

Her faltering hand upon the balustrade,
Old Angela was feeling for the stair,
When Madeline, St. Agnes' charmed maid,
Rose, like a mission'd spirit, unaware :
With silver taper's light, and pious care,
She turn'd, and down the aged gossip led
To a safe level matting.   Now prepare,
Young Porphyro, for gazing on that bed ;
She comes, she comes again, like ring-dove fray'd and fled.

Out went the taper as she hurried in ;
Its little smoke, in pallid moonshine, died :
She closed the door, she panted, all akin
To spirits of the air, and visions wide :
No utter'd syllable, or, woe betide !
But to her heart, her heart was voluble,
Paining with eloquence her balmy side ;
As though a tongueless nightingale should swell
Her throat in vain, and die, heart-stifled, in her dell.

A casement high and triple-arch'd there was,
All garlanded with carven imageries,
Of fruits and flowers, and bunches of knot-grass,
And diamonded with panes of quaint device,
Innumerable of stains and splendid dyes,
As are the tiger-moth's deep-damask'd wings ;
And in the midst, 'mong thousand heraldries,
And twilight saints, and dim emblazonings,
A shielded scutcheon blush'd with blood of queens and
  kings.

Full on this casement shone the wintry moon,
And threw warm gules on Madeline's fair breast,
As down she knelt for Heaven's grace and boon ;
Rose-bloom fell on her hands, together prest,
And on her silver cross soft amethyst,
And on her hair a glory, like a saint :
She seem'd a splendid angel, newly drest,
Save wings, for heaven :—Porphyro grew faint :
She knelt, so pure a thing, so free from mortal taint.

Anon his heart revives : her vespers done,
Of all its wreathed pearls her hair she frees ;
Unclasps her warmed jewels one by one ;
Loosens her fragrant boddice ; by degrees
Her rich attire creeps rustling to her knees :
Half-hidden, like a mermaid in sea-weed,
Pensive awhile she dreams awake, and sees,
In fancy, fair St. Agnes in her bed,
But dares not look behind, or all the charm is fled.

Soon, trembling in her soft and chilly nest,
In sort of wakeful swoon, perplex'd she lay,
Until the poppied warmth of sleep oppress'd
Her soothed limbs, and soul fatigued away ;
Flown, like a thought, until the morrow-day ;
Blissfully haven'd both from joy and pain ;
Clasp'd like a missal where swart Paynims pray ;
Blinded alike from sunshine and from rain,
As though a rose should shut, and be a bud again.

Stolen to this paradise, and so entranced,
Porphyro gazed upon her empty dress,
And listen'd to her breathing, if it chanced
To wake into a slumberous tenderness ;
Which when he heard, that minute did he bless,
And breath'd himself : then from the closet crept,
Noiseless as fear in a wide wilderness,
And over the hush'd carpet, silent, stept,
And 'tween the curtains peep'd, where, lo !—how fast she
slept !

Then by the bed-side, where the faded moon
Made a dim, silver twilight, soft he set
A table, and, half anguish'd, threw thereon
A cloth of woven crimson, gold, and jet :—
O for some drowsy Morphean amulet !
The boisterous, midnight, festive clarion,
The kettle-drum, and far-heard clarionet,
Affray his ears, though but in dying tone :—
The hall-door shuts again, and all the noise is gone.

And still she slept an azure-lidded sleep,
In blanched linen, smooth, and lavender'd,
While he from forth the closet brought a heap
Of candied apple, quince, and plum, and gourd ;
With jellies soother than the creamy curd,
And lucent syrops, tinct with cinnamon ;
Manna and dates, in argosy transferr'd
From Fez ; and spiced dainties, every one,
From silken Samarcand to cedar'd Lebanon.

These delicates he heap'd with glowing hand
On golden dishes and in baskets bright
Of wreathed silver : sumptuous they stand
In the retired quiet of the night,
Filling the chilly room with perfume light.—
" And now, my love, my seraph fair, awake !
Thou art my heaven, and I thine eremite :
Open thine eyes, for meek St. Agnes' sake,
Or I shall drowse beside thee, so my soul doth ache."

Thus whispering, his warm, unnerved arm
Sank in her pillow.   Shaded was her dream
By the dusk curtains :—'twas a midnight charm
Impossible to melt as iced stream :
The lustrous salvers in the moonlight gleam ;
Broad golden fringe upon the carpet lies :
It seem'd he never, never could redeem
From such a steadfast spell his lady's eyes ;
So mused awhile, entoil'd in woofed phantasies.

Awakening up, he took her hollow lute,—
Tumultuous,—and, in chords that tenderest be,

K

He play'd an ancient ditty, long since mute,
In Provence call'd "La belle dame sans mercy":
Close to her ear touching the melody;—
Wherewith disturb'd, she utter'd a soft moan:
He ceased—she panted quick—and suddenly
Her blue affrayed eyes wide open shone:
Upon his knees he sank, pale as smooth-sculptured stone.

Her eyes were open, but she still beheld,
Now wide awake, the vision of her sleep:
There was a painful change, that nigh expell'd
The blisses of her dream so pure and deep.
At which fair Madeline began to weep,
And moan forth witless words with many a sigh,
While still her gaze on Porphyro would keep;
Who knelt, with joined hands and piteous eye,
Fearing to move or speak, she look'd so dreamingly.

"Ah, Porphyro!" said she, "but even now
Thy voice was at sweet tremble in mine ear,
Made tunable with every sweetest vow;
And those sad eyes were spiritual and clear:
How changed thou art! how pallid, chill, and drear!
Give me that voice again, my Porphyro,
Those looks immortal, those complainings dear!
Oh leave me not in this eternal woe,
For if thou diest, my Love, I know not where to go."

Beyond a mortal man impassion'd far
At these voluptuous accents, he arose,
Ethereal, flush'd, and like a throbbing star
Seen 'mid the sapphire heaven's deep repose;
Into her dream he melted, as the rose
Blendeth its odour with the violet,—
Solution sweet: meantime the frost-wind blows
Like Love's alarum, pattering the sharp sleet
Against the window-panes; St. Agnes' moon hath set.

'Tis dark: quick pattereth the flaw-blown sleet.
"This is no dream, my bride, my Madeline!"
'Tis dark: the iced gusts still rave and beat:
"No dream, alas! alas! and woe is mine!

Porphyro will leave me here to fade and pine.
Cruel! what traitor could thee hither bring?
I curse not, for my heart is lost in thine,
Though thou forsakest a deceived thing;—
A dove forlorn and lost with sick unpruned wing."

"My Madeline! sweet dreamer! lovely bride!
Say, may I be for aye thy vassal blest?
Thy beauty's shield, heart-shaped and vermeil-dyed?
Ah, silver shrine, here will I take my rest
After so many hours of toil and quest,
A famish'd pilgrim,—saved by miracle.
Though I have found, I will not rob thy nest,
Saving of thy sweet self; if thou think'st well
To trust, fair Madeline, to no rude infidel.

"Hark! 'tis an elfin storm from faery land,
Of haggard seeming, but a boon indeed:
Arise—arise! the morning is at hand;—
The bloated wassailers will never heed;—
Let us away, my love, with happy speed;
There are no ears to hear, or eyes to see,—
Drown'd all in Rhenish and the sleepy mead.
Awake! arise! my love, and fearless be,
For o'er the southern moors I have a home for thee."

She hurried at his words, beset with fears,
For there were sleeping dragons all around
At glaring watch, perhaps, with ready spears.
Down the wide stairs a darkling way they found;
In all the house was heard no human sound.
A chain-droop'd lamp was flickering by each door;
The arras, rich with horsemen, hawk, and hound,
Flutter'd in the besieging wind's uproar;
And the long carpets rose along the gusty floor.

They glide, like phantoms, into the wide hall!
Like phantoms to the iron porch they glide,
Where lay the Porter, in uneasy sprawl,
With a huge empty flagon by his side:
The wakeful bloodhound rose, and shook his hide,

But his sagacious eye an inmate owns :
By one, and one, the bolts full easy slide :—
The chains lie silent on the footworn stones ;
The key turns, and the door upon its hinges groans.

And they are gone : ay, ages long ago
These lovers fled away into the storm.
That night the Baron dreamt of many a woe,
And all his warrior-guests with shade and form
Of witch, and demon, and large coffin-worm,
Were long be-nightmared.   Angela the old
Died palsy-twitch'd, with meagre face deform ;
The Beadsman, after thousand aves told,
For aye unsought-for slept among his ashes cold.

LAMIA

PART I

Upon a time, before the faery broods
Drove Nymph and Satyr from the prosperous woods,
Before King Oberon's bright diadem,
Sceptre, and mantle, clasp'd with dewy gem,
Frighted away the Dryads and the Fauns
From rushes green, and brakes, and cowslipp'd lawns,
The ever-smitten Hermes empty left
His golden throne, bent warm on amorous theft:
From high Olympus had he stolen light,
On this side of Jove's clouds, to escape the sight
Of his great summoner, and made retreat
Into a forest on the shores of Crete.
For somewhere in that sacred island dwelt
A nymph to whom all hoofed Satyrs knelt;
At whose white feet the languid Tritons pour'd
Pearls, while on land they wither'd and adored.
Fast by the springs where she to bathe was wont,
And in those meads where sometimes she might haunt,
Were strewn rich gifts, unknown to any Muse,
Though Fancy's casket were unlock'd to choose.
Ah, what a world of love was at her feet!
So Hermes thought, and a celestial heat
Burn'd from his winged heels to either ear,
That, from a whiteness as the lily clear,
Blush'd into roses 'mid his golden hair,
Fallen in jealous curls about his shoulders bare.
From vale to vale, from wood to wood, he flew,
Breathing upon the flowers his passion new,
And wound with many a river to its head,
To find where this sweet nymph prepared her secret bed
In vain; the sweet nymph might nowhere be found,
And so he rested on the lonely ground,
Pensive, and full of painful jealousies
Of the Wood-Gods, and even the very trees.

There as he stood he heard a mournful voice,
Such as, once heard, in gentle heart destroys
All pain but pity ; thus the lone voice spake :
" When from this wreathed tomb shall I awake ?
When move in a sweet body fit for life,
And love, and pleasure, and the ruddy strife
Of hearts and lips ?   Ah, miserable me ! "
The God, dove-footed, glided silently
Round bush and tree, soft-brushing in his speed
The taller grasses and full-flowering weed,
Until he found a palpitating snake,
Bright and cirque-couchant, in a dusky brake.

She was a gordian shape of dazzling hue,
Vermilion-spotted, golden, green, and blue ;
Striped like a zebra, freckled like a pard,
Eyed like a peacock, and all crimson-barr'd ;
And full of silver moons, that, as she breathed,
Dissolved, or brighter shone, or interwreathed
Their lustres with the gloomier tapestries—
So rainbow-sided, touch'd with miseries,
She seem'd at once, some penanced lady elf,
Some demon's mistress, or the demon's self.
Upon her crest she wore a wannish fire
Sprinkled with stars, like Ariadne's tiar :
Her head was serpent, but ah, bitter-sweet !
She had a woman's mouth with all its pearls complete ;
And for her eyes—what could such eyes do there
But weep and weep, that they were born so fair,
As Proserpine still weeps for her Sicilian air ?
Her throat was serpent, but the words she spake
Came, as through bubbling honey, for Love's sake,
And thus ; while Hermes on his pinions lay,
Like a stoop'd falcon ere he takes his prey :

" Fair Hermes ! crown'd with feathers, fluttering light,
I had a splendid dream of thee last night !
I saw thee sitting, on a throne of gold,
Among the Gods, upon Olympus old,
The only sad one ; for thou didst not hear
The soft lute-finger'd Muses chanting clear,
Nor even Apollo when he sang alone,

Deaf to his throbbing throat's long, long melodious moan.
I dreamt I saw thee, robed in purple flakes,
Break amorous through the clouds, as morning breaks,
And swiftly as a bright Phœbean dart
Strike for the Cretan isle; and here thou art!
Too gentle Hermes, hast thou found the maid?"
Whereat the star of Lethe not delay'd
His rosy eloquence, and thus inquired:
"Thou smooth-lipp'd serpent, surely high-inspired!
Thou beauteous wreath, with melancholy eyes,
Possess whatever bliss thou canst devise,
Telling me only where my nymph is fled—
Where she doth breathe!" "Bright planet, thou hast said,"
Return'd the snake, "but seal with oaths, fair God!"
"I swear," said Hermes, "by my serpent rod,
And by thine eyes, and by thy starry crown!"
Light flew his earnest words, among the blossoms blown.
Then thus again the brilliance feminine:
"Too frail of heart! for this lost nymph of thine,
Free as the air, invisibly she strays
About these thornless wilds; her pleasant days
She tastes unseen; unseen her nimble feet
Leave traces in the grass and flowers sweet:
From weary tendrils and bow'd branches green
She plucks the fruit unseen, she bathes unseen:
And by my power is her beauty veil'd
To keep it unaffronted, unassail'd
By the love-glances of unlovely eyes,
Of Satyrs, Fauns, and blear'd Silenus' sighs.
Pale grew her immortality, for woe
Of all these lovers, and she grieved so
I took compassion on her, bade her steep
Her hair in weird syrops, that would keep
Her loveliness invisible, yet free
To wander as she loves, in liberty.
Thou shalt behold her, Hermes, thou alone,
If thou wilt, as thou swearest, grant my boon."
Then, once again, the charmed God began
An oath, and through the serpent's ears it ran
Warm, tremulous, devout, psalterian.
Ravish'd she lifted her Circean head,
Blush'd a live damask, and swift-lisping said,

"I was a woman, let me have once more
A woman's shape, and charming as before.
I love a youth of Corinth—O the bliss !
Give me my woman's form, and place me where he is.
Stoop, Hermes, let me breathe upon thy brow,
And thou shalt see thy sweet nymph even now."
The God on half-shut feathers sank serene,
She breathed upon his eyes, and swift was seen
Of both the guarded nymph near-smiling on the green.
It was no dream ; or say a dream it was,
Real are the dreams of Gods, and smoothly pass
Their pleasures in a long immortal dream.
One warm, flush'd moment, hovering, it might seem,
Dash'd by the wood-nymph's beauty, so he burn'd ;
Then, lighting on the printless verdure, turn'd
To the swoon'd serpent, and with languid arm,
Delicate, put to proof the lithe Caducean charm.
So done, upon the nymph his eyes he bent
Full of adoring tears and blandishment,
And towards her stept : she, like a moon in wane,
Faded before him, cower'd, nor could restrain
Her fearful sobs, self-folding like a flower
That faints into itself at evening hour :
But the God fostering her chilled hand,
She felt the warmth, her eyelids open'd bland,
And, like new flowers at morning song of bees,
Bloom'd, and gave up her honey to the lees.
Into the green-recessed woods they flew ;
Nor grew they pale, as mortal lovers do.

    Left to herself, the serpent now began
To change ; her elfin blood in madness ran ;
Her mouth foam'd, and the grass, therewith besprent,
Wither'd at dew so sweet and virulent ;
Her eyes in torture fix'd and anguish drear,
Hot, glazed, and wide, with lid-lashes all sear,
Flash'd phosphor and sharp sparks, without one cooling
    tear.
The colours all inflamed throughout her train,
She writhed about, convulsed with scarlet pain :
A deep volcanian yellow took the place,
Of all her milder-mooned body's grace ;

And, as the lava ravishes the mead,
Spoilt all her silver mail, and golden brede:
Made gloom of all her frecklings, streaks and bars,
Eclipsed her crescents, and lick'd up her stars:
So that, in moments few, she was undrest
Of all her sapphires, greens, and amethyst,
And rubious-argent: of all these bereft,
Nothing but pain and ugliness were left.
Still shone her crown; that vanish'd, also she
Melted and disappear'd as suddenly;
And in the air, her new voice luting soft,
Cried, "Lycius! gentle Lycius!"—borne aloft
With the bright mists about the mountains hoar
These words dissolved: Crete's forests heard no more.

Whither fled Lamia, now a lady bright,
A full-born beauty new and exquisite?
She fled into that valley they pass o'er
Who go to Corinth from Cenchreas' shore;
And rested at the foot of those wild hills,
The rugged founts of the Peræan rills,
And of that other ridge whose barren back
Stretches, with all its mist and cloudy rack,
South-westward to Cleone. There she stood,
About a young bird's flutter from a wood,
Fair, on a sloping green of mossy tread,
By a clear pool, wherein she passioned
To see herself escaped from so sore ills,
While her robes flaunted with the daffodils.

Ah, happy Lycius!—for she was a maid
More beautiful than ever twisted braid,
Or sigh'd, or blush'd, or on spring-flower'd lea
Spread a green kirtle to the minstrelsy:
A virgin purest lipp'd, yet in the lore
Of love deep learned to the red heart's core:
Not one hour old, yet of sciential brain
To unperplex bliss from its neighbour pain;
Define their pettish limits, and estrange
Their points of contact, and swift counterchange;
Intrigue with the specious chaos, and dispart
Its most ambiguous atoms with sure art;

As though in Cupid's college she had spent
Sweet days a lovely graduate, still unshent,
And kept his rosy terms in idle languishment.

Why this fair creature chose so fairily
By the wayside to linger, we shall see ;
But first 'tis fit to tell how she could muse
And dream, when in the serpent prison-house,
Of all she list, strange or magnificent :
How, ever, where she will'd her spirit went ;
Whether to faint Elysium, or where
Down through tress-lifting waves the Nereids fair
Wind into Thetis' bower by many a pearly stair ;
Or where God Bacchus drains his cups divine,
Stretch'd out, at ease, beneath a glutinous pine ;
Or where in Pluto's gardens palatine
Mulciber's columns gleam in far piazzian line.
And sometimes into cities she would send
Her dream, with feast and rioting to blend ;
And once, while among mortals dreaming thus,
She saw the young Corinthian Lycius
Charioting foremost in the envious race,
Like a young Jove with calm uneager face,
And fell into a swooning love of him.
Now on the moth-time of that evening dim
He would return that way, as well she knew,
To Corinth from the shore ; for freshly blew
The eastern soft-wind, and his galley now
Grated the quay-stones with her brazen prow
In port Cenchreas, from Egina isle
Fresh anchor'd ; whither he had been awhile
To sacrifice to Jove, whose temple there
Waits with high marble doors for blood and incense rare.

Jove heard his vows, and better'd his desire ;
For by some freakful chance he made retire
From his companions, and set forth to walk,
Perhaps grown wearied of their Corinth talk :
Over the solitary hills he fared,
Thoughtless, at first, but ere eve's star appear'd
His phantasy was lost, where reason fades,
In the calm'd twilight of Platonic shades.

Lamia beheld him coming, near, more near—
Close to her passing, in indifference drear,
His silent sandals swept the mossy green;
So neighbour'd to him, and yet so unseen,
She stood : he pass'd, shut up in mysteries,
His mind wrapp'd like his mantle, while her eyes
Follow'd his steps, and her neck regal white
Turn'd—syllabling thus : " Ah, Lycius bright !
And will you leave me on the hills alone ?
Lycius, look back ! and be some pity shown."
He did ; not with cold wonder, fearingly,
But Orpheus-like at an Eurydice ;
For so delicious were the words she sung
It seem'd he had loved them a whole summer long.
And soon his eyes had drunk her beauty up,
Leaving no drop in the bewildering cup,
And still the cup was full,—while he, afraid
Lest she should vanish ere his lip had paid
Due adoration, thus began to adore,—
Her soft look growing coy, she saw his chain so sure :
" Leave thee alone ! Look back ! Ah, Goddess, see
Whether my eyes can ever turn from thee !
For pity do not this sad heart belie—
Even as thou vanishest so I shall die.
Stay ! though a Naiad of the rivers, stay !
To thy far wishes will thy streams obey :
Stay ! though the greenest woods be thy domain,
Alone they can drink up the morning rain ;
Though a descended Pleiad, will not one
Of thine harmonious sisters keep in tune
Thy spheres, and as thy silver proxy shine?
So sweetly to these ravish'd ears of mine
Came thy sweet greeting, that if thou shouldst fade,
Thy memory will waste me to a shade.
For pity do not melt !" " If I should stay,"
Said Lamia, " here, upon this floor of clay,
And pain my steps upon these flowers too rough,
What canst thou say or do of charm enough
To dull the nice remembrance of my home?
Thou canst not ask me with thee here to roam
Over these hills and vales, where no joy is,—
Empty of immortality and bliss !

Thou art a scholar, Lycius, and must know
That finer spirits cannot breathe below
In human climes, and live.   Alas ! poor youth,
What taste of purer air hast thou to soothe
My essence ?   What serener palaces,
Where I may all my many senses please
And by mysterious sleights a hundred thirsts appease ?
It cannot be—adieu ! "   So said, she rose
Tiptoe, with white arms spread.   He, sick to lose
The amorous promise of her lone complain,
Swoon'd murmuring of love and pale with pain.
The cruel lady, without any show
Of sorrow for her tender favourite's woe,
But rather, if her eyes could brighter be,
With brighter eyes and slow amenity,
Put her new lips to his, and gave afresh
The life she had so tangled in her mesh :
And as he from one trance was wakening
Into another, she began to sing,—
Happy in beauty, life, and love, and everything,—
A song of love, too sweet for earthly lyres,
While, like held breath, the stars drew in their panting fires.
And then she whisper'd in such trembling tone
As those who, safe together met alone
For the first time through many anguish'd days,
Use other speech than looks ; bidding him raise
His drooping head, and clear his soul of doubt,
For that she was a woman, and without
Any more subtle fluid in her veins
Than throbbing blood, and that the self-same pains
Inhabited her frail-strung heart as his.
And next she wonder'd how his eyes could miss
Her face so long in Corinth, where, she said,
She dwelt but half retired, and there had led
Days happy as the gold coin could invent
Without the aid of love ; yet in content,
Till she saw him, as once she pass'd him by
Where 'gainst a column he leant thoughtfully
At Venus' temple porch, 'mid baskets heap'd
Of amorous herbs and flowers, newly reap'd
Late on that eve, as 'twas the night before
The Adonian feast ; whereof she saw no more,

But wept alone those days,—for why should she adore?
Lycius from death awoke into amaze
To see her still, and singing so sweet lays;
Then from amaze into delight he fell
To hear her whisper woman's lore so well;
And every word she spake enticed him on
To unperplex'd delight and pleasure known.
Let the mad poets say whate'er they please
Of the sweets of Fairies, Peris, Goddesses,
There is not such a treat among them all—
Haunters of cavern, lake, and waterfall—
As a real woman, lineal indeed
From Pyrrha's pebbles or old Adam's seed.
Thus gentle Lamia judged, and judged aright,
That Lycius could not love in half a fright,
So threw the goddess off, and won his heart
More pleasantly by playing woman's part,
With no more awe than what her beauty gave,
That, while it smote, still guaranteed to save.
Lycius to all made eloquent reply,
Marrying to every word a twin-born sigh;
And last, pointing to Corinth, ask'd her sweet,
If 'twas too far that night for her soft feet.
The way was short, for Lamia's eagerness
Made, by a spell, the triple league decrease
To a few paces; not at all surmised
By blinded Lycius. So, in her comprised,
They pass'd the city gates, he knew not how,
So noiseless, and he never thought to know.

As men talk in a dream, so Corinth all,
Throughout her palaces imperial,
And all her populous streets and temples lewd,
Mutter'd, like tempest in the distance brew'd,
To the wide-spreaded night above her towers.
Men, women, rich and poor, in the cool hours,
Shuffled their sandals o'er the pavement white,
Companion'd or alone; while many a light
Flared, here and there, from wealthy festivals,
And threw their moving shadows on the walls,
Or found them cluster'd in the corniced shade
Of some arch'd temple door or dusky colonnade.

Muffling his face, of greeting friends in fear,
Her finger he press'd hard, as one came near
With curl'd grey beard, sharp eyes, and smooth bald crown,
Slow-stepp'd, and robed in philosophic gown :
Lycius shrank closer, as they met and past,
Into his mantle, adding wings to haste,
While hurried Lamia trembled.   "Ah !" said he,
"Why do you shudder, love, so ruefully ?
Why does your tender palm dissolve in dew ?"—
"I'm wearied," said fair Lamia : "tell me who
Is that old man ?   I cannot bring to mind
His features :—Lycius ! wherefore did you blind
Yourself from his quick eyes ?"   Lycius replied,
"'Tis Apollonius sage, my trusty guide
And good instructor ; but to-night he seems
The ghost of Folly haunting my sweet dreams."

While yet he spake they had arrived before
A pillar'd porch, with lofty portal door,
Where hung a silver lamp, whose phosphor glow
Reflected in the slabbed steps below,
Mild as a star in water ; for so new
And so unsullied was the marble hue,
So through the crystal polish, liquid fine,
Ran the dark veins, that none but feet divine
Could e'er have touch'd there.   Sounds Æolian
Breathed from the hinges, as the ample span
Of the wide doors disclosed a place unknown
Some time to any, but those two alone,
And a few Persian mutes, who that same year
Were seen about the markets : none knew where
They could inhabit ; the most curious
Were foil'd, who watch'd to trace them to their house :
And but the flitter-winged verse must tell,
For truth's sake what woe afterwards befell.
'Twould humour many a heart to leave them thus
Shut from the busy world of more incredulous.

PART II

LOVE in a hut, with water and a crust,
Is—Love, forgive us !—cinders, ashes, dust ;
Love in a palace is perhaps at last
More grievous torment than a hermit's fast :—
That is a doubtful tale from faery land,
Hard for the non-elect to understand.
Had Lycius lived to hand his story down,
He might have given the moral a fresh frown,
Or clench'd it quite : but too short was their bliss
To breed distrust and hate, that make the soft voice hiss.
Besides, there, nightly, with terrific glare,
Love, jealous grown of so complete a pair,
Hover'd and buzz'd his wings, with fearful roar,
Above the lintel of their chamber door,
And down the passage cast a glow upon the floor.

For all this came a ruin : side by side
They were enthroned, in the even tide,
Upon a couch, near to a curtaining
Whose airy texture, from a golden string,
Floated into the room, and let appear
Unveil'd the summer heaven, blue and clear,
Betwixt two marble shafts :—there they reposed,
Where use had made it sweet, with eyelids closed,
Saving a tithe which love still open kept,
That they might see each other while they almost slept ;
When from the slope side of a suburb hill,
Deafening the swallow's twitter, came a thrill
Of trumpets.   Lycius started—the sounds fled,
But left a thought, a buzzing in his head.
For the first time, since first he harbour'd in
That purple-lined palace of sweet sin,
His spirit pass'd beyond its golden bourn
Into the noisy world almost forsworn.
The lady, ever watchful, penetrant,
Saw this with pain, so arguing a want
Of something more, more than her empery
Of joys ; and she began to moan and sigh
Because he mused beyond her, knowing well,
That but a moment's thought is passion's passing bell.
" Why do you sigh, fair creature ? " whisper'd he :

"Why do you think ?" return'd she tenderly :
"You have deserted me ; where am I now ?
Not in your heart while care weighs on your brow :
No, no, you have dismiss'd me, and I go,
From your breast houseless : ay, it must be so."
He answer'd, bending to her open eyes,
Where he was mirror'd small in paradise,—
"My silver planet, both of eve and morn !
Why will you plead yourself so sad forlorn,
While I am striving how to fill my heart
With deeper crimson and a double smart ?
How to entangle, trammel up, and snare
Your soul in mine, and labyrinth you there,
Like the hid scent in an unbudded rose ?
Ay, a sweet kiss—you see your mighty woes.
My thoughts ! shall I unveil them ? Listen then.
What mortal hath a prize, that other men
May be confounded and abash'd withal,
But lets it sometimes pace abroad majestical,
And triumph, as in thee I should rejoice
Amid the hoarse alarm of Corinth's voice.
Let my foes choke, and my friends shout afar,
While through the thronged streets your bridal car
Wheels round its dazzling spokes."—The lady's cheek
Trembled ; she nothing said, but, pale and meek,
Arose and knelt before him, wept a rain
Of sorrows at his words ; at last with pain
Beseeching him, the while his hand she wrung,
To change his purpose. He thereat was stung,
Perverse, with stronger fancy to reclaim
Her wild and timid nature to his aim ;
Besides, for all his love, in self despite,
Against his better self, he took delight
Luxurious in her sorrows, soft and new.
His passion, cruel grown, took on a hue
Fierce and sanguineous as 'twas possible
In one whose brow had no dark veins to swell.
Fine was the mitigated fury, like
Apollo's presence when in act to strike
The serpent—Ha ! the serpent ! certes, she
Was none. She burnt, she loved the tyranny,
And, all subdued, consented to the hour

When to the bridal he should lead his paramour.
Whispering in midnight silence, said the youth,
"Sure some sweet name thou hast, though, by my truth,
I have not ask'd it, ever thinking thee
Not mortal, but of heavenly progeny,
As still I do. Hast any mortal name,
Fit appellation for this dazzling frame?
Or friends or kinsfolk on the citied earth,
To share our marriage feast and nuptial mirth?"
"I have no friends," said Lamia, "no, not one;
My presence in wide Corinth hardly known.
My parents' bones are in their dusty urns
Sepulchred, where no kindled incense burns,
Seeing all their luckless race are dead save me,
And I neglect the holy rite for thee.
Even as you list invite your many guests;
But if, as now it seems, your vision rests
With any pleasure on me, do not bid
Old Apollonius—from him keep me hid."
Lycius, perplex'd at words so blind and blank,
Made close inquiry; from whose touch she shrank,
Feigning a sleep; and he to the dull shade
Of deep sleep in a moment was betray'd.

It was the custom then to bring away
The bride from home at blushing shut of day,
Veil'd, in a chariot, heralded along
By strewn flowers, torches, and a marriage song,
With other pageants: but this fair unknown
Had not a friend. So being left alone
(Lycius was gone to summon all his kin),
And knowing surely she could never win
His foolish heart from its mad pompousness,
She set herself, high-thoughted, how to dress
The misery in fit magnificence.
She did so, but 'tis doubtful how and whence
Came and who were her subtle servitors.
About the halls, and to and from the doors,
There was a noise of wings, till in short space
The glowing banquet-room shone with wide-arched grace;
A haunting music, sole perhaps and lone
Supportress of the faery-roof, made moan

Throughout, as fearful the whole charm might fade.
Fresh carved cedar, mimicking a glade
Of palm and plantain, met from either side,
High in the midst, in honour of the bride :
Two palms and then two plantains, and so on,
From either side their stems branch'd one to one
All down the aisled place ; and beneath all
There ran a stream of lamps straight on from wall to wall.
So canopied, lay an untasted feast
Teeming with odours.   Lamia, regal drest,
Silently paced about, and as she went,
In pale contented sort of discontent,
Mission'd her viewless servants to enrich
The fretted splendour of each nook and niche.
Between the tree-stems, marbled plain at first,
Came jasper panels ; then anon there burst
Forth creeping imagery of slighter trees,
And with the larger wove in small intricacies.
Approving all, she faded at self-will,
And shut the chamber up, close, hush'd and still,
Complete and ready for the revels rude,
When dreadful guests would come to spoil her solitude.

    The day appear'd, and all the gossip rout.
O senseless Lycius ! Madman ! wherefore flout
The silent-blessing fate, warm cloister'd hours,
And show to common eyes these secret bowers ?
The herd approach'd ; each guest, with busy brain,
Arriving at the portal, gazed amain,
And enter'd marvelling : for they knew the street,
Remember'd it from childhood all complete
Without a gap, yet ne'er before had seen
That royal porch, that high-built fair demesne ;
So in they hurried all, mazed, curious and keen ;
Save one, who look'd thereon with eye severe,
And with calm-planted steps walk'd in austere ;
'Twas Apollonius : something too he laugh'd,
As though some knotty problem, that had daft
His patient thought, had now begun to thaw
And solve and melt : 'twas just as he foresaw.

    He met within the murmurous vestibule
His young disciple.   " 'Tis no common rule,

Lycius," said he, " for uninvited guest
To force himself upon you, and infest
With an unbidden presence the bright throng
Of younger friends; yet must I do this wrong,
And you forgive me." Lycius blush'd, and led
The old man through the inner doors broad-spread;
With reconciling words and courteous mien
Turning into sweet milk the sophist's spleen.

Of wealthy lustre was the banquet-room,
Fill'd with pervading brilliance and perfume:
Before each lucid panel fuming stood
A censer fed with myrrh and spiced wood,
Each by a sacred tripod held aloft,
Whose slender feet wide-swerved upon the soft
Wool-woofed carpets: fifty wreaths of smoke
From fifty censers their light voyage took
To the high roof, still mimick'd as they rose
Along the mirror'd walls by twin-clouds odorous.
Twelve sphered tables by silk seats insphered,
High as the level of a man's breast rear'd
On libbard's paws, upheld the heavy gold
Of cups and goblets, and the store thrice told
Of Ceres' horn, and, in huge vessels, wine
Came from the gloomy tun with merry shine.
Thus loaded with a feast the tables stood,
Each shrining in the midst the image of a God.

When in an antechamber every guest
Had felt the cold full sponge to pleasure press'd
By ministering slaves upon his hands and feet,
And fragrant oils with ceremony meet
Pour'd on his hair, they all moved to the feast
In white robes, and themselves in order placed
Around the silken couches, wondering
Whence all this mighty cost and blaze of wealth could spring.

Soft went the music the soft air along,
While fluent Greek a vowel'd under-song
Kept up among the guests, discoursing low
At first, for scarcely was the wine at flow;
But when the happy vintage touch'd their brains,
Louder they talk, and louder come the strains

Of powerful instruments :—the gorgeous dyes,
The space, the splendour of the draperies,
The roof of awful richness, nectarous cheer,
Beautiful slaves, and Lamia's self, appear.
Now, when the wine has done its rosy deed
And every soul from human trammels freed,
No more so strange ; for merry wine, sweet wine,
Will make Elysian shades not too fair, too divine.
Soon was God Bacchus at meridian height ;
Flush'd were their cheeks, and bright eyes double bright ;
Garlands of every green and every scent
From vales deflower'd or forest-trees branch-rent,
In baskets of bright osier'd gold were brought,
High as the handles heap'd, to suit the thought
Of every guest ; that each, as he did please.
Might fancy-fit his brows, silk-pillow'd at his ease.

What wreath for Lamia ? What for Lycius ?
What for the sage, old Apollonius ?
Upon her aching forehead be there hung
The leaves of willow and of adder's tongue ;
And for the youth, quick, let us strip for him
The thyrsus, that his watching eyes may swim
Into forgetfulness ; and, for the sage,
Let spear-grass and the spiteful thistle wage
War on his temples.   Do not all charms fly
At the mere touch of cold philosophy ?
There was an awful rainbow once in heaven :
We know her woof, her texture ; she is given
In the dull catalogue of common things.
Philosophy will clip an Angel's wings,
Conquer all mysteries by rule and line,
Empty the haunted air and gnomed mine—
Unweave a rainbow, as it erewhile made
The tender-person'd Lamia melt into a shade.

By her glad Lycius sitting, in chief place,
Scarce saw in all the room another face,
Till, checking his love trance, a cup he took
Full brimm'd, and opposite sent forth a look
'Cross the broad table, to beseech a glance
From his old teacher's wrinkled countenance,
And pledge him.   The bald-head philosopher

Had fix'd his eye, without a twinkle or a stir,
Full on the alarmed beauty of the bride,
Brow-beating her fair form and troubling her sweet pride.
Lycius then press'd her hand, with devout touch,
As pale it lay upon the rosy couch:
'Twas icy, and the cold ran through his veins;
Then sudden it grew hot, and all the pains
Of an unnatural heat shot to his heart.
"Lamia, what means this?   Wherefore dost thou start?
Know'st thou that man?"   Poor Lamia answer'd not.
He gazed into her eyes, and not a jot
Own'd they the lovelorn piteous appeal:
More, more he gazed: his human senses reel:
Some hungry spell that loveliness absorbs;
There was no recognition in those orbs.
"Lamia!" he cried—and no soft-toned reply.
The many heard, and the loud revelry
Grew hush; the stately music no more breathes;
The myrtle sicken'd in a thousand wreaths.
By faint degrees, voice, lute, and pleasure ceased;
A deadly silence step by step increased
Until it seem'd a horrid presence there,
And not a man but felt the terror in his hair.
"Lamia!" he shriek'd; and nothing but the shriek
With its sad echo did the silence break.
"Begone, foul dream!" he cried, gazing again
In the bride's face, where now no azure vein
Wander'd on fair-spaced temples, no soft bloom
Misted the cheek, no passion to illume
The deep-recessed vision:—all was blight:
Lamia, no longer fair, there sat, a deadly white.
"Shut, shut those juggling eyes, thou ruthless man!
Turn them aside, wretch! or the righteous ban
Of all the Gods, whose dreadful images
Here represent their shadowy presences,
May pierce them on the sudden with the thorn
Of painful blindness; leaving thee forlorn,
In trembling dotage to the feeblest fright
Of conscience, for their long-offended might,
For all thine impious proud-heart sophistries,
Unlawful magic, and enticing lies.
Corinthians! look upon that grey-beard wretch!

Mark how, possess'd, his lashless eyelids stretch
Around his demon eyes!   Corinthians, see!
My sweet bride withers at their potency."
"Fool!" said the sophist, in an under-tone,
Gruff with contempt; which a death-nighing moan
From Lycius answer'd, as, heart-struck and lost,
He sank supine beside the aching ghost.
"Fool! Fool!" repeated he, while his eyes still
Relented not, nor moved; "from every ill
Of life have I preserved thee to this day,
And shall I see thee made a serpent's prey?"
Then Lamia breathed death-breath; the sophist's eye,
Like a sharp spear, went through her utterly,
Keen, cruel, perceant, stinging: she, as well
As her weak hand could any meaning tell,
Motion'd him to be silent; vainly so;
He look'd and look'd again a level—No!
"A serpent!" echoed he.   No sooner said,
Than with a frightful scream she vanished;
And Lycius' arms were empty of delight,
As were his limbs of life, from that same night.
On the high couch he lay—his friends came round—
Supported him; no pulse or breath they found,
And in its marriage robe the heavy body wound.[1]

---

[1] "Philostratus, in his fourth book, *De Vita Apollonii*, hath a memorable instance in this kind, which I may not omit, of one Menippus Lycius, a young man twenty-five years of age, that, going betwixt Cenchreas and Corinth, met such a phantasm in the habit of a fair gentlewoman, which, taking him by the hand, carried him home to her house, in the suburbs of Corinth, and told him she was a Phœnician by birth, and if he would tarry with her he should hear her sing and play, and drink such wine as never any drank, and no man should molest him; but she, being fair and lovely, would die with him, that was fair and lovely to behold. The young man, a philosopher, otherwise staid and discreet, able to moderate his passions, though not this of love, tarried with her awhile to his great content, and at last married her; to whose wedding, amongst other guests, came Apollonius, who, by some probable conjectures, found her out to be a serpent, a *lamia*, and that all her furniture was, like Tantalus' gold, described by Homer, no substance, but mere illusions. When she saw herself descried she wept, and desired Apollonius to be silent, but he would not be moved, and thereupon she, plate, house, and all that was in it, vanished in an instant. Many thousands took notice of this fact, for it was done in the midst of Greece."—BURTON'S *Anatomy of Melancholy*, Part 3, Sect. 2, Memb. I. Subs. I.

ISABELLA ;

OR,

THE POT OF BASIL

A STORY, FROM BOCCACCIO

FAIR Isabel, poor simple Isabel !
   Lorenzo, a young palmer in Love's eye !
They could not in the self-same mansion dwell
   Without some stir of heart, some malady ;
They could not sit at meals but feel how well
   It soothed each to be the other by ;
They could not, sure, beneath the same roof sleep,
But to each other dream, and nightly weep.

With every morn their love grew tenderer,
   With every eve deeper and tenderer still ;
He might not in house, field, or garden stir,
   But her full shape would all his seeing fill ;
And his continual voice was pleasanter
   To her, than noise of trees or hidden rill ;
Her lute-string gave an echo of his name,
She spoilt her half-done broidery with the same.

He knew whose gentle hand was at the latch,
   Before the door had given her to his eyes ;
And from her chamber-window he would catch
   Her beauty farther than the falcon spies ;
And constant as her vespers would he watch,
   Because her face was turn'd to the same skies ;
And with sick longing all the night outwear,
To hear her morning-step upon the stair.

A whole long month of May in this sad plight
   Made their cheeks paler by the break of June :
" To-morrow will I bow to my delight,
   To-morrow will I ask my lady's boon."—

"O may I never see another night,
  Lorenzo, if thy lips breathe not love's tune."—
So spake they to their pillows; but, alas,
Honeyless days and days did he let pass;

Until sweet Isabella's untouch'd cheek
  Fell sick within the rose's just domain,
Fell thin as a young mother's, who doth seek
  By every lull to cool her infant's pain:
"How ill she is!" said he, "I may not speak
  And yet I will, and tell my love all plain:
If looks speak love-laws, I will drink her tears,
And at the least 'twill startle off her cares."

So said he one fair morning, and all day
  His heart beat awfully against his side;
And to his heart he inwardly did pray
  For power to speak; but still the ruddy tide
Stifled his voice, and pulsed resolve away—
  Fever'd his high conceit of such a bride,
Yet brought him to the meekness of a child:
Alas! when passion is both meek and wild!

So once more he had waked and anguished
  A dreary night of love and misery,
If Isabel's quick eye had not been wed
  To every symbol on his forehead high;
She saw it waxing very pale and dead,
  And straight all flush'd; so, lisped tenderly,
"Lorenzo!"—here she ceased her timid quest,
But in her tone and look he read the rest.

"O Isabella! I can half perceive
  That I may speak my grief into thine ear;
If thou didst ever anything believe,
  Believe how I love thee, believe how near
My soul is to its doom: I would not grieve
  Thy hand by unwelcome pressing, would not fear
Thine eyes by gazing; but I cannot live
Another night, and not my passion shrive.

"Love: thou art leading me from wintry cold,
  Lady! thou leadest me to summer clime,

And I must taste the blossoms that unfold
 In its ripe warmth this gracious morning time."
So said, his erewhile timid lips grew bold,
 And poesied with hers in dewy rhyme :
Great bliss was with them, and great happiness
Grew, like a lusty flower in June's caress.

Parting they seem'd to tread upon the air,
 'Twin roses by the zephyr blown apart
Only to meet again more close, and share
 The inward fragrance of each other's heart.
She, to her chamber gone, a ditty fair
 Sang, of delicious love and honey'd dart ;
He with light steps went up a western hill,
And bade the sun farewell, and joy'd his fill.

All close they met again, before the dusk
 Had taken from the stars its pleasant veil,
All close they met, all eves, before the dusk
 Had taken from the stars its pleasant veil,
Close in a bower of hyacinth and musk,
 Unknown of any, free from whispering tale.
Ah ! better had it been for ever so,
Than idle ears should pleasure in their woe.

Were they unhappy then ?—It cannot be—
 Too many tears for lovers have been shed,
Too many sighs give we to them in fee,
 Too much of pity after they are dead,
Too many doleful stories do we see,
 Whose matter in bright gold were best be read ;
Except in such a page where Theseus' spouse
Over the pathless waves towards him bows.

But for the general award of love,
 The little sweet doth kill much bitterness ;
Though Dido silent is in under-grove,
 And Isabella's was a great distress,
Though young Lorenzo in warm Indian clove
 Was not embalm'd, this truth is not the less—
Even bees, the little almsmen of spring-bowers,
Know there is richest juice in poison-flowers.

With her two brothers this fair lady dwelt,
  Enriched from ancestral merchandise,
And for them many a weary hand did swelt
  In torched mines and noisy factories,
And many once proud-quiver'd loins did melt
  In blood from stinging whip; with hollow eyes
Many all day in dazzling river stood,
To take the rich-ored driftings of the flood.

For them the Ceylon diver held his breath,
  And went all naked to the hungry shark;
For them his ears gush'd blood; for them in death
  The seal on the cold ice with piteous bark
Lay full of darts; for them alone did seethe
  A thousand men in troubles wide and dark:
Half-ignorant, they turn'd an easy wheel,
That set sharp racks at work, to pinch and peel.

Why were they proud? Because their marble founts
  Gush'd with more pride than do a wretch's tears?
Why were they proud? Because fair orange-mounts
  Were of more soft ascent than lazar stairs?
Why were they proud? Because red-lined accounts
  Were richer than the songs of Grecian years?
Why were they proud? again we ask aloud,
Why in the name of Glory were they proud?

Yet were these Florentines as self-retired
  In hungry pride and gainful cowardice,
As two close Hebrews in that land inspired,
  Paled in and vineyarded from beggar-spies;
The hawks of ship-mast forests—the untired
  And pannier'd mules for ducats and old lies—
Quick cat's-paws on the generous stray-away,—
Great wits in Spanish, Tuscan, and Malay.

How was it these same ledger-men could spy
  Fair Isabella in her downy nest?
How could they find out in Lorenzo's eye
  A straying from his toil? Hot Egypt's pest
Into their vision covetous and sly!
  How could these money-bags see east and west?
Yet so they did—and every dealer fair
Must see behind, as doth the hunted hare.

O eloquent and famed Boccaccio!
  Of thee we now should ask forgiving boon,
And of thy spicy myrtles as they blow,
  And of thy roses amorous of the moon,
And of thy lilies, that do paler grow
  Now they can no more hear thy ghittern's tune,
For venturing syllables that ill beseem
The quiet glooms of such a piteous theme.

Grant thou a pardon here, and then the tale
  Shall move on soberly, as it is meet;
There is no other crime, no mad assail
  To make old prose in modern rhyme more sweet;
But it is done—succeed the verse or fail—
  To honour thee, and thy gone spirit greet;
To stead thee as a verse in English tongue,
An echo of thee in the north-wind sung.

These brethren having found by many signs
  What love Lorenzo for their sister had,
And how she loved him too, each unconfines
  His bitter thoughts to other, well-nigh mad
That he, the servant of their trade designs,
  Should in their sister's love be blithe and glad,
When 'twas their plan to coax her by degrees
To some high noble and his olive-trees.

And many a jealous conference had they,
  And many times they bit their lips alone,
Before they fix'd upon a surest way
  To make the youngster for his crime atone;
And at the last, these men of cruel clay
  Cut Mercy with a sharp knife to the bone;
For they resolved in some forest dim
To kill Lorenzo, and there bury him.

So on a pleasant morning, as he leant
  Into the sun-rise, o'er the balustrade
Of the garden-terrace, towards him they bent
  Their footing through the dews; and to him said,
"You seem there in the quiet of content,
  Lorenzo, and we are most loth to invade
Calm speculation; but if you are wise,
Bestride your steed while cold is in the skies.

"To-day we purpose, ay, this hour we mount
    To spur three leagues towards the Apennine;
Come down, we pray thee, ere the hot sun count
    His dewy rosary on the eglantine."
Lorenzo, courteously as he was wont,
    Bow'd a fair greeting to these serpents' whine,
And went in haste, to get in readiness,
With belt, and spur, and bracing huntsman's dress.

And as he to the court-yard pass'd along,
    Each third step did he pause, and listen'd oft
If he could hear his lady's matin-song,
    Or the light whisper of her footstep soft;
And as he thus over his passion hung,
    He heard a laugh full musical aloft;
When, looking up, he saw her features bright
Smile through an in-door lattice all delight.

"Love, Isabel!" said he, "I was in pain
    Lest I should miss to bid thee a good morrow:
Ah! what if I should lose thee, when so fain
    I am to stifle all the heavy sorrow
Of a poor three hours' absence? but we'll gain
    Out of the amorous dark what day doth borrow.
Good bye! I'll soon be back."—"Good bye!" said she:
And as he went she chanted merrily.

So the two brothers and their murder'd man
    Rode past fair Florence, to where Arno's stream
Gurgles through straiten'd banks, and still doth fan
    Itself with dancing bulrush, and the bream
Keeps head against the freshets. Sick and wan
    The brothers' faces in the ford did seem,
Lorenzo's flush with love. They pass'd the water
Into a forest quiet for the slaughter.

There was Lorenzo slain and buried in,
    There in that forest did his great love cease;
Ah! when a soul doth thus its freedom win,
    It aches in loneliness—is ill at peace
As the break-covert blood-hounds of such sin:
    They dipp'd their swords in the water, and did tease
Their horses homeward, with convulsed spur,
Each richer by his being a murderer.

They told their sister how, with sudden speed,
  Lorenzo had ta'en ship for foreign lands,
Because of some great urgency and need
  In their affairs, requiring trusty hands.
Poor girl! put on thy stifling widow's weed,
  And 'scape at once from Hope's accursed bands;
To-day thou wilt not see him, nor to-morrow,
And the next day will be a day of sorrow.

She weeps alone for pleasures not to be;
  Sorely she wept until the night came on,
And then, instead of love, O misery!
  She brooded o'er the luxury alone:
His image in the dusk she seem'd to see,
  And to the silence made a gentle moan,
Spreading her perfect arms upon the air,
And on her couch low murmuring, "Where? O where?"

But Selfishness, Love's cousin, held not long
  Its fiery vigil in her single breast;
She fretted for the golden hour, and hung
  Upon the time with feverish unrest—
Not long; for soon into her heart a throng
  Of higher occupants, a richer zest,
Came tragic; passion not to be subdued,
And sorrow for her love in travels rude.

In the mid days of autumn, on their eves
  The breath of Winter comes from far away,
And the sick west continually bereaves
  Of some gold tinge, and plays a roundelay
Of death among the bushes and the leaves,
  To make all bare before he dares to stray
From his north cavern. So sweet Isabel
By gradual decay from beauty fell,

Because Lorenzo came not. Oftentimes
  She ask'd her brothers, with an eye all pale
Striving to be itself, what dungeon climes
  Could keep him off so long? They spake a tale
Time after time, to quiet her. Their crimes
  Came on them, like a smoke from Hinnom's vale;
And every night in dreams they groan'd aloud,
To see their sister in her snowy shroud.

And she had died in drowsy ignorance,
    But for a thing more deadly dark than all;
It came like a fierce potion, drunk by chance,
    Which saves a sick man from the feather'd pall
For some few gasping moments; like a lance,
    Waking an Indian from his cloudy hall
With cruel pierce, and bringing him again
Sense of the gnawing fire at heart and brain.

It was a vision.   In the drowsy gloom,
    The dull of midnight, at her couch's foot
Lorenzo stood, and wept: the forest tomb
    Had marr'd his glossy hair which once could shoot
Lustre into the sun, and put cold doom
    Upon his lips, and taken the soft lute
From his lorn voice, and past his loamed ears
Had made a miry channel for his tears.

Strange sound it was, when the pale shadow spake,
    For there was striving, in its piteous tongue,
To speak as when on earth it was awake,
    And Isabella on its music hung:
Languor there was in it, and tremulous shake,
    As in a palsied Druid's harp unstrung;
And through it moan'd a ghostly under-song,
Like hoarse night-gusts sepulchral briars among.

Its eyes, though wild, were still all dewy bright
    With love, and kept all phantom fear aloof
From the poor girl by magic of their light,
    The while it did unthread the horrid woof
Of the late darken'd time—the murderous spite
    Of pride and avarice—the dark pine roof
In the forest—and the sodden turfed dell,
Where, without any word, from stabs he fell.

Saying moreover, "Isabel, my sweet!
    Red whortle-berries droop above my head,
And a large flint-stone weighs upon my feet;
    Around me beeches and high chestnuts shed
Their leaves and prickly-nuts; a sheep-fold bleat
    Comes from beyond the river to my bed:
Go, shed one tear upon my heather-bloom,
And it shall comfort me within the tomb.

"I am a shadow now, alas! alas!
  Upon the skirts of human nature dwelling
Alone: I chant alone the holy mass,
  While little sounds of life are round me knelling,
And glossy bees at noon do fieldward pass,
  And many a chapel bell the hour is telling,
Paining me through: those sounds grow strange to me,
And thou art distant in Humanity.

"I know what was, I feel full well what is,
  And I should rage, if spirits could go mad;
Though I forget the taste of earthly bliss,
  That paleness warms my grave, as though I had
A seraph chosen from the bright abyss
  To be my spouse: thy paleness makes me glad:
Thy beauty grows upon me, and I feel
A greater love through all my essence steal."

The Spirit mourn'd "Adieu!"—dissolved, and left
  The atom darkness in a slow turmoil;
As when of healthful midnight sleep bereft,
  Thinking on rugged hours and fruitless toil,
We put our eyes into a pillowy cleft,
  And see the spangly gloom froth up and boil:
It made sad Isabella's eyelids ache,
And in the dawn she started up awake;

"Ha! ha!" said she, 'I knew not this hard life,
  I thought the worst was simple misery;
I thought some Fate with pleasure or with strife
  Portion'd us—happy days, or else to die;
But there is crime—a brother's bloody knife!
  Sweet Spirit, thou hast school'd my infancy:
I'll visit thee for this, and kiss thine eyes,
And greet thee morn and even in the skies."

When the full morning came, she had devised
  How she might secret to the forest hie;
How she might find the clay, so dearly prized,
  And sing to it one latest lullaby;
How her short absence might be unsurmised,
  While she the inmost of the dream would try.
Resolved, she took with her an aged nurse,
And went into that dismal forest-hearse.

See, as they creep along the river side,
　　How she doth whisper to that aged dame,
And, after looking round the champaign wide,
　　Shows her a knife.—"What feverous hectic flame
Burns in thee, child?—what good can thee betide
　　That thou shouldst smile again?"—The evening came,
And they had found Lorenzo's earthly bed;
The flint was there, the berries at his head.

Who hath not loiter'd in a green church-yard,
　　And let his spirit, like a demon mole,
Work through the clayey soil and gravel hard,
　　To see skull, coffin'd bones, and funeral stole;
Pitying each form that hungry Death had marr'd,
　　And filling it once more with human soul?
Ah! this is holiday to what was felt
When Isabella by Lorenzo knelt.

She gazed into the fresh-thrown mould, as though
　　One glance did fully all its secrets tell;
Clearly she saw, as other eyes would know
　　Pale limbs at bottom of a crystal well;
Upon the murderous spot she seem'd to grow,
　　Like to a native lily of the dell:
Then with her knife, all sudden she began
To dig more fervently than misers can.

Soon she turn'd up a soiled glove, whereon
　　Her silk had play'd in purple phantasies;
She kiss'd it with a lip more chill than stone,
　　And put it in her bosom, where it dries
And freezes utterly unto the bone
　　Those dainties made to still an infant's cries:
Then 'gan she work again; nor stay'd her care,
But to throw back at times her veiling hair.

That old nurse stood beside her wondering,
　　Until her heart felt pity to the core
At sight of such a dismal labouring,
　　And so she kneeled, with her locks all hoar,
And put her lean hands to the horrid thing:
　　Three hours they labour'd at this travail sore;
At last they felt the kernel of the grave,
And Isabella did not stamp and rave.

Ah! wherefore all this wormy circumstance?
  Why linger at the yawning tomb so long?
O for the gentleness of old Romance,
  The simple plaining of a minstrel's song!
Fair reader, at the old tale take a glance,
  For here, in truth, it doth not well belong
To speak:—O turn thee to the very tale,
And taste the music of that vision pale.

With duller steel than the Perséan sword
  They cut away no formless monster's head,
But one, whose gentleness did well accord
  With death, as life. The ancient harps have said,
Love never dies, but lives, immortal Lord:
  If Love impersonate was ever dead,
Pale Isabella kiss'd it, and low moan'd.
'Twas love; cold,—dead indeed, but not dethroned.

In anxious secrecy they took it home,
  And then the prize was all for Isabel:
She calm'd its wild hair with a golden comb,
  And all around each eye's sepulchral cell
Pointed each fringed lash; the smeared loam
  With tears, as chilly as a dripping well,
She drench'd away: and still she comb'd and kept
Sighing all day—and still she kiss'd and wept.

Then in a silken scarf,—sweet with the dews
  Of precious flowers pluck'd in Araby,
And divine liquids come with odorous ooze
  Through the cold serpent-pipe refreshfully,—
She wrapp'd it up; and for its tomb did choose
  A garden-pot, wherein she laid it by,
And cover'd it with mould, and o'er it set
Sweet Basil, which her tears kept ever wet.

And she forgot the stars, the moon, and sun,
  And she forgot the blue above the trees,
And she forgot the dells where waters run,
  And she forgot the chilly autumn breeze;
She had no knowledge when the day was done,
  And the new morn she saw not: but in peace
Hung over her sweet Basil evermore,
And moisten'd it with tears unto the core.

F

And so she ever fed it with thin tears,
    Whence thick, and green, and beautiful it grew,
So that it smelt more balmy than its peers
    Of Basil-tufts in Florence ; for it drew
Nurture besides, and life, from human fears,
    From the fast mouldering head there shut from view :
So that the jewel, safely casketed,
Came forth, and in perfumed leaflets spread.

O Melancholy, linger here awhile !
    O Music, Music, breathe despondingly !
O Echo, Echo, from some sombre isle,
    Unknown, Lethean, sigh to us—O sigh !
Spirits in grief, lift up your heads, and smile ;
    Lift up your heads, sweet Spirits, heavily,
And make a pale light in your cypress glooms,
Tinting with silver wan your marble tombs.

Moan hither, all ye syllables of woe,
    From the deep throat of sad Melpomene !
Through bronzed lyre in tragic order go,
    And touch the strings into a mystery ;
Sound mournfully upon the winds and low ;
    For simple Isabel is soon to be
Among the dead : She withers, like a palm
Cut by an Indian for its juicy balm.

O leave the palm to wither by itself ;
    Let not quick Winter chill its dying hour !—
It may not be—those Baâlites of pelf,
    Her brethren, noted the continual shower
From her dead eyes ; and many a curious elf,
    Among her kindred, wonder'd that such dower
Of youth and beauty should be thrown aside
By one mark'd out to be a Noble's bride.

And, furthermore, her brethren wonder'd much
    Why she sat drooping by the Basil green,
And why it flourish'd, as by magic touch ;
    Greatly they wonder'd what the thing might mean :
They could not surely give belief, that such
    A very nothing would have power to wean
Her from her own fair youth, and pleasures gay,
And even remembrance of her love's delay.

Therefore they watch'd a time when they might sift
  This hidden whim; and long they watch'd in vain;
For seldom did she go to chapel-shrift,
  And seldom felt she any hunger-pain:
And when she left, she hurried back, as swift
  As bird on wing to breast its eggs again:
And, patient as a hen-bird, sat her there
Beside her Basil, weeping through her hair.

Yet they contrived to steal the Basil-pot,
  And to examine it in secret place:
The thing was vile with green and livid spot,
  And yet they knew it was Lorenzo's face:
The guerdon of their murder they had got,
  And so left Florence in a moment's space,
Never to turn again.—Away they went,
With blood upon their heads, to banishment.

O Melancholy, turn thine eyes away!
  O Music, Music, breathe despondingly!
O Echo, Echo, on some other day,
  From isles Lethean, sigh to us—O sigh!
Spirits of grief, sing not your "Well-a-way!"
  For Isabel, sweet Isabel, will die;
Will die a death too lone and incomplete,
Now they have ta'en away her Basil sweet.

Piteous she look'd on dead and senseless things,
  Asking for her lost Basil amorously:
And with melodious chuckle in the strings
  Of her lorn voice, she oftentimes would cry
After the Pilgrim in his wanderings,
  To ask him where her Basil was; and why
'Twas hid from her: "For cruel 'tis," said she,
"To steal my Basil-pot away from me."

And so she pin'd, and so she died forlorn,
  Imploring for her Basil to the last.
No heart was there in Florence but did mourn
  In pity of her love, so overcast.
And a sad ditty of this story borne
  From mouth to mouth through all the country pass'd:
Still is the burthen sung—"O cruelty,
To steal my Basil-pot away from me!"

ENDYMION

BOOK I

A THING of beauty is a joy for ever:
Its loveliness increases; it will never
Pass into nothingness; but still will keep
A bower quiet for us, and a sleep
Full of sweet dreams, and health, and quiet breathing
Therefore, on every morrow, are we wreathing
A flowery band to bind us to the earth,
Spite of despondence, of the inhuman dearth
Of noble natures, of the gloomy days,
Of all the unhealthy and o'er-darken'd ways
Made for our searching: yes, in spite of all,
Some shape of beauty moves away the pall
From our dark spirits. Such the sun, the moon,
Trees old and young, sprouting a shady boon
For simple sheep; and such are daffodils
With the green world they live in; and clear rills
That for themselves a cooling covert make
'Gainst the hot season; the mid-forest brake,
Rich with a sprinkling of fair musk-rose blooms:
And such too is the grandeur of the dooms
We have imagined for the mighty dead;
All lovely tales that we have heard or read:
An endless fountain of immortal drink,
Pouring unto us from the heaven's brink.

Nor do we merely feel these essences
For one short hour; no, even as the trees
That whisper round a temple become soon
Dear as the temple's self, so does the moon,
The passion poesy, glories infinite,
Haunt us till they become a cheering light
Unto our souls, and bound to us so fast,
That, whether there be shine, or gloom o'ercast,
They alway must be with us, or we die.

Therefore, 'tis with full happiness that I
Will trace the story of Endymion.
The very music of the name has gone
Into my being, and each pleasant scene
Is growing fresh before me as the green
Of our own valleys: so I will begin
Now while I cannot hear the city's din;
Now while the early budders are just new,
And run in mazes of the youngest hue
About old forests; while the willow trails
Its delicate amber; and the dairy pails
Bring home increase of milk.   And, as the year
Grows lush in juicy stalks, I'll smoothly steer
My little boat, for many quiet hours,
With streams that deepen freshly into bowers.
Many and many a verse I hope to write,
Before the daisies, vermeil rimm'd and white,
Hide in deep herbage; and ere yet the bees
Hum about globes of clover and sweet peas,
I must be near the middle of my story.
O may no wintry season, bare and hoary,
See it half-finish'd: but let Autumn bold,
With universal tinge of sober gold,
Be all about me when I make an end.
And now at once, adventuresome, I send
My herald thought into a wilderness:
There let its trumpet blow, and quickly dress
My uncertain path with green, that I may speed
Easily onward, thorough flowers and weed.

Upon the sides of Latmos was outspread
A mighty forest; for the moist earth fed
So plenteously all weed-hidden roots
Into o'erhanging boughs, and precious fruits.
And it had gloomy shades, sequester'd deep,
Where no man went; and if from shepherd's keep
A lamb stray'd far a-down those inmost glens,
Never again saw he the happy pens
Whither his brethren, bleating with content,
Over the hills at every night-fall went.
Among the shepherds 'twas believed ever,
That not one fleecy lamb which thus did sever

From the white flock, but pass'd unworried
By any wolf, or pard with prying head,
Until it came to some unfooted plains
Where fed the herds of Pan : ay, great his gains
Who thus one lamb did lose.   Paths there were many,
Winding through palmy fern, and rushes fenny,
And ivy banks ; all leading pleasantly
To a wide lawn, whence one could only see
Stems thronging all around between the swell
Of tuft and slanting branches : who could tell
The freshness of the space of heaven above,
Edged round with dark tree-tops ? through which a dove
Would often beat its wings, and often too
A little cloud would move across the blue.

Full in the middle of this pleasantness
There stood a marble altar, with a tress
Of flowers budded newly ; and the dew
Had taken fairy phantasies to strew
Daisies upon the sacred sward last eve,
And so the dawned light in pomp receive.
For 'twas the morn : Apollo's upward fire
Made every eastern cloud a silvery pyre
Of brightness so unsullied, that therein
A melancholy spirit well might win
Oblivion, and melt out his essence fine
Into the winds : rain-scented eglantine
Gave temperate sweets to that well-wooing sun :
The lark was lost in him ; cold springs had run
To warm their chilliest bubbles in the grass ;
Man's voice was on the mountains ; and the mass
Of nature's lives and wonders pulsed tenfold,
To feel this sun-rise and its glories old.

Now while the silent workings of the dawn
Were busiest, into that self-same lawn
All suddenly, with joyful cries, there sped
A troop of little children garlanded ;
Who gathering round the altar, seem'd to pry
Earnestly round as wishing to espy
Some folk of holiday : nor had they waited
For many moments, ere their ears were sated

With a faint breath of music, which even then
Fill'd out its voice, and died away again.
Within a little space again it gave
Its airy swellings, with a gentle wave,
To light-hung leaves, in smoothest echoes breaking
Through copse-clad valleys,—ere their death, o'er-taking
The surgy murmurs of the lonely sea.

And now, as deep into the wood as we
Might mark a lynx's eye, there glimmer'd light
Fair faces and a rush of garments white,
Plainer and plainer showing, till at last
Into the widest alley they all past,
Making directly for the woodland altar.
O kindly muse! let not my weak tongue falter
In telling of this goodly company,
Of their old piety, and of their glee:
But let a portion of ethereal dew
Fall on my head, and presently unmew
My soul; that I may dare, in wayfaring,
To stammer where old Chaucer used to sing.

Leading the way, young damsels danced along,
Bearing the burden of a shepherd's song;
Each having a white wicker, overbrimm'd
With April's tender younglings: next, well trimm'd,
A crowd of shepherds with as sunburnt looks
As may be read of in Arcadian books;
Such as sat listening round Apollo's pipe,
When the great deity, for earth too ripe,
Let his divinity o'erflowing die
In music, through the vales of Thessaly:
Some idly trail'd their sheep-hooks on the ground,
And some kept up a shrilly mellow sound
With ebon-tipped flutes: close after these,
Now coming from beneath the forest trees,
A venerable priest full soberly
Begirt, with ministering looks: alway his eye
Steadfast upon the matted turf he kept,
And after him his sacred vestments swept.
From his right hand there swung a vase, milk-white,
Of mingled wine, out-sparkling generous light;

And in his left he held a basket full
Of all sweet herbs that searching eye could cull:
Wild thyme, and valley-lilies whiter still
Than Leda's love, and cresses from the rill.
His aged head, crowned with beechen wreath,
Seem'd like a poll of ivy in the teeth
Of winter hoar.   Then came another crowd
Of shepherds, lifting in due time aloud
Their share of the ditty.   After them appear'd,
Up-follow'd by a multitude that rear'd
Their voices to the clouds, a fair-wrought car,
Easily rolling, so as scarce to mar
The freedom of three steeds of dapple brown:
Who stood therein did seem of great renown
Among the throng.   His youth was fully blown,
Showing like Ganymede to manhood grown;
And, for those simple times, his garments were
A chieftain king's: beneath his breast, half bare,
Was hung a silver bugle, and between
His nervy knees there lay a boar-spear keen.
A smile was on his countenance; he seem'd
To common lookers-on, like one who dream'd
Of idleness in groves Elysian:
But there were some who feelingly could scan
A lurking trouble in his nether lip,
And see that oftentimes the reins would slip
Through his forgotten hands: then would they sigh
And think of yellow leaves, of owlets' cry,
Of logs piled solemnly.—Ah, well-a-day,
Why should our young Endymion pine away!

Soon the assembly, in a circle ranged,
Stood silent round the shrine: each look was changed
To sudden veneration: women meek
Beckon'd their sons to silence; while each cheek
Of virgin bloom paled gently for slight fear.
Endymion too, without a forest peer,
Stood, wan, and pale, and with an awed face,
Among his brothers of the mountain chase.
In midst of all, the venerable priest
Eyed them with joy from greatest to the least,
And, after lifting up his aged hands,

Thus spake he: "Men of Latmos! shepherd bands
Whose care it is to guard a thousand flocks:
Whether descended from beneath the rocks
That overtop your mountains; whether come
From valleys where the pipe is never dumb;
Or from your swelling downs, where sweet air stirs
Blue hare-bells lightly, and where prickly furze
Buds lavish gold; or ye, whose precious charge
Nibble their fill at ocean's very marge,
Whose mellow reeds are touch'd with sounds forlorn
By the dim echoes of old Triton's horn:
Mothers and wives! who day by day prepare
The scrip, with needments, for the mountain air;
And all ye gentle girls who foster up
Udderless lambs, and in a little cup
Will put choice honey for a favour'd youth:
Yea, every one attend! for in good truth
Our vows are wanting to our great god Pan.
Are not our lowing heifers sleeker than
Night-swollen mushrooms? Are not our wide plains
Speckled with countless fleeces? Have not rains
Green'd over April's lap? No howling sad
Sickens our fearful ewes; and we have had
Great Bounty from Endymion our lord.
The earth is glad: the merry lark has pour'd
His early song against yon breezy sky,
That spreads so clear o'er our solemnity."

Thus ending, on the shrine he heap'd a spire
Of teeming sweets, enkindling sacred fire;
Anon he stain'd the thick and spongy sod
With wine, in honour of the shepherd-god.
Now while the earth was drinking it, and while
Bay leaves were crackling in the fragrant pile,
And gummy frankincense was sparkling bright
'Neath smothering parsley, and a hazy light
Spread greyly eastward, thus a chorus sang:

"O thou, whose mighty palace roof doth hang
From jagged trunks, and overshadoweth
Eternal whispers, glooms, the birth, life, death
Of unseen flowers in heavy peacefulness;

Who lovest to see the hamadryads dress
Their ruffled locks where meeting hazels darken;
And through whole solemn hours dost sit, and hearken
The dreary melody of bedded reeds—
In desolate places, where dank moisture breeds
The pipy hemlock to strange overgrowth,
Bethinking thee, how melancholy loth
Thou wast to lose fair Syrinx—do thou now,
By thy love's milky brow!
By all the trembling mazes that she ran,
Hear us, Great Pan!

"O thou, for whose soul-soothing quiet, turtles
Passion their voices cooingly 'mong myrtles,
What time thou wanderest at eventide
Through sunny meadows, that outskirt the side
Of thine enmossed realms: O thou, to whom
Broad-leaved fig-trees even now foredoom
Their ripen'd fruitage; yellow-girted bees
Their golden honeycombs; our village leas
Their fairest-blossom'd beans and poppied corn;
The chuckling linnet its five young unborn,
To sing for thee; low-creeping strawberries
Their summer coolness; pent-up butterflies
Their freckled wings; yea, the fresh-budding year
All its completions—be quickly near,
By every wind that nods the mountain pine,
O forester divine!

"Thou, to whom every faun and satyr flies
For willing service; whether to surprise
The squatted hare while in half-sleeping fit;
Or upward ragged precipices flit
To save poor lambkins from the eagle's maw;
Or by mysterious enticement draw
Bewilder'd shepherds to their path again;
Or to tread breathless round the frothy main,
And gather up all fancifullest shells
For thee to tumble into Naiads' cells,
And, being hidden, laugh at their out-peeping;
Or to delight thee with fantastic leaping,
The while they pelt each other on the crown

With silvery oak-apples, and fir-cones brown—
By all the echoes that about thee ring,
Hear us, O satyr king!

"O Hearkener to the loud-clapping shears,
While ever and anon to his shorn peers
A ram goes bleating: Winder of the horn,
When snouted wild-boars routing tender corn
Anger our huntsman: Breather round our farms,
To keep off mildews, and all weather harms:
Strange ministrant of undescribed sounds,
That come a-swooning over hollow grounds,
And wither drearily on barren moors:
Dread opener of the mysterious doors
Leading to universal knowledge—see,
Great son of Dryope,
The many that are come to pay their vows
With leaves about their brows!

"Be still the unimaginable lodge
For solitary thinkings; such as dodge
Conception to the very bourne of heaven,
Then leave the naked brain: be still the leaven
That spreading in this dull and clodded earth,
Gives it a touch ethereal—a new birth:
Be still a symbol of immensity;
A firmament reflected in a sea;
An element filling the space between;
An unknown—but no more: we humbly screen
With uplift hands our foreheads, lowly bending,
And giving out a shout most heaven-rending,
Conjure thee to receive our humble Pæan,
Upon thy Mount Lycean!"

Even while they brought the burden to a close,
A shout from the whole multitude arose,
That linger'd in the air like dying rolls
Of abrupt thunder, when Ionian shoals
Of dolphins bob their noses through the brine.
Meantime, on shady levels, mossy fine,
Young companies nimbly began dancing
To the swift treble pipe, and humming string.

Ay, those fair living forms swam heavenly
To tunes forgotten—out of memory:
Fair creatures! whose young children's children bred
Thermopylæ its heroes—not yet dead,
But in old marbles ever beautiful.
High genitors, unconscious did they cull
Time's sweet firstfruits—they danced to weariness,
And then in quiet circles did they press
The hillock turf, and caught the latter end
Of some strange history, potent to send
A young mind from its bodily tenement.
Or they might watch the quoit-pitchers, intent
On either side ; pitying the sad death
Of Hyacinthus, when the cruel breath
Of Zephyr slew him,—Zephyr penitent,
Who now, ere Phœbus mounts the firmament,
Fondles the flower amid the sobbing rain.
The archers too, upon a wider plain,
Beside the feathery whizzing of the shaft,
And the dull twanging bowstring, and the raft
Branch down sweeping from a tall ash top,
Call'd up a thousand thoughts to envelop
Those who would watch.   Perhaps, the trembling knee
And frantic gape of lonely Niobe,
Poor, lonely Niobe ! when her lovely young
Were dead and gone, and her caressing tongue
Lay a lost thing upon her paly lip,
And very, very deadliness did nip
Her motherly cheeks.   Aroused from this sad mood
By one, who at a distance loud halloo'd,
Uplifting his strong bow into the air,
Many might after brighter visions stare :
After the Argonauts, in blind amaze
Tossing about on Neptune's restless ways,
Until, from the horizon's vaulted side,
There shot a golden splendour far and wide,
Spangling those million poutings of the brine
With quivering ore : 'twas even an awful shine
From the exaltation of Apollo's bow ;
A heavenly beacon in their dreary woe.
Who thus were ripe for high contemplating,
Might turn their steps towards the sober ring

Where sat Endymion and the aged priest
'Mong shepherds gone in eld, whose looks increased
The silvery setting of their mortal star.
There they discoursed upon the fragile bar
That keeps us from our homes ethereal;
And what our duties there: to nightly call
Vesper, the beauty-crest of summer weather;
To summon all the downiest clouds together
For the sun's purple couch; to emulate
In ministering the potent rule of fate
With speed of fire-tail'd exhalations;
To tint her pallid cheek with bloom, who cons
Sweet poesy by moonlight: besides these,
A world of other unguess'd offices.
Anon they wander'd, by divine converse,
Into Elysium; vying to rehearse
Each one his own anticipated bliss.
One felt heart-certain that he could not miss
His quick-gone love, among fair blossom'd boughs,
Where every zephyr-sigh pouts, and endows
Her lips with music for the welcoming.
Another wish'd, 'mid that eternal spring,
To meet his rosy child, with feathery sails,
Sweeping, eye-earnestly, through almond vales:
Who, suddenly, should stoop through the smooth wind,
And with the balmiest leaves his temples bind;
And, ever after, through those regions be
His messenger, his little Mercury.
Some were athirst in soul to see again
Their fellow-huntsmen o'er the wide champaign
In times long past; to sit with them, and talk
Of all the chances in their earthly walk;
Comparing, joyfully, their plenteous stores
Of happiness, to when upon the moors,
Benighted, close they huddled from the cold,
And shared their famish'd scrips.   Thus all out-told
Their fond imaginations,—saving him
Whose eyelids curtain'd up their jewels dim,
Endymion: yet hourly had he striven
To hide the cankering venom, that had riven
His fainting recollections.   Now indeed
His senses had swoon'd off: he did not heed

The sudden silence, or the whispers low,
Or the old eyes dissolving at his woe,
Or anxious calls, or close of trembling palms,
Or maiden's sigh, that grief itself embalms;
But in the self-same fixed trance he kept,
Like one who on the earth had never stept,
Ay, even as dead-still as a marble man,
Frozen in that old tale Arabian.

Who whispers him so pantingly and close?
Peona, his sweet sister: of all those,
His friends, the dearest. Hushing signs she made,
And breathed a sister's sorrow to persuade
A yielding up, a cradling on her care.
Her eloquence did breathe away the curse.
She led him, like some midnight spirit nurse
Of happy changes in emphatic dreams,
Along a path between two little streams,—
Guarding his forehead, with her round elbow,
From low-grown branches, and his footsteps slow
From stumbling over stumps and hillocks small;
Until they came to where these streamlets fall,
With mingled bubblings and a gentle rush,
Into a river, clear, brimful, and flush
With crystal mocking of the trees and sky.
A little shallop, floating there hard by,
Pointed its beak over the fringed bank;
And soon it lightly dipt, and rose, and sank,
And dipt again, with the young couple's weight,—
Peona guiding, through the water straight,
Towards a bowery island opposite;
Which gaining presently, she steered light
Into a shady, fresh, and ripply cove,
Where nested was an arbour, overwove
By many a summer's silent fingering;
To whose cool bosom she was used to bring
Her playmates, with their needle broidery,
And minstrel memories of times gone by.

So she was gently glad to see him laid
Under her favourite bower's quiet shade,
On her own couch, new made of flower leaves,
Dried carefully on the cooler side of sheaves

When last the sun his autumn tresses shook,
And the tann'd harvesters rich armfuls took.
Soon was he quieted to slumbrous rest:
But, ere it crept upon him, he had prest
Peona's busy hand against his lips,
And still, a-sleeping, held her finger-tips
In tender pressure. And as a willow keeps
A patient watch over the stream that creeps
Windingly by it, so the quiet maid
Held her in peace: so that a whispering blade
Of grass, a wailful gnat, a bee bustling
Down in the blue-bells, or a wren light rustling
Among sere leaves and twigs, might all be heard.

O magic sleep! O comfortable bird,
That broodest o'er the troubled sea of the mind
Till it is hush'd and smooth! O unconfined
Restraint! imprison'd liberty! great key
To golden palaces, strange minstrelsy,
Fountains grotesque, new trees, bespangled caves,
Echoing grottoes, full of tumbling waves
And moonlight; ay, to all the mazy world
Of silvery enchantment!—who, upfurl'd
Beneath thy drowsy wing a triple hour,
But renovates and lives?—Thus, in the bower,
Endymion was calm'd to life again.
Opening his eyelids with a healthier brain,
He said: "I feel this thine endearing love
All through my bosom: thou art as a dove
Trembling its closed eyes and sleeked wings
About me; and the pearliest dew not brings
Such morning incense from the fields of May,
As do those brighter drops that twinkling stray
From those kind eyes,—the very home and haunt
Of sisterly affection. Can I want
Aught else, aught nearer heaven, than such tears?
Yet dry them up, in bidding hence all fears
That, any longer, I will pass my days
Alone and sad. No, I will once more raise
My voice upon the mountain-heights; once more
Make my horn parley from their foreheads hoar:
Again my trooping hounds their tongues shall loll

Around the breathed boar : again I'll poll
The fair-grown yew-tree, for a chosen bow :
And, when the pleasant sun is getting low,
Again I'll linger in a sloping mead
To hear the speckled thrushes, and see feed
Our idle sheep.   So be thou cheered, sweet !
And, if thy lute is here, softly entreat
My soul to keep in its resolved course.

    Hereat Peona, in their silver source
Shut her pure sorrow-drops with glad exclaim,
And took a lute, from which there pulsing came
A lively prelude, fashioning the way
In which her voice should wander.   'Twas a lay
More subtle-cadenced, more forest wild
Than Dryope's lone lulling of her child ;
And nothing since has floated in the air
So mournful strange.   Surely some influence rare
Went, spiritual, through the damsel's hand ;
For still, with Delphic emphasis, she spann'd
The quick invisible strings, even though she saw
Endymion's spirit melt away and thaw
Before the deep intoxication.
But soon she came, with sudden burst, upon
Her self-possession—swung the lute aside,
And earnestly said : "Brother, 'tis vain to hide
That thou dost know of things mysterious,
Immortal, starry ; such alone could thus
Weigh down thy nature.   Hast thou sinn'd in aught
Offensive to the heavenly powers ?   Caught
A Paphian dove upon a message sent ?
Thy deathful bow against some deer-herd bent,
Sacred to Dian ?   Haply, thou hast seen
Her naked limbs among the alders green ;
And that, alas ! is death.   No, I can trace
Something more high perplexing in thy face !"

    Endymion look'd at her, and press'd her hand,
And said, "Art thou so pale, who was so bland
And merry in our meadows ?   How is this ?
Tell me thine ailment : tell me all amiss !
Ah ! thou hast been unhappy at the change
Wrought suddenly in me.   What indeed more strange ?

Or more complete to overwhelm surmise?
Ambition is no sluggard: 'tis no prize,
That toiling years would put within my grasp,
That I have sigh'd for:·with so deadly gasp
No man e'er panted for a mortal love.
So all have set my heavier grief above
These things which happen. Rightly have they done:
I, who still saw the horizontal sun
Heave his broad shoulder o'er the edge of the world,
Out-facing Lucifer, and then had hurl'd
My spear aloft, as signal for the chase—
I, who, for very sport of heart, would race
With my own steed from Araby; pluck down
A vulture from his towery perching; frown
A lion into growling, loth retire—
To lose, at once, all my toil-breeding fire,
And sink thus low! but I will ease my breast
Of secret grief, here in this bowery nest.

"This river does not see the naked sky,
Till it begins to progress silverly
Around the western border of the wood,
Whence, from a certain spot, its winding flood
Seems at the distance like a crescent moon:
And in that nook, the very pride of June,
Had I been used to pass my weary eves;
The rather for the sun unwilling leaves
So dear a picture of his sovereign power,
And I could witness his most kingly hour,
When he doth tighten up the golden reins,
And paces leisurely down amber plains
His snorting four. Now when his chariot last
Its beams against the zodiac-lion cast,
There blossom'd suddenly a magic bed
Of sacred dittany, and poppies red:
At which I wonder'd greatly, knowing well
That but one night had wrought this flowery spell;
And, sitting down close by, began to muse
What it might mean. Perhaps, thought I, Morpheus,
In passing here, his owlet pinions shook;
Or, it may be, ere matron Night uptook
Her ebon urn, young Mercury, by stealth,

Had dipp'd his rod in it : such garland wealth
Came not by common growth.   Thus on I thought,
Until my head was dizzy and distraught.
Moreover, through the dancing poppies stole
A breeze most softly lulling to my soul ;
And shaping visions all about my sight
Of colours, wings, and bursts of spangly light :
The which became more strange, and strange, and dim,
And then were gulf'd in a tumultuous swim :
And then I fell asleep.   Ah, can I tell
The enchantment that afterwards befel ?
Yet it was but a dream : yet such a dream
That never tongue, although it overteem
With mellow utterance, like a cavern spring,
Could figure out and to conception bring
All I beheld and felt.   Methought I lay
Watching the zenith, where the milky way
Among the stars in virgin splendour pours ;
And travelling my eye, until the doors
Of heaven appear'd to open for my flight,
I became loth and fearful to alight
From such high soaring by a downward glance ;
So kept me stedfast in that airy trance,
Spreading imaginary pinions wide.
When, presently, the stars began to glide,
And faint away, before my eager view :
At which I sigh'd that I could not pursue,
And dropp'd my vision to the horizon's verge ;
And lo ! from opening clouds, I saw emerge
The loveliest moon, that ever silver'd o'er
A shell for Neptune's goblet ; she did soar
So passionately bright, my dazzled soul
Commingling with her argent spheres did roll
Through clear and cloudy, even when she went
At last into a dark and vapoury tent—
Whereat, methought, the lidless-eyed train
Of planets all were in the blue again.
To commune with those orbs, once more I raised
My sight right upward : but it was quite dazed
By a bright something, sailing down apace,
Making me quickly veil my eyes and face :
Again I look'd, and, O ye deities,

Who from Olympus watch our destinies!
Whence that completed form of all completeness?
Whence came that high perfection of all sweetness?
Speak, stubborn earth, and tell me where, O where
Hast thou a symbol of her golden hair?
Not oat-sheaves drooping in the western sun;
Not—thy soft hand, fair sister! let me shun
Such follying before thee—yet she had,
Indeed, locks bright enough to make me mad;
And they were simply gordian'd up and braided,
Leaving, in naked comeliness, unshaded,
Her pearl round ears, white neck, and orbed brow;
The which were blended in, I know not how,
With such a paradise of lips and eyes,
Blush-tinted cheeks, half smiles, and faintest sighs,
That, when I think thereon, my spirit clings
And plays about its fancy, till the stings
Of human neighbourhood envenom all.
Unto what awful power shall I call?
To what high fane?—Ah! see her hovering feet,
More bluely vein'd, more soft, more whitely sweet
Than those of sea-born Venus, when she rose
From out her cradle shell. The wind outblows
Her scarf into a fluttering pavilion;
'Tis blue, and over-spangled with a million
Of little eyes, as though thou wert to shed,
Over the darkest, lushest blue-bell bed,
Handfuls of daisies."—" Endymion, how strange!
Dream within dream!"—"She took an airy range,
And then, towards me, like a very maid,
Came blushing, waning, willing, and afraid,
And press'd me by the hand: Ah! 'twas too much;
Methought I fainted at the charmed touch,
Yet held my recollection, even as one
Who dives three fathoms where the waters run
Gurgling in beds of coral: for anon,
I felt upmounted in that region
Where falling stars dart their artillery forth,
And eagles struggle with the buffeting north
That balances the heavy meteor-stone;—
Felt too, I was not fearful, nor alone,
But lapp'd and lull'd along the dangerous sky.

Soon, as it seem'd, we left our journeying high,
And straightway into frightful eddies swoop'd;
Such as aye muster where grey Time has scoop'd
Huge dens and caverns in a mountain's side:
There hollow sounds aroused me, and I sigh'd
To faint once more by looking on my bliss—
I was distracted; madly did I kiss
The wooing arms which held me, and did give
My eyes at once to death: but 'twas to live,
To take in draughts of life from the gold fount
Of kind and passionate looks; to count, and count
The moments, by some greedy help that seem'd
A second self, that each might be redeem'd
And plunder'd of its load of blessedness.
Ah, desperate mortal! I even dared to press
Her very cheek against my crowned lip,
And, at that moment, felt my body dip
Into a warmer air: a moment more,
Our feet were soft in flowers. There was store
Of newest joys upon that alp. Sometimes
A scent of violets, and blossoming limes,
Loiter'd around us; then of honey cells,
Made delicate from all white-flower bells,—
And once, above the edges of our nest,
An arch face peep'd,—an Oread as I guess'd.

"Why did I dream that sleep o'erpower'd me
In midst of all this heaven? Why not see,
Far off, the shadows of his pinions dark,
And stare them from me? But no, like a spark
That needs must die, although its ltitle beam
Reflects upon a diamond, my sweet dream
Fell into nothing—into stupid sleep.
And so it was, until a gentle creep,
A careful moving caught my waking ears,
And up I started: Ah! my sighs, my tears,
My clenched hands;—for lo! the poppies hung
Dew-dabbled on their stalks, the ouzel sung
A heavy ditty, and the sullen day
Had chidden herald Hesperus away,
With leaden looks: the solitary breeze
Bluster'd, and slept, and its wild self did tease

With wayward melancholy; and I thought,
Mark me, Peona! that sometimes it brought
Faint fare-thee-wells, and sigh-shrilled adieus!—
Away I wander'd—all the pleasant hues
Of heaven and earth had faded: deepest shades
Were deepest dungeons; heaths and sunny glades
Were full of pestilent light; our taintless rills
Seem'd sooty, and o'erspread with upturn'd gills
Of dying fish; the vermeil rose had blown
In frightful scarlet, and its thorns outgrown
Like spiked aloe.   If an innocent bird
Before my heedless footsteps stirr'd, and stirr'd
In little journeys, I beheld in it
A disguised demon, missioned to knit
My soul with under darkness; to entice
My stumblings down some monstrous precipice:
Therefore I eager follow'd, and did curse
The disappointment.   Time, that aged nurse,
Rock'd me to patience.   Now, thank gentle heaven
These things, with all their comfortings, are given
To my down-sunken hours, and with thee,
Sweet sister, help to stem the ebbing sea
Of weary life."
                        Thus ended he, and both
Sat silent: for the maid was very loth
To answer; feeling well that breathed words
Would all be lost, unheard, and vain as swords
Against the enchased crocodile, or leaps
Of grasshoppers against the sun.   She weeps,
And wonders; struggles to devise some blame
To put on such a look as would say, *Shame
On this poor weakness!* but, for all her strife,
She could as soon have crush'd away the life
From a sick dove.   At length, to break the pause,
She said with trembling chance: " Is this the cause?
This all?   Yet it is strange, and sad, alas!
That one who through this middle earth should pass
Most like a sojourning demi-god, and leave
His name upon the harp-string, should achieve
No higher bard than simple maidenhood,
Singing alone, and fearfully,—how the blood
Left his young cheek; and how he used to stray

He knew not where: and how he would say, *nay*,
If any said 'twas love: and yet 'twas love;
What could it be but love? How a ring-dove
Let fall a sprig of yew-tree in his path
And how he died: and then, that love doth scathe
The gentle heart, as northern blasts do roses;
And then the ballad of his sad life closes
With sighs, and an alas!—Endymion!
Be rather in the trumpet's mouth,—anon
Among the winds at large—that all may hearken!
Although, before the crystal heavens darken,
I watch and dote upon the silver lakes
Pictured in western cloudiness, that takes
The semblance of gold rocks and bright gold sands,
Islands, and creeks, and amber-fretted strands
With horses prancing o'er them, palaces
And towers of amethyst,—would I so tease
My pleasant days, because I could not mount
Into those regions? The Morphean fount
Of that fine element that visions, dreams,
And fitful whims of sleep are made of, streams
Into its airy channels with so subtle,
So thin a breathing, not the spider's shuttle,
Circled a million times within the space
Of a swallow's nest-door, could delay a trace,
A tinting of its quality: how light
Must dreams themselves be; seeing they're more slight
Than the mere nothing that engenders them!
Then wherefore sully the entrusted gem
Of high and noble life with thoughts so sick?
Why pierce high-fronted honour to the quick
For nothing but a dream?" Hereat the youth
Look'd up: a conflicting of shame and ruth
Was in his plaited brow: yet his eyelids
Widen'd a little, as when Zephyr bids
A little breeze to creep between the fans
Of careless butterflies: amid his pains
He seem'd to taste a drop of manna-dew,
Full palatable; and a colour grew
Upon his cheek, while thus he lifeful spake.

"Peona! ever have I long'd to slake
My thirst for the world's praises: nothing base,

No merely slumberous phantasm, could unlace
The stubborn canvas for my voyage prepared—
Though now 'tis tatter'd ; leaving my bark bared
And sullenly drifting : yet my higher hope
Is of too wide, too rainbow-large a scope,
To fret at myriads of earthly wrecks.
Wherein lies happiness ?   In that which becks
Our ready minds to fellowship divine,
A fellowship with essence ; till we shine,
Full alchemized, and free of space.   Behold
The clear religion of heaven !   Fold
A rose-leaf round thy finger's taperness,
And soothe thy lips : hist ! when the airy stress
Of music's kiss impregnates the free winds,
And with a sympathetic touch unbinds
Æolian magic from their lucid wombs :
Then old songs waken from enclouded tombs ;
Old ditties sigh above their father's grave ;
Ghosts of melodious prophesyings rave
Round every spot where trod Apollo's foot ;
Bronze clarions awake, and faintly bruit,
Where long ago a giant battle was ;
And, from the turf, a lullaby doth pass
In every place where infant Orpheus slept.
Feel we these things !—that moment have we stept
Into a sort of oneness, and our state
Is like a floating spirit's.   But there are
Richer entanglements, enthralments far
More self-destroying, leading, by degrees,
To the chief intensity : the crown of these
Is made of love and friendship, and sits high
Upon the forehead of humanity.
All its more ponderous and bulky worth
Is friendship, whence there ever issues forth
A steady splendour ; but at the tip-top,
There hangs by unseen film, an orbed drop
Of light, and that is love : its influence
Thrown in our eyes genders a novel sense,
At which we start and fret ; till in the end,
Melting into its radiance, we blend,
Mingle, and so become a part of it,—
Nor with aught else can our souls interknit

So wingedly: when we combine therewith,
Life's self is nourish'd by its proper pith,
And we are nurtured like a pelican brood.
Ay, so delicious is the unsating food,
That men, who might have tower'd in the van
Of all the congregated world, to fan
And winnow from the coming step of time
All chaff of custom, wipe away all slime
Left by men-slugs and human serpentry,
Have been content to let occasion die,
Whilst they did sleep in love's Elysium.
And, truly, I would rather be struck dumb
Than speak against this ardent listlessness:
For I have ever thought that it might bless
The world with benefits unknowingly;
As does the nightingale, up-perched high,
And cloister'd among cool and bunched leaves—
She sings but to her love, nor e'er conceives
How tiptoe Night holds back her dark-grey hood.
Just so may love, although 'tis understood
The mere commingling of passionate breath,
Produce more than our searching witnesseth:
What I know not: but who, of men, can tell
That flowers would bloom, or that green fruit would swell
To melting pulp, that fish would have bright mail,
The earth its dower of river, wood, and vale,
The meadows runnels, runnels pebble-stones,
The seed its harvest, or the lute its tones,
Tones ravishment, or ravishment its sweet,
If human souls did never kiss and greet?

"Now, if this earthly love has power to make
Men's being mortal, immortal; to shake
Ambition from their memories, and brim
Their measure of content; what merest whim,
Seems all this poor endeavour after fame,
To one, who keeps within his stedfast aim
A love immortal, an immortal too.
Look not so wilder'd; for these things are true,
And never can be born of atomies
That buzz about our slumbers, like brain-flies,
Leaving us fancy-sick.   No, no, I'm sure,

My restless spirit never could endure
To brood so long upon one luxury,
Unless it did, though fearfully, espy
A hope beyond the shadow of a dream.
My sayings will the less obscured seem
When I have told thee how my waking sight
Has made me scruple whether that same night
Was pass'd in dreaming.   Hearken, sweet Peona!
Beyond the matron-temple of Latona,
Which we should see but for these darkening boughs,
Lies a deep hollow, from whose ragged brows
Bushes and trees do lean all round athwart,
And meet so nearly, that with wings outraught,
And spreaded tail, a vulture could not glide
Past them, but he must brush on every side.
Some moulder'd steps lead into this cool cell,
Far as the slabbed margin of a well,
Whose patient level peeps its crystal eye
Right upward, through the bushes, to the sky.
Oft have I brought thee flowers, on their stalks set
Like vestal primroses, but dark velvet
Edges them round, and they have golden pits:
'Twas there I got them, from the gaps and slits
In a mossy stone, that sometimes was my seat,
When all above was faint with mid-day heat.
And there in strife no burning thoughts to heed,
I'd bubble up the water through a reed;
So reaching back to boyhood: make me ships
Of moulted feathers, touchwood, alder chips,
With leaves stuck in them; and the Neptune be
Of their petty ocean.   Oftener, heavily,
When lovelorn hours had left me less a child,
I sat contemplating the figures wild
Of o'erhead clouds melting the mirror through.
Upon a day, while thus I watch'd, by flew
A cloudy Cupid, with his bow and quiver;
So plainly character'd, no breeze would shiver
The happy chance: so happy, I was fain
To follow it upon the open plain,
And, therefore, was just going; when, behold!
A wonder, fair as any I have told—
The same bright face I tasted in my sleep,

Smiling in the clear well. My heart did leap
Through the cool depth.—It moved as if to flee—
I started up, when lo! refreshfully,
There came upon my face, in plenteous showers,
Dew-drops, and dewy buds, and leaves, and flowers,
Wrapping all objects from my smother'd sight,
Bathing my spirit in a new delight.
Ay, such a breathless honey-feel of bliss
Alone preserved me from the drear abyss
Of death, for the fair form had gone again.
Pleasure is oft a visitant; but pain
Clings cruelly to us, like the gnawing sloth
On the deer's tender haunches: late, and loth,
'Tis scared away by slow-returning pleasure.
How sickening, how dark the dreadful leisure
Of weary days, made deeper exquisite,
By a foreknowledge of unslumbrous night!
Like sorrow came upon me, heavier still,
Than when I wander'd from the poppy hill:
And a whole age of lingering moments crept
Sluggishly by, ere more contentment swept
Away at once the deadly yellow spleen.
Yes, thrice have I this fair enchantment seen;
Once more been tortured with renewed life.
When last the wintry gusts gave over strife
With the conquering sun of spring, and left the skies
Warm and serene, but yet with moisten'd eyes
In pity of the shatter'd infant buds,—
That time thou didst adorn, with amber studs,
My hunting-cap, because I laugh'd and smiled,
Chatted with thee, and many days exiled
All torment from my breast;—'twas even then,
Straying about, yet, coop'd up in the den
Of helpless discontent,—hurling my lance
From place to place, and following at chance,
At last, by hap, through some young trees it struck,
And, plashing among bedded pebbles, stuck
In the middle of a brook,—whose silver ramble
Down twenty little falls through reeds and bramble,
Tracing along, it brought me to a cave,
Whence it ran brightly forth, and white did lave
The nether sides of mossy stones and rock,—

'Mong which it gurgled blithe adieus, to mock
Its own sweet grief at parting.   Overhead
Hung a lush screen of drooping weeds, and spread
Thick, as to curtain up some wood-nymph's home.
'Ah! impious mortal, whither do I roam!'
Said I, low-voiced : 'Ah, whither !   'Tis the grot
Of Proserpine, when Hell, obscure and hot,
Doth her resign : and where her tender hands
She dabbles on the cool and sluicy sands;
Or 'tis the cell of Echo, where she sits,
And babbles thorough silence, till her wits
Are gone in tender madness, and anon,
Faints into sleep, with many a dying tone
Of sadness.   O that she would take my vows,
And breathe them sighingly among the boughs,
To sue her gentle ears for whose fair head,
Daily, I pluck sweet flowerets from their bed,
And weave them dyingly—send honey-whispers
Round every leaf, that all those gentle lispers
May sigh my love unto her pitying !
O charitable Echo ! hear, and sing
This ditty to her !—tell her'—So I stay'd
My foolish tongue, and listening, half afraid,
Stood stupefied with my own empty folly,
And blushing for the freaks of melancholy.
Salt tears were coming, when I heard my name
Most fondly lipp'd, and then these accents came :
'Endymion ! the cave is secreter
Than the isle of Delos.   Echo hence shall stir
No sighs but sigh-warm kisses, or light noise
Of thy combing hand, the while it travelling cloys
And trembles through my labyrinthine hair.'
At that oppress'd, I hurried in.—Ah ! where
Are those swift moments ?   Whither are they fled ?
I'll smile no more, Peona ; nor will wed
Sorrow, the way to death ; but patiently
Bear up against it : so farewell, sad sigh ;
And come instead demurest meditation,
To occupy me wholly, and to fashion
My pilgrimage for the world's dusky brink.
No more will I count over, link by link,
My chain of grief : no longer strive to find

A half-forgetfulness in mountain wind
Blustering about my ears : ay, thou shalt see,
Dearest of sisters, what my life shall be ;
What a calm round of hours shall make my days.
There is a paly flame of hope that plays
Where'er I look : but yet, I'll say 'tis nought—
And here I bid it die.   Have not I caught,
Already, a more healthy countenance ?
By this the sun is setting ; we may chance
Meet some of our near-dwellers with my car."

    This said, he rose, faint-smiling like a star
Through autumn mists, and took Peona's hand :
They stept into the boat, and launch'd from land.

BOOK II

O SOVEREIGN power of love !   O grief !   O balm !
All records, saving thine, come cool, and calm,
And shadowy, through the mist of passed years :
For others, good or bad, hatred and tears
Have become indolent ; but touching thine,
One sigh doth echo, one poor sob doth pine,
One kiss brings honey-dew from buried days.
The woes of Troy, towers smothering o'er their blaze,
Stiff-holden shields, far-piercing spears, keen blades,
Struggling, and blood, and shrieks—all dimly fades
Into some backward corner of the brain ;
Yet, in our very souls, we feel amain
The close of Troïlus and Cressid sweet.
Hence, pageant history ! hence, gilded cheat !
Swart planet in the universe of deeds !
Wide sea, that one continuous murmur breeds
Along the pebbled shore of memory !
Many old rotten-timber'd boats there be
Upon thy vaporous bosom, magnified
To goodly vessels ; many a sail of pride,
And golden-keel'd, is left unlaunch'd and dry.
But wherefore this ?   What care, though owl did fly
About the great Athenian admiral's mast ?

What care, though striding Alexander past
The Indus with his Macedonian numbers?
Though old Ulysses tortured from his slumbers
The glutted Cyclops, what care?—Juliet leaning
Amid her window-flowers,—sighing,—weaning
Tenderly her fancy from its maiden snow,
Doth more avail than these: the silver flow
Of Hero's tears, the swoon of Imogen,
Fair Pastorella in the bandit's den,
Are things to brood on with more ardency
Than the death-day of empires.   Fearfully
Must such conviction come upon his head,
Who, thus far, discontent, has dared to tread,
Without one muse's smile, or kind behest,
The path of love and poesy.   But rest,
In chafing restlessness, is yet more drear
Than to be crush'd, in striving to uprear
Love's standard on the battlements of song.
So once more, days and nights, aid me along,
Like legion'd soldiers.

                    Brain-sick shepherd prince!
What promise hast thou faithful guarded since
The day of sacrifice?   Or, have new sorrows
Come with the constant dawn upon thy morrows?
Alas! 'tis his old grief.   For many days,
Has he been wandering in uncertain ways:
Through wilderness, and woods of mossed oaks;
Counting his woe-worn minutes, by the strokes
Of the lone wood-cutter; and listening still,
Hour after hour, to each lush-leaved rill.
Now he is sitting by a shady spring,
And elbow-deep with feverous fingering
Stems the upbursting cold: a wild rose-tree
Pavilions him in bloom, and he doth see
A bud which snares his fancy: lo! but now
He plucks it, dips its stalk in the water: how!
It swells, it buds, it flowers beneath his sight;
And, in the middle, there is softly pight
A golden butterfly; upon whose wings
There must be surely character'd strange things,
For with wide eye he wonders, and smiles oft.

Lightly this little herald flew aloft,
Follow'd by glad Endymion's clasped hands:
Onward it flies.   From languor's sullen bands
His limbs are loosed, and eager, on he hies
Dazzled to trace it in the sunny skies.
It seem'd he flew, the way so easy was;
And like a new-born spirit did he pass
Through the green evening quiet in the sun
O'er many a heath, through many a woodland dun,
Through buried paths, where sleepy twilight dreams
The summer time away.   One track unseams
A wooded cleft, and, far away, the blue
Of ocean fades upon him; then, anew,
He sinks adown a solitary glen,
Where there was never sound of mortal men,
Saving, perhaps, some snow-light cadences
Melting to silence, when upon the breeze
Some holy bark let forth an anthem sweet,
To cheer itself to Delphi.   Still his feet
Went swift beneath the merry-winged guide,
Until it reach'd a splashing fountain's side
That, near a cavern's mouth, for ever pour'd
Unto the temperate air; then high it soar'd,
And, downward, suddenly began to dip,
As if, athirst with so much toil, 'twould sip
The crystal spout-head: so it did, with touch
Most delicate, as though afraid to smutch
Even with mealy gold the waters clear.
But, at that very touch, to disappear
So fairy-quick, was strange!   Bewildered,
Endymion sought around, and shook each bed
Of covert flowers in vain; and then he flung
Himself along the grass.   What gentle tongue,
What whisperer disturb'd his gloomy rest?
It was a nymph uprisen to the breast
In the fountain's pebbly margin, and she stood
'Mong lilies, like the youngest of the brood.
To him her dripping hand she softly kist,
And anxiously began to plait and twist
Her ringlets round her fingers, saying: " Youth !
Too long, alas, hast thou starved on the ruth,
The bitterness of love: too long indeed,

Seeing thou art so gentle.   Could I weed
Thy soul of care, by heavens, I would offer
All the bright riches of my crystal coffer
To Amphitrite; all my clear-eyed fish,
Golden, or rainbow-sided, or purplish,
Vermilion-tail'd, or finn'd with silvery gauze;
Yea, or my veined pebble-floor, that draws
A virgin-light to the deep; my grotto-sands,
Tawny and gold, oozed slowly from far lands
By my diligent springs: my level lilies, shells,
My charming-rod, my potent river spells;
Yes, everything, even to the pearly cup
Meander gave me,—for I bubbled up
To fainting creatures in a desert wild.
But woe is me, I am but as a child
To gladden thee; and all I dare to say,
Is, that I pity thee; that on this day
I've been thy guide; that thou must wander far
In other regions, past the scanty bar
To mortal steps, before thou canst be ta'en
From every wasting sigh, from every pain,
Into the gentle bosom of thy love.
Why it is thus, one knows in heaven above:
But, a poor Naiad, I guess not.   Farewell!
I have a ditty for my hollow cell."

Hereat she vanish'd from Endymion's gaze,
Who brooded o'er the water in amaze:
The dashing fount pour'd on, and where its pool
Lay, half asleep, in grass and rushes cool,
Quick waterflies and gnats were sporting still,
And fish were dimpling, as if good nor ill
Had fallen out that hour.   The wanderer,
Holding his forehead, to keep off the burr
Of smothering fancies, patiently sat down;
And, while beneath the evening's sleepy frown
Glow-worms began to trim their starry lamps,
Thus breathed he to himself: "Whoso encamps
To take a fancied city of delight,
O what a wretch is he! and when 'tis his,
After long toil and travelling, to miss
The kernel of his hopes, how more than vile!

Yet, for him there's refreshment even in toil
Another city doth he set about,
Free from the smallest pebble-bead of doubt
That he will seize on trickling honey-combs :
Alas ! he finds them dry ; and then he foams,
And onward to another city speeds.
But this is human life : the war, the deeds,
The disappointment, the anxiety,
Imagination's struggles, far and nigh,
All human ; bearing in themselves this good,
That they are still the air, the subtle food,
To make us feel existence, and to show
How quiet death is.   Where soil is men grow,
Whether to weeds or flowers ; but for me,
There is no depth to strike in : I can see
Nought earthly worth my compassing ; so stand
Upon a misty, jutting head of land—
Alone ? No, no ; and by the Orphean lute,
When mad Eurydice is listening to't,
I'd rather stand upon this misty peak,
With not a thing to sigh for, or to seek,
But the soft shadow of my thrice-seen love,
Than be—I care not what.   O meekest dove
Of heaven ! O Cynthia, ten-times bright and fair !
From thy blue throne, now filling all the air,
Glance but one little beam of temper'd light
Into my bosom, that the dreadful night
And tyranny of love be somewhat scared !
Yet do not so, sweet queen ; one torment spared
Would give a pang to jealous misery,
Worse than the torment's self : but rather tie
Large wings upon my shoulders, and point out
My love's far dwelling.   Though the playful rout
Of Cupids shun thee, too divine art thou,
Too keen in beauty, for thy silver prow
Not to have dipp'd in love's most gentle stream
O be propitious, nor severely deem
My madness impious ; for, by all the stars
That tend thy bidding, I do think the bars
That kept my spirit in are burst—that I
Am sailing with thee through the dizzy sky !
How beautiful thou art ! The world how deep !

How tremulous-dazzlingly the wheels sweep
Around their axle! Then these gleaming reins,
How lithe! When this thy chariot attains
Its airy goal, haply some bower veils
Those twilight eyes? Those eyes!—my spirit fails;
Dear goddess, help! or the wide-gaping air
Will gulf me—help!"—At this, with madden'd stare,
And lifted hands, and trembling lips, he stood;
Like old Deucalion mountain'd o'er the flood,
Or blind Orion hungry for the morn.
And, but from the deep cavern there was borne
A voice, he had been froze to senseless stone;
Nor sigh of his, nor plaint, nor passion'd moan
Had more been heard. Thus swell'd it forth: "Descend,
Young mountaineer! descend where alleys bend
Into the sparry hollows of the world!
Oft hast thou seen bolts of the thunder hurl'd
As from thy threshold; day by day hast been
A little lower than the chilly sheen
Of icy pinnacles, and dipp'dst thine arms
Into the deadening ether that still charms
Their marble being: now, as deep profound
As those are high, descend! He ne'er is crown'd
With immortality, who fears to follow
Where airy voices lead: so through the hollow,
The silent mysteries of earth, descend!"

He heard but the last words, nor could contend
One moment in reflection: for he fled
Into the fearful deep, to hide his head
From the clear moon, the trees, and coming madness.

'Twas far too strange and wonderful for sadness;
Sharpening, by degrees, his appetite
To dive into the deepest. Dark, nor light,
The region; nor bright, nor sombre wholly,
But mingled up; a gleaming melancholy;
A dusky empire and its diadems;
One faint eternal eventide of gems.
Ay, millions sparkled on a vein of gold,
Along whose track the prince quick footsteps told,

G

With all its lines abrupt and angular :
Out-shooting sometimes, like a meteor-star,
Through a vast antre ; then the metal woof,
Like Vulcan's rainbow, with some monstrous roof
Curves hugely : now, far in the deep abyss,
It seems an angry lightning, and doth hiss
Fancy into belief : anon it leads
Through winding passages, where sameness breeds
Vexing conceptions of some sudden change ;
Whether to silver grots, or giant range
Of sapphire columns, or fantastic bridge
Athwart a flood of crystal.   On a ridge
Now fareth he, that o'er the vast beneath
Towers like an ocean-cliff, and whence he seeth
A hundred waterfalls, whose voices come
But as the murmuring surge.   Chilly and numb
His bosom grew, when first he, far away,
Described an orbed diamond, set to fray
Old Darkness from his throne : 'twas like the sun
Uprisen o'er chaos : and with such a stun
Came the amazement, that, absorb'd in it,
He saw not fiercer wonders—past the wit
Of any spirit to tell, but one of those
Who, when this planet's sphering time doth close
Will be its high remembrancers : who they ?
The mighty ones who have made eternal day
For Greece and England.   While astonishment
With deep-drawn sighs was quieting, he went
Into a marble gallery, passing through
A mimic temple, so complete and true
In sacred custom, that he well-nigh fear'd
To search it inwards ; whence far off appear'd
Through a long pillar'd vista, a fair shrine,
And, just beyond, on light tiptoe divine,
A quiver'd Dian.   Stepping awfully,
The youth approach'd ; oft turning his veil'd eye
Down sidelong aisles, and into niches old :
And, when more near against the marble cold
He had touch'd his forehead, he began to thread
All courts and passages, where silence dead,
Roused by his whispering footsteps, murmur'd faint :
And long he traversed to and fro, to acquaint

Himself with every mystery, and awe;
Till, weary, he sat down before the maw
Of a wide outlet, fathomless and dim,
To wild uncertainty and shadows grim.
There, when new wonders ceased to float before,
And thoughts of self came on, how crude and sore
The journey homeward to habitual self!
A mad-pursuing of the fog-born elf,
Whose flitting lantern, through rude nettle-brier,
Cheats us into a swamp, into a fire,
Into the bosom of a hated thing.

What misery most drowningly doth sing
In lone Endymion's ear, now he has caught
The goal of consciousness? Ah, 'tis the thought,
The deadly feel of solitude: for lo!
He cannot see the heavens, nor the flow
Of rivers, nor hill-flowers running wild
In pink and purple chequer, nor, up-piled,
The cloudy rack slow journeying in the west,
Like herded elephants; nor felt, nor prest
Cool grass, not tasted the fresh slumberous air;
But far from such companionship to wear
An unknown time, surcharged with grief, away,
Was now his lot. And must he patient stay,
Tracing fantastic figures with his spear?
"No!" exclaim'd he, "why should I tarry here?"
No! loudly echoed times innumerable.
At which he straightway started, and 'gan tell
His paces back into the temple's chief;
Warming and glowing strong in the belief
Of help from Dian: so that when again
He caught her airy form, thus did he plain,
Moving more near the while: "O Haunter chaste
Of river sides, and woods, and heathy waste,
Where with thy silver bow and arrows keen
Art thou now forested? O woodland Queen,
What smoothest air thy smoother forehead woos?
Where dost thou listen to the wide halloos
Of thy disparted nymphs? Through what dark tree
Glimmers thy crescent? Wheresoe'er it be,
'Tis in the breath of heaven: thou dost taste

Freedom as none can taste it, nor dost waste
Thy loveliness in dismal elements;
But, finding in our green earth sweet contents,
There livest blissfully. Ah, if to thee
It feels Elysian, how rich to me,
An exiled mortal, sounds its pleasant name!
Within my breast there lives a choking flame—
O let me cool it zephyr-boughs among!
A homeward fever parches up my tongue—
O let me slake it at the running springs!
Upon my ear a noisy nothing rings—
O let me once more hear the linnet's note!
Before mine eyes thick films and shadows float—
O let me 'noint them with the heaven's light:
Dost thou now lave thy feet and ankles white?
O think how sweet to me the freshening sluice!
Dost thou now please thy thirst with berry-juice?
O think how this dry palate would rejoice!
If in soft slumber thou dost hear my voice,
O think how I should love a bed of flowers!—
Young goddess! let me see my native bowers!
Deliver me from this rapacious deep!"

    Thus ending loudly, as he would o'erleap
His destiny, alert he stood: but when
Obstinate silence came heavily again,
Feeling about for its old couch of space
And airy cradle, lowly bow'd his face,
Desponding, o'er the marble floor's cold thrill.
But 'twas not long; for, sweeter than the rill
To its old channel, or a swollen tide
To margin sallows, where the leaves he spied,
And flowers, and wreaths, and ready myrtle crowns
Up heaping through the slab: refreshment drowns
Itself, and strives its own delights to hide—
Nor in one spot alone; the floral pride
In a long whispering birth enchanted grew
Before his footsteps; as when heaved anew
Old ocean rolls a lengthen'd wave to the shore,
Down whose green back the short-lived foam, all
        hoar,
Bursts gradual, with a wayward indolence.

Increasing still in heart, and pleasant sense,
Upon his fairy journey on he hastes ;
So anxious for the end, he scarcely wastes
One moment with his hand among the sweets :
Onward he goes—he stops—his bosom beats
As plainly in his ear, as the faint charm
Of which the throbs were born.   This still alarm,
This sleepy music, forced him walk tiptoe ;
For it came more softly than the east could blow
Arion's magic to the Atlantic isles ;
Or than the west, made jealous by the smiles
Of throned Apollo, could breathe back the lyre
To seas Ionian and Tyrian.

O did he ever live, that lonely man,
Who loved—and music slew not ? 'Tis the pest
Of love, that fairest joys give most unrest ;
That things of delicate and tenderest worth
Are swallow'd all, and make a seared dearth,
By one consuming flame : it doth immerse
And suffocate true blessings in a curse.
Half-happy, by comparison of bliss,
Is miserable.   'Twas even so with this
Dew-dropping melody, in the Carian's ear ;
First heaven, then hell, and then forgotten clear,
Vanish'd in elemental passion.

And down some swart abysm he had gone,
Had not a heavenly guide benignant led
To where thick myrtle branches, 'gainst his head
Brushing, awaken'd : then the sounds again
Went noiseless as a passing noontide rain
Over a bower, where little space he stood ;
For as the sunset peeps into a wood,
So saw he panting light, and towards it went
Through winding alleys ; and lo, wonderment !
Upon soft verdure saw, one here, one there,
Cupids a-slumbering on their pinions fair.

After a thousand mazes overgone,
At last, with sudden step, he came upon
A chamber, myrtle-wall'd, embower'd high,
Full of light, incense, tender minstrelsy,

And more of beautiful and strange beside:
For on a silken couch of rosy pride,
In midst of all, there lay a sleeping youth
Of fondest beauty; fonder, in fair sooth,
Than sighs could fathom, or contentment reach:
And coverlids gold-tinted like the peach,
Or ripe October's faded marigolds,
Fell sleek about him in a thousand folds—
Not hiding up an Apollonian curve
Of neck and shoulder, nor the tenting swerve
Of knee from knee, nor ankles pointing light;
But rather, giving them to the fill'd sight
Officiously. Sideway his face reposed
On one white arm, and tenderly unclos'd,
By tenderest pressure, a faint damask mouth
To slumbery pout: just as the morning south
Disparts a dew-lipp'd rose. Above his head,
Four lily stalks did their white honours wed
To make a coronal; and round him grew
All tendrils green, of every bloom and hue,
Together intertwined and trammell'd fresh:
The vine of glossy sprout; the ivy mesh,
Shading its Ethiop berries; and woodbine,
Of velvet leaves and bugle-blooms divine;
Convolvulus in streaked vases flush;
The creeper, mellowing for an autumn blush;
And virgin's bower, trailing airily;
With others of the sisterhood. Hard by,
Stood serene Cupids watching silently.
One, kneeling to a lyre, touch'd the strings,
Muffling to death the pathos with his wings;
And, ever and anon, uprose to look
At the youth's slumber; while another took
A willow bough, distilling odorous dew,
And shook it on his hair; another flew
In through the woven roof, and fluttering-wise
Rain'd violets upon his sleeping eyes.

At these enchantments, and yet many more,
The breathless Latmian wonder'd o'er and o'er;
Until impatient in embarrassment,
His forthright pass'd, and lightly treading went

To that same feather'd lyrist, who straightway,
Smiling, thus whisper'd: "Though from upper day
Thou art a wanderer, and thy presence here
Might seem unholy, be of happy cheer!
For 'tis the nicest touch of human honour,
When some ethereal and high-favour:ng donor
Presents immortal bowers to mortal sense;
As now 'tis done to thee, Endymion.   Hence
Was I in no wise startled.   So recline
Upon these living flowers.   Here is wine,
Alive with sparkles—never, I aver,
Since Ariadne was a vintager,
So cool a purple: taste these juicy pears,
Sent me by sad Vertumnus, when his fears
Were high about Pomona; here is cream,
Deepening to richness from a snowy gleam;
Sweeter than that nurse Amalthea skimm'd
For the boy Jupiter: and here, undimm'd
By any touch, a bunch of blooming plums
Ready to melt between an infant's gums:
And here is manna pick'd from Syrian trees,
In starlight, by the three Hesperides.
Feast on, and meanwhile I will let thee know
Of all these things around us."   He did so,
Still brooding o'er the cadence of his lyre;
And thus: "I need not any hearing tire
By telling how the sea-born goddess pined
For a mortal youth, and how she strove to bind
Him all in all unto her doting self.
Who would not be so prison'd? but, fond elf,
He was content to let her amorous plea
Faint through his careless arms; content to see
An unseized heaven dying at his feet;
Content, O fool! to make a cold retreat,
When on the pleasant grass such love, lovelorn,
Lay sorrowing; when every tear was born
Of diverse passion; when her lips and eyes
Were closed in sullen moisture, and quick sighs
Came vex'd and pettish through her nostrils small.
Hush! no exclaim—yet, justly might'st thou call
Curses upon his head.—I was half glad,
But my poor mistress went distract and mad,

When the boar tusk'd him : so away she flew
To Jove's high throne, and by her plainings drew
Immortal tear-drops down the Thunderer's beard ;
Whereon, it was decreed he should be rear'd
Each summer-time to life.   Lo ! this is he,
That same Adonis, safe in the privacy
Of this still region all his winter-sleep.
Ay, sleep ; for when our love-sick queen did weep
Over his waned corse, the tremulous shower
Heal'd up the wound, and, with a balmy power,
Medicined death to a lengthen'd drowsiness :
The which she fills with visions, and doth dress
In all this quiet luxury ; and hath set
Us young immortals, without any let,
To watch his slumber through.   'Tis well-nigh pass'd,
Even to a moment's filling up, and fast
She scuds with summer breezes, to pant through
The first long kiss, warm firstling, to renew
Embower'd sports in Cytherea's isle.
Look, how those winged listeners all this while
Stand anxious : see ! behold ! "—This clamant word
Broke through the careful silence ; for they heard
A rustling noise of leaves, and out there flutter'd
Pigeons and doves : Adonis something mutter'd,
The while one hand, that erst upon his thigh
Lay dormant, moved convulsed and gradually
Up to his forehead.   Then there was a hum
Of sudden voices, echoing, "Come ! come !
Arise ! awake !   Clear summer has forth walk'd
Unto the clover-sward, and she has talk'd
Full soothingly to every nested finch :
Rise, Cupids ! or we'll give the blue-bell pinch
To your dimpled arms.   Once more sweet life begin !"
At this, from every side they hurried in,
Rubbing their sleepy eyes with lazy wrists,
And doubling overhead their little fists
In backward yawns.   But all were soon alive :
For as delicious wine doth, sparkling, dive
In nectar'd clouds and curls through water fair,
So from the arbour roof down swell'd an air
Odorous and enlivening ; making all
To laugh, and play, and sing, and loudly call

For their sweet queen : when lo ! the wreathed green
Disparted, and far upward could be seen
Blue heaven, and a silver car, air-borne,
Whose silent wheels, fresh wet from clouds of morn,
Spun off a drizzling dew,—which falling chill
On soft Adonis' shoulders, made him still
Nestle and turn uneasily about.
Soon were the white doves plain, with necks stretched out,
And silken traces lighten'd in descent ;
And soon, returning from love's banishment,
Queen Venus leaning downward open-arm'd :
Her shadow fell upon his breast, and charm'd
A tumult to his heart, and a new life
Into his eyes.   Ah, miserable strife,
But for her comforting ! unhappy sight,
But meeting her blue orbs !   Who, who can write
Of these first minutes ?   The unchariest muse
To embracements warm as theirs makes coy excuse.

O it has ruffled every spirit there,
Saving love's self, who stands superb to share
The general gladness : awfully he stands ;
A sovereign quell is in his waving hands ;
No sight can bear the lightning of his bow ;
His quiver is mysterious, none can know
What themselves think of it ; from forth his eyes
There darts strange light of varied hues and dyes :
A scowl is sometimes on his brow, but who
Look full upon it feel anon the blue
Of his fair eyes run liquid through their souls.
Endymion feels it, and no more controls
The burning prayer within him ; so, bent low,
He had begun a plaining of his woe.
But Venus, bending forward, said : " My child,
Favour this gentle youth ; his days are wild
With love—he—but alas ! too well I see
Thou know'st the deepness of his misery.
Ah, smile not so, my son : I tell thee true,
That when through heavy hours I used to rue
The endless sleep of this new-born Adon',
This stranger aye I pitied.   For upon
A dreary morning once I fled away

Into the breezy clouds, to weep and pray
For this my love : for vexing Mars had teased
Me even to tears : thence, when a little eased,
Down-looking, vacant, through a Lazy wood,
I saw this youth as he despairing stood :
Those same dark curls blown vagrant in the wind :
Those same full fringed lids a constant blind
Over his sullen eyes : I saw him throw
Himself on wither'd leaves, even as though
Death had come sudden ; for no jot he moved,
Yet mutter'd wildly. I could hear he loved
Some fair immortal, and that his embrace
Had zoned her through the night. There is no trace
Of this in heaven : I have mark'd each cheek,
And find it is the vainest thing to seek ;
And that of all things 'tis kept secretest.
Endymion ! one day thou wilt be blest :
So still obey the guiding hand that fends
Thee safely through these wonders for sweet ends.
'Tis a concealment needful in extreme ;
And if I guess'd not so, the sunny beam
Thou shouldst mount up to with me. Now adieu !
Here must we leave thee."—At these words up flew
The impatient doves, up rose the floating car,
Up went the hum celestial. High afar
The Latmian saw them minish into nought ;
And, when all were clear vanish'd, still he caught
A vivid lightning from that dreadful bow.
When all was darken'd, with Ætnean throe
The earth closed—gave a solitary moan—
And left him once again in twilight lone.

He did not rave, he did not stare aghast,
For all those visions were o'ergone, and past,
And he in loneliness : he felt assured
Of happy times, when all he had endured
Would seem a feather to the mighty prize.
So, with unusual gladness, on he hies
Through caves, and palaces of mottled ore,
Gold dome, and crystal wall, and turquois floor,
Black polish'd porticoes of awful shade,
And, at the last, a diamond balustrade,

Leading afar past wild magnificence,
Spiral through ruggedest loop-holes, and thence
Stretching across a void, then guiding o'er
Enormous chasms, where, all foam and roar,
Streams subterranean tease their granite beds;
Then heighten'd just above the silvery heads
Of a thousand fountains, so that he could dash
The waters with his spear; but at the splash,
Done heedlessly, those spouting columns rose
Sudden a poplar's height, and 'gan to inclose
His diamond path with fretwork streaming round
Alike, and dazzling cool, and with a sound,
Haply, like dolphin tumults, when sweet shells
Welcome the float of Thetis.   Long he dwells
On this delight; for, every minute's space,
The streams with changed magic interlace:
Sometimes like delicatest lattices,
Cover'd with crystal vines; then weeping trees,
Moving about as in a gentle wind,
Which, in a wink, to watery gauze refined,
Pour'd into shapes of curtain'd canopies,
Spangled, and rich with liquid broideries
Of flowers, peacocks, swans, and naiads fair.
Swifter than lightning went these wonders rare;
And then the water, into stubborn streams
Collecting, mimick'd the wrought oaken beams,
Pillars, and frieze, and high fantastic roof,
Of those dusk places in times far aloof
Cathedrals call'd.   He bade a loath farewell
To these founts Protean, passing gulf, and dell,
And torrent, and ten thousand jutting shapes,
Half seen through deepest gloom, and grizly gapes,
Blackening on every side, and overhead
A vaulted dome like heaven's far bespread
With starlight gems: ay, all so huge and strange,
The solitary felt a hurried change
Working within him into something dreary,—
Vex'd like a morning eagle, lost and weary,
And purblind amid foggy midnight wolds.
But he revives at once: for who beholds
New sudden things, nor casts his mental slough?
Forth from a rugged arch, in the dusk below,

Came mother Cybele! alone—alone—
In sombre chariot; dark foldings thrown
About her majesty, and front death-pale,
With turrets crown'd. Four maned lions hale
The sluggish wheels; solemn their toothed maws,
Their surly eyes brow-hidden, heavy paws
Uplifted drowsily, and nervy tails
Cowering their tawny brushes. Silent sails
This shadowy queen athwart, and faints away
In another gloomy arch.

                 Wherefore delay,
Young traveller, in such a mournful place?
Art thou wayworn, or canst not further trace
The diamond path? And does it indeed end
Abrupt in middle air? Yet earthward bend
Thy forehead, and to Jupiter cloud-borne
Call ardently! He was indeed wayworn;
Abrupt, in middle air, his way was lost;
To cloud-borne Jove he bowed, and there crost
Towards him a large eagle, 'twixt whose wings,
Without one impious word, himself he flings,
Committed to the darkness and the gloom:
Down, down, uncertain to what pleasant doom,
Swift as a fathoming plummet down he fell
Through unknown things; till exhaled asphodel,
And rose, with spicy fannings interbreathed,
Came swelling forth where little caves were wreathed
So thick with leaves and mosses, that they seem'd
Large honeycombs of green, and freshly teem'd
With airs delicious. In the greenest nook
The eagle landed him, and farewell took.

    It was a jasmine bower, all bestrown
With golden moss. His every sense had grown
Ethereal for pleasure; 'bove his head
Flew a delight half graspable; his tread
Was Hesperean; to his capable ears
Silence was music from the holy spheres;
A dewy luxury was in his eyes;
The little flowers felt his pleasant sighs
And stirr'd them faintly. Verdant cave and cell
He wander'd through, oft wondering at such swell

Of sudden exaltation : but, " Alas ! "
Said he, " will all this gush of feeling pass
Away in solitude ?   And must they wane,
Like melodies upon a sandy plain,
Without an echo ?   Then shall I be left
So sad, so melancholy, so bereft !
Yet still I feel immortal !   O my love,
My breath of life, where art thou ? High above,
Dancing before the morning gates of heaven ?
Or keeping watch among those starry seven,
Old Atlas' children ?   Art a maid of the waters,
One of shell-winding Triton's bright-hair'd daughters ?
Or art, impossible ! a nymph of Dian's,
Weaving a coronal of tender scions
For very idleness ?   Where'er thou art,
Methinks it now is at my will to start
Into thine arms ; to scare Aurora's train,
And snatch thee from the morning ; o'er the main
To scud like a wild bird, and take thee off
From thy sea-foamy cradle ; or to doff
Thy shepherd vest, and woo thee 'mid fresh leaves.
No, no, too eagerly my soul deceives
Its powerless self : I know this cannot be.
O let me then by some sweet dreaming flee
To her entrancements : hither sleep awhile !
Hither, most gentle sleep ! and soothing foil
For some few hours the coming solitude."

Thus spake he, and that moment felt endued
With power to dream deliciously ; so wound
Through a dim passage, searching till he found
The smoothest mossy bed and deepest, where
He threw himself, and just into the air
Stretching his indolent arms, he took, O bliss !
A naked waist : " Fair Cupid, whence is this ? "
A well-known voice sigh'd, " Sweetest, here am I ! "
At which soft ravishment, with doting cry
They trembled to each other.—Helicon !
O fountain'd hill !   Old Homer's Helicon !
That thou would'st spout a little streamlet o'er
These sorry pages ; then the verse would soar
And sing above this gentle pair, like lark

Over his nested young : but all is dark
Around thine aged top, and thy clear fount
Exhales in mists to heaven.   Ay, the count
Of mighty Poets is made up ; the scroll
Is folded by the Muses ; the bright roll
Is in Apollo's hand : our dazed eyes
Have seen a new tinge in the western skies :
The world has done its duty.   Yet, oh yet,
Although the sun of poesy is set,
These lovers did embrace, and we must weep
That there is no old power left to steep
A quill immortal in their joyous tears.
Long time in silence did their anxious fears
Question that thus it was ; long time they lay
Fondling and kissing every doubt away ;
Long time ere soft caressing sobs began
To mellow into words, and then there ran
Two bubbling springs of talk from their sweet lips.
"O known Unknown ! from whom my being sips
Such darling essence, wherefore may I not
Be ever in these arms ? in this sweet spot
Pillow my chin for ever ? ever press
These toying hands and kiss their smooth excess ?
Why not for ever and for ever feel
That breath about my eyes ?   Ah, thou wilt steal
Away from me again, indeed, indeed—
Thou wilt be gone away, and wilt not heed
My lonely madness.   Speak, my kindest fair !
Is—is it to be so ?   No !   Who will dare
To pluck thee from me ?   And, of thine own will,
Full well I feel thou wouldst not leave me.   Still
Let me entwine thee surer, surer—now
How can we part ?   Elysium !   Who art thou ?
Who, that thou canst not be for ever here,
Or lift me with thee to some starry sphere ?
Enchantress ! tell me by this soft embrace,
By the most soft complexion of thy face,
Those lips, O slippery blisses ! twinkling eyes,
And by these tenderest, milky sovereignties—
These tenderest, and by the nectar-wine,
The passion "——   "O loved Ida the divine !
Endymion ! dearest !   Ah, unhappy me !

His soul will 'scape us—O felicity!
How he does love me! His poor temples beat
To the very tune of love—how sweet, sweet, sweet!
Revive, dear youth, or I shall faint and die;
Revive, or these soft hours will hurry by
In tranced dulness; speak, and let that spell
Affright this lethargy! I cannot quell
Its heavy pressure, and will press at least
My lips to thine, that they may richly feast
Until we taste the life of love again.
What! dost thou move? dost kiss? O bliss! O pain!
I love thee, youth, more than I can conceive;
And so long absence from thee doth bereave
My soul of any rest: yet must I hence:
Yet, can I not to starry eminence
Uplift thee; nor for very shame can own
Myself to thee. Ah, dearest! do not groan,
Or thou wilt force me from this secrecy,
And I must blush in heaven. O that I
Had done it already! that the dreadful smiles
At my lost brightness, my impassion'd wiles,
Had waned from Olympus' solemn height,
And from all serious Gods; that our delight
Was quite forgotten, save of us alone!
And wherefore so ashamed? 'Tis but to atone
For endless pleasure, by some coward blushes:
Yet must I be a coward! Horror rushes
Too palpable before me—the sad look
Of Jove—Minerva's start—no bosom shook
With awe of purity—no Cupid pinion
In reverence veil'd—my crystalline dominion
Half lost, and all old hymns made nullity!
But what is this to love? Oh! I could fly
With thee into the ken of heavenly powers,
So thou wouldst thus, for many sequent hours,
Press me so sweetly. Now I swear at once
That I am wise, that Pallas is a dunce—
Perhaps her love like mine is but unknown—
Oh! I do think that I have been alone
In chastity! yes, Pallas has been sighing,
While every eve saw me my hair uptying
With fingers cool as aspen leaves. Sweet love!

I was as vague as solitary dove,
Nor knew that nests were built.　Now a soft kiss—
Ay, by that kiss, I vow an endless bliss,
An immortality of passion's thine :
Ere long I will exalt thee to the shine
Of heaven ambrosial ; and we will shade
Ourselves whole summers by a river glade ;
And I will tell thee stories of the sky,
And breathe thee whispers of its minstrelsy.
My happy love will overwing all bounds !
O let me melt into thee ! let the sounds
Of our close voices marry at their birth ;
Let us entwine hoveringly !　O dearth
Of human words ! roughness of mortal speech
Lispings empyrean will I sometimes teach
Thine honey'd tongue—lute-breathings which I gasp
To have thee understand, now while I clasp
Thee thus, and weep for fondness—I am pain'd,
Endymion : woe ! woe ! is grief contain'd
In the very deeps of pleasure, my sole life ? "—
Hereat, with many sobs, her gentle strife
Melted into a languor.　He return'd
Entranced vows and tears.

　　　　　　　　　　　Ye who have yearn'd
With too much passion, will here stay and pity,
For the mere sake of truth ; as 'tis a ditty
Not of these days, but long ago 'twas told
By a cavern wind unto a forest old ;
And then the forest told it in a dream
To a sleeping lake, whose cool and level gleam
A poet caught as he was journeying
To Phœbus' shrine ; and in it he did fling
His weary limbs, bathing an hour's space,
And after, straight in that inspired place
He sang the story up into the air,
Giving it universal freedom.　There
Has it been ever sounding for those ears
Whose tips are glowing hot.　The legend cheers
Yon sentinel stars ; and he who listens to it
Must surely be self-doom'd or he will rue it :
For quenchless burnings come upon the heart,

Made fiercer by a fear lest any part
Should be engulfed in the eddying wind.
As much as here is penn'd doth always find
A resting-place, thus much comes clear and plain ;
Anon the strange voice is upon the wane—
And 'tis but echoed from departing sound,
That the fair visitant at last unwound
Her gentle limbs, and left the youth asleep.—
Thus the tradition of the gusty deep.

Now turn we to our former chroniclers.—
Endymion awoke, that grief of hers
Sweet paining on his ear : he sickly guess'd
How lone he was once more, and sadly press'd
His empty arms together, hung his head,
And most forlorn upon that widow'd bed
Sat silently.   Love's madness he had known :
Often with more than tortured lion's groan
Moanings had burst from him ; but now that rage
Had pass'd away : no longer did he wage
A rough-voiced war against the dooming stars.
No, he had felt too much for such harsh jars :
The lyre of his soul Æolian tuned
Forgot all violence, and but communed
With melancholy thought : O he had swoon'd
Drunken from pleasure's nipple ! and his love
Henceforth was dove-like.—Loth was he to move
From the imprinted couch, and when he did,
'Twas with slow, languid paces, and face hid
In muffling hands.   So temper'd, out he stray'd,
Half seeing visions that might have dismay'd
Alecto's serpents ; ravishments more keen
Than Hermes' pipe, when anxious he did lean
Over eclipsing eyes : and at the last
It was a sounding grotto, vaulted, vast,
O'erstudded with a thousand, thousand pearls,
And crimson-mouthed shells with stubborn curls
Of every shape and size, even to the bulk
In which whales harbour close, to brood and sulk
Against an endless storm.   Moreover too,
Fish-semblances of green and azure hue,
Ready to snort their streams.   In this cool wonder

Endymion sat down, and 'gan to ponder
On all his life: his youth, up to the day
When 'mid acclaim, and feasts, and garlands gay,
He stepp'd upon his shepherd throne: the look
Of his white palace in wild forest nook,
And all the revels he had lorded there:
Each tender maiden whom he once thought fair,
With every friend and fellow-woodlander—
Pass'd like a dream before him.   Then the spur
Of the old bards to mighty deeds: his plans
To nurse the golden age 'mong shepherd clans:
That wondrous night: the great Pan-festival:
His sister's sorrow; and his wanderings all,
Until into the earth's deep maw he rush'd:
Then all its buried magic, till it flush'd
High with excessive love.   "And now," thought he,
"How long must I remain in jeopardy
Of blank amazements that amaze no more?
Now I have tasted her sweet soul to the core,
All other depths are shallow: essences,
Once spiritual, are like muddy lees,
Meant but to fertilize my earthly root,
And make my branches lift a golden fruit
Into the bloom of heaven: other light,
Though it be quick and sharp enough to blight
The Olympian eagle's vision, is dark,
Dark as the parentage of chaos.   Hark!
My silent thoughts are echoing from these shells;
Or they are but the ghosts, the dying swells
Of noises far away?—list!"—Hereupon
He kept an anxious ear.   The humming tone
Came louder, and behold, there as he lay,
On either side outgush'd, with misty spray,
A copious spring; and both together dash'd
Swift, mad, fantastic round the rocks, and lash'd
Among the conchs and shells of the lofty grot,
Leaving a trickling dew.   At last they shot
Down from the ceiling's height, pouring a noise
As of some breathless racers whose hopes poise
Upon the last few steps, and with spent force
Along the ground they took a winding course.
Endymion follow'd—for it seem'd that one

Ever pursued, the other strove to shun—
Follow'd their languid mazes, till well-nigh
He had left thinking of the mystery,—
And was now rapt in tender hoverings
Over the vanish'd bliss.   Ah! what is it sings
His dream away?   What melodies are these?
They sound as through the whispering of trees,
Not native in such barren vaults.   Give ear!

"O Arethusa, peerless nymph! why fear
Such tenderness as mine?   Great Dian, why,
Why didst thou hear her prayer?   O that I
Were rippling round her dainty fairness now,
Circling about her waist, and striving how
To entice her to a dive! then stealing in
Between her luscious lips and eyelids thin.
O that her shining hair was in the sun,
And I distilling from it thence to run
In amorous rillets down her shrinking form!
To linger on her lily shoulders, warm
Between her kissing breasts, and every charm
Touch raptured!—See how painfully I flow:
Fair maid, be pitiful to my great woe.
Stay, stay thy weary course, and let me lead,
A happy wooer, to the flowery mead
Where all that beauty snared me."—"Cruel god,
Desist! or my offended mistress' nod
Will stagnate all thy fountains :—tease me not
With syren words—Ah, have I really got
Such power to madden thee?   And is it true—
Away, away, or I shall dearly rue
My very thoughts : in mercy then away,
Kindest Alpheus, for should I obey
My own dear will, 'twould be a deadly bane."—
"O, Oread-Queen! would that thou hadst a pain
Like this of mine, then would I fearless turn
And be a criminal."—"Alas, I burn,
I shudder—gentle river, get thee hence.
Alpheus! thou enchanter! every sense
Of mine was once made perfect in these woods.
Fresh breezes, bowery lawns, and innocent floods,
Ripe fruits, and lonely couch, contentment gave ;

But ever since I heedlessly did lave
In thy deceitful stream, a panting glow
Grew strong within me; wherefore serve me so,
And call it love? Alas! 'twas cruelty.
Not once more did I close my happy eyes
Amid the thrush's song. Away! avaunt!
O 'twas a cruel thing."—" Now thou dost taunt
So softly, Arethusa, that I think
If thou wast playing on my shady brink,
Thou wouldst bathe once again. Innocent maid
Stifle thine heart no more;—nor be afraid
Of angry powers: there are deities
Will shade us with their wings. Those fitful sighs
'Tis almost death to hear: O let me pour
A dewy balm upon them!—fear no more,
Sweet Arethusa! Dian's self must feel,
Sometimes, these very pangs. Dear maiden, steal
Blushing into my soul, and let us fly
These dreary caverns for the open sky.
I will delight thee all my winding course,
From the green sea up to my hidden source
About Arcadian forests; and will show
The channels where my coolest waters flow
Through mossy rocks; where 'mid exuberant green
I roam in pleasant darkness, more unseen
Than Saturn in his exile; where I brim
Round flowery islands, and take thence a skim
Of mealy sweets, which myriads of bees
Buzz from their honey'd wings: and thou should please
Thyself to choose the richest, where we might
Be incense-pillow'd every summer night.
Doff all sad fears, thou white deliciousness,
And let us be thus comforted; unless
Thou couldst rejoice to see my hopeless stream
Hurry distracted from Sol's temperate beam,
And pour to death along some hungry sands."—
" What can I do, Alpheus? Dian stands
Severe before me: persecuting fate!
Unhappy Arethusa! thou wast late
A huntress free in—" At this, sudden fell
Those two sad streams adown a fearful dell.
The Latmian listen'd, but he heard no more,

Save echo, faint repeating o'er and o'er
The name of Arethusa.   On the verge
Of that dark gulf he wept, and said : " I urge
Thee, gentle Goddess of my pilgrimage,
By our eternal hopes, to soothe, to assuage,
If thou art powerful, these lovers' pains ;
And make them happy in some happy plains."
He turn'd—there was a whelming sound—he stept,
There was a cooler light ; and so he kept
Towards it by a sandy path, and lo !
More suddenly than doth a moment go,
The visions of the earth were gone and fled—
He saw the giant sea above his head.

BOOK III

THERE are who lord it o'er their fellow-men
With most prevailing tinsel : who unpen
Their baaing vanities, to browse away
The comfortable green and juicy hay
From human pastures ; or, O torturing fact !
Who, through an idiot blink, will see unpack'd
Fire-branded foxes to sear up and singe
Our gold and ripe-ear'd hopes.   With not one tinge
Of sanctuary splendour, not a sight
Able to face an owl's, they still are dight
By the blear-eyed nations in empurpled vests,
And crowns, and turbans.   With unladen breasts,
Save of blown self-applause, they proudly mount
To their spirit's perch, their being's high account,
Their tip-top nothings, their dull skies, their thrones—
Amid the fierce intoxicating tones
Of trumpets, shoutings, and belabour'd drums,
And sudden cannon.   Ah ! how all this hums,
In wakeful ears, like uproar past and gone—
Like thunder-clouds that spake to Babylon,
And set those old Chaldeans to their tasks.—
Are then regalities all gilded masks ?
No, there are throned seats unscalable
But by a patient wing, a constant spell,
Or by ethereal things that, unconfined,

Can make a ladder of the eternal wind,
And poise about in cloudy thunder-tents
To watch the abysm-birth of elements.
Ay, 'bove the withering of old-lipp'd Fate
A thousand Powers keep religious state,
In water, fiery realm, and airy bourne ;
And, silent as a consecrated urn,
Hold sphery sessions for a season due.
Yet few of these far majesties, ah, few !
Have bared their operations to this globe—
Few, who with gorgeous pageantry enrobe
Our piece of heaven—whose benevolence
Shakes hand with our own Ceres ; every sense
Filling with spiritual sweets to plenitude,
As bees gorge full their cells.   And by the feud
'Twixt Nothing and Creation, I here swear,
Eterne Apollo ! that thy Sister fair
Is of all these the gentlier-mightiest.
When thy gold breath is misting in the west,
She unobserved steals unto her throne,
And there she sits most meek and most alone ;
As if she had not pomp subservient ;
As if thine eye, high Poet ! was not bent
Towards her with the Muses in thine heart ;
As if the minist'ring stars kept not apart,
Waiting for silver-footed messages.
O Moon ! the oldest shades 'mong oldest trees
Feel palpitations when thou lookest in.
O Moon ! old boughs lisp forth a holier din
The while they feel thine airy fellowship.
Thou dost bless everywhere, with silver lip
Kissing dead things to life.   The sleeping kine,
Couch'd in thy brightness, dream of fields divine :
Innumerable mountains rise, and rise,
Ambitious for the hallowing of thine eyes ;
And yet thy benediction passeth not
One obscure hiding-place, one little spot
Where pleasure may be sent : the nested wren
Has thy fair face within its tranquil ken,
And from beneath a sheltering ivy leaf
Takes glimpses of thee ; thou art a relief
To the poor patient oyster, where it sleeps,

Within its pearly house ;—The mighty deeps,
The monstrous sea is thine—the myriad sea !
O Moon ! far spooming Ocean bows to thee,
And Tellus feels her forehead's cumbrous load.

Cynthia ! where art thou now ? What far abode
Of green or silvery bower doth enshrine
Such utmost beauty ? Alas, thou dost pine
For one as sorrowful : thy cheek is pale
For one whose cheek is pale : thou dost bewail
His tears who weeps for thee ! Where dost thou sigh?
Ah ! surely that light peeps from Vesper's eye,
Or, what a thing is love ! 'Tis She, but lo !
How changed, how full of ache, how gone in woe !
She dies at the thinnest cloud ; her loveliness
Is wan on Neptune's blue : yet there's a stress
Of love-spangles, just off yon cape of trees,
Dancing upon the waves, as if to please
The curly foam with amorous influence.
O, not so idle ! for down glancing thence,
She fathoms eddies, and runs wild about
O'erwhelming water-courses ; scaring out
The thorny sharks from hiding-holes, and fright'ning
Their savage eyes with unaccustom'd lightning.
Where will the splendour be content to reach ?
O love ! how potent hast thou been to teach
Strange journeyings ! Wherever beauty dwells,
In gulf or aerie, mountains or deep dells,
In light, in gloom, in star or blazing sun,
Thou pointest out the way, and straight 'tis won.
Amid his toil thou gavest Leander breath ;
Thou leddest Orpheus through the gleams of death ;
Thou madest Pluto bear thin element :
And now, O winged Chieftain ! thou hast sent
A moon-beam to the deep, deep water-world,
To find Endymion.

On gold sand impearl'd
With lily shells, and pebbles milky white,
Poor Cynthia greeted him, and soothed her light
Against his pallid face : he felt the charm
To breathlessness, and suddenly a warm
Of his heart's blood : 'twas very sweet ; he stay'd

His wandering steps, and half-entranced laid
His head upon a tuft of straggling weeds,
To taste the gentle moon, and freshening beads,
Lash'd from the crystal roof by fishes' tails.
And so he kept, until the rosy veils
Mantling the east, by Aurora's peering hand
Were lifted from the water's breast, and fann'd
Into sweet air; and sober'd morning came
Meekly through billows :—when like taper-flame
Left sudden by a dallying breath of air,
He rose in silence, and once more 'gan fare
Along his fated way.

               Far had he roam'd,
With nothing save the hollow vast, that foam'd
Above, around, and at his feet; save things
More dead than Morpheus' imaginings :
Old rusted anchors, helmets, breastplates large
Of gone sea-warriors; brazen beaks and targe;
Rudders that for a hundred years had lost
The sway of human hand; gold vase emboss'd
With long-forgotten story, and wherein
No reveller had ever dipp'd a chin
But those of Saturn's vintage; mouldering scrolls,
Writ in the tongue of heaven, by those souls
Who first were on the earth; and sculptures rude
In ponderous stone, developing the mood
Of ancient Nox ;—then skeletons of man,
Of beast, behemoth, and leviathan,
And elephant, and eagle, and huge jaw
Of nameless monster. A cold leaden awe
These secrets struck into him; and unless
Dian had chased away that heaviness,
He might have died : but now, with cheered feel,
He onward kept; wooing these thoughts to steal
About the labyrinth in his soul of love.

" What is there in thee, Moon ! that thou shouldst move
My heart so potently? When yet a child
I oft have dried my tears when thou hast smiled.
Thou seem'dst my sister : hand in hand we went
From eve to morn across the firmament.
No apples would I gather from the tree,

Till thou hadst cool'd their cheeks deliciously:
No tumbling water ever spake romance,
But when my eyes with thine thereon could dance:
No woods were green enough, no bower divine,
Until thou liftedst up thine eyelids fine:
In sowing-time ne'er would I dibble take,
Or drop a seed, till thou wast wide awake;
And, in the summer-tide of blossoming,
No one but thee hath heard me blithely sing
And mesh my dewy flowers all the night.
No melody was like a passing spright
If it went not to solemnise thy reign.
Yes, in my boyhood, every joy and pain
By thee were fashion'd to the self-same end;
And as I grew in years, still didst thou blend
With all my ardours: thou wast the deep glen—
Thou wast the mountain-top—the sage's pen—
The poet's harp—the voice of friends—the sun;
Thou wast the river—thou wast glory won;
Thou wast my clarion's blast—thou wast my steed—
My goblet full of wine—my topmost deed:—
Thou wast the charm of women, lovely Moon!
O what a wild and harmonised tune
My spirit struck from all the beautiful!
On some bright essence could I lean, and lull
Myself to immortality: I prest
Nature's soft pillow in a wakeful rest.
But gentle Orb! there came a nearer bliss—
My strange love came—Felicity's abyss!
She came, and thou didst fade, and fade away—
Yet not entirely; no, thy starry sway
Has been an under-passion to this hour.
Now I begin to feel thine orby power
Is coming fresh upon me: O be kind!
Keep back thine influence, and do not blind
My sovereign vision.—Dearest love, forgive
That I can think away from thee and live!—
Pardon me, airy planet, that I prize
One thought beyond thine argent luxuries!
How far beyond!"   At this a surprised start
Frosted the springing verdure of his heart;
For as he lifted up his eyes to swear

How his own goddess was past all things fair,
He saw far in the concave green of the sea
An old man sitting calmly and peacefully.
Upon a weeded rock this old man sat,
And his white hair was awful, and a mat
Of weeds were cold beneath his cold thin feet;
And, ample as the largest winding-sheet,
A cloak of blue wrapp'd up his aged bones,
O'erwrought with symbols by the deepest groans
Of ambitious magic: every ocean-form
Was woven in with black distinctness; storm,
And calm, and whispering, and hideous roar
Were emblem'd in the woof; with every shape
That skims, or dives, or sleeps, 'twixt cape and cape
The gulphing whale was like a dot in the spell,
Yet look upon it, and 'twould size and swell
To its huge self; and the minutest fish
Would pass the very hardest gazer's wish,
And show his little eye's anatomy.
Then there was pictured the regality
Of Neptune; and the sea-nymphs round his state,
In beauteous vassalage, look up and wait.
Beside this old man lay a pearly wand,
And in his lap a book, the which he conn'd
So steadfastly, that the new denizen
Had time to keep him in amazed ken,
To mark these shadowings, and stand in awe.

  The old man raised his hoary head and saw
The wilder'd stranger—seeming not to see,
His features were so lifeless.   Suddenly
He woke as from a trance; his snow-white brows
Went arching up, and like two magic ploughs
Furrow'd deep wrinkles in his forehead large,
Which kept as fixedly as rocky marge,
Till round his wither'd lips had gone a smile.
Then up he rose, like one whose tedious toil
Had watch'd for years in forlorn hermitage,
Who had not from mid-life to utmost age
Eased in one accent his o'erburden'd soul,
Even to the trees.   He rose: he grasp'd his stole,
With convulsed clenches waving it abroad,

And in a voice of solemn joy, that awed
Echo into oblivion, he said :—

"Thou art the man! Now shall I lay my head
In peace upon my watery pillow : now
Sleep will come smoothly to my weary brow.
O Jove! I shall be young again, be young!
O shell-borne Neptune, I am pierced and stung
With new-born life! What shall I do? Where go,
When I have cast this serpent-skin of woe?—
I'll swim to the syrens, and one moment listen
Their melodies, and see their long hair glisten;
Anon upon that giant's arm I'll be,
That writhes about the roots of Sicily;
To northern seas I'll in a twinkling sail,
And mount upon the snortings of a whale
To some black cloud; thence down I'll madly sweep
On forked lightning to the deepest deep,
Where through some sucking pool I will be hurl'd
With rapture to the other side of the world!
O, I am full of gladness! Sisters three,
I bow full-hearted to your old decree!
Yes, every god be thank'd, and power benign,
For I no more shall wither, droop, and pine.
Thou art the man!"   Endymion started back
Dismay'd; and like a wretch from whom the rack
Tortures hot breath, and speech of agony,
Mutter'd : "What lonely death am I to die
In this cold region?   Will he let me freeze,
And float my brittle limbs o'er polar seas?
Or will he touch me with his searing hand,
And leave a black memorial on the sand?
Or tear me piecemeal with a bony saw,
And keep me as a chosen food to draw
His magian fish through hated fire and flame?
O misery of hell! resistless, tame,
Am I to be burn'd up? No, I will shout,
Until the gods through heaven's blue look out!—
O Tartarus! but some few days agone
Her soft arms were entwining me, and on
Her voice I hung like fruit among green leaves :
Her lips were all my own, and—ah, ripe sheaves

Of happiness ! ye on the stubble droop,
But never may be garner'd.   I must stoop
My head, and kiss death's foot.   Love ! love, farewell !
Is there no hope from thee ?   This horrid spell
Would melt at thy sweet breath.—By Dian's hind
Feeding from her white fingers, on the wind
I see thy streaming hair ! and now, by Pan,
I care not for this old mysterious man ! "

He spake, and walking to that aged form,
Look'd high defiance.   Lo ! his heart 'gan warm
With pity, for the grey-hair'd creature wept.
Had he then wrong'd a heart where sorrow kept ?
Had he though blindly contumelious, brought
Rheum to kind eyes, a sting to human thought,
Convulsion to a mouth of many years ?
He had in truth ; and he was ripe for tears.
The penitent shower fell, as down he knelt
Before that care-worn sage, who trembling felt
About his large dark locks, and faltering spake :

"Arise, good youth, for sacred Phœbus' sake !
I know thine inmost bosom, and I feel
A very brother's yearning for thee steal
Into mine own : for why ? thou openest
The prison-gates that have so long oppress'd
My weary watching.   Though thou know'st it not,
Thou art commission'd to this fated spot
For great enfranchisement.   O weep no more !
I am a friend to love, to loves of yore :
Ay, hadst thou never loved an unknown power,
I had been grieving at this joyous hour.
But even now, most miserable old,
I saw thee, and my blood no longer cold
Gave mighty pulses : in this tottering case
Grew a new heart, which at this moment plays
As dancingly as thine.   Be not afraid,
For thou shalt hear this secret all display'd,
Now as we speed towards our joyous task."

So saying, this young soul in age's mask
Went forward with the Carian side by side :

Resuming quickly thus ; while ocean's tide
Hung swollen at their backs, and jewell'd sands
Took silently their foot-prints.

                     " My soul stands
Now past the midway from mortality,
And so I can prepare without a sigh
To tell thee briefly all my joy and pain.
I was a fisher once, upon this main,
And my boat danced in every creek and bay ;
Rough billows were my home by night and day,—
The sea-gulls not more constant ; for I had
No housing from the storm and tempests mad,
But hollow rocks,—and they were palaces
Of silent happiness, of slumberous ease :
Long years of misery have told me so.
Ay, thus it was one thousand years ago.
One thousand years !—Is it then possible
To look so plainly through them ? to dispel
A thousand years with backward glance sublime ?
To breathe away as 'twere all scummy slime
From off a crystal pool, to see its deep,
And one's own image from the bottom peep ?
Yes : now I am no longer wretched thrall,
My long captivity and moanings all
Are but a slime, a thin-pervading scum,
The which I breathe away, and thronging come
Like things of yesterday my youthful pleasures.

    " I touch'd no lute, I sang not, trod no measures :
I was a lonely youth on desert shores.
My sports were lonely, 'mid continuous roars,
And craggy isles, and seamews' plaintive cry
Plaining discrepant between sea and sky.
Dolphins were still my playmates ; shapes unseen
Would let me feel their scales of gold and green
Nor be my desolation ; and, full oft,
When a dread waterspout had rear'd aloft
Its hungry hugeness, seeming ready ripe
To burst with hoarsest thunderings, and wipe
My life away like a vast sponge of fate,
Some friendly monster pitying my sad state,

Has dived to its foundations, gulf'd it down,
And left me tossing safely.   But the crown
Of all my life was utmost quietude :
More did I love to lie in cavern rude,
Keeping in wait whole days for Neptune's voice,
And if it came at last, hark, and rejoice !
There blush'd no summer eve but I would steer
My skiff along green shelving coasts, to hear
The shepherd's pipe come clear from aery steep,
Mingled with ceaseless bleatings of his sheep :
And never was a day of summer shine,
But I beheld its birth upon the brine :
For I would watch all night to see unfold
Heaven's gates, and Æthon snort his morning gold
Wide o'er the swelling streams : and constantly
At brim of day-tide, on some grassy lea,
My nets would be spread out, and I at rest.
The poor folk of the sea-country I blest
With daily boon of fish most delicate :
They knew not whence this bounty, and elate
Would strew sweet flowers on a sterile beach.

"Why was I not contented ?   Wherefore reach
At things which, but for thee, O Latmian !
Had been my dreary death ! Fool ! I began
To feel distemper'd longings : to desire
The utmost privilege that ocean's sire
Could grant in benediction : to be free
Of all his kingdom.   Long in misery
I wasted, ere in one extremest fit
I plunged for life or death.   To interknit
One's senses with so dense a breathing stuff
Might seem a work of pain ; so not enough
Can I admire how crystal-smooth it felt,
And buoyant round my limbs.   At first I dwelt
Whole days and days in sheer astonishment ;
Forgetful utterly of self-intent ;
Moving but with the mighty ebb and flow.
Then, like a new-fledged bird that first doth show
His spreaded feathers to the morrow chill,
I tried in fear the pinions of my will.
'Twas freedom ! and at once I visited

The ceaseless wonders of this ocean-bed.
No need to tell thee of them, for I see
That thou hast been a witness—it must be.
For these I know thou canst not feel a drouth,
By the melancholy corners of that mouth.
So I will in my story straightway pass
To more immediate matter.   Woe, alas!
That love should be my bane!   Ah, Scylla, fair!
Why did poor Glaucus ever—ever dare
To sue thee to his heart?   Kind stranger-youth!
I loved her to the very white of truth,
And she would not conceive it.   Timid thing!
She fled me swift as sea-bird on the wing,
Round every isle, and point, and promontory,
From where large Hercules wound up his story
Far as Egyptian Nile.   My passion grew
The more, the more I saw her dainty hue
Gleam delicately through the azure clear:
Until 'twas too fierce agony to bear;
And in that agony, across my grief
It flash'd, that Circe might find some relief—
Cruel enchantress!   So above the water
I rear'd my head, and look'd for Phœbus' daughter.
Æææ's isle was wondering at the moon:—
It seem'd to whirl around me, and a swoon
Left me dead-drifting to that fatal power.

   " When I awoke, 'twas in a twilight bower;
Just when the light of morn, with hum of bees,
Stole through its verdurous matting of fresh trees.
How sweet, and sweeter! for I heard a lyre,
And over it a sighing voice expire.
It ceased—I caught light footsteps; and anon
The fairest face that morn e'er looked upon
Push'd through a screen of roses.   Starry Jove!
With tears, and smiles, and honey-words she wove
A net whose thraldom was more bliss than all
The range of flower'd Elysium.   Thus did fall
The dew of her rich speech: 'Ah! art awake?
O let me hear thee speak, for Cupid's sake!
I am so oppress'd with joy!   Why, I have shed
An urn of tears, as though thou wert cold dead;

And now I find thee living, I will pour
From these devoted eyes their silver store,
Until exhausted of the latest drop,
So it will pleasure thee, and force thee stop
Here, that I too may live ; but if beyond
Such cool and sorrowful offerings, thou art fond
Of soothing warmth, of dalliance supreme ;
If thou art ripe to taste a long love-dream ;
If smiles, if dimples, tongues for ardour mute,
Hang in thy vision like a tempting fruit,
O let me pluck it for thee !'   Thus she link'd
Her charming syllables, till indistinct
Their music came to my o'er-sweeten'd soul ;
And then she hover'd over me, and stole
So near, that if no nearer it had been
This furrow'd visage thou hadst never seen.

"Young man of Latmos ! thus particular
Am I, that thou may'st plainly see how far
This fierce temptation went : and thou may'st not
Exclaim, How then ? was Scylla quite forgot ?

"Who could resist ?   Who in this universe ?
She did so breathe ambrosia ; so immerse
My fine existence in a golden clime.
She took me like a child of suckling time,
And cradled me in roses.   Thus condemn'd,
The current of my former life was stemm'd,
And to this arbitrary queen of sense
I bow'd a tranced vassal : nor would thence
Have moved, even though Amphion's harp had woo'd
Me back to Scylla o'er the billows rude.
For as Apollo each eve doth devise
A new apparelling for western skies ;
So every eve, nay, every spendthrift hour
Shed balmy consciousness within that bower.
And I was free of haunts umbrageous ;
Could wander in the mazy forest-house
Of squirrels, foxes shy, and antler'd deer,
And birds from coverts innermost and drear
Warbling for very joy mellifluous sorrow—
To me new-born delights !

"Now let me borrow
For moments few, a temperament as stern
As Pluto's sceptre, that my words not burn
These uttering lips, while I in calm speech tell
How specious heaven was changed to real hell.

"One morn she left me sleeping : half awake
I sought for her smooth arms and lips, to slake
My greedy thirst with nectarous camel-draughts ;
But she was gone.   Whereat the barbed shafts
Of disappointment stuck in me so sore,
That out I ran and search'd the forest o'er.
Wandering about in pine and cedar gloom
Damp awe assail'd me, for there 'gan to boom
A sound of moan, an agony of sound
Sepulchral, from the distance all around.
Then came a conquering earth-thunder, and rumbled
That fierce complain to silence ; while I stumbled
Down a precipitous path, as if impell'd.
I came to a dark valley.   Groanings swell'd
Poisonous about my ears, and louder grew,
The nearer I approach'd a flame's gaunt blue,
That glared before me through a thorny brake.
This fire, like the eye of Gordian snake,
Bewitch'd me towards ; and I soon was near
A sight too fearful for the feel of fear :
In thicket hid I cursed the haggard scene—
The banquet of my arms, my arbour queen,
Seated upon an uptorn forest root ;
And all around her shapes, wizard and brute,
Laughing, and wailing, grovelling, serpenting,
Showing tooth, tusk, and venom-bag, and sting.
O such deformities ! old Charon's self,
Should he give up awhile his penny pelf,
And take a dream 'mong rushes Stygian,
It could not be so fantasied.   Fierce, wan,
And tyrannising was the lady's look,
As over them a gnarled staff she shook.
Oft-times upon the sudden she laugh'd out,
And from a basket emptied to the rout
Clusters of grapes, the which they raven'd quick
And roar'd for more ; with many a hungry lick

H

About their shaggy jaws.   Avenging, slow,
Anon she took a branch of mistletoe,
And emptied on't a black dull-gurgling phial :
Groan'd one and all, as if some piercing trial
Was sharpening for their pitiable bones.
She lifted up the charm : appealing groans
From their poor breasts went suing to her ear
In vain ; remorseless as an infant's bier
She whisk'd against their eyes the sooty oil,
Whereat was heard a noise of painful toil,
Increasing gradual to a tempest rage,
Shrieks, yells, and groans of torture pilgrimage ;
Until their grieved bodies 'gan to bloat
And puff from the tail's end to stifled throat :
Then was appalling silence : then a sight
More wildering than all that hoarse affright ;
For the whole herd, as by a whirlwind writhen,
Went through the dismal air like one huge Python
Antagonising Boreas,—and so vanish'd.
Yet there was not a breath of wind : she banish'd
These phantoms with a nod.   Lo ! from the dark
Came waggish fauns, and nymphs, and satyrs stark
With dancing and loud revelry,—and went
Swifter then centaurs after rapine bent.—
Sighing an elephant appear'd and bow'd
Before the fierce witch, speaking thus aloud
In human accent : ' Potent goddess ! chief
Of pains resistless ! make my being brief,
Or let me from this heavy prison fly :
Or give me to the air, or let me die !
I sue not for my happy crown again ;
I sue not for my phalanx on the plain ;
I sue not for my lone, my widow'd wife ;
I sue not for my ruddy drops of life,
My children fair, my lovely girls and boys !
I will forget them ; I will pass these joys ;
Ask nought so heavenward, so too—too high ,
Only I pray, as fairest boon, to die,
Or be deliver'd from this cumbrous flesh,
From this gross, detestable, filthy mesh,
And merely given to the cold bleak air.
Have mercy, Goddess ! Circe, feel my prayer !'

"That curst magician's name fell icy numb
Upon my wild conjecturing : truth had come
Naked and sabre-like against my heart.
I saw a fury whetting a death-dart ;
And my slain spirit, overwrought with fright,
Fainted away in that dark lair of night.
Think, my deliverer, how desolate
My waking must have been ! disgust and hate
And terrors manifold divided me
A spoil amongst them.   I prepared to flee
Into the dungeon core of that wild wood :
I fled three days—when lo ! before me stood
Glaring the angry witch.   O Dis, even now,
A clammy dew is beading on my brow,
At mere remembering her pale laugh, and curse.
'Ha ! ha ! Sir Dainty ! there must be a nurse
Made of rose-leaves and thistle-down, express,
To cradle thee, my sweet, and lull thee : yes,
I am too flinty-hard for thy nice touch :
My tenderest squeeze is but a giant's clutch.
So, fairy-thing, it shall have lullabies
Unheard of yet ; and it shall still its cries
Upon some breast more lily-feminine.
Oh, no—it shall not pine, and pine, and pine
More than one pretty, trifling thousand years ;
And then 'twere pity, but fate's gentle shears
Cut short its immortality.   Sea-flirt !
Young dove of the waters ! truly I'll not hurt
One hair of thine : see how I weep and sigh,
That our heart-broken parting is so nigh.
And must we part ?   Ah, yes, it must be so.
Yet ere thou leavest me in utter woe,
Let me sob over thee my last adieus,
And speak a blessing : Mark me ! thou hast thews
Immortal, for thou art of heavenly race :
But such a love is mine, that here I chase
Eternally away from thee all bloom
Of youth, and destine thee towards a tomb.
Hence shalt thou quickly to the watery vast ;
And there, ere many days be overpast,
Disabled age shall seize thee ; and even then
Thou shalt not go the way of aged men ;

But live and wither, cripple and still breathe
Ten hundred years : which gone, I then bequeath
Thy fragile bones to unknown burial.
Adieu, sweet love, adieu !'—As shot stars fall,
She fled ere I could groan for mercy.   Stung
And poison'd was my spirit : despair sung
A war-song of defiance 'gainst all hell.
A hand was at my shoulder to compel
My sullen steps ; another 'fore my eyes
Moved on with pointed finger.   In this guise
Enforced, at the last by ocean's foam
I found me ; by my fresh, my native home,
Its tempering coolness, to my life akin,
Came salutary as I waded in ;
And, with a blind voluptuous rage, I gave
Battle to the swollen billow-ridge, and drave
Large froth before me, while there yet remain'd
Hale strength, nor from my bones all marrow drain'd.

"Young lover, I must weep—such hellish spite
With dry cheek who can tell ?   Why thus my might
Proving upon this element, dismay'd,
Upon a dead thing's face my hand I laid ;
I look'd—'twas Scylla !   Cursed, cursed Circe !
O vulture-witch, hast never heard of mercy !
Could not thy harshest vengeance be content,
But thou must nip this tender innocent
Because I loved her ?—Cold, O cold indeed
Were her fair limbs, and like a common weed
The sea-swell took her hair.   Dead as she was
I clung about her waist, nor ceased to pass
Fleet as an arrow through unfathom'd brine,
Until there shone a fabric crystalline,
Ribb'd and inlaid with coral, pebble, and pearl.
Headlong I darted ; at one eager swirl
Gain'd its bright portal, enter'd, and behold !
'Twas vast, and desolate, and icy-cold ;
And all around—But wherefore this to thee
Who in few minutes more thyself shalt see ?—
I left poor Scylla in a niche and fled.
My fever'd parchings up, my scathing dread
Met palsy half way : soon these limbs became
Gaunt, wither'd, sapless, feeble, cramp'd, and lame.

"Now let me pass a cruel, cruel space,
Without one hope, without one faintest trace
Of mitigation, or redeeming bubble
Of colour'd phantasy ; for I fear 'twould trouble
Thy brain to loss of reason : and next tell
How a restoring chance came down to quell
One half of the witch in me.

                                "On a day,
Sitting upon a rock above the spray,
I saw grow up from the horizon's brink
A gallant vessel : soon she seem'd to sink
Away from me again, as though her course
Had been resumed in spite of hindering force—
So vanish'd : and not long, before arose
Dark clouds, and muttering of winds morose.
Old Æolus would stifle his mad spleen,
But could not, therefore, all the billows green
Toss'd up the silver spume against the clouds
The tempest came : I saw that vessel's shrouds
In perilous bustle ; while upon the deck
Stood trembling creatures.   I beheld the wreck ;
The final gulfing ; the poor struggling souls :
I heard their cries amid loud thunder-rolls.
O they had all been saved but crazed eld
Annull'd my vigorous cravings : and thus quell'd
And curb'd, think on't, O Latmian ! did I sit
Writhing with pity, and a cursing fit
Against that hell-born Circe.   The crew had gone,
By one and one, to pale oblivion ;
And I was gazing on the surges prone,
With many a scalding tear, and many a groan,
When at my feet emerged an old man's hand,
Grasping this scroll, and this same slender wand.
I knelt with pain—reach'd out my hand—had grasp'd
These treasures—touch'd the knuckles—they unclasp'd—
I caught a finger : but the downward weight
O'erpower'd me—it sank.   Then 'gan abate
The storm, and through chill aguish gloom outburst
The comfortable sun.   I was athirst
To search the book, and in the warming air
Parted its dripping leaves with eager care.

Strange matters did it treat of, and drew on
My soul page after page, till well-nigh won
Into forgetfulness ; when, stupefied,
I read these words, and read again, and tried
My eyes against the heavens, and read again.
O what a load of misery and pain
Each Atlas-line bore off !—a shine of hope
Came gold around me, cheering me to cope
Strenuous with hellish tyranny.   Attend !
For thou hast brought their promise to an end.

    " ' In the wide sea there lives a forlorn wretch,
Doom'd with enfeebled carcase to outstretch
His loathed existence through ten centuries,
And then to die alone.   Who can devise
A total opposition ?   No one.   So
One million times ocean must ebb and flow,
And he oppressed.   Yet he shall not die,
These things accomplish'd :—If he utterly
Scans all the depths of magic, and expounds
The meanings of all motions, shapes, and sounds ;
If he explores all forms and substances
Straight homeward to their symbol-essences ;
He shall not die.   Moreover, and in chief,
He must pursue this task of joy and grief
Most piously ;—all lovers tempest-tost,
And in the savage overwhelming lost,
He shall deposit side by side, until
Time's creeping shall the dreary space fulfil :
Which done, and all these labours ripened,
A youth, by heavenly power loved and led,
Shall stand before him ; whom he shall direct
How to consummate all.   The youth elect
Must do the thing, or both will be destroy'd. ' "

    " Then," cried the young Endymion, overjoy'd,
" We are twin brothers in this destiny !
Say, I entreat thee, what achievement high
Is, in this restless world, for me reserved.
What ! if from thee my wandering feet had swerved,
Had we both perish'd ? "—" Look ! " the sage replied,
" Dost thou not mark a gleaming through the tide,

Of divers brilliances? 'tis the edifice
I told thee of, where lovely Scylla lies;
And where I have enshrined piously
All lovers, whom fell storms have doom'd to die
Throughout my bondage." Thus discoursing, on
They went till unobscured the porches shone;
Which hurryingly they gain'd, and enter'd straight.
Sure never since king Neptune held his state
Was seen such wonder underneath the stars.
Turn to some level plain where haughty Mars
Has legion'd all his battle; and behold
How every soldier, with firm foot, doth hold
His even breast: see, many steeled squares,
And rigid ranks of iron—whence who dares
One step? Imagine further, line by line,
These warrior thousands on the field supine:—
So in that crystal place, in silent rows,
Poor lovers lay at rest from joys and woes,
The stranger from the mountains, breathless, traced
Such thousands of shut eyes in order placed;
Such ranges of white feet, and patient lips
All ruddy,—for here death no blossom nips.
He mark'd their brows and foreheads; saw their hair
Put sleekly on one side with nicest care;
And each one's gentle wrists, with reverence,
Put cross-wise to its heart.

          "Let us commence
(Whisper'd the guide, stuttering with joy) even now."
He spake, and, trembling like an aspen-bough,
Began to tear his scroll in pieces small,
Uttering the while some mumblings funeral.
He tore it into pieces small as snow
That drifts unfeather'd when bleak northerns blow;
And having done it, took his dark blue cloak
And bound it round Endymion: then struck
His wand against the empty air times nine.
"What more there is to do, young man, is thine:
But first a little patience; first undo
This tangled thread, and wind it to a clue.
Ah, gentle! 'tis as weak as spider's skein;
And shouldst thou break it—What, is it done so clean?

A power overshadows thee !   Oh, brave !
The spite of hell is tumbling to its grave.
Here is a shell ; 'tis pearly blank to me,
Nor mark'd with any sign or charactery—
Canst thou read aught ?   O read for pity's sake !
Olympus ! we are safe !   Now, Carian, break
This wand against yon lyre on the pedestal. "

   'Twas done : and straight with sudden swell and fall
Sweet music breathed her soul away, and sigh'd
A lullaby to silence.—" Youth ! now strew
These minced leaves on me, and passing through
Those files of dead, scatter the same around,
And thou wilt see the issue."—'Mid the sound
Of flutes and viols, ravishing his heart,
Endymion from Glaucus stood apart,
And scatter'd in his face some fragments light.
How lightning-swift the change ! a youthful wight
Smiling beneath a coral diadem,
Out-sparkling sudden like an upturn'd gem,
Appear'd, and, stepping to a beauteous corse,
Kneel'd down beside it, and with tenderest force
Press'd its cold hand, and wept—and Scylla sigh'd !
Endymion, with quick hand, the charm applied—
The nymph arose : he left them to their joy,
And onward went upon his high employ,
Showering those powerful fragments on the dead,
And, as he pass'd, each lifted up its head,
As doth a flower at Apollo's touch.
Death felt it to his inwards ; 'twas too much :
Death fell a-weeping in his charnel-house.
The Latmian persevered along, and thus
All were reanimated.   There arose
A noise of harmony, pulses and throes
Of gladness in the air—while many, who
Had died in mutual arms devout and true,
Sprang to each other madly ; and the rest
Felt a high certainty of being blest.
They gazed upon Endymion.   Enchantment
Grew drunken, and would have its head and bent.
Delicious symphonies, like airy flowers,
Budded, and swell'd, and, full-blown, shed full showers

Of light, soft, unseen leaves of sounds divine.
The two deliverers tasted a pure wine
Of happiness, from fairy press oozed out.
Speechless they eyed each other, and about
The fair assembly wander'd to and fro,
Distracted with the richest overflow
Of joy that ever pour'd from heaven.

                                        ——"Away!"
Shouted the new-born god; "Follow, and pay
Our piety to Neptunus supreme!"
Then Scylla, blushing sweetly from her dream,
They led on first, bent to her meek surprise,
Through portal columns of a giant size
Into the vaulted, boundless emerald.
Joyous all follow'd, as the leader call'd,
Down marble steps; pouring as easily
As hour-glass sand—and fast, as you might see
Swallows obeying the south summer's call,
Or swans upon a gentle waterfall.

Thus went that beautiful multitude, nor far,
Ere from among some rocks of glittering spar,
Just within ken, they saw descending thick
Another multitude. Whereat more quick
Moved either host. On a wide sand they met,
And of those numbers every eye was wet;
For each their old love found. A murmuring rose,
Like what was never heard in all the throes
Of wind and waters: 'tis past human wit
To tell; 'tis dizziness to think of it.

This mighty consummation made, the host
Moved on for many a league; and gain'd and lost
Huge sea-marks; vanward swelling in array,
And from the rear diminishing away,
Till a faint dawn surprised them. Glaucus cried,
"Behold! behold, the palace of his pride!
God Neptune's palaces!" With noise increased,
They shoulder'd on towards that brightening east,
At every onward step proud domes arose
In prospect, diamond gleams and golden glows
Of amber 'gainst their faces levelling.

Joyous, and many as the leaves in spring,
Still onward; still the splendour gradual swell'd.
Rich opal domes were seen, on high upheld
By jasper pillars, letting through their shafts
A blush of coral. Copious wonder-draughts
Each gazer drank; and deeper drank more near:
For what poor mortals fragment up, as mere
As marble was there lavish, to the vast
Of one fair palace, that far, far surpass'd,
Even for common bulk, those olden three,
Memphis, and Babylon, and Nineveh.

As large, as bright, as colour'd as the bow
Of Iris, when unfading it doth show
Beyond a silvery shower, was the arch
Through which this Paphian army took its march
Into the outer courts of Neptune's state:
Whence could be seen, direct, a golden gate,
To which the leaders sped; but not half raught
Ere it burst open swift as fairy thought,
And made those dazzled thousands veil their eyes
Like callow eagles at the first sunrise.
Soon with an eagle nativeness their gaze
Ripe from hue-golden swoons took all the blaze,
And then, behold! large Neptune on his throne
Of emerald deep: yet not exalt alone;
At his right hand stood winged Love, and on
His left sat smiling Beauty's paragon.

Far as the mariner on highest mast
Can see all round upon the calmed vast,
So wide was Neptune's hall: and as the blue
Doth vault the waters, so the waters drew
Their doming curtains, high, magnificent,
Awed from the throne aloof;—and when storm-rent
Disclosed the thunder-gloomings in Jove's air;
But soothed as now, flash'd sudden everywhere,
Noiseless, sub-marine cloudlets, glittering
Death to a human eye: for there did spring
From natural west, and east, and south, and north,
A light as of four sunsets, blazing forth
A gold-green zenith 'bove the Sea-God's head.
Of lucid depth the floor, and far outspread

As breezeless lake, on which the slim canoe
Of feather'd Indian darts about, as through
The delicatest air : air verily,
But for the portraiture of clouds and sky :
This palace floor breath-air,—but for the amaze
Of deep-seen wonders motionless,—and blaze
Of the dome pomp, reflected in extremes,
Globing a golden sphere.

                      They stood in dreams
Till Triton blew his horn. The palace rang;
The Nereids danced ; the Syrens faintly sang ;
And the great Sea-King bow'd his dripping head.
Then Love took wing, and from his pinions shed
On all the multitude a nectarous dew.
The ooze-born Goddess beckoned and drew
Fair Scylla and her guides to conference ;
And when they reach'd the throned eminence
She kiss'd the sea-nymph's cheek, who sat her down
A toying with the doves. Then, "Mighty crown
And sceptre of this kingdom !" Venus said,
"Thy vows were on a time to Nais paid :
Behold !"—Two copious tear-drops instant fell
From the God's large eyes ; he smiled delectable,
And over Glaucus held his blessing hands.—
"Endymion ! Ah ! still wandering in the bands
Of love ? Now this is cruel. Since the hour
I met thee in earth's bosom, all my power
Have I put forth to serve thee. What, not yet
Escaped from dull mortality's harsh net ?
A little patience, youth ! 'twill not be long,
Or I am skilless quite : an idle tongue,
A humid eye, and steps luxurious,
Where these are new and strange, are ominous.
Ay, I have seen these signs in one of heaven,
When others were all blind ; and were I given
To utter secrets, haply I might say
Some pleasant words : but Love will have his day
So wait awhile expectant. Pr'ythee soon,
Even in the passing of thine honey-moon,
Visit my Cytherea : thou wilt find
Cupid well-natured. my Adonis kind ;

And pray persuade with thee—Ah, I have done,
All blisses be upon thee, my sweet son!"—
Thus the fair Goddess: while Endymion
Knelt to receive those accents halcyon.

Meantime a glorious revelry began
Before the Water-Monarch.   Nectar ran
In courteous fountains to all cups outreach'd;
And plunder'd vines, teeming exhaustless, pleach'd
New growth about each shell and pendent lyre;
The which, in entangling for their fire,
Pull'd down fresh foliage and coverture
For dainty toy.   Cupid, empire-sure,
Flutter'd and laugh'd, and oft-times through the throng
Made a delighted way.   Then dance, and song,
And garlanding, grew wild; and pleasure reign'd.
In harmless tendril they each other chain'd,
And strove who should be smother'd deepest in
Fresh crush of leaves.

                                    O 'tis a very sin
For one so weak to venture his poor verse
In such a place as this.   O do not curse,
High Muses! let him hurry to the ending.

All suddenly were silent.   A soft blending
Of dulcet instruments came charmingly;
And then a hymn.

                              "King of the stormy sea!
Brother of Jove, and co-inheritor
Of elements!   Eternally before
Thee the waves awful bow.   Fast, stubborn rock,
At thy fear'd trident shrinking, doth unlock
Its deep foundations, hissing into foam.
All mountain-rivers lost, in the wide home
Of thy capacious bosom ever flow.
Thou frownest, and old Æolus thy foe
Skulks to his cavern, 'mid the gruff complaint
Of all his rebel tempests.   Dark clouds faint
When, from thy diadem, a silver gleam
Slants over blue dominion.   Thy bright team
Gulfs in the morning light, and scuds along
To bring thee nearer to that golden song

Apollo singeth, while his chariot
Waits at the doors of heaven.   Thou art not
For scenes like this : an empire stern hast thou ;
And it hath furrow'd that large front : yet now,
As newly come of heaven, dost thou sit
To blend and interknit
Subdued majesty with this glad time.
O shell-born King sublime !
We lay our hearts before thee evermore—
We sing, and we adore !

" Breathe softly, flutes,
Be tender of your strings, ye soothing lutes ;
Nor be the trumpet heard ! O vain, O vain !
Not flowers budding in an April rain,
Nor breath of sleeping dove, nor river's flow—
No, nor the Æolian twang of Love's own bow,
Can mingle music fit for the soft ear
Of goddess Cytherea !
Yet deign, white Queen of Beauty, thy fair eyes
On our souls' sacrifice.

" Bright-winged Child !
Who has another care when thou hast smiled ?
Unfortunates on earth, we see at last
All death-shadows, and glooms that overcast
Our spirits, fann'd away by thy light pinions.
O sweetest essence ! sweetest of all minions !
God of warm pulses, and dishevell'd hair,
And panting bosoms bare !
Dear unseen light in darkness ! eclipser
Of light in light ! delicious poisoner !
Thy venom'd goblet will we quaff until
We fill—we fill !
And by thy Mother's lips——"

Was heard no more
For clamour, when the golden palace-door
Open'd again, and from without, in shone
A new magnificence.   On oozy throne
Smooth-moving came Oceanus the old,
To take a latest glimpse at his sheep-fold,
Before he went into his quiet cave
To muse for ever—Then, a lucid wave,

Scoop'd from its trembling sisters of mid-sea,
Afloat, and pillowing up the majesty
Of Doris, and the Ægean seer, her spouse—
Next, on a dolphin, clad in laurel boughs,
Theban Amphion leaning on his lute.
His fingers went across it—All were mute
To gaze on Amphitrite, queen of pearls,
And Thetis pearly too.—

                  The palace whirls
Around giddy Endymion ; seeing he
Was there far strayed from mortality.
He could not bear it—shut his eyes in vain ;
Imagination gave a dizzier pain.
"O I shall die ! sweet Venus, be my stay !
Where is my lovely mistress ? Well away !
I die—I hear her voice—I feel my wing—"
At Neptune's feet he sank. A sudden ring
Of Nereids were about him, in kind strife
To usher back his spirit into life :
But still he slept. At last they interwove
Their cradling arms, and purposed to convey
Towards a crystal bower far away.

Lo ! while slow carried through the pitying crowd,
To his inward senses these words spake aloud ;
Written in star-light on the dark above :
"Dearest Endymion ! my entire love !
How have I dwelt in fear of fate ; 'tis done—
Immortal bliss for me too hast thou won.
Arise then ! for the hen-dove shall not hatch
Her ready eggs, before I'll kissing snatch
Thee into endless heaven. Awake ! awake !"

The youth at once arose : a placid lake
Came quiet to his eyes ; and forest green,
Cooler than all the wonder he had seen,
Lull'd with its simple song his fluttering breast.
How happy once again in grassy nest !

BOOK IV

MUSE of my native land! loftiest Muse!
O first-born on the mountains! By the hues
Of heaven on the spiritual air begot:
Long didst thou sit alone in northern grot,
While yet our England was a wolfish den;
Before our forests heard the talk of men;
Before the first of Druids was a child;—
Long didst thou sit amid our regions wild,
Rapt in a deep prophetic solitude.
There came an eastern voice of solemn mood:—
Yet wast thou patient. Then sang forth the Nine,
Apollo's garland:—yet didst thou divine
Such home-bred glory, that they cried in vain,
"Come hither, Sister of the Island!" Plain
Spake fair Ausonia; and once more she spake
A higher summons:—still didst thou betake
Thee to thy native hopes. O thou hast won
A full accomplishment! The thing is done,
Which undone, these our latter days had risen
On barren souls. Great Muse, thou know'st what prison
Of flesh and bone, curbs, and confines, and frets
Our spirits' wings: despondency besets
Our pillows; and the fresh to-morrow morn
Seems to give forth its light in very scorn
Of our dull, uninspired, snail-paced lives.
Long have I said, how happy he who shrives
To thee! But then I thought on poets gone,
And could not pray:—nor can I now—so on
I move to the end in lowliness of heart.—

   "Ah, woe is me! that I should fondly part
From my dear native land! Ah, foolish maid!
Glad was the hour, when, with thee, myriads bade
Adieu to Ganges and their pleasant fields!
To one so friendless the clear freshet yields
A bitter coolness; the ripe grape is sour:
Yet I would have, great Gods! but one short hour
Of native air—let me but die at home."

Endymion to heaven's airy dome
Was offering up a hecatomb of vows,
When these words reach'd him.   Whereupon he bows
His head through thorny-green entanglement
Of underwood, and to the sound is bent,
Anxious as hind towards her hidden fawn.

"Is no one near to help me?   No fair dawn
Of life from charitable voice?   No sweet saying
To set my dull and sadden'd spirit playing!
No hand to toy with mine?   No lips so sweet
That I may worship them?   No eyelids meet
To twinkle on my bosom?   No one dies
Before me, till from these enslaving eyes
Redemption sparkles!—I am sad and lost."

Thou, Carian lord, hadst better have been tost
Into a whirlpool.   Vanish into air,
Warm mountaineer! for canst thou only bear
A woman's sigh alone and in distress?
See not her charms!   Is Phœbe passionless?
Phœbe is fairer far—O gaze no more:—
Yet if thou wilt behold all beauty's store,
Behold her panting in the forest grass!
Do not those curls of glossy jet surpass
For tenderness the arms so idly lain
Amongst them?   Feelest not a kindred pain,
To see such lovely eyes in swimming search
After some warm delight, that seems to perch
Dovelike in the dim cell lying beyond
Their upper lids?—Hist!

                    "O for Hermes' wand,
To touch this flower into human shape!
That woodland Hyacinthus could escape
From his green prison, and here kneeling down
Call me his queen, his second life's fair crown!
Ah me, how I could love!—My soul doth melt
For the unhappy youth—Love! I have felt
So faint a kindness, such a meek surrender
To what my own full thoughts had made too tender,
That but for tears my life had fled away!—
Ye deaf and senseless minutes of the day,

And thou, old forest, hold ye this for true,
There is no lightning, no authentic dew
But in the eye of love : there's not a sound,
Melodious howsoever, can confound
The heavens and earth in one to such a death
As doth the voice of love : there's not a breath
Will mingle kindly with the meadow air,
Till it has panted round, and stolen a share
Of passion from the heart !"—

                          Upon a bough
He leant, wretched. He surely cannot now
Thirst for another love : O impious,
That he can even dream upon it thus!
Thought he, "Why am I not as are the dead,
Since to a woe like this I have been led
Through the dark earth, and through the wondrous sea?
Goddess ! I love thee not the less : from thee,
By Juno's smile, I turn not—no, no, no—
While the great waters are at ebb and flow,—
I have a triple soul ! O fond pretence—
For both, for both my love is so immense,
I feel my heart is cut in twain for them."

    And so he groan'd, as one by beauty slain.
The lady's heart beat quick, and he could see
Her gentle bosom heave tumultuously.
He sprang from his green covert : there she lay,
Sweet as a musk-rose upon new-made hay ;
With all her limbs on tremble, and her eyes
Shut softly up alive. To speak he tries :
"Fair damsel, pity me ! forgive that I
Thus violate thy bower's sanctity !
O pardon me, for I am full of grief—
Grief born of thee, young angel ! fairest thief !
Who stolen hast away the wings wherewith
I was to top the heavens. Dear maid, sith
Thou art my executioner, and I feel
Loving and hatred, misery and weal,
Will in a few short hours be nothing to me,
And all my story that much passion slew me ;
Do smile upon the evening of my days ;
And, for my tortured brain begins to craze,

Be thou my nurse ; and let me understand
How dying I shall kiss that lily hand.—
Dost weep for me ! Then should I be content.
Scowl on, ye fates ! until the firmament
Outblackens Erebus, and the full-cavern'd earth
Crumbles into itself. By the cloud-girth
Of Jove, those tears have given me a thirst
To meet oblivion."—As her heart would burst
The maiden sobb'd awhile, and then replied :
"Why must such desolation betide
As that thou speakest of ? Are not these green nooks
Empty of all misfortune ? Do the brooks
Utter a gorgon voice ? Does yonder thrush,
Schooling its half-fledged little ones to brush
About the dewy forest, whisper tales ?—
Speak not of grief, young stranger, or cold snails
Will slime the rose to-night. Though if thou wilt,
Methinks 'twould be a guilt—a very guilt—
Not to companion thee, and sigh away
The light—the dusk—the dark—till break of day !"
"Dear lady," said Endymion, "'tis past :
I love thee ! and my days can never last.
That I may pass in patience still speak :
Let me have music dying, and I seek
No more delight—I bid adieu to all.
Didst thou not after other climates call,
And murmur about Indian streams ? "—Then she,
Sitting beneath the midmost forest tree,
For pity sang this roundelay——

  "O Sorrow !
  Why dost borrow
The natural hue of health, from vermeil lips ?—
   To give maiden blushes
   To the white rose bushes ?
Or is it thy dewy hand the daisy tips ?

  "O Sorrow !
  Why dost borrow
The lustrous passion from a falcon-eye ?—
   To give the glow-worm light ?
   Or, on a moonless night,
To tinge, on syren shores, the salt sea-spry ?

        " O Sorrow!
        Why dost borrow
The mellow ditties from a mourning tongue?
        To give at evening pale
        Unto the nightingale,
That thou mayst listen the cold dews among?

        " O Sorrow!
        Why dost borrow
Heart's lightness from the merriment of May?
        A lover would not tread
        A cowslip on the head,
Though he should dance from eve till peep of day,
        Nor any drooping flower
        Held sacred for thy bower,
Wherever he may sport himself and play.

        " To Sorrow
        I bade good morrow,
And thought to leave her far away behind;
        But cheerly, cheerly,
        She loves me dearly;
She is so constant to me, and so kind:
        I would deceive her,
        And so leave her,
But ah! she is so constant and so kind.

" Beneath my palm-trees, by the river side,
I sat a-weeping: in the whole world wide
There was no one to ask me why I wept—
        And so I kept
Brimming the water-lily cups with tears
        Cold as my fears.

" Beneath my palm-trees, by the river side,
I sat a-weeping: what enamour'd bride,
Cheated by shadowy wooer from the clouds,
        But hides and shrouds
Beneath dark palm-trees by a river side?

" And as I sat, over the light blue hills
There came a noise of revellers: the rills
Into the wide stream came of purple hue—
        'Twas Bacchus and his crew!

The earnest trumpet spake, and silver thrills
From kissing cymbals made a merry din—
  'Twas Bacchus and his kin!
Like to a moving vintage down they came,
Crown'd with green leaves, and faces all on flame;
All madly dancing through the pleasant valley,
  To scare thee, Melancholy!
O then, O then, thou wast a simple name!
And I forgot thee, as the berried holly
By shepherds is forgotten, when in June,
Tall chestnuts keep away the sun and moon:—
  I rush'd into the folly!

"Within his car, aloft, young Bacchus stood,
Trifling his ivy-dart, in dancing mood,
  With sidelong laughing;
And little rills of crimson wine imbrued
His plump white arms, and shoulders, enough white,
  For Venus' pearly bite;
And near him rode Silenus on his ass,
Pelted with flowers as he on did pass
  Tipsily quaffing.

"Whence came ye, merry Damsels! whence came ye,
So many, and so many, and such glee?
Why have ye left your bowers desolate,
  Your lutes, and gentler fate?
'We follow Bacchus!   Bacchus on the wing,
  A-conquering!
Bacchus, young Bacchus! good or ill betide,
We dance before him thorough kingdoms wide:—
Come hither, lady fair, and joined be
  To our wild minstrelsy!'

"Whence came ye, jolly Satyrs! whence came ye,
So many, and so many, and such glee?
Why have ye left your forest haunts, why left
  Your nuts in oak-tree cleft?—
'For wine, for wine we left our kernel tree;
For wine we left our heath, and yellow brooms,
  And cold mushrooms;
For wine we follow Bacchus through the earth;

Great god of breathless cups and chirping mirth!
Come hither, lady fair, and joined be
To our mad minstrelsy!'

"Over wide streams and mountains great we went
And, save when Bacchus kept his ivy tent,
Onward the tiger and the leopard pants,
With Asian elephants:
Onward these myriads—with song and dance,
With zebras striped, and sleek Arabians' prance,
Web-footed alligators, crocodiles,
Bearing upon their scaly backs, in files,
Plump infant laughers mimicking the coil
Of seamen, and stout galley-rowers' toil:
With toying oars and silken sails they glide,
Nor care for wind and tide.

"Mounted on panthers' furs and lions' manes,
From rear to van they scour about the plains;
A three days' journey in a moment done;
And always, at the rising of the sun,
About the wilds they hunt with spear and horn,
On spleenful unicorn.

"I saw Osirian Egypt kneel adown
Before the vine-wreath crown!
I saw parch'd Abyssinia rouse and sing
To the silver cymbals' ring!
I saw the whelming vintage hotly pierce
Old Tartary the fierce!
The kings of Ind their jewel-sceptres vail,
And from their treasures scatter pearled hail;
Great Brahma from his mystic heaven groans,
And all his priesthood moans,
Before young Bacchus' eye-wink turning pale.
Into these regions came I, following him,
Sick-hearted, weary—so I took a whim
To stray away into these forests drear,
Alone, without a peer:
And I have told thee all thou mayest hear.

"Young stranger!
I've been a ranger
In search of pleasure throughout every clime;

Alas ! 'tis not for me :
Bewitch'd I sure must be,
To lose in grieving all my maiden prime.

"Come then, Sorrow,
Sweetest Sorrow !
Like an own babe I nurse thee on my breast :
I thought to leave thee,
And deceive thee,
But now of all the world I love thee best.

"There is not one,
No, no, not one
But thee to comfort a poor lonely maid ;
Thou art her mother,
And her brother,
Her playmate, and her wooer in the shade."

O what a sigh she gave in finishing,
And look, quite dead to every worldly thing !
Endymion could not speak, but gazed on her ;
And listen'd to the wind that now did stir
About the crisped oaks full drearily,
Yet with as sweet a softness as might be
Remember'd from its velvet summer song.
At last he said : "Poor lady ! how thus long
Have I been able to endure that voice ?
Fair Melody ! kind Syren ! I've no choice ;
I must be thy sad servant evermore :
I cannot choose but kneel here and adore.
Alas, I must not think—by Phœbe, no !
Let me not think, soft Angel ! shall it be so ?
Say, beautifullest shall I never think ?
O thou couldst foster me beyond the brink
Of recollection ! make my watchful care
Close up its bloodshot eyes, nor see despair !
Do gently murder half my soul, and I
Shall feel the other half so utterly :—
I'm giddy at that cheek so fair and smooth ;
O let it blush so ever : let it soothe
My madness ; let it mantle rosy-warm
With the tinge of love, panting in safe alarm.

This cannot be thy hand, and yet it is!
And this is sure thine other softling—this
Thine own fair bosom, and I am so near!
Wilt fall asleep? O let me sip that tear!
And whisper one sweet word that I may know
This is this world—sweet dewy blossom!"—WOE!
WOE! WOE TO THAT ENDYMION: WHERE IS HE?—
Even these words went echoing dismally
Through the wide forest—a most fearful tone,
Like one repenting in his latest moan;
And while it died away a shade pass'd by,
As of a thunder-cloud. When arrows fly
Through the thick branches, poor ring-doves sleek forth
Their timid necks and tremble; so these both
Leant to each other trembling, and sat so
Waiting for some destruction—when lo!
Foot-feather'd Mercury appeared sublime
Beyond the tall tree tops; and in less time
Than shoots the slanted hail-storm, down he dropp'd
Towards the ground; but rested not, nor stopp'd
One moment from his home: only the sward
He with his wand light touch'd, and heavenward
Swifter than sight was gone—even before
The teeming earth a sudden witness bore
Of his swift magic. Diving swans appear
Above the crystal circlings white and clear;
And catch the cheated eye in wild surprise,
How they can dive in sight and unseen rise—
So from the turf outsprang two steeds jet-black,
Each with large dark blue wings upon his back.
The youth of Caria placed the lovely dame
On one, and felt himself in spleen to tame
The other's fierceness. Through the air they flew,
High as the eagles. Like two drops of dew
Exhaled to Phœbus' lips, away they are gone,
Far from the earth away—unseen, alone,
Among cool clouds and winds, but that the free
The buoyant life of song can floating be
Above their heads, and follow them untired.
Muse of my native land! am I inspired?
This is the giddy air, and I must spread
Wide pinions to keep here; nor do I dread

Or height, or depth, or width, or any chance
Precipitous : I have beneath my glance
Those towering horses and their mournful freight.
Could I thus sail, and see, and thus await
Fearless for power of thought, without thine aid?
There is a sleepy dusk, an odorous shade
From some approaching wonder, and behold
Those winged steeds, with snorting nostrils bold
Snuff at its faint extreme, and seem to tire,
Dying to embers from their native fire !

    There curl'd a purple mist around them ; soon,
It seem'd as when around the pale new moon
Sad Zephyr droops the clouds like weeping willow :
'Twas Sleep slow journeying with head on pillow,
For the first time, since he came nigh dead-born
From the old womb of night, his cave forlorn
Had he left more forlorn ; for the first time,
He felt aloof the day and morning's prime—
Because into his depth Cimmerian
There came a dream, showing how a young man,
Ere a lean bat could plump its wintry skin,
Would at high Jove's empyreal footstool win
An immortality, and how espouse
Jove's daughter, and be reckon'd of his house.
Now was he slumbering towards heaven's gate,
That he might at the threshold one hour wait
To hear the marriage melodies, and then
Sink downward to his dusky cave again :
His litter of smooth semilucent mist,
Diversely tinged with rose and amethyst,
Puzzled those eyes that for the centre sought ;
And scarcely for one moment could be caught
His sluggish form reposing motionless.
Those two on winged steeds, with all the stress
Of vision search'd for him, as one would look
Athwart the sallows of a river nook
To catch a glance at silver-throated eels,—
Or from old Skiddaw's top, when fog conceals
His rugged forehead in a mantle pale,
With an eye-guess towards some pleasant vale,
Descry a favourite hamlet faint and far.

These raven horses, though they foster'd are
Of earth's splenetic fire, dully drop
Their full-vein'd ears, nostrils blood wide, and stop;
Upon the spiritless mist have they outspread
Their ample feathers, are in slumber dead,—
And on those pinions, level in mid-air
Endymion sleepeth and the lady fair.
Slowly they sail, slowly as icy isle
Upon a calm sea drifting: and meanwhile
The mournful wanderer dreams.   Behold! he walks
On heaven's pavement, brotherly he talks
To divine powers: from his hand full fain
Juno's proud birds are pecking pearly grain:
He tries the nerve of Phœbus' golden bow,
And asketh where the golden apples grow:
Upon his arm he braces Pallas' shield,
And strives in vain to unsettle and wield
A Jovian thunderbolt: arch Hebe brings
A full-brimm'd goblet, dances lightly, sings
And tantalises long; at last he drinks,
And lost in pleasure, at her feet he sinks,
Touching with dazzled lips her star-light hand;
He blows a bugle,—an ethereal band
Are visible above: the Seasons four,—
Green-kirtled Spring, flush Summer, golden store
In Autumn's sickle, Winter frosty hoar,
Join dance with shadowy Hours; while still the blast,
In swells unmitigated, still doth last
To sway their floating morris.   " Whose is this ?
Whose bugle ? " he inquires : they smile—" O Dis !
Why is this mortal here ?   Dost thou not know
Its mistress' lips ?   Not thou ?—'Tis Dian's : lo !
She rises crescented ! "   He looks, 'tis she,
His very goddess : good-bye earth, and sea,
And air, and pains, and care, and suffering ;
Good-bye to all but love !   Then doth he spring
Towards her, and awakes—and, strange, o'erhead,
Of those same fragrant exhalations bred,
Beheld awake his very dream : the gods
Stood smiling ; merry Hebe laughs and nods ;
And Phœbe bends towards him crescented.
O state perplexing !   On the pinion bed,

Too well awake, he feels the panting side
Of his delicious lady.   He who died
For soaring too audacious in the sun,
Where that same treacherous wax began to run,
Felt not more tongue-tied than Endymion.
His heart leapt up as to its rightful throne,
To that fair-shadow'd passion pulsed its way—
Ah, what perplexity ! Ah, well a-day !
So fond, so beauteous was his bed-fellow,
He could not help but kiss her : then he grew
Awhile forgetful of all beauty save
Young Phœbe's, golden-hair'd ; and so 'gan crave
Forgiveness : yet he turn'd once more to look
At the sweet sleeper,—all his soul was shook,—
She press'd his hand in slumber ; so once more
He could not help but kiss her and adore.
At this the shadow wept, melting away.
The Latmian started up : "Bright goddess, stay !
Search my most hidden breast !   By truth's own tongue
I have no dædale heart ; why is it wrung
To desperation ?   Is there nought for me
Upon the bourne of bliss, but misery ? "

     These words awoke the stranger of dark tresses :
Her dawning love-look rapt Endymion blesses
With 'haviour soft.   Sleep yawn'd from underneath.
"Thou swan of Ganges, let us no more breathe
This murky phantasm ! thou contented seem'st,
Pillow'd in lovely idleness, nor dream'st
What horrors may discomfort thee and me.
Ah, shouldst thou die from my heart-treachery !—
Yet did she merely weep—her gentle soul
Hath no revenge in it ; as it is whole
In tenderness, would I were whole in love !
Can I prize thee, fair maid, all price above,
Even when I feel as true as innocence !
I do, I do.—What is this soul then ?   Whence
Came it ?   It does not seem my own, and I
Have no self-passion or identity.
Some fearful end must be ; where, where is it ?
By Nemesis ! I see my spirit flit
Alone about the dark—Forgive me, sweet !

Shall we away?" He roused the steeds; they beat
Their wings chivalrous into the clear air,
Leaving old Sleep within his vapoury lair.

The good-night blush of eve was waning slow,
And Vesper, risen star, began to throe
In the dusk heavens silvery, when they
Thus sprang direct towards the Galaxy.
Nor did speed hinder converse soft and strange—
Eternal oaths and vows they interchange,
In such wise, in such temper, so aloof
Up in the winds, beneath a starry roof,
So witless of their doom, that verily
'Tis well nigh past man's search their hearts to see;
Whether they wept, or laugh'd or grieved, or toy'd—
Most like with joy gone mad, with sorrow cloy'd.

Full facing their swift flight, from ebon streak,
The moon put forth a little diamond peak,
No bigger than an unobserved star,
Or tiny point of fairy scimetar;
Bright signal that she only stoop'd to tie
Her silver sandals, ere deliciously
She bow'd into the heavens her timid head.
Slowly she rose, as though she would have fled,
While to his lady meek the Carian turn'd,
To mark if her dark eyes had yet discern'd
This beauty in its birth—Despair! despair!
He saw her body fading gaunt and spare
In the cold moonshine. Straight he seized her wrist;
It melted from his grasp; her hand he kiss'd,
And, horror! kiss'd his own—he was alone.
Her steed a little higher soar'd, and then
Dropt hawk-wise to the earth.

There lies a den,
Beyond the seeming confines of the space
Made for the soul to wander in and trace
Its own existence, of remotest glooms.
Dark regions are around it, where the tombs
Of buried griefs the spirit sees, but scarce
One hour doth linger weeping, for the pierce

Of new-born woe it feels more inly smart;
And in these regions many a venom'd dart
At random flies; they are the proper home
Of every ill: the man is yet to come
Who hath not journey'd in this native hell.
But few have ever felt how calm and well
Sleep may be had in that deep den of all.
There anguish does not sting, nor pleasure pall;
Woe-hurricanes beat ever at the gate.
Yet all is still within and desolate.
Beset with painful gusts, within ye hear
No sound so loud as when on curtain'd bier
The death-watch tick is stifled.   Enter none
Who strive therefore; on the sudden it is won.
Just when the sufferer begins to burn,
Then it is free to him; and from an urn,
Still fed by melting ice, he takes a draught—
Young Semele such richness never quaff'd
In her maternal longing.   Happy gloom!
Dark Paradise! where pale becomes the bloom
Of health by due; where silence dreariest
Is most articulate; where hopes infest;
Where those eyes are the brightest far that keep
Their lids shut longest in a dreamless sleep.
O happy spirit-home!   O wondrous soul!
Pregnant with such a den to save the whole
In thine own depth.   Hail, gentle Carian!
For, never since thy griefs and woes began,
Hast thou felt so content: a grievous feud
Hath led thee to this Cave of Quietude.
Ay, his lull'd soul was there, although upborne
With dangerous speed: and so he did not mourn
Because he knew not whither he was going.
So happy was he, not the aerial blowing
Of trumpets at clear parley from the east
Could rouse from that fine relish, that high feast.
They stung the feather'd horse; with fierce alarm
He flapped towards the sound.   Alas! no charm
Could lift Endymion's head, or he had view'd
A skyey mask, a pinion'd multitude,—
And silvery was its passing: voices sweet
Warbling the while as if to lull and greet

The wanderer in his path. Thus warbled they,
While past the vision went in bright array.

"Who, who from Dian's feast would be away?
For all the golden bowers of the day
Are empty left? Who, who away would be
From Cynthia's wedding and festivity?
Not Hesperus: lo! upon his silver wings
He leans away for highest heaven and sings,
Snapping his lucid fingers merrily!—
Ah, Zephyrus! art here, and Flora too?
Ye tender bibbers of the rain and dew,
Young playmates of the rose and daffodil,
Be careful, ere ye enter in, to fill
      Your baskets high
With fennel green, and balm, and golden pines,
Savoury, latter-mint, and columbines,
Cool parsley, basil sweet, and sunny thyme;
Yea, every flower and leaf of every clime,
All gather'd in the dewy morning: hie
      Away! fly, fly!—
Crystalline brother of the belt of heaven,
Aquarius! to whom king Jove has given
Two liquid pulse streams 'stead of feather'd wings,
Two fanlike fountains,—thine illuminings
      For Dian play:
Dissolve the frozen purity of air;
Let thy white shoulders silvery and bare
Show cold through watery pinions; make more bright
The Star-Queen's crescent on her marriage night:
      Haste, haste away!
Castor has tamed the planet Lion, see!
And of the Bear has Pollux mastery:
A third is in the race! who is the third,
Speeding away swift as the eagle bird?
      The ramping Centaur!
The Lion's mane's on end: the Bear how fierce!
The Centaur's arrow ready seems to pierce
Some enemy: far forth his bow is bent
Into the blue of heaven. He'll be shent,
      Pale unrelentor,
When he shall hear the wedding lutes a-playing.—

Andromeda! sweet woman! why delaying
So timidly among the stars: come hither!
Join this bright throng, and nimbly follow whither
   They all are going.
Danae's Son, before Jove newly bow'd,
Has wept for thee, calling to Jove aloud.
Thee, gentle lady, did he disenthral:
Ye shall for ever live and love, for all
   Thy tears are flowing.—
By Daphne's fright, behold Apollo!"—

         More
Endymion heard not: down his steed him bore
Prone to the green head of a misty hill.

 His first touch of the earth went nigh to kill.
"Alas!" said he, "were I but always borne
Through dangerous winds, had but my footsteps worn
A path in hell, for ever would I bless
Horrors which nourish an uneasiness
For my own sullen conquering: to him
Who lives beyond earth's boundary, grief is dim,
Sorrow is but a shadow: now I see
The grass; I feel the solid ground—Ah, me!
It is thy voice—divinest! Where?—who? who
Left thee so quiet on this bed of dew?
Behold upon this happy earth we are;
Let us aye love each other; let us fare
On forest-fruits, and never, never go
Among the abodes of mortals here below,
Or be by phantoms duped. O destiny!
Into a labyrinth now my soul would fly,
But with thy beauty will I deaden it.
Where didst thou melt to? By thee will I sit
For ever: let our fate stop here—a kid
I on this spot will offer: Pan will bid
Us live in peace, in love and peace among
His forest wildernesses. I have clung
To nothing, loved a nothing, nothing seen
Or felt but a great dream! Oh, I have been
Presumptuous against love, against the sky,
Against all elements, against the tie
Of mortals each to each, against the blooms

Of flowers, rush of rivers, and the tombs
Of heroes gone! Against his proper glory
Has my own soul conspired: so my story
Will I to children utter, and repent.
There never lived a mortal man, who bent
His appetite beyond his natural sphere,
But starved and died. My sweetest Indian, here,
Here will I kneel, for thou redeemed hast
My life from too thin breathing: gone and past
Are cloudy phantasms. Caverns lone, farewell!
And air of visions, and the monstrous swell
Of visionary seas! No, never more
Shall airy voices cheat me to the shore
Of tangled wonder, breathless and aghast.
Adieu, my daintiest Dream! although so vast
My love is still for thee. The hour may come
When we shall meet in pure elysium.
On earth I may not love thee, and therefore
Doves will I offer up, and sweetest store
All through the teeming year: so thou wilt shine
On me, and on this damsel fair of mine,
And bless our simple lives. My Indian bliss!
My river-lily bud! one human kiss!
One sigh of real breath—one gentle squeeze,
Warm as a dove's nest among summer trees,
And warm with dew at ooze from living blood!
Whither didst melt? Ah, what of that!—all good
We'll talk about—no more of dreaming.—Now,
Where shall our dwelling be? Under the brow
Of some steep mossy hill, where ivy dun
Would hide us up, although spring leaves were none;
And where dark yew-trees, as we rustle through,
Will drop their scarlet-berry cups of dew!
O thou wouldst joy to live in such a place!
Dusk for our loves, yet light enough to grace
Those gentle limbs on mossy bed reclined:
For by one step the blue sky shouldst thou find,
And by another, in deep dell below,
See, through the trees, a little river go
All in its mid-way gold and glimmering.
Honey from out the gnarled hive I'll bring,
And apples, wan with sweetness, gather thee,—

Cresses that grow where no man may them see,
And sorrel untorn by the dew-claw'd stag:
Pipes will I fashion of the syrinx flag,
That thou mayst always know whither I roam,
When it shall please thee in our quiet home
To listen and think of love.   Still let me speak;
Still let me dive into the joy I seek,—
For yet the past doth prison me.   The rill,
Thou haply mayst delight in, will I fill
With fairy fishes from the mountain tarn,
And thou shalt feed them from the squirrel's barn.
Its bottom will I strew with amber shells,
And pebbles blue from deep enchanted wells.
Its sides I'll plant with dew-sweet eglantine,
And honeysuckles full of clear bee-wine.
I will entice this crystal rill to trace
Love's silver name upon the meadow's face.
I'll kneel to Vesta, for a flame of fire;
And to god Phœbus, for a golden lyre;
To Empress Dian, for a hunting-spear,
To Vesper, for a taper silver-clear,
That I may see thy beauty through the night;
To Flora, and a nightingale shall light
Tame on thy finger; to the River-gods,
And they shall bring thee taper fishing-rods
Of gold, and lines of naiads' long bright tress.
Heaven shield thee for thine utter loveliness!
Thy mossy footstool shall the altar be
'Fore which I'll bend, bending, dear love, to thee:
Those lips shall be my Delphos, and shall speak
Laws to my footsteps, colour to my cheek,
Trembling or steadfastness to this same voice,
And of three sweetest pleasurings the choice:
And that affectionate light, those diamond things,
Those eyes, those passions, those supreme pearl springs,
Shall be my grief, or twinkle me to pleasure.
Say, is not bliss within our perfect seizure?
O that I could not doubt!"

The mountaineer
Thus strove by fancies vain and crude to clear
His brier'd path to some tranquillity.

It gave bright gladness to his lady's eye,
And yet the tears she wept were tears of sorrow;
Answering thus, just as the golden morrow
Beam'd upward from the valleys of the east:
"O that the flutter of his heart had ceased,
Or the sweet name of love had pass'd away!
Young feather'd tyrant! by a swift decay
Wilt thou devote this body to the earth:
And I do think that at my very birth
I lisp'd thy blooming titles inwardly;
For at the first, first dawn and thought of thee,
With uplift hands I bless'd the stars of heaven.
Art thou not cruel? ever have I striven
To think thee kind, but ah, it will not do!
When yet a child, I heard that kisses drew
Favour from thee, and so I kisses gave
To the void air, bidding them find out love:
But when I came to feel how far above
All fancy, pride, and fickle maidenhood,
All earthly pleasure, all imagined good,
Was the warm tremble of a devout kiss,—
Even then that moment, at the thought of this,
Fainting I fell into a bed of flowers,
And languish'd there three days.   Ye milder powers,
Am I not cruelly wrong'd?   Believe, believe
Me, dear Endymion, were I to weave
With my own fancies garlands of sweet life,
Thou shouldst be one of all.   Ah, bitter strife!
I may not be thy love: I am forbidden—
Indeed I am—thwarted, affrighted, chidden,
By things I trembled at, and gorgon wrath.
Twice hast thou ask'd whither I went: henceforth
Ask me no more! I may not utter it,
Nor may I be thy love.   We might commit
Ourselves at once to vengeance; we might die;
We might embrace and die: voluptuous thought!
Enlarge not to my hunger, or I'm caught
In trammels of perverse deliciousness.
No, no, that shall not be: thee will I bless,
And bid a long adieu."

The Carian

No word return'd: both lovelorn, silent, wan,
I

Into the valleys green together went.
Far wandering, they were perforce content
To sit beneath a fair lone beechen tree;
Nor at each other gazed, but heavily
Pored on its hazel cirque of shedded leaves.

Endymion! unhappy! it nigh grieves
Me to behold thee thus in last extreme:
Enskied ere this, but truly that I deem
Truth the best music in a first-born song.
Thy lute-voiced brother will I sing ere long,
And thou shalt aid—hast thou not aided me?
Yes, moonlight Emperor! felicity
Has been thy meed for many thousand years;
Yet often have I, on the brink of tears,
Mourn'd as if yet thou wert a forester;—
Forgetting the old tale.

He did not stir
His eyes from the dead leaves, or one small pulse
Of joy he might have felt. The spirit culls
Unfaded amaranth, when wild it strays
Through the old garden-ground of boyish days
A little onward ran the very stream
By which he took his first soft poppy dream;
And on the very bark 'gainst which he leant
A crescent he had carved, and round it spent
His skill in little stars. The teeming tree
Had swoll'n and green'd the pious charactery,
But not ta'en out. Why, there was not a slope
Up which he had not fear'd the antelope;
And not a tree, beneath whose rooty shade
He had not with his tamed leopards play'd;
Nor could an arrow light, or javelin,
Fly in the air where his had never been—
And yet he knew it not.

O treachery!
Why does his lady smile, pleasing her eye
With all his sorrowing? He sees her not.
But who so stares on him? His sister sure!
Peona of the woods!—Can she endure?—

Impossible—how dearly they embrace!
His lady smiles; delight is in her face;
It is no treachery.

     "Dear brother mine!
Endymion, weep not so! Why shouldst thou pine
When all great Latmos so exalt will be?
Thank the great gods, and look not bitterly;
And speak not one pale word, and sigh no more.
Sure I will not believe thou hast such store
Of grief, to last thee to my kiss again.
Thou surely canst not bear a mind in pain,
Come hand in hand with one so beautiful.
Be happy both of you! for I will pull
The flowers of autumn for your coronals.
Pan's holy priest for young Endymion calls;
And when he is restored, thou, fairest dame,
Shalt be our queen. Now, is it not a shame
To see ye thus,—not very, very sad?
Perhaps ye are too happy to be glad:
O feel as if it were a common day;
Free-voiced as one who never was away.
No tongue shall ask, whence come ye? but ye shall
Be gods of your own rest imperial.
Not even I, for one whole month, will pry
Into the hours that have pass'd us by,
Since in my arbour I did sing to thee.
O Hermes! on this very night will be
A hymning up to Cynthia, queen of light;
For the soothsayers old saw yesternight
Good visions in the air,—whence will befal,
As say these sages, health perpetual
To shepherds and their flocks; and furthermore
In Dian's face they read the gentle lore:
Therefore for her these vesper-carols are.
Our friends will all be there from nigh and far.
Many upon thy death have ditties made;
And many, even now, their foreheads shade
With cypress, on a day of sacrifice.
New singing for our maids shalt thou devise,
And pluck the sorrow from our huntsmen's brows.
Tell me, my lady-queen, how to espouse

This wayward brother to his rightful joys!
His eyes are on thee bent, as thou didst poise
His fate most goddess-like.　Help me, I pray,
To lure—Endymion, dear brother, say
What ails thee?"　He could bear no more, and so
Bent his soul fiercely like a spiritual bow,
And twang'd it inwardly, and calmly said:
"I would have thee my only friend, sweet maid!
My only visitor! not ignorant though,
That those deceptions which for pleasure go
'Mong men, are pleasures real as real may be:
But there are higher ones I may not see,
If impiously an earthly realm I take.
Since I saw thee, I have been wide awake
Night after night, and day by day, until
Of the empyrean I have drunk my fill.
Let it content thee, Sister, seeing me
More happy than betides mortality.
A hermit young, I'll live in mossy cave,
Where thou alone shalt come to me, and lave
Thy spirit in the wonders I shall tell.
Through me the shepherd realm shall prosper well;
For to thy tongue will I all health confide.
And for my sake, let this young maid abide
With thee as a dear sister.　Thou alone,
Peona, mayst return to me.　I own
This may sound strangely: but when, dearest girl,
Thou seest it for my happiness, no pearl
Will trespass down those cheeks.　Companion fair!
Wilt be content to dwell with her, to share
This sister's love with me?"　Like one resign'd
And bent by circumstances, and thereby blind
In self-commitment, thus, that meek unknown:
"Ay, but a buzzing by my ears has flown,
Of jubilee to Dian:—truth I heard!
Well then, I see there is no little bird,
Tender soever, but is Jove's own care.
Long have I sought for rest, and unaware,
Behold I find it! so exalted too!
So after my own heart! I knew, I knew
There was a place untenanted in it;
In that same void white Chastity shall sit,

And monitor me nightly to lone slumber.
With sanest lips I vow me to the number
Of Dian's sisterhood ; and, kind lady,
With thy good help, this very night shall see
My future days to her fane consecrate."

As feels a dreamer what doth most create
His own particular fright, so these three felt.
Or like one who, in after ages, knelt
To Lucifer or Baal, when he'd pine
After a little sleep : or when in mine
Far under-ground, a sleeper meets his friends
Who know him not.   Each diligently bends
Towards common thoughts and things for very fear ;
Striving their ghastly malady to cheer,
By thinking it a thing of yes and no,
That housewives talk of.   But the spirit-blow
Was struck, and all were dreamers.   At the last
Endymion said : "Are not our fates all cast ?
Why stand we here ?   Adieu, ye tender pair !
Adieu !"   Whereat those maidens, with wild stare,
Walk'd dizzily away.   Pained and hot
His eyes went after them, until they got
Near to a cypress grove, whose deadly maw,
In one swift moment, would what then he saw
Engulf for ever.   "Stay !" he cried, "ah, stay !
Turn, damsels ! hist ! one word I have to say :
Sweet Indian, I would see thee once again.
It is a thing I dote on : so I'd fain,
Peona, ye should hand in hand repair
Into those holy groves that silent are
Behind great Dian's temple.   I'll be yon,
At vesper's earliest twinkle—they are gone—
But once, once, once again—" At this he prest
His hands against his face, and then did rest
His head upon a mossy hillock green,
And so remain'd as he a corpse had been
All the long day ; save when he scantily lifted
His eyes abroad, to see how shadows shifted
With the slow move of time,—sluggish and weary
Until the poplar tops, in journey dreary,
Had reach'd the river's brim.   Then up he rose,

And, slowly as that very river flows,
Walk'd towards the temple-grove with this lament:
"Why such a golden eve? The breeze is sent
Careful and soft, that not a leaf may fall
Before the serene father of them all
Bows down his summer head below the west.
Now am I of breath, speech, and speed possest,
But at the setting I must bid adieu
To her for the last time. Night will strew
On the damp grass myriads of lingering leaves,
And with them shall I die; nor much it grieves
To die, when summer dies on the cold sward.
Why, I have been a butterfly, a lord
Of flowers, garlands, love-knots, silly posies,
Groves, meadows, melodies, and arbour-roses;
My kingdom's at its death, and just it is
That I should die with it: so in all this
We miscal grief, bale, sorrow, heart-break, woe,
What is there to plain of? By Titan's foe
I am but rightly served." So saying, he
Tripp'd lightly on, in sort of deathful glee;
Laughing at the clear stream and setting sun,
As though they jests had been: nor had he done
His laugh at nature's holy countenance,
Until that grove appear'd, as if perchance,
And then his tongue with sober seemlihed
Gave utterance as he enter'd: "Ha!" he said,
"King of the butterflies; but by this gloom,
And by old Rhadamanthus' tongue of doom,
This dusk religion, pomp of solitude,
And the Promethean clay by thief endued,
By old Saturnus' forelock, by his head
Shook with eternal palsy, I did wed
Myself to things of light from infancy;
And thus to be cast out, thus lorn to die,
Is sure enough to make a mortal man
Grow impious." So he inwardly began
On things for which no wording can be found
Deeper and deeper sinking, until drown'd
Beyond the reach of music: for the choir
Of Cynthia he heard not, though rough brier
Nor muffling thicket interposed to dull

The vesper hymn, far swollen, soft and full,
Through the dark pillars of those sylvan aisles.
He saw not the two maidens, nor their smiles,
Wan as primroses gather'd at midnight
By chilly-finger'd spring.   Unhappy wight!
"Endymion!" said Peona, "we are here!
What wouldst thou ere we all are laid on bier?"
Then he embraced her, and his lady's hand
Press'd, saying: "Sister, I would have command,
If it were heaven's will, on our sad fate."
At which that dark-eyed stranger stood elate
And said, in a new voice, but sweet as love,
To Endymion's amaze: "By Cupid's dove,
And so thou shalt! and by the lily truth
Of my own breast thou shalt, beloved youth!"
And as she spake, into her face there came,
Light, as reflected from a silver flame:
Her long black hair swell'd ampler, in display
Full golden; in her eyes a brighter day
Dawn'd blue, and full of love.   Ay, he beheld
Phœbe, his passion! joyous she upheld
Her lucid bow, continuing thus: "Drear, drear
Has our delaying been; but foolish fear
Withheld me first; and then decrees of fate:
And then 'twas fit that from this mortal state
Thou shouldst, my love, by some unlook'd-for change
Be spiritualised.   Peona, we shall range
These forests, and to thee they safe shall be
As was thy cradle; hither shalt thou flee
To meet us many a time."   Next Cynthia bright
Peona kiss'd, and bless'd with fair good night:
Her brother kiss'd her too, and knelt adown
Before his goddess, in a blissful swoon.
She gave her fair hands to him, and behold,
Before three swiftest kisses he had told,
They vanish'd far away!—Peona went
Home through the gloomy wood in wonderment.

HYPERION

BOOK I

DEEP in the shady sadness of a vale
Far sunken from the healthy breath of morn,
Far from the fiery noon, and eve's one star,
Sat grey-hair'd Saturn, quiet as a stone,
Still as the silence round about his lair;
Forest on forest hung about his head
Like cloud on cloud.   No stir of air was there,
Not so much life as on a summer's day
Robs not one light seed from the feather'd grass,
But where the dead leaf fell, there did it rest.
A stream went voiceless by, still deadened more
By reason of his fallen divinity,
Spreading a shade : the Naiad 'mid her reeds
Press'd her cold finger closer to her lips.

Along the margin-sand large foot-marks went,
No further than to where his feet had stray'd,
And slept there since.   Upon the sodden ground
His old right hand lay nerveless, listless, dead,
Unsceptred; and his realmless eyes were closed;
While his bow'd head seem'd list'ning to the Earth,
His ancient mother, for some comfort yet.

It seem'd no force could wake him from his place;
But there came one, who with a kindred hand
Touch'd his wide shoulders, after bending low
With reverence, though to one who knew it not.
She was a Goddess of the infant world;
By her in stature the tall Amazon
Had stood a pigmy's height : she would have ta'en
Achilles by the hair and bent his neck;

Or with a finger stay'd Ixion's wheel.
Her face was large as that of Memphian sphinx,
Pedestal'd haply in a palace-court,
When sages look'd to Egypt for their lore.
But oh! how unlike marble was that face:
How beautiful, if sorrow had not made
Sorrow more beautiful than Beauty's self.
There was a listening fear in her regard,
As if calamity had but begun;
As if the vanward clouds of evil days
Had spent their malice, and the sullen rear
Was with its stored thunder labouring up.
One hand she press'd upon that aching spot
Where beats the human heart, as if just there,
Though an immortal, she felt cruel pain:
The other upon Saturn's bended neck
She laid, and to the level of his ear
Leaning with parted lips, some words she spake
In solemn tenour and deep organ tone:
Some mourning words, which in our feeble tongue
Would come in these like accents; O how frail
To that large utterance of the early Gods!
"Saturn, look up!—though wherefore, poor old King?
I have no comfort for thee, no not one:
I cannot say, "O wherefore sleepest thou?"
For heaven is parted from thee, and the earth
Knows thee not, thus afflicted, for a God;
And ocean too, with all its solemn noise,
Has from thy sceptre pass'd; and all the air
Is emptied of thine hoary majesty.
Thy thunder, conscious of the new command,
Rumbles reluctant o'er our fallen house;
And thy sharp lightning in unpractised hands
Scorches and burns our once serene domain.
O aching time! O moments big as years!
All as ye pass swell out the monstrous truth,
And press it so upon our weary griefs
That unbelief has not a space to breathe.
Saturn, sleep on:—O thoughtless, why did I
Thus violate thy slumbrous solitude?
Why should I ope thy melancholy eyes?
Saturn, sleep on! while at thy feet I weep."

As when, upon a tranced summer-night,
Those green-robed senators of mighty woods,
Tall oaks, branch-charmed by the earnest stars,
Dream, and so dream all night without a stir,
Save from one gradual solitary gust
Which comes upon the silence, and dies off,
As if the ebbing air had but one wave :
So came these words and went ; the while in tears
She touch'd her fair large forehead to the ground,
Just where her falling hair might be outspread
A soft and silken mat for Saturn's feet.
One moon, with alternations slow, had shed
Her silver seasons four upon the night,
And still these two were postured motionless,
Like natural sculpture in cathedral cavern ;
The frozen God still couchant on the earth,
And the sad Goddess weeping at his feet :
Until at length old Saturn lifted up
His faded eyes, and saw his kingdom gone,
And all the gloom and sorrow of the place,
And that fair kneeling Goddess ; and then spake
As with a palsied tongue, and while his beard
Shook horrid with such aspen malady :
" O tender spouse of gold Hyperion,
Thea, I feel thee ere I see thy face ;
Look up, and let me see our doom in it ;
Look up, and tell me, if this feeble shape
Is Saturn's ; tell me, if thou hear'st the voice
Of Saturn ; tell me, if this wrinkling brow,
Naked and bare of its great diadem,
Peers like the front of Saturn ?   Who had power
To make me desolate ? whence came the strength ?
How was it nurtured to such bursting forth,
While Fate seem'd strangled in my nervous grasp ?
But it is so ; and I am smother'd up,
And buried from all godlike exercise
Of influence benign on planets pale,
Of admonitions to the winds and seas,
Of peaceful sway above man's harvesting,
And all those acts which Deity supreme
Doth ease its heart of love in.   I am gone
Away from my own bosom : I have left

My strong identity, my real self,
Somewhere between the throne, and where I sit
Here on this spot of earth. Search, Thea, search,
Open thine eyes eterne, and sphere them round
Upon all space : space starr'd, and lorn of light,
Space region'd with life-air, and barren void,
Spaces of fire, and all the yawn of hell.
Search, Thea, search ! and tell me if thou seest
A certain shape or shadow, making way
With wings or chariot fierce to repossess
A heaven he lost erewhile : it must—it must
Be of ripe progress—Saturn must be king !
Yes, there must be a golden victory ;
There must be Gods thrown down, and trumpets blown
Of triumph calm, and hymns of festival
Upon the gold clouds metropolitan,
Voices of soft proclaim, and silver stir
Of strings in hollow shells ; and there shall be
Beautiful things made new, for the surprise
Of the sky-children ; I will give command :
Thea !   Thea !   Thea ! where is Saturn ? "

    This passion lifted him upon his feet,
And made his hands to struggle in the air,
His Druid locks to shake and ooze with sweat,
His eyes to fever out, his voice to cease.
He stood, and heard not Thea's sobbing deep ;
A little time, and then again he snatch'd
Utterance thus :—" But cannot I create ?
Cannot I form ? Cannot I fashion forth
Another world, another universe,
To overbear and crumble this to nought ?
Where is another chaos ? Where ? " That word
Found way unto Olympus, and made quake
The rebel three. Thea was startled up,
And in her bearing was a sort of hope,
As thus she quick-voiced spake, yet full of awe.

    " This cheers our fallen house : come to our friends,
O Saturn ! come away, and give them heart ;
I know the covert, for thence came I hither."
Thus brief ; then with beseeching eyes she went

With backward footing through the shade a space:
He follow'd, and she turn'd to lead the way
Through aged boughs, that yielded like the mist
Which eagles cleave, upmounting from their nest.

Meanwhile in other realms big tears were shed,
More sorrow like to this, and such like woe,
Too huge for mortal tongue or pen of scribe:
The Titans fierce, self-hid or prison-bound,
Groan'd for the old allegiance once more,
And listen'd in sharp pain for Saturn's voice.
But one of the whole mammoth-brood still kept
His sovereignty, and rule, and majesty;
Blazing Hyperion on his orbed fire
Still sat, still snuff'd the incense, teeming up
From man to the sun's God, yet unsecure:
For as among us mortals omens drear
Fright and perplex, so also shudder'd he,
Not at dog's howl, or gloom-bird's hated screech,
Or the familiar visiting of one
Upon the first toll of his passing-bell,
Or prophesyings of the midnight lamp;
But horrors, portion'd to a giant nerve,
Oft made Hyperion ache.　His palace bright,
Bastion'd with pyramids of glowing gold,
And touched with shade of bronzed obelisks,
Glared a blood-red through all its thousand courts,
Arches, and domes, and fiery galleries;
And all its curtains of Aurorian clouds
Flush'd angerly: while sometimes eagles' wings,
Unseen before by Gods or wondering men,
Darken'd the place; and neighing steeds were heard,
Not heard before by Gods or wondering men.
Also, when he would taste the spicy wreaths
Of incense, breathed aloft from sacred hills,
Instead of sweets, his ample palate took
Savour of poisonous brass and metal sick:
And so, when harbour'd in the sleepy west,
After the full completion of fair day,
For rest divine upon exalted couch,
And slumber in the arms of melody,
He paced away the pleasant hours of ease

With stride colossal, on from hall to hall ;
While far within each aisle and deep recess,
His winged minions in close clusters stood,
Amazed and full of fear ; like anxious men
Who on wide plains gather in panting troops,
When earthquakes jar their battlements and towers.
Even now, while Saturn, raised from icy trance,
Went step for step with Thea through the woods,
Hyperion, leaving twilight in the rear,
Came slope upon the threshold of the west ;
Then, as was wont, his palace-door flew ope
In smoothed silence, save what solemn tubes,
Blown by the serious Zephyrs, gave of sweet,
And wandering sounds, slow-breathed melodies ;
And like a rose in vermeil tint and shape,
In fragrance soft, and coolness to the eye,
That inlet to severe magnificence
Stood full blown, for the God to enter in.

He enter'd, but he enter'd full of wrath ;
His flaming robes streamed out beyond his heels,
And gave a roar, as if of earthly fire,
That scared away the meek ethereal Hours
And made their dove-wings tremble.   On he flared
From stately nave to nave, from vault to vault,
Through bowers of fragrant and enwreathed light,
And diamond-paved lustrous long arcades,
Until he reached the great main cupola ;
There standing fierce beneath, he stampt his foot,
And from the basements deep to the high towers
Jarr'd his own golden region ; and before
The quavering thunder thereupon had ceased,
His voice leapt out, despite of godlike curb,
To this result : "O dreams of day and night !
O monstrous forms !   O effigies of pain !
O spectres busy in a cold, cold gloom !
O lank-ear'd Phantoms of black-weeded pools !
Why do I know ye? why have I seen ye? why
Is my eternal essence thus distraught
To see and to behold these horrors new?
Saturn is fallen, am I too to fall?
Am I to leave this haven of my rest,

This cradle of my glory, this soft clime,
This calm luxuriance of blissful light,
These crystalline pavilions, and pure fanes,
Of all my lucent empire? It is left
Deserted, void, nor any haunt of mine.
The blaze, the splendour, and the symmetry,
I cannot see—but darkness, death and darkness.
Even here, into my centre of repose,
The shady visions come to domineer,
Insult, and blind, and stifle up my pomp—
Fall!—No, by Tellus and her briny robes!
Over the fiery frontier of my realms
I will advance a terrible right arm
Shall scare that infant thunderer, rebel Jove,
And bid old Saturn take his throne again."
He spake, and ceased, the while a heavier threat
Held struggle with his throat, but came not forth;
For as in theatres of crowded men
Hubbub increases more they call out "Hush!"
So at Hyperion's words the Phantoms pale
Bestirr'd themselves, thrice horrible and cold;
And from the mirror'd level where he stood
A mist arose, as from a scummy marsh.
At this, through all his bulk an agony
Crept gradual, from the feet unto the crown,
Like a lithe serpent vast and muscular
Making slow way, with head and neck convulsed
From over-strained might. Released, he fled
To the eastern gates, and full six dewy hours
Before the dawn in season due should blush,
He breathed fierce breath against the sleepy portals,
Clear'd them of heavy vapours, burst them wide
Suddenly on the ocean's chilly streams.
The planet orb of fire, whereon he rode
Each day from east to west the heavens through,
Spun round in sable curtaining of clouds;
Not therefore veiled quite, blindfold and hid,
But ever and anon the glancing spheres,
Circles, and arcs, and broad-belting colure,
Glow'd through, and wrought upon the muffling dark
Sweet-shaped lightnings from the nadir deep
Up to the zenith—hieroglyphics old,

Which sages and keen-eyed astrologers
Then living on the earth, with labouring thought
Won from the gaze of many centuries:
Now lost, save what we find on remnants huge
Of stone, or marble swart; their import gone,
Their wisdom long since fled.   Two wings this orb
Possess'd for glory, two fair argent wings,
Ever exalted at the God's approach:
And now, from forth the gloom their plumes immense
Rose, one by one, till all outspreaded were;
While still the dazzling globe maintain'd eclipse,
Awaiting for Hyperion's command.
Fain would he have commanded, fain took throne
And bid the day begin, if but for change.
He might not:—No, though a primeval God
The sacred seasons might not be disturb'd,
Therefore the operations of the dawn
Stay'd in their birth, even as here 'tis told.
Those silver wings expanded sisterly,
Eager to sail their orb; the porches wide
Open'd upon the dusk demesnes of night;
And the bright Titan, frenzied with new woes,
Unused to bend, by hard compulsion bent
His spirit to the sorrow of the time;
And all along a dismal rack of clouds,
Upon the boundaries of day and night,
He stretch'd himself in grief and radiance faint.
There as he lay, the Heaven with its stars
Look'd down on him with pity, and the voice
Of Cœlus, from the universal space,
Thus whisper'd low and solemn in his ear:
"O brightest of my children dear, earth-born
And sky-engender'd, Son of Mysteries!
All unrevealed even to the powers
Which met at thy creating! at whose joys
And palpitations sweet, and pleasures soft,
I, Cœlus, wonder how they came and whence;
And at the fruits thereof what shapes they be,
Distinct, and visible; symbols divine,
Manifestations of that beauteous life
Diffused unseen throughout eternal space;
Of these new-form'd art thou, oh brightest child!

Of these, thy brethren and the Goddesses!
There is sad feud among ye, and rebellion
Of son against his sire.   I saw him fall,
I saw my firstborn tumbled from his throne!
To me his arms were spread, to me his voice
Found way from forth the thunders round his head!
Pale wox I, and in vapours hid my face.
Art thou, too, near such doom? vague fear there is:
For I have seen my sons most unlike Gods.
Divine ye were created, and divine
In sad demeanour, solemn, undisturb'd
Unruffled, like high Gods, ye lived and ruled:
Now I behold in you fear, hope, and wrath;
Actions of rage and passions; even as
I see them, on the mortal world beneath,
In men who die.—This is the grief, O Son!
Sad sign of ruin, sudden dismay, and fall!
Yet do thou strive; as thou art capable,
As thou canst move about, an evident God,
And canst oppose to each malignant hour
Ethereal presence:—I am but a voice;
My life is but the life of winds and tides,—
No more than winds and tides can I avail:—
But thou canst.—Be thou therefore in the van
Of circumstance; yea, seize the arrow's barb
Before the tense string murmur.—To the earth!
For there thou wilt find Saturn, and his woes.
Meantime I will keep watch on thy bright sun,
And of thy seasons be a careful nurse."—
Ere half this region-whisper had come down
Hyperion arose, and on the stars
Lifted his curvèd lids, and kept them wide
Until it ceased; and still he kept them wide:
And still they were the same bright, patient stars.
Then with a slow incline of his broad breast,
Like to a diver in the pearly seas,
Forward he stoop'd over the airy shore,
And plunged all noiseless into the deep night.

BOOK II

Just at the self-same beat of Time's wide wings
Hyperion slid into the rustled air,
And Saturn gain'd with Thea that sad place
Where Cybele and the bruised Titans mourn'd.
It was a den where no insulting light
Could glimmer on their tears; where their own groans
They felt, but heard not, for the solid roar
Of thunderous waterfalls and torrents hoarse,
Pouring a constant bulk, uncertain where.
Crag jutting forth to crag, and rocks that seem'd
Ever as if just rising from a sleep,
Forehead to forehead held their monstrous horns;
And thus in thousand hugest phantasies
Made a fit roofing to this nest of woe.
Instead of thorns, hard flint they sat upon,
Couches of rugged stone, and slaty ridge
Stubborn'd with iron. All were not assembled:
Some chain'd in torture, and some wandering.
Cœus, and Gyges, and Briareüs,
Typhon and Dolor, and Porphyrion,
With many more, the brawniest in assault,
Were pent in regions of laborious breath;
Dungeon'd in opaque element to keep
Their clenched teeth still clench'd, and all their limbs
Lock'd up like veins of metal, cramp'd and screw'd;
Without a motion, save of their big hearts
Heaving in pain, and horribly convulsed
With sanguine, feverous, boiling gurge of pulse.
Mnemosyne was straying in the world;
Far from her moon had Phœbe wander'd;
And many else were free to roam abroad,
But for the main, here found they covert drear.
Scarce images of life, one here, one there,
Lay vast and edgeways; like a dismal cirque
Of Druid stones, upon a forlorn moor,
When the chill rain begins at shut of eve,
In dull November, and their chancel vault,
The heaven itself, is blinded throughout night.

Each one kept shroud, nor to his neighbour gave
Or word or look, or action of despair.
Creüs was one; his ponderous iron mace
Lay by him, and a shatter'd rib of rock
Told of his rage, ere he thus sank and pined.
Iapetus another; in his grasp,
A serpent's plashy neck; its barbed tongue
Squeezed from the gorge, and all its uncurl'd length
Dead: and because the creature could not spit
Its poison in the eyes of conquering Jove.
Next Cottus: prone he lay, chin uppermost,
As though in pain; for still upon the flint
He ground severe his skull, with open mouth
And eyes at horrid working. Nearest him
Asia, born of most enormous Caf,
Who cost her mother Tellus keener pangs,
Though feminine, than any of her sons:
More thought than woe was in her dusky face,
For she was prophesying of her glory;
And in her wide imagination stood
Palm-shaded temples, and high rival fanes
By Oxus or in Ganges' sacred isles.
Even as Hope upon her anchor leans,
So leant she, not so fair, upon a tusk
Shed from the broadest of her elephants.
Above her, on a crag's uneasy shelve,
Upon his elbow raised, all prostrate else,
Shadow'd Enceladus; once tame and mild
As grazing ox unworried in the meads;
Now tiger-passion'd, lion-thoughted, wroth,
He meditated, plotted, and even now
Was hurling mountains in that second war,
Not long delay'd, that scared the younger Gods
To hide themselves in forms of beast and bird.
Not far hence Atlas; and beside him prone
Phorcus, the sire of Gorgons. Neighbour'd close
Oceanus, and Tethys, in whose lap
Sobbed Clymene among her tangled hair.
In midst of all lay Themis, at the feet
Of Ops the queen all clouded round from sight;
No shape distinguishable, more than when
Thick night confounds the pine-tops with the clouds:

And many else whose names may not be told.
For when the muse's wings are air-ward spread,
Who shall delay her flight?   And she must chant
Of Saturn, and his guide, who now had climb'd
With damp and slippery footing from a depth
More horrid still.   Above a sombre cliff
Their heads appear'd, and up their stature grew
Till on the level height their steps found ease;
Then Thea spread abroad her trembling arms
Upon the precincts of this nest of pain,
And sidelong fix'd her eye on Saturn's face:
There saw she direst strife; the supreme God
At war with all the frailty of grief,
Of rage, of fear, anxiety, revenge,
Remorse, spleen, hope, but most of all despair.
Against these plagues he strove in vain; for Fate
Had pour'd a mortal oil upon his head,
A disanointing poison: so that Thea,
Affrighted, kept her still, and let him pass
First onwards in, among the fallen tribe.

As with us mortal men, the laden heart
Is persecuted more, and fever'd more,
When it is nighing to the mournful house
Where other hearts are sick of the same bruise;
So Saturn, as he walk'd into the midst,
Felt faint, and would have sunk among the rest,
But that he met Enceladus's eye,
Whose mightiness, and awe of him, at once
Came like an inspiration; and he shouted,
"Titans, behold your God!" at which some groan'd;
Some started on their feet; some also shouted,
Some wept, some wail'd—all bowed with reverence;
And Ops, uplifting her black folded veil,
Show'd her pale cheeks, and all her forehead wan,
Her eyebrows thin and jet, and hollow eyes.
There is a roaring in the bleak-grown pines
When Winter lifts his voice; there is a noise
Among immortals when a God gives sign,
With hushing finger, how he means to load
His tongue with the full weight of utterless thought,
With thunder, and with music, and with pomp:

Such noise is like the roar of bleak-grown pines,
Which, when it ceases in this mountain'd world,
No other sound succeeds; but ceasing here,
Among these fallen, Saturn's voice therefrom
Grew up like organ, that begins anew
Its strain, when other harmonies, stopt short,
Leave the dinn'd air vibrating silverly.
Thus grew it up:—"Not in my own sad breast,
Which is its own great judge and searcher out,
Can I find reason why ye should be thus:
Not in the legends of the first of days,
Studied from that old spirit-leaved book
Which starry Uranus with finger bright
Saved from the shores of darkness, when the waves
Low-ebb'd still hid it up in shallow gloom;
And the which book ye know I ever kept
For my firm-based footstool:—Ah, infirm!
Not there, nor in sign, symbol, or portent
Of element, earth, water, air, and fire,—
At war, at peace, or inter-quarrelling
One against one, or two, or three, or all,
Each several one against the other three.
As fire with air loud warring when rain-floods
Drown both, and press them both against earth's face,
Where, finding sulphur, a quadruple wrath
Unhinges the poor world;—not in that strife,
Wherefrom I take strange lore, and read it deep,
Can I find reason why ye should be thus:
No, nowhere can unriddle, though I search,
And pore on Nature's universal scroll
Even to swooning, why ye, Divinities,
The first-born of all shaped and palpable Gods,
Should cower beneath what, in comparison,
Is untremendous might. Yet ye are here,
O'erwhelm'd and spurn'd, and batter'd, ye are here!
O Titans, shall I say, 'Arise!'—Ye groan:
Shall I say 'Crouch!'—Ye groan. What can I then?
O Heaven wide! O unseen parent dear!
What can I? Tell me, all ye brethren Gods.
How we can war, how engine our great wrath!
O speak your counsel now, for Saturn's ear
Is all a-hunger'd. Thou, Oceanus,

Ponderest high and deep; and in thy face
I see, astonied, that severe content
Which comes of thought and musing : give us help!"

So ended Saturn; and the God of the Sea,
Sophist and sage, from no Athenian grove,
But cogitation in his watery shades,
Arose, with locks not oozy, and began,
In murmurs, which his first endeavouring tongue
Caught infant-like from the far-foamed sands.
"O ye, whom wrath consumes! who, passion-stung,
Writhe at defeat, and nurse your agonies!
Shut up your senses, stifle up your ears,
My voice is not a bellows unto ire.
Yet listen, ye who will, whilst I bring proof
How ye, perforce, must be content to stoop :
And in the proof much comfort will I give,
If ye will take that comfort in its truth.
We fall by course of Nature's law, not force
Of thunder, or of Jove.   Great Saturn, thou
Hast sifted well the atom-universe;
But for this reason, that thou art the King,
And only blind from sheer supremacy,
One avenue was shaded from thine eyes,
Through which I wander'd to eternal truth.
And first, as thou wast not the first of powers,
So art thou not the last; it cannot be.
Thou art not the beginning nor the end.
From chaos and parental darkness came
Light, the first fruits of that intestine broil,
That sullen ferment, which for wondrous ends
Was ripening in itself.   The ripe hour came,
And with it light, and light engendering
Upon its own producer, forthwith touch'd
The whole enormous matter into life.
Upon that very hour, our parentage,
The Heavens and the Earth, were manifest :
Then thou first-born, and we the giant-race,
Found ourselves ruling new and beauteous realms.
Now comes the pain of truth, to whom 'tis pain ;
O folly! for to bear all naked truths,
And to envisage circumstance, all calm,

That is the top of sovereignty.   Mark well!
As Heaven and Earth are fairer, fairer far
Than Chaos and blank Darkness, though once chief.
And as we show beyond that Heaven and Earth
In form and shape compact and beautiful,
In will, in action free, companionship,
And thousand other signs of purer life;
So on our heels a fresh perfection treads,
A power more strong in beauty, born of us
And fated to excel us, as we pass
In glory that old Darkness: nor are we
Thereby more conquer'd than by us the rule
Of shapeless Chaos.   Say, doth the dull soil
Quarrel with the proud forests it hath fed,
And feedeth still, more comely than itself?
Can it deny the chiefdom of green groves?
Or shall the tree be envious of the dove
Because it cooeth, and hath snowy wings
To wander wherewithal and find its joys?
We are such forest-trees, and our fair boughs
Have bred forth, not pale solitary doves,
But eagles golden-feather'd, who do tower
Above us in their beauty, and must reign
In right thereof; for 'tis the eternal law
That first in beauty should be first in might;
Yea, by that law, another race may drive
Our conquerors to mourn as we do now.
Have ye beheld the young God of the Seas,
My dispossessor?   Have ye seen his face?
Have ye beheld his chariot, foam'd along
By noble wing'd creatures he hath made?
I saw him on the calmed waters scud,
With such a glow of beauty in his eyes,
That it enforced me to bid sad farewell
To all my empire: farewell sad I took,
And hither came, to see how dolorous fate
Had wrought upon ye; and how I might best
Give consolation in this woe extreme,
Receive the truth, and let it be your balm."

Whether through pozed conviction, or disdain,
They guarded silence, when Oceanus

Left murmuring, what deepest thought can tell?
But so it was, none answer'd for a space,
Save one whom none regarded, Clymene :
And yet she answer'd not, only complain'd,
With hectic lips, and eyes up-looking mild,
Thus wording timidly among the fierce :
"O Father! I am here the simplest voice,
And all my knowledge is that joy is gone,
And this thing woe crept in among our hearts,
There to remain for ever, as I fear :
I would not bode of evil, if I thought
So weak a creature could turn off the help
Which by just right should come of mighty Gods ;
You let me tell my sorrow, let me tell
Of what I heard, and how it made me weep,
And know that we had parted from all hope.
I stood upon a shore, a pleasant shore,
Where a sweet clime was breathed from a land
Of fragrance, quietness, and trees, and flowers.
Full of calm joy it was, as I of grief;
Too full of joy and soft delicious warmth ;
So that I felt a movement in my heart
To chide, and to reproach that solitude
With songs of misery, music of our woes ;
And sat me down, and took a mouthed shell
And murmur'd into it, and made melody—
O melody no more! for while I sang,
And with poor skill let pass into the breeze
The dull shell's echo, from a bowery strand
Just opposite, an island of the sea,
There came enchantment with the shifting wind
That did both drown and keep alive my ears.
I threw my shell away upon the sand,
And a wave fill'd it, as my sense was fill'd
With that new blissful golden melody.
A living death was in each gush of sounds,
Each family of rapturous hurried notes,
That fell, one after one, yet all at once,
Like pearl beads dropping sudden from their string :
And then another, then another strain,
Each like a dove leaving its olive perch,
With music wing'd instead of silent plumes,

To hover round my head, and make me sick
Of joy and grief at once.   Grief overcame,
And I was stopping up my frantic ears,
When, past all hindrance of my trembling hands,
A voice came, sweeter, sweeter than all tune,
And still it cried, 'Apollo! young Apollo!
The morning-bright Apollo! young Apollo!'
I fled, it follow'd me and cried 'Apollo!'
O Father, and O Brethren! had ye felt
Those pains of mine! O Saturn, hadst thou felt,
Ye would not call this too indulged tongue
Presumptuous, in thus venturing to be heard!"

So far her voice flow'd on, like timorous brook
That, lingering along a pebbled coast,
Doth fear to meet the sea : but sea it met,
And shudder'd ; for the overwhelming voice
Of huge Enceladus swallow'd it in wrath :
The ponderous syllables, like sullen waves
In the half-glutted hollows of reef-rocks,
Came booming thus, while still upon his arm
He lean'd ; not rising, from supreme contempt.
"Or shall we listen to the over-wise,
Or to the over-foolish giant, Gods ?
Not thunderbolt on thunderbolt, till all
That rebel Jove's whole armoury were spent,
Not world on world upon these shoulders piled,
Could agonise me more than baby-words
In midst of this dethronement horrible.
Speak! roar! shout! yell! ye sleepy Titans all.
Do ye forget the blows, the buffets vile?
Are ye not smitten by a youngling arm?
Dost thou forget, sham Monarch of the Waves,
Thy scalding in the seas? What! have I roused
Your spleens with so few simple words as these?
O joy! for now I see ye are not lost:
O joy! for now I see a thousand eyes
Wide glaring for revenge."—As this he said,
He lifted up this stature vast, and stood,
Still without intermission speaking thus :
"Now ye are flames, I'll tell ye how to burn,
And purge the ether of our enemies :

How to feed fierce the crooked stings of fire,
And singe away the swollen clouds of Jove,
Stifling that puny essence in its tent,
O let him feel the evil he hath done!
For though I scorn Oceanus's lore,
Much pain have I for more than loss of realms:
The days of peace and slumberous calm are fled;
Those days, all innocent of scathing war,
When all the fair Existences of heaven
Came open-eyed to guess what we would speak:—
That was before our brows were taught to frown,
Before our lips knew else but solemn sounds;
That was before we knew the winged thing,
Victory, might be lost, or might be won.
And be ye mindful that Hyperion,
Our brightest brother, still is undisgraced—
Hyperion, lo! his radiance is here!"

All eyes were on Enceladus's face,
And they beheld, while still Hyperion's name
Flew from his lips up to the vaulted rocks,
A pallid gleam across his features stern:
Not savage, for he saw full many a God
Wroth as himself.   He look'd upon them all,
And in each face he saw a gleam of light,
But splendider in Saturn's, whose hoar locks
Shone like the bubbling foam about a keel
When the prow sweeps into a midnight cove.
In pale and silver silence they remain'd,
Till suddenly a splendour, like the morn,
Pervaded all the beetling gloomy steeps,
All the sad spaces of oblivion,
And every gulf, and every chasm old,
And every height, and every sullen depth,
Voiceless, or hoarse with loud tormented streams
And all the everlasting cataracts,
And all the headlong torrents far and near,
Mantled before in darkness and huge shade,
Now saw the light and made it terrible.
It was Hyperion:—a granite peak
His bright feet touch'd, and there he staid to view
The misery his brilliance had betray'd

To the most hateful seeing of itself.
Golden his hair of short Numidian curl,
Regal his shape majestic, a vast shade
In midst of his own brightness, like the bulk
Of Memnon's image at the set of sun
To one who travels from the dusking East:
Sighs, too, as mournful as that Memnon's harp,
He utter'd, while his hands, contemplative,
He press'd together, and in silence stood.
Despondence seized again the fallen Gods
At sight of the dejected King of Day,
And many hid their faces from the light:
But fierce Enceladus sent forth his eyes
Among the brotherhood; and, at their glare,
Uprose Iapetus, and Creüs too,
And Phorcus, sea-born, and together strode
To where he tower'd on his eminence.
There those four shouted forth old Saturn's name.
Hyperion from the peak loud answer'd, "Saturn!"
Saturn sat near the Mother of the Gods,
In whose face was no joy, though all the Gods
Gave from their hollow throats the name of "Saturn!"

BOOK III

THUS, in alternate uproar and sad peace,
Amazed were those Titans utterly.
O leave them, Muse! O leave them to their woes
For thou art weak to sing such tumults dire:
A solitary sorrow best befits
Thy lips, and antheming a lonely grief.
Leave them, O Muse! for thou anon wilt find
Many a fallen old Divinity
Wandering in vain about bewilder'd shores.
Meantime touch piously the Delphic harp,
And not a wind of heaven but will breathe
In aid soft warble from the Dorian flute;
For lo! 'tis for the Father of all verse.
Flush everything that hath a vermeil hue,
Let the rose glow intense and warm the air,

And let the clouds of even and of morn
Float in voluptuous fleeces o'er the hills;
Let the red wine within the goblet boil,
Cold as a bubbling well; let faint-lipp'd shells,
On sands or in great deeps, vermilion turn
Through all their labyrinths; and let the maid
Blush keenly, as with some warm kiss surprised.
Chief isle of the embowered Cyclades,
Rejoice, O Delos, with thine olives green,
And poplars, and lawn-shading palms, and beech,
In which the Zephyr breathes the loudest song,
And hazels thick dark-stemm'd beneath the shade:
Apollo is once more the golden theme!
Where was he, when the Giant of the Sun
Stood bright, amid the sorrow of his peers?
Together had he left his mother fair
And his twin-sister sleeping in their bower,
And in the morning twilight wander'd forth
Beside the osiers of a rivulet,
Full ankle-deep in lilies of the vale.
The nightingale had ceased, and a few stars
Were lingering in the heavens, while the thrush
Began calm-throated.   Throughout all the isle
There was no covert, no retired cave,
Unhaunted by the murmurous noise of waves,
Though scarcely heard in many a green recess.
He listen'd, and he wept, and his bright tears
Went trickling down the golden bow he held.
Thus with half-shut suffused eyes he stood,
While from beneath some cumbrous boughs hard by
With solemn step an awful Goddess came,
And there was purport in her looks for him,
Which he with eager guess began to read
Perplex'd, the while melodiously he said:
"How camest thou over the unfooted sea?
Or hath that antique mien and robed form
Moved in these vales invisible till now?
Sure I have heard those vestments sweeping o'er
The fallen leaves, when I have sat alone
In cool mid-forest.   Surely I have traced
The rustle of those ample skirts about
These grassy solitudes, and seen the flowers

Lift up their heads, as still the whisper pass'd.
Goddess! I have beheld those eyes before,
And their eternal calm, and all that face,
Or I have dream'd."   "Yes," said the supreme shape,
"Thou hast dream'd of me; and awaking up
Didst find a lyre all golden by thy side,
Whose strings touch'd by thy fingers, all the vast
Unwearied ear of the whole universe
Listen'd in pain and pleasure at the birth
Of such new tuneful wonder. Is't not strange
That thou shouldst weep, so gifted? Tell me, youth,
What sorrow thou canst feel; for I am sad
When thou dost shed a tear: explain thy griefs
To one who in this lonely isle hath been
The watcher of thy sleep and hours of life,
From the young day when first thy infant hand
Pluck'd witless the weak flowers, till thine arm
Could bend that bow heroic to all times.
Show thy heart's secrets to an ancient Power
Who hath forsaken old and sacred thrones
For prophecies of thee, and for the sake
Of loveliness new-born."—Apollo then,
With sudden scrutiny and gloomless eyes.
Thus answer'd, while his white melodious throat
Throbb'd with the syllables :—"Mnemosyne!
Thy name is on my tongue, I know not how;
Why should I tell thee what thou so well seest?
Why should I strive to show what from my lips
Would come no mystery? For me, dark, dark,
And painful vile oblivion seals my eyes:
I strive to search wherefore I am so sad,
Until a melancholy numbs my limbs;
And then upon the grass I sit, and moan,
Like one who once had wings.   O why should I
Feel cursed and thwarted, when the liegeless air
Yields to my step aspirant? why should I
Spurn the green turf as hateful to my feet?
Goddess benign! point forth some unknown thing.
Are there not other regions than this isle?
What are the stars?   There is the sun, the sun!
And the most patient brilliance of the moon!
And stars by thousands!   Point me out the way

To any one particular beauteous star,
And I will flit into it with my lyre,
And make its silvery splendour pant with bliss.
I have heard the cloudy thunder : where is power ?
Whose hand, whose essence, what divinity
Makes this alarum in the elements,
While I here idle listen on the shores
In fearless yet in aching ignorance ?
O tell me, lonely Goddess ! by thy harp,
That waileth every morn and eventide,
Tell me why thus I rave about these groves.
Mute thou remainest—mute ? yet I can read
A wondrous lesson in thy silent face :
Knowledge enormous makes a God of me.
Names, deeds, grey legends, dire events, rebellions,
Majesties, sovran voices, agonies,
Creations and destroyings, all at once
Pour into the wide hollows of my brain,
And deify me, as if some blithe wine
Or bright elixir peerless I had drunk,
And so become immortal."—Thus the God,
While his enkindled eyes, with level glance
Beneath his white soft temples, steadfast kept,
Trembling with light, upon Mnemosyne.
Soon wild commotions shook him, and made flush
All the immortal fairness of his limbs :
Most like the struggle at the gate of death ;
Or liker still to one who should take leave
Of pale immortal death, and with a pang
As hot as death's is chill, with fierce convulse
Die into life : so young Apollo anguish'd ;
His very hair, his golden tresses famed,
Kept undulation round his eager neck.
During the pain Mnemosyne upheld
Her arms as one who prophesied.   At length
Apollo shriek'd ;—and lo ! from all his limbs
Celestial   .   .   .   .   .
        .   .   .   .

HYPERION, A VISION

CANTO I

FANATICS have their dreams, wherewith they weave
A paradise for a sect; the savage, too,
From forth the loftiest fashion of his sleep
Guesses at heaven; pity these have not
Traced upon vellum or wild Indian leaf
The shadows of melodious utterance,
But bare of laurel they live, dream, and die;
For Poesy alone can tell her dreams,—
With the fine spell of words alone can save
Imagination from the sable chain
And dumb enchantment.   Who alive can say,
"Thou art no Poet—mayst not tell thy dreams?"
Since every man whose soul is not a clod
Hath visions and would speak, if he had loved,
And been well nurtured in his mother tongue.
Whether the dream now purposed to rehearse
Be poet's or fanatic's will be known
When this warm scribe, my hand, is in the grave.

    Methought I stood where trees of every clime,
Palm, myrtle, oak, and sycamore, and beech,
With plantane and spice-blossoms, made a screen,
In neighbourhood of fountains (by the noise
Soft-showering in mine ears), and (by the touch
Of scent) not far from roses.   Twining round
I saw an arbour with a drooping roof
Of trellis vines, and bells, and larger blooms,
Like floral censers, swinging light in air;
Before its wreathed doorway, on a mound
Of moss, was spread a feast of summer fruits,
Which, nearer seen, seem'd refuse of a meal
By angel tasted or our Mother Eve;
For empty shells were scatter'd on the grass,
And grapestalks but half-bare, and remnants more
Sweet-smelling, whose pure kinds I could not know.

Still was more plenty than the fabled horn
Thrice emptied could pour forth at banqueting.
For Proserpine return'd to her own fields,
Where the white heifers low.   And appetite,
More yearning than on earth I ever felt,
Growing within, I ate deliciously,—
And, after not long thirsted ; for thereby
Stood a cool vessel of transparent juice
Sipp'd by the wander'd bee, the which I took,
And pledging all the mortals of the world,
And all the dead whose names are in our lips,
Drank.   That full draught is parent of my theme.
No Asian poppy or elixir fine
Of the soon-fading, jealous Caliphat,
No poison gender'd in close monkish cell,
To thin the scarlet conclave of old men,
Could so have rapt unwilling life away.
Among the fragrant husks and berries crush'd
Upon the grass, I struggled hard against
The domineering potion, but in vain.
The cloudy swoon came on, and down I sank,
Like a Silenus on an antique vase.
How long I slumber'd 'tis a chance to guess.
When sense of life return'd, I started up
As if with wings, but the fair trees were gone,
The mossy mound and arbour were no more !
I look'd around upon the curved sides
Of an old sanctuary, with roof august,
Builded so high, it seem'd that filmed clouds
Might spread beneath as o'er the stars of heaven.
So old the place was, I remember'd none
The like upon the earth : what I had seen
Of grey cathedrals, buttress'd walls, rent towers,
The superannuations of sunk realms,
Or Nature's rocks toil'd hard in waves and winds,
Seem'd but the faulture of decrepit things
To that eternal domed monument.
Upon the marble at my feet there lay
Store of strange vessels and large draperies,
Which needs had been of dyed asbestos wove,
Or in that place the moth could not corrupt,
So white the linen, so, in some, distinct

Ran imageries from a sombre loom.
All in a mingled heap confused there lay
Robes, golden tongs, censer and chafing-dish,
Girdles, and chains, and holy jewelries.

    Turning from these with awe, once more I raised
My eyes to fathom the space every way:
The embossed roof, the silent massy range
Of columns north and south, ending in mist
Of nothing; then to eastward, where black gates
Were shut against the sunrise evermore;
Then to the west I look'd, and saw far off
An image, huge of feature as a cloud,
At level of whose feet an altar slept,
To be approach'd on either side by steps
And marble balustrade, and patient travail
To count with toil the innumerable degrees.
Towards the altar sober-paced I went,
Repressing haste as too unholy there;
And, coming nearer, saw beside the shrine
One ministering; and there arose a flame.
When in midday the sickening east-wind
Shifts sudden to the south, the small warm rain
Melts out the frozen incense from all flowers
And fills the air with so much pleasant health
That even the dying man forgets his shroud;—
Even so that lofty sacrificial fire,
Sending forth Maian incense, spread around
Forgetfulness of everything but bliss,
And clouded all the altar with soft smoke;
From whose white fragrant curtains thus I heard
Language pronounced: "If thou canst not ascend
These steps, die on that marble where thou art.
Thy flesh, near cousin to the common dust,
Will parch for lack of nutriment; thy bones
Will wither in few years, and vanish so
That not the quickest eye could find a grain
Of what thou now art on that pavement cold.
The sands of thy short life are spent this hour,
And no hand in the universe can turn
Thy hour-glass, if these gummed leaves be burnt
Ere thou canst mount up these immortal steps."
I heard, I look'd: two senses both at once,

So fine, so subtle, felt the tyranny
Of that fierce threat and the hard task proposed,
Prodigious seem'd the toil; the leaves were yet
Burning, when suddenly a palsied chill
Struck from the paved level up my limbs,
And was ascending quick to put cold grasp
Upon those streams that pulse beside the throat.
I shriek'd, and the sharp anguish of my shriek
Stung my own ears; I strove hard to escape
The numbness, strove to gain the lowest step.
Slow, heavy, deadly was my pace: the cold
Grew stifling, suffocating at the heart;
And when I clasp'd my hands I felt them not.
One minute before death my iced foot touch'd
The lowest stair; and, as it touch'd, life seem'd
To pour in at the toes; I mounted up
As once fair angels on a ladder flew
From the green turf to heaven.   "Holy Power,"
Cried I, approaching near the horned shrine,
"What am I that should so be saved from death?
What am I that another death come not
To choke my utterance, sacrilegious, here?"
Then said the veiled shadow: "Thou hast felt
What 'tis to die and live again before
Thy fated hour; that thou hadst power to do so
Is thine own safety; thou hast dated on
Thy doom."   "High Prophetess," said I, "purge off,
Benign, if so it please thee, my mind's film."
"None can usurp this height," returned that shade,
"But those to whom the miseries of the world
Are misery, and will not let them rest.
All else who find a haven in the world,
Where they may thoughtless sleep away their days,
If by a chance into this fane they come,
Rot on the pavement where thou rottedst half."
"Are there not thousands in the world," said I,
Encouraged by the sooth voice of the shade,
"Who love their fellows even to the death,
Who feel the giant agony of the world,
And more, like slaves to poor humanity,
Labour for mortal good?   I sure should see
Other men here, but I am here alone."

K

"Those whom thou spakest of are no visionaries,"
Rejoin'd that voice; "they are no dreamers weak;
They seek no wonder but the human face,
No music but a happy-noted voice:
They come not here, they have no thought to come;
And thou are here, for thou art less than they.
What benefit canst thou do, or all thy tribe,
To the great world?   Thou art a dreaming thing,
A fever of thyself: think of the earth;
What bliss, even in hope, is there for thee?
What haven? every creature hath its home,
Every sole man hath days of joy and pain,
Whether his labours be sublime or low—
The pain alone, the joy alone, distinct:
Only the dreamer venoms all his days,
Bearing more woe than all his sins deserve.
Therefore, that happiness be somewhat shared,
Such things as thou art are admitted oft
Into like gardens thou didst pass erewhile,
And suffer'd in these temples: for that cause
Thou standest safe beneath this statue's knees."
"That I am favour'd for unworthiness,
By such propitious parley medicined
In sickness not ignoble, I rejoice,
Ay, and could weep for love of such award."
So answer'd I, continuing, "If it please,
Majestic shadow, tell me where I am,
Whose altar this, for whom this incense curls;
What image this whose face I cannot see
For the broad marble knees; and who thou art,
Of accent feminine, so courteous?"
     Then the tall shade, in drooping linen veil'd,
Spoke out, so much more earnest, that her breath
Stirr'd the thin folds of gauze that drooping hung
About a golden censer from her hand
Pendent; and by her voice I knew she shed
Long-treasured tears.   "This temple, sad and lone,
Is all spared from the thunder of a war
Foughten long since by giant hierarchy
Against rebellion: this old image here,
Whose carved features wrinkled as he fell,
Is Saturn's; I, Moneta, left supreme,

Sole goddess of this desolation."
I had no words to answer, for my tongue,
Useless, could find about its roofed home
No syllable of a fit majesty
To make rejoinder to Moneta's mourn:
There was a silence, while the altar's blaze
Was fainting for sweet food. I look'd thereon,
And on the paved floor, where nigh were piled
Faggots of cinnamon, and many heaps
Of other crisped spicewood: then again
I look'd upon the altar, and its horns
Whiten'd with ashes, and its languorous flame,
And then upon the offerings again;
And so, by turns, till sad Moneta cried:
"The sacrifice is done, but not the less
Will I be kind to thee for thy good will.
My power, which to me is still a curse,
Shall be to thee a wonder, for the scenes
Still swooning vivid through my globed brain,
With an electral changing misery,
Thou shalt with these dull mortal eyes behold
Free from all pain, if wonder pain thee not."
As near as an immortal's sphered words
Could to a mother's soften were these last:
And yet I had a terror of her robes,
And chiefly of the veils that from her brow
Hung pale, and curtain'd her in mysteries,
That made my heart too small to hold its blood.
This saw that Goddess, and with sacred hand
Parted the veils.   Then saw I a wan face,
Not pined by human sorrows, but bright-blanch'd
By an immortal sickness which kills not;
It works a constant change, which happy death
Can put no end to; deathwards progressing
To no death was that visage; it had past
The lily and the snow; and beyond these
I must not think now, though I saw that face.
But for her eyes I should have fled away;
They held me back with a benignant light,
Soft, mitigated by divinest lids
Half-closed, and visionless entire they seem'd
Of all external things; they saw me not,

But in blank splendour beam'd, like the mild moon,
Who comforts those she sees not, who knows not
What eyes are upward cast.   As I had found
A grain of gold upon a mountain's side,
And, twinged with avarice, strain'd out my eyes
To search its sullen entrails rich with ore,
So, at the view of sad Moneta's brow,
I ask'd to see what things the hollow brow
Behind environ'd : what high tragedy
In the dark secret chambers of her skull
Was acting, that could give so dread a stress
To her cold lips, and fill with such a light
Her planetary eyes, and touch her voice
With such a sorrow ?   "Shade of Memory !"
Cried I, with act adorant at her feet,
"By all the gloom hung round thy fallen house,
By this last temple, by the golden age,
By great Apollo, thy dear foster-child,
And by thyself, forlorn divinity,
The pale Omega of a wither'd race,
Let me behold, according as thou saidst,
What in thy brain so ferments to and fro !"
No sooner had this conjuration past
My devout lips, than side by side we stood
(Like a stunt bramble by a solemn pine)
Deep in the shady sadness of a vale
Far sunken from the healthy breath of morn,
Far from the fiery noon and eve's one star.
Onward I look'd beneath the gloomy boughs,
And saw what first I thought an image huge,
Like to the image pedestal'd so high
In Saturn's temple ; then Moneta's voice
Came brief upon mine ear.   "So Saturn sat
When he had lost his realms ;" whereon there grew
A power within me of enormous ken
To see as a god sees, and take the depth
Of things as nimbly as the outward eye
Can size and shape pervade.   The lofty theme
Of those few words hung vast before my mind
With half-unravell'd web.   I sat myself
Upon an eagle's watch, that I might see,
And seeing ne'er forget.   No stir of life

Was in this shrouded vale,—not so much air
As in the zoning of a summer's day
Robs not one light seed from the feather'd grass;
But where the dead leaf fell there did it rest.
A stream went noiseless by, still deaden'd more
By reason of the fallen divinity
Spreading more shade; the Naiad 'mid her reeds
Prest her cold finger closer to her lips.

Along the margin-sand large foot-marks went
No further than to where old Saturn's feet
Had rested, and there slept how long a sleep!
Degraded, cold, upon the sodden ground
His old right hand lay nerveless, listless, dead,
Unsceptred, and his realmless eyes were closed;
While his bow'd head seem'd listening to the Earth,
His ancient mother, for some comfort yet.

It seem'd no force could wake him from his place;
But there came one who, with a kindred hand,
Touch'd his wide shoulders, after bending low
With reverence, though to one who knew it not.
Then came the grieved voice of Mnemosyne,
And grieved I hearken'd. "That divinity
Whom thou saw'st step from yon forlornest wood,
And with slow pace approach our fallen king,
Is Thea, softest-natured of our brood."
I mark'd the Goddess, in fair statuary
Surpassing wan Moneta by the head,
And in her sorrow nearer woman's tears.
There was a list'ning fear in her regard,
As if calamity had but begun;
As if the venom'd clouds of evil days
Had spent their malice, and the sullen rear
Was with its stored thunder labouring up.
One hand she press'd upon that aching spot
Where beats the human heart, as if just there,
Though an immortal, she felt cruel pain;
The other upon Saturn's bended neck
She laid, and to the level of his ear
Leaning, with parted lips some words she spoke
In solemn tenour and deep organ-tone;
Some mourning words, which in our feeble tongue
Would come in this like accenting; how frail

To that large utterance of the early gods!
    "Saturn, look up! and for what, poor lost king?
I have no comfort for thee; no, not one;
I cannot say, wherefore thus sleepest thou?
For Heaven is parted from thee, and the Earth
Knows thee not, so afflicted, for a god.
The Ocean, too, with all its solemn noise,
Has from thy sceptre pass'd; and all the air
Is emptied of thy hoary majesty.
Thy thunder, captious at the new command,
Rumbles reluctant o'er our fallen house;
And thy sharp lightning, in unpractised hands,
Scourges and burns our once serene domain.
With such remorseless speed still come new woes,
That unbelief has not a space to breathe.
Saturn! sleep on: me thoughtless, why should I
Thus violate thy slumbrous solitude?
Why should I ope thy melancholy eyes?
Saturn! sleep on, while at thy feet I weep."

    As when upon a tranced summer-night
Forests, branch-charmed by the earnest stars,
Dream, and so dream all night without a noise.
Save from one gradual solitary gust
Swelling upon the silence, dying off,
As if the ebbing air had but one wave,
So came these words and went; the while in tears
She prest her fair large forehead to the earth,
Just where her fallen hair might spread in curls
A soft and silken net for Saturn's feet.
Long, long these two were postured motionless,
Like sculpture builded-up upon the grave
Of their own power. A long awful time
I look'd upon them: still they were the same;
The frozen God still bending to the earth,
And the sad Goddess weeping at his feet;
Moneta silent. Without stay or prop
But my own weak mortality, I bore
The load of this eternal quietude,
The unchanging gloom and the three fixed shapes
Ponderous upon my senses, a whole moon;
For by my burning brain I measured sure
Her silver seasons shedded on the night,

And every day by day methought I grew
More gaunt and ghostly. Oftentimes I pray'd
Intense, that death would take me from the vale
And all its burthens; gasping with despair
Of change, hour after hour I cursed myself,
Until old Saturn raised his faded eyes,
And look'd around and saw his kingdom gone,
And all the gloom and sorrow of the place,
And that fair kneeling Goddess at his feet.
As the moist scent of flowers, and grass, and leaves,
Fills forest-dells with a pervading air,
Known to the woodland nostril, so the words
Of Saturn fill'd the mossy glooms around,
Even to the hollows of time-eaten oaks,
And to the windings of the foxes' hole,
With sad, low tones, while thus he spoke, and sent
Strange moanings to the solitary Pan.
"Moan, brethren, moan, for we are swallow'd up
And buried from all godlike exercise
Of influence benign on planets pale,
And peaceful sway upon man's harvesting,
And all those acts which Deity supreme
Doth ease its heart of love in. Moan and wail;
Moan, brethren, moan; for lo, the rebel spheres
Spin round; the stars their ancient courses keep;
Clouds still with shadowy moisture haunt the earth,
Still suck their fill of light from sun and moon;
Still buds the tree, and still the seashores murmur;
There is no death in all the universe,
No smell of death.—There shall be death. Moan, moan;
Moan, Cybele, moan; for thy pernicious babes
Have changed a god into an aching palsy.
Moan, brethren, moan, for I have no strength left;
Weak as the reed, weak, feeble as my voice.
Oh! oh! the pain, the pain of feebleness;
Moan, moan, for still I thaw; or give me help;
Throw down those imps, and give me victory.
Let me hear other groans, and trumpets blown
Of triumph calm, and hymns of festival,
From the gold peaks of heaven's high-piled clouds;
Voices of soft proclaim, and silver stir
    Of strings in hollow shells; and there shall be

Beautiful things made new, for the surprise
Of the sky-children." So he feebly ceased,
With such a poor and sickly-sounding pause,
Methought I heard some old man of the earth
Bewailing earthly loss; nor could my eyes
And ears act with that unison of sense
Which marries sweet sound with the grace of form,
And dolorous accent from a tragic harp
With large-limb'd visions. More I scrutinised.
Still fixt he sat beneath the sable trees,
Whose arms spread straggling in wild serpent forms,
With leaves all hush'd ; his awful presence there
(Now all was silent) gave a deadly lie
To what I erewhile heard : only his lips
Trembled amid the white curls of his beard ;
They told the truth, though round the snowy locks
Hung nobly, as upon the face of heaven
A mid-day fleece of clouds. Thea arose,
And stretcht her white arm through the hollow dark.
Pointing some whither : whereat he too rose,
Like a vast giant, seen by men at sea
To grow pale from the waves at dull midnight.
They melted from my sight into the woods ;
Ere I could turn, Moneta cried, "These twain
Are speeding to the families of grief,
Where, rooft in by black rocks, they waste in pain
And darkness, for no hope." And she spake on,
As ye may read who can unwearied pass
Onward from the antechamber of this dream,
Where, even at the open doors, awhile
I must delay, and glean my memory
Of her high phrase—perhaps no further dare.

END OF CANTO I

CANTO II

" MORTAL, that thou mayst understand aright,
I humanize my sayings to thine ear,
Making comparisons of earthly things ;
Or thou mightst better listen to the wind,
Whose language is to thee a barren noise,
Though it blows legend-laden thro' the trees.
In melancholy realms big tears are shed,
More sorrow like to this, and such like woe,
Too huge for mortal tongue or pen of scribe.
The Titans fierce, self-hid or prison-bound,
Groan for the old allegiance once more,
Listening in their doom for Saturn's voice.
But one of the whole eagle-brood still keeps
His sovereignty, and rule, and majesty :
Blazing Hyperion on his orbed fire
Still sits, still snuffs the incense teeming up
From Man to the Sun's God—yet insecure,
For as upon the earth dire prodigies
Fright and perplex, so also shudders he ;
Not at dog's howl or gloom-bird's hated screech,
Or the familiar visiting of one
Upon the first toll of his passing bell,
Or prophesyings of the midnight lamp ;
But horrors, portioned to a giant nerve,
Make great Hyperion ache.   His palace bright,
Bastion'd with pyramids of shining gold,
And touch'd with shade of bronzed obelisks,
Glares a blood-red thro' all the thousand courts,
Arches, and domes, and fiery galleries ;
And all its curtains of Aurorian clouds
Flash angerly ; when he would taste the wreaths
Of incense breathed aloft from sacred hills
Instead of sweets, his ample palate takes
Savour of poisonous brass and metals sick ;
Wherefore when harbour'd in the sleepy West,
After the full completion of fair day,
For rest divine upon exalted couch,
And slumber in the arms of melody,

He paces through the pleasant hours of ease,
With strides colossal, from hall to hall,
While far within each aisle and deep recess
His winged minions in close clusters stand
Amazed, and full of fear ; like anxious men
Who on a wide plain gather in sad troops,
When earthquakes jar their battlements and towers.
Even now where Saturn, roused from icy trance,
Goes step for step with Thea from yon woods,
Hyperion, leaving twilight in the rear,
Is sloping to the threshold of the West.
Thither we tend."   Now in clear light I stood,
Relieved from the dusk vale.   Mnemosyne
Was sitting on a square-edged polish'd stone,
That in its lucid depth reflected pure
Her priestess' garments.   My quick eyes ran on
From stately nave to nave, from vault to vault,
Through bow'rs of fragrant and enwreathed light,
And diamond-paned lustrous long arcades.
Anon rush'd by the bright Hyperion ;
His flaming robes stream'd out beyond his heels,
And gave a roar as if of earthly fire,
That scared away the meek ethereal hours,
And made their dove-wings tremble.   On he flared.

HERE MS. ENDS

OTHO THE GREAT

A TRAGEDY IN FIVE ACTS

DRAMATIS PERSONÆ

OTHO THE GREAT, *Emperor of Germany.*
LUDOLPH, *his Son.*
CONRAD, *Duke of Franconia.*
ALBERT, *a Knight, favoured by Otho.*
SIGIFRED, *an Officer, friend of Ludolph.*
THEODORE } *Officers.*
GONFRID }
ETHELBERT, *an Abbot.*

GERSA, *Prince of Hungary.*
An Hungarian Captain.
Physician.
Page.
Nobles, Knights, Attendants, and Soldiers.

ERMINIA, *Niece of Otho.*
AURANTHE, *Conrad's Sister.*
Ladies and Attendants.

SCENE: *The Castle of Friedburg, its vicinity, and the Hungarian Camp.*

TIME, *One Day.*

ACT I

SCENE I.—*An Apartment in the Castle.*

Enter CONRAD

So, I am safe emergèd from these broils!
Amid the wreck of thousands I am whole;
For every crime I have a laurel-wreath,
For every lie a lordship.   Nor yet has
My ship of fortune furled her silken sails,—
Let her glide on!   This dangered neck is saved,
By dexterous policy from the rebels' axe;
And of my ducal palace not one stone
Is bruised by the Hungarian petards.
Toil hard, ye slaves, and from the miser-earth
Bring forth once more my bullion, treasured deep,
With all my jewelled salvers, silver and gold
And precious goblets that make rich the wine.
But why do I stand babbling to myself?
Where is Auranthe?   I have news for her
Shall——

Enter AURANTHE

   Auranthe. Conrad! what tidings?   Good, if I may guess
From your alert eyes and high-lifted brows.
What tidings of the battle?   Albert? Ludolph?
Otho?
   Conrad. You guess aright.   And, sister, slurring o'er
Our by-gone quarrels, I confess my heart
Is beating with a child's anxiety,
To make our golden fortune known to you.
   Auranthe. So serious?
   Conrad.   Yes, so serious, that before
I utter even the shadow of a hint
Concerning what will make that sin-worn cheek
Blush joyous blood through every lineament,
You must make here a solemn vow to me.
   Auranthe. I pr'ythee, Conrad, do not overact
The hypocrite.   What vow would you impose?
   Conrad. Trust me for once.   That you may be assured
'Tis not confiding in a broken reed,
A poor court-bankrupt, outwitted and lost,
Revolve these facts in your acutest mood,
In such a mood as now you listen to me:
A few days since, I was an open rebel,—
Against the Emperor had suborned his son,—
Drawn off his nobles to revolt,—and shown
Contented fools causes for discontent,
Fresh hatched in my ambition's eagle-nest;
So thrived I as a rebel,—and, behold!
Now I am Otho's favourite, his dear friend,
His right hand, his brave Conrad!
   Auranthe.   I confess
You have intrigued with these unsteady times
To admiration.   But to be a favourite!
   Conrad. I saw my moment.   The Hungarians,
Collected silently in holes and corners,
Appeared, a sudden host, in the open day.
I should have perished in our empire's wreck,
But, calling interest loyalty, swore faith
To most believing Otho; and so helped
His blood-stained ensigns to the victory

In yesterday's hard fight, that it has turned
The edge of his sharp wrath to eager kindness.

Auranthe. So far yourself. But what is this to me
More than that I am glad? I gratulate you.

Conrad. Yes, sister, but it does regard you greatly,
Nearly, momentously,—aye, painfully!
Make me this vow——

Auranthe. Concerning whom or what?

Conrad. Albert!

Auranthe. I would inquire somewhat of him.
You had a letter from me touching him?
No treason 'gainst his head in deed or word!
Surely you spared him at my earnest prayer?
Give me the letter—it should not exist.

Conrad. At one pernicious charge of the enemy
I for a moment-whiles, was prisoner ta'en
And rifled,—stuff! the horse's hoofs have minced it!

Auranthe. He is alive?

Conrad. He is! but here make oath
To alienate him from your scheming brain,
Divorce him from your solitary thoughts,
And cloud him in such utter banishment,
That when his person meets again your eye
Your vision shall quite lose its memory,
And wander past him as through vacancy.

Auranthe. I'll not be perjured.

Conrad. No, nor great, nor mighty;
You would not wear a crown, or rule a kingdom.
To you it is indifferent.

Auranthe. What means this?

Conrad. You'll not be perjured! Go to Albert then,
That camp-mushroom—dishonour of our house.
Go, page his dusty heels upon a march,
Furbish his jingling baldric while he sleeps,
And share his mouldy ration in a siege.
Yet stay,—perhaps a charm may call you back,
And make the widening circlets of your eyes
Sparkle with healthy fevers.—The Emperor
Hath given consent that you should marry Ludolph.

Auranthe. Can it be, brother? For a golden crown
With a queen's awful lips I doubly thank you!
This is to wake in Paradise! Farewell,

Thou clod of yesterday!—'twas not myself!
Not till this moment did I ever feel
My spirit's faculties! I'll flatter you
For this, and be you ever proud of it;
Thou, Jove-like, struck'dst thy forehead,
And from the teeming marrow of thy brain
I spring complete Minerva! But the prince—
His highness Ludolph—where is he?

  Conrad.   I know not
When, lackeying my counsel at a beck,
The rebel lords, on bended knees, received
The Emperor's pardon, Ludolph kept aloof,
Sole, in a stiff, fool-hardy, sulky pride;
Yet, for all this. I never saw a father
In such a sickly longing for his son.
We shall soon see him; for the Emperor
He will be here this morning.

  Auranthe.   That I heard
Among the midnight rumours from the camp.

  Conrad. You give up Albert to me?

  Auranthe.   Harm him not!
E'en for his highness Ludolph's sceptry hand,
I would not Albert suffer any wrong.

  Conrad. Have I not laboured, plotted——?

  Auranthe.   See you spare him:
Nor be pathetic, my kind benefactor!
On all the many bounties of your hand,
'Twas for yourself you laboured—not for me!
Do you not count, when I am queen, to take
Advantage of your chance discoveries
Of my poor secrets, and so hold a rod
Over my life?

  Conrad.   Let not this slave—this villain—
Be cause of feud between us. See! he comes!
Look, woman, look, your Albert is quite safe!
In haste it seems. Now shall I be in the way,
And wished with silent curses in my grave,
Or side by side with 'whelmèd mariners.

Enter ALBERT

  Albert. Fair on your graces fall this early morrow!
So it is like to do, without my prayers,

For your right noble names, like favourite tunes,
Have fallen full frequent from our Emperor's lips,
High commented with smiles.

Auranthe.   Noble Albert!

Conrad (*aside*). Noble!

Auranthe. Such salutation argues a glad heart
In our prosperity.   We thank you, sir.

Albert.   Lady,
O, would to Heaven your poor servant
Could do you better service than mere words!
But I have other greeting than mine own,—
From no less man than Otho, who has sent
This ring as pledge of dearest amity;
'Tis chosen, I hear, from Hymen's jewel'ry,
And you will prize it, lady, I doubt not,
Beyond all pleasures past, and all to come.
To you, great duke—

Conrad.   To me!   What of me, ha?

Albert. What pleased your grace to say?

Conrad.   Your message, sir!

Albert. You mean not this to me?

Conrad.   Sister, this way;
For there shall be no "gentle Alberts" now,   [*Aside.*
No "sweet Auranthes!"

                         [*Exeunt* CONRAD *and* AURANTHE.

Albert (*solus*). The duke is out of temper; if he knows
More than a brother of a sister ought
I should not quarrel with his peevishness.
Auranthe—Heaven preserve her always fair!—
Is in the heady, proud, ambitious vein;
I bicker not with her,—bid her farewell;
She has taken flight from me, then let her soar,—
He is a fool who stands at pining gaze!
But for poor Ludolph, he is food for sorrow:
No levelling bluster of my licensed thoughts,
No military swagger of my mind,
Can smother from myself the wrong I've done him,—
Without design, indeed,—yet it is so,—
And opiate for the conscience have I none!   [*Exit.*

SCENE II.—*The Court-yard of the Castle.*

Martial Music. Enter, from the outer gate, OTHO, *Nobles, Knights, and Attendants. The Soldiers halt at the gate, with Banners in sight.*

Otho. Where is my noble herald?

Enter CONRAD, *from the Castle, attended by two Knights and Servants.* ALBERT *following.*

Well, hast told
Auranthe our intent imperial?
Lest our rent banners, too o' the sudden shown,
Should fright her silken casements and dismay
Her household to our lack of entertainment.
A victory!
Conrad. God save illustrious Otho!
Otho. Aye, Conrad, it will pluck out all grey hairs;
It is the best physician for the spleen;
The courtliest inviter to a feast;
The subtlest excuser of small faults;
And a nice judge in the age and smack of wine.

Enter from the Castle, AURANTHE, *followed by Pages holding up her robes, and a train of Women. She kneels.*

Hail, my sweet hostess! I do thank the stars,
Or my good soldiers, or their ladies' eyes,
That, after such a merry battle fought,
I can, all safe in body and in soul,
Kiss your fair hand and lady fortune's too.
My ring! now, on my life, it doth rejoice
These lips to feel 't on this soft ivory!
Keep it, my brightest daughter; it may prove
The little prologue to a line of kings.
I strove against thee and my hot-blood son,
Dull blockhead that I was to be so blind;
But now my sight is clear; forgive me, lady.
Auranthe. My lord, I was a vassal to your frown,
And now your favour makes me but more humble;

In wintry winds the simple snow is safe,
But fadeth at the greeting of the sun:
Unto thine anger I might well have spoken,
Taking on me a woman's privilege,
But this so sudden kindness makes me dumb.

Otho. What need of this? Enough, if you will be
A potent tutoress to my wayward boy,
And teach him, what it seems his nurse could not,
To say, for once, I thank you. Sigifred!

Albert. He has not yet returned, my gracious liege.

Otho. What then! No tidings of my friendly Arab?

Conrad. None, mighty Otho.

      [To one of his Knights, who goes out.
        Send forth instantly.

An hundred horsemen from my honoured gates,
To scour the plains and search the cottages.
Cry a reward to him who shall first bring
News of that vanishèd Arabian,—
A full-heaped helmet of the purest gold.

Otho. More thanks, good Conrad; for, except my son's,
There is no face I rather would behold
Than that same quick-eyed pagan's. By the saints,
This coming night of banquets must not light
Her dazzling torches; nor the music breathe
Smooth, without clashing cymbal, tones of peace
And indoor melodies; nor the ruddy wine
Ebb spouting to the lees; if I pledge not,
In my first cup, that Arab!

Albert.   Mighty monarch,
I wonder not this stranger's victor-deeds
So hang upon your spirit. Twice in the fight
It was my chance to meet his olive brow,
Triumphant in the enemy's shattered rhomb;
And, to say truth, in any Christian arm
I never saw such prowess.

Otho.   Did you ever?
O, 'tis a noble boy!—tut!—what do I say?
I mean a triple Saladin, whose eyes,
When in the glorious scuffle they met mine,
Seemed to say, "Sleep, old man, in safety sleep;
I am the victory!"

Conrad.   Pity he's not here.

Otho. And my son too, pity he is not here.
Lady Auranthe, I would not make you blush,
But can you give a guess where Ludolph is?
Know you not of him?

 Auranthe.   Indeed, my liege, no secret——

 Otho. Nay, nay, without more words, dost know of him?

 Auranthe. I would I were so over-fortunate,
Both for his sake and mine, and to make glad
A father's ears with tidings of his son.

 Otho. I see 'tis like to be a tedious day.
Were Theodore and Gonfrid and the rest
Sent forth with my commands?

 Albert.   Aye, my lord.

 Otho. And no news! No news! 'Faith! 'tis very
  strange
He thus avoids us. Lady, is't not strange?
Will he be truant to you too? It is a shame.

 Conrad. Wilt please your highness enter, and accept
The unworthy welcome of your servant's house?
Leaving your cares to one whose diligence
May in few hours make pleasures of them all.

 Otho. Not so tedious, Conrad. No, no, no,—
I must see Ludolph or the—what's that shout?

 Voices without. Huzza! huzza! Long live the Emperor!
 Other voices. Fall back! Away there!
 Otho.   Say, what noise is that!

  [ALBERT *advancing from the back of the Stage,
   whither he had hastened on hearing the cheers
   of the soldiery.*

 Albert. It is young Gersa, the Hungarian prince,
Picked like a red stag from the fallow herd
Of prisoners. Poor prince, forlorn he steps,
Slow, and demure, and proud in his despair.
If I may judge by his so tragic bearing,
His eye not downcast, and his folded arm,
He doth this moment wish himself asleep
Among his fallen captains on yon plains.

   Enter GERSA, *in chains, and guarded*

 Otho. Well said, Sir Albert.
 Gersa.   Not a word of greeting?
No welcome to a princely visitor,

Most mighty Otho? Will not my great host
Vouchsafe a syllable, before he bids
His gentlemen conduct me with all care
To some securest lodging—cold perhaps!

Otho. What mood is this? Hath fortune touched thy
brain?

Gersa. O kings and princes of this fev'rous world,
What abject things, what mockeries must ye be,
What nerveless minions of safe palaces,
When here, a monarch, whose proud foot is used
To fallen princes' necks as to his stirrup,
Must needs exclaim that I am mad forsooth,
Because I cannot flatter with bent knees
My conqueror!

Otho. Gersa, I think you wrong me:
I think I have a better fame abroad.

Gersa. I pr'ythee mock me not with gentle speech,
But, as a favour, bid me from thy presence;
Let me no longer be the wondering food
Of all these eyes; pr'ythee, command me hence!

Otho. Do not mistake me, Gersa. That you may not,
Come, fair Auranthe, try if your soft hands
Can manage those hard rivets, to set free
So brave a prince and soldier.

Auranthe (*sets him free*). Welcome task!

Gersa. I am wound up in deep astonishment!
Thank you, fair lady. Otho! emperor!
You rob me of myself; my dignity
Is now your infant; I am a weak child.

Otho. Give me your hand, and let this kindly grasp
Live in our memories.

Gersa. In mine it will.
I blush to think of my unchastened tongue;
But I was haunted by the monstrous ghost
Of all our slain battalions. Sire, reflect,
And pardon you will grant, that, at this hour,
The bruisèd remnants of our stricken camp
Are huddling undistinguished, my dear friends,
With common thousands, into shallow graves.

Otho. Enough, most noble Gersa. You are free
To cheer the brave remainder of your host
By your own healing presence, and that, too,

Not as their leader merely, but their king;
For, as I hear, the wily enemy
Who eased the crownet from your infant brows,
Bloody Taraxa, is among the dead.

 Gersa. Then I retire, so generous Otho, please,
Bearing with me a weight of benefits
Too heavy to be borne.

 Otho.   It is not so;
Still, understand me, King of Hungary,
Nor judge my open purposes awry.
Though I did hold you high in my esteem
For your self's sake, I do not personate
The stage-play emperor to entrap applause,
To set the silly sort o' the world agape,
And make the politic smile; no, I have heard
How in the Council you condemned this war,
Urging the perfidy of broken faith,—
For that I am your friend.

 Gersa.   If ever, sire,
You are my enemy, I dare here swear
'Twill not be Gersa's fault. Otho, farewell!

 Otho. Will you return, prince, to our banqueting?

 Gersa. As to my father's board I will return.

 Otho. Conrad, with all due ceremony, give
The prince a regal escort to his camp;
Albert, go thou and bear him company.
Gersa, farewell!

 Gersa.   All happiness attend you!

 Otho. Return with what good speed you may, for soon
We must consult upon our terms of peace.
        [*Exeunt* GERSA *and* ALBERT *with others.*
And thus a marble column do I build
To prop my empire's dome. Conrad, in thee
I have another steadfast one, to uphold
The portals of my state; and, for my own
Pre-eminence and safety, I will strive
To keep thy strength upon its pedestal.
For, without thee, this day I might have been
A show-monster about the streets of Prague,
In chains, as just now stood that noble prince:
And then to me no mercy had been shown,
For when the conquered lion is once dungeoned

Who lets him forth again, or dares to give
An old lion sugar-cakes of mild reprieve?
Not to thine ear alone I make confession,
But to all here, as, by experience,
I know how the great basement of all power
Is frankness, and a true tongue to the world;
And how intriguing secrecy is proof
Of fear and weakness, and a hollow state.
Conrad, I owe thee much.

Conrad.   To kiss that hand,
My Emperor, is ample recompense
For a mere act of duty.

Otho.   Thou art wrong;
For what can any man on earth do more?
We will make trial of your house's welcome,
My bright Auranthe!

Conrad.   How is Friedburg honoured!

Enter ETHELBERT *and six Monks*

Ethelbert. The benison of Heaven on your head,
Imperial Otho!

Otho.   Who stays me? Speak! Quick!

Ethelbert. Pause but one moment, mighty conqueror,
Upon the threshold of this house of joy.

Otho. Pray, do not prose, good Ethelbert, but speak
What is your purpose.

Ethelbert. The restoration of some captive maids,
Devoted to Heaven's pious ministries,
Who, driven forth from their religious cells
And kept in thraldom by our enemy,
When late this province was a lawless spoil,
Still weep amid the wild Hungarian camp,
Though hemmed around by thy victorious arms.

Otho. Demand the holy sisterhood in our name
From Gersa's tents. Farewell, old Ethelbert.

Ethelbert. The saints will bless you for this pious care.

Otho. Daughter, your hand; Ludolph's would fit it best.

Conrad. Ho! let the music sound!

[*Music.* ETHELBERT *raises his hands, as in benediction
of* OTHO. *Exeunt severally. The scene closes on them.*

SCENE III.—*The Country, with the Castle in the distance.*

Enter LUDOLPH *and* SIGIFRED

Ludolph. You have my secret ; let it not be breathed.

Sigifred. Still give me leave to wonder that the Prince
Ludolph and the swift Arab are the same ;
Still to rejoice that 'twas a German arm
Death doing in a turbaned masquerade.

Ludolph. The Emperor must not know it, Sigifred.

Sigifred. I pr'ythee, why ? What happier hour of time
Could thy pleased star point down upon from heaven
With silver index, bidding thee make peace ?

Ludolph. Still it must not be known, good Sigifred ;
The star may point oblique.

Sigifred.   If Otho knew
His son to be that unknown Mussulman
After whose spurring heels he sent me forth,
With one of his well-pleased Olympian oaths,
The charters of man's greatness, at this hour
He would be watching round the castle walls,
And, like an anxious warder, strain his sight
For the first glimpse of such a son returned—
Ludolph !—that blast of the Hungarians,
That Saracenic meteor of the fight,
That silent fury, whose fell scymitar
Kept danger all aloof from Otho's head,
And left him space for wonder.

Ludolph.   Say no more.
Not as a swordsman would I pardon claim,
But as a son.   The bronzed centurion,
Long toiled in foreign wars, and whose high deeds
Are shaded in a forest of tall spears,
Known only to his troop, hath greater plea
Of favour with my sire than I can have.

Sigifred. My lord, forgive me that I cannot see
How this proud temper with clear reason squares.
What made you then, with such an anxious love,
Hover around that life, whose bitter days
You vext with bad revolt ?   Was 't opium,
Or the mad-fumêd wine ?   Nay, do not frown,
I rather would grieve with you than upbraid.

Ludolph. I do believe you. No, 'twas not to make
A father his son's debtor, or to heal
His deep heart-sickness for a rebel child.
'Twas done in memory of my boyish days,
Poor cancel for his kindness to my youth,
For all his calming of my childish griefs,
And all his smiles upon my merriment.
No, not a thousand foughten fields could sponge
Those days paternal from my memory,
Though now upon my head he heaps disgrace.
 Sigifred. My Prince, you think too harshly—
 Ludolph.   Can I so?
Hath he not galled my spirit to the quick?
And with a sullen rigour obstinate
Poured out a phial of wrath upon my faults;
Hunted me as the Tartar does the boar,
Driven me to the very edge o' the world,
And almost put a price upon my head?
 Sigifred. Remember how he spared the rebel lords.
 Ludolph. Yes, yes, I know he hath a noble nature
That cannot trample on the fallen. But his
Is not the only proud heart in his realm.
He hath wronged me, and I have done him wrong;
He hath loved me, and I have shown him kindness;
We should be almost equal.
 Sigifred.   Yet for all this,
I would you had appeared among those lords,
And ta'en his favour.
 Ludolph.   Ha! Till now I thought
My friend had held poor Ludolph's honour dear.
What! Would you have me sue before his throne
And kiss, the courtier's missal, its silk steps?
Or hug the golden housings of his steed,
Amid a camp whose steelèd swarms I dared
But yesterday? and, at the trumpet sound,
Bow, like some unknown mercenary's flag,
And lick the soilèd grass? No, no, my friend,
I would not, I, be pardoned in the heap,
And bless indemnity with all that scum,—
Those men I mean, who on my shoulders propped
Their weak rebellion, winning me with lies,
And pitying forsooth my many wrongs;

Poor self-deceivèd wretches, who must think
Each one himself a king in embryo,
Because some dozen vassals cried, My lord!
Cowards, who never knew their little hearts
Till flurried danger held the mirror up,
And then they owned themselves without a blush,
Curling, like spaniels, round my father's feet.
Such things deserted me and are forgiven,
While I, least guilty, am an outcast still,—
And will be, for I love such fair disgrace.

   Sigifred. I know the clear truth; so would Otho see,
For he is just and noble. Fain would I
Be pleader for you—

   Ludolph.   He'll hear none of it;
You know his temper, hot, proud, obstinate;
Endanger not yourself so uselessly.
I will encounter this thwart spleen myself,
To-day at the Duke Conrad's, where he keeps
His crowded state after the victory.
There will I be, a most unwelcome guest,
And parley with him, as a son should do
Who doubly loathes a father's tyranny;
Tell him how feeble is that tyranny;
How the relationship of father and son
Is no more valued than a silken leash
Where lions tug averse, if love grow not
From interchangèd love through many years.
Ay, and those turreted Franconian walls,
Like to a jealous casket, hold my pearl—
My fair Auranthe! Yes, I will be there.

   Sigifred. Be not so rash! wait till his wrath shall pass,
Until his royal spirit softly ebbs,
Self-influenced; then, in his morning dreams
He will forgive thee, and awake in grief
To have not thy good-morrow.

   Ludolph.   Yes, to-day
I must be there, while her young pulses beat
Among the new-plumed minions of war.
Have you seen her of late? No? Auranthe,
Franconia's fair sister, 'tis I mean.
She should be paler for my troublous days—
And there it is—my father's iron lips

Have sworn divorcement 'twixt me and my right.

Sigifred (aside). Auranthe! I had hoped this whim had passed.

Ludolph. And, Sigifred, with all his love of justice,
When will he take that grandchild in his arms,
That, by my love I swear, shall soon be his?
This reconcilement is impossible,
For see—but who are these?

Sigifred. They are messengers
From our great emperor; to you, I doubt not,
For couriers are abroad to seek you out.

Enter THEODORE *and* GONFRID

Theodore. Seeing so many vigilant eyes explore
The province to invite your highness back
To your high dignities, we are too happy.

Gonfrid. We have no eloquence to colour justly
The emperor's anxious wishes.

Ludolph. Go. I follow you.

[*Exeunt* THEODORE *and* GONFRID.

I play the prude: it is but venturing—
Why should he be so earnest? Come, my friend,
Let us to Friedburg castle.

ACT II

SCENE I.—*An Ante-chamber in the Castle.*

Enter LUDOLPH *and* SIGIFRED

Ludolph. No more advices, no more cautioning;
I leave it all to fate—to anything!
I cannot square my conduct to time, place,
Or circumstance; to me 'tis all a mist!

Sigifred. I say no more.

Ludolph. It seems I am to wait
Here in the ante-room;—that may be a trifle.
You see now how I dance attendance here,
Without that tyrant temper, you so blame,
Snapping the rein. You have medicined me
With good advices; and I here remain,

In this most honourable ante-room,
Your patient scholar.

    Sigifred,   Do not wrong me, Prince.
By heavens, I'd rather kiss Duke Conrad's slipper,
When in the morning he doth yawn with pride,
Than see you humbled but a half-degree !
Truth is, the Emperor would fain dismiss
The nobles ere he sees you.

        Enter GONFRID, *from the Council-room*

    Ludolph.   Well, sir ! what ?
    Gonfrid. Great honour to the Prince !   The Emperor,
Hearing that his brave son had re-appeared,
Instant dismissed the Council from his sight,
As Jove fans off the clouds.   Even now they pass.

                                    [*Exit.*

Enter the Nobles from the Council-room.   They cross the
    stage, bowing with respect to LUDOLPH, *he frowning on*
    them.   CONRAD *follows.   Exeunt.*

    Ludolph. Not the discoloured poisons of a fen,
Which he who breathes feels warning of his death,
Could taste so nauseous to the bodily sense,
As these prodigious sycophants disgust
The soul's fine palate.

    Conrad.   Princely Ludolph, hail !
Welcome, thou younger sceptre to the realm !
Strength to thy virgin crownet's golden buds,
That they, against the winter of thy sire,
May burst, and swell, and flourish round thy brows,
Maturing to a weighty diadem !
Yet be that hour far off ! and may he live,
Who waits for thee, as the chapped earth for rain.
Set my life's star !   I have lived long enough,
Since under my glad roof, propitiously,
Father and son each other repossess.

    Ludolph. Fine wording, Duke ! but words could never
        yet
Forestall the fates ; have you not learnt that yet ?
Let me look well : your features are the same ;
Your gait the same : your hair of the same shade ;
As one I knew some passèd weeks ago,

Who sung far different notes into mine ears.
I have mine own particular comments on 't;
You have your own, perhaps.
   Conrad.   My gracious Prince,
All men may err. In truth I was deceived
In your great father's nature, as you were.
Had I known that of him I have since known,
And what you soon will learn, I would have turned
My sword to my own throat, rather than held
Its threatening edge against a good King's quiet:
Or with one word fevered you, gentle Prince,
Who seemed to me, as rugged times then went,
Indeed too much oppressed. May I be bold
To tell the Emperor you will haste to him?
   Ludolph. Your Dukedom's privilege will grant so much.
                                   [*Exit* CONRAD.

He's very close to Otho,—a tight leech!
Your hand—I go. Ha! here the thunder comes
Sullen against the wind! If in two angry brows
My safety lies, then, Sigifred, I'm safe.

           Enter OTHO *and* CONRAD

   Otho. Will you make Titan play the lackey-page
To chattering pigmies? I would have you know
That such neglect of our high Majesty
Annuls all feel of kindred. What is son,—
Or friend,—or brother,—or all ties of blood,—
When the whole kingdom, centred in ourself,
Is rudely slighted? Who am I to wait?
By Peter's chair! I have upon my tongue
A word to fright the proudest spirit here!—
Death!—and slow tortures to the hardy fool
Who dares take such large charter from our smiles!
Conrad, we would be private. Sigifred,
Off! And none pass this way on pain of death!
               [*Exeunt* CONRAD *and* SIGIFRED.
   Ludolph. This was but half expected, my good sire,
Yet I am grieved at it, to the full height,
As though my hopes of favour had been whole.
   Otho. How you indulge yourself! What can you hope
    for?
   Ludolph. Nothing, my liege; I have to hope for nothing.

I come to greet you as a loving son,
And then depart, if I may be so free,
Seeing that blood of yours in my warm veins
Has not yet mitigated into milk.

   Otho. What would you, sir?

   Ludolph.   A lenient banishment.
So please you, let me unmolested pass
This Conrad's gates to the wide air again.
I want no more. A rebel wants no more.

   Otho. And shall I let a rebel loose again
To muster kites and eagles 'gainst my head?
No, obstinate boy, you shall be kept caged up,
Served with harsh food, with scum for Sunday drink.

   Ludolph. Indeed!

   Otho.   And chains too heavy for your life:
I'll choose a gaoler whose swart monstrous face
Shall be a hell to look upon, and she——

   Ludolph. Ha!

   Otho. Shall be your fair Auranthe.

   Ludolph.   Amaze! Amaze!

   Otho. To-day you marry her.

   Ludolph.   This is a sharp jest!

   Otho. No. None at all. When have I said a lie?

   Ludolph. If I sleep not, I am a waking wretch.

   Otho. Not a word more. Let me embrace my child.

   Ludolph. I dare not. 'Twould pollute so good a father!
O heavy crime!—that your son's blinded eyes
Could not see all his parent's love aright,
As now I see it! Be not kind to me—
Punish me not with favour.

   Otho.   Are you sure,
Ludolph, you have no saving plea in store?

   Ludolph. My father, none!

   Otho.   Then you astonish me.

   Ludolph. No, I have no plea. Disobedience,
Rebellion, obstinacy, blasphemy,
Are all my counsellors. If they can make
My crooked deeds show good and plausible,
Then grant me loving pardon, but not else,
Good gods! not else, in any way, my liege!

   Otho. You are a most perplexing noble boy.

   Ludolph. You not less a perplexing noble father.

Otho. Well, you shall have free passport through the
    gates.
Farewell!
    Ludolph. Farewell! and by these tears believe,
And still remember, I repent in pain
All my misdeeds!
    Otho.   Ludolph, I will! I will!
But, Ludolph, ere you go, I would inquire
If you, in all your wandering, ever met
A certain Arab haunting in these parts.
    Ludolph. No, my good lord, I cannot say I did.
    Otho. Make not your father blind before his time;
Nor let these arms paternal hunger more
For an embrace, to dull the appetite
Of my great love for thee, my supreme child!
Come close, and let me breathe into thine ear.
I knew you through disguise. You are the Arab!
You can't deny it.   [*Embracing him*
    Ludolph.   Happiest of days!
    Otho. We'll make it so.
    Ludolph.   'Stead of one fatted calf
Ten hecatombs shall bellow out their last,
Smote 'twixt the horns by the death-stunning mace
Of Mars, and all the soldiery shall feast
Nobly as Nimrod's masons, when the towers
Of Nineveh new kissed the parted clouds!
    Otho. Large as a God speak out, where all is thine.
    Ludolph. Ay, father, but the fire in my sad breast
Is quenched with inward tears! I must rejoice
For you, whose wings so shadow over me
In tender victory, but for myself
I still must mourn. The fair Auranthe mine!
Too great a boon! I pr'ythee let me ask
What more than I know of could so have changed
Your purpose touching her?
    Otho.   At a word, this:
In no deed did you give me more offence
Than your rejection of Erminia.
To my appalling, I saw too good proof
Of your keen-eyed suspicion,—she is naught.
    Ludolph. You are convinced?
    Otho.   Ay, spite of her sweet looks.

O that my brother's daughter should so fall !
Her fame has passed into the grosser lips
Of soldiers in their cups.

Ludolph.   'Tis very sad.

Otho. No more of her.   Auranthe—Ludolph, come !
This marriage be the bond of endless peace !   [*Exeunt.*

SCENE II.—*The entrance of* GERSA'S *Tent in the Hungarian Camp.*

Enter ERMINIA

Erminia. Where—where—where shall I find a messenger?
A trusty soul—a good man, in the camp ?
Shall I go myself ?   Monstrous wickedness !
O cursed Conrad ! devilish Auranthe !
Here is proof palpable as the bright sun !
O for a voice to reach the Emperor's ears !

[*Shouts in the Camp.*

Enter an HUNGARIAN CAPTAIN

Captain. Fair prisoner, you hear these joyous shouts ?
The King—aye, now our King—but still your slave,
Young Gersa, from a short captivity
Has just returned.   He bids me say, bright dame,
That even the homage of his rangèd chiefs
Cures not his keen impatience to behold
Such beauty once again.   What ails you, lady ?

Erminia. Say, is not that a German, yonder ?   There !

Captain. Methinks by his stout bearing he should be ;
Yes—it is Albert ; a brave German Knight,
And much in the Emperor's favour.

Erminia.   I would fain
Inquire of friends and kinsfolk,—how they fared
In these rough times.   Brave soldier, as you pass
To royal Gersa with my humble thanks.
Will you send yonder knight to me ?

Captain.   I will   [*Exit.*

Erminia. Yes, he was ever known to be a man
Frank, open, generous ; Albert, I may trust.
O proof ! proof ! proof !   Albert's an honest man ;

Not Ethelbert the monk, if he were here,
Would I hold more trustworthy.   Now——

Enter ALBERT

Albert.   Good gods !
Lady Erminia ! are you prisoner
In this beleaguered camp ? or are you here
Of your own will ?   You pleased to send for me.
By Venus, 'tis a pity I knew not
Your plight before, and, by her son, I swear
To do you every service you can ask.
What would the fairest—— ?
 Erminia.   Albert, will you swear ?
 Albert. I have.   Well ?
 Erminia.   Albert, you have fame to lose.
If men, in court and camp, lie not outright,
You should be, from a thousand, chosen forth
To do an honest deed.   Shall I confide—— ?
 Albert. Aye, anything to me, fair creature.   Do ;
Dictate my task.   Sweet woman,——
 Erminia.   Truce with that.
You understand me not ; and, in your speech,
I see how far the slander is abroad.
Without proof could you think me innocent ?
 Albert. Lady, I should rejoice to know you so.
 Erminia. If you have any pity for a maid
Suffering a daily death from evil tongues ;
Any compassion for that Emperor's niece
Who, for your bright sword and clear honesty,
Lifted you from the crowd of common men
Into the lap of honour,—save me, knight !
 Albert. How ?   Make it clear, if it be possible,
I, by the banner of Saint Maurice, swear
To right you.
 Erminia.   Possible !—Easy.   O my heart !
This letter's not so soiled but you may read it ;—
Possible !   There—that letter !   Read it.
        [*Gives him a letter.*

ALBERT (*reading*)

"To the Duke Conrad,—Forget the threat you made
at parting and I will forget to send the Emperor letters and

papers of yours I have become possessed of. His life is no trifle to me; his death you shall find none to yourself."

(*Speaks to himself:*) 'Tis me—my life that's pleaded for!

(*Reads.*)

"He, for his own sake, will be dumb as the grave. Erminia has my shame fixed upon her, sure as a wen. We are safe. AURANTHE."

A she-devil! A dragon! I her imp!
Fire of hell! Auranthe—lewd demon!
Where got you this? Where? when?
 Erminia. I found it in the tent, among some spoils
Which, being noble, fell to Gersa's lot.
Come in, and see.   [*They go in and return.*
 Albert.   Villainy! Villainy!
Conrad's sword, his corslet and his helm,
And his letter. Caitiff, he shall feel——
 Erminia. I see you are thunderstruck. Haste, haste, away!
 Albert. O I am tortured by this villainy.
 Erminia. You needs must be. Carry it swift to Otho;
Tell him, moreover, I am prisoner
Here in this camp, where all the sisterhood,
Forced from their quiet cells, are parcelled out
For slaves among these Huns. Away! Away!
 Albert. I am gone.
 Erminia. Swift be your steed! Within this hour
The Emperor will see it.
 Albert.   Ere I sleep:
That I can swear.   [*Hurries out.*
 Gersa (*without*). Brave captains! thanks. Enough
Of loyal homage now!

Enter GERSA

 Erminia.   Hail, royal Hun!
 Gersa. What means this, fair one? Why in such alarm?
Who was it hurried by me so distract?
It seemed you were in deep discourse together;
Your doctrine has not been so harsh to him

As to my poor deserts.   Come, come, be plain.
I am no jealous fool to kill you both,
Or, for such trifles, rob th' adorned woild
Of such a beauteous vestal.
    Erminia.   I grieve, my lord.
To hear you condescend to ribald-phrase.
    Gersa. This is too much !   Hearken, my lady pure !
    Erminia. Silence ! and hear the magic of a name—
Erminia !   I am she,—the Emperor's niece !
Praisèd be the heavens, I now dare own myself !
    Gersa. Erminia !   Indeed !   I've heard of her.
Pr'ythee, fair lady, what chance brought you here ?
    Erminia. Ask your own soldiers.
    Gersa. And you dare own your name.
For loveliness you may—and for the rest
My vein is not censorious.
    Erminia.   Alas ! poor me !
'Tis false indeed.
    Gersa.   Indeed you are too fair :
The swan, soft leaning on her fledgy breast,
When to the stream she launches, looks not back
With such a tender grace ; nor are her wings
So white as your soul is, if that but be
Twin picture to your face.   Erminia !
To-day, for the first day, I am a king,
Yet would I give my unworn crown away
To know you spotless.
    Erminia.   Trust me one day more,
Generously, without more certain guarantee
Than this poor face you deign to praise so much ;
After that, say and do whate'er you please.
If I have any knowledge of you, sir,
I think, nay I am sure, you will grieve much
To hear my story.   O, be gentle to me,
For I am sick and faint with many wrongs,
Tired out and weary-worn with contumelies.
    Gersa. Poor lady !

Enter ETHELBERT

    Erminia. Gentle Prince, 'tis false indeed.
Good morrow, holy father !   I have had
Your prayers, though I looked for you in vain.
    L

Ethelbert. Blessings upon you, daughter! Sure you look
Too cheerful for these foul pernicious days.
Young man, you heard this virgin say 'twas false.—
'Tis false I say. What! can you not employ
Your temper elsewhere, 'mong these burly tents,
But you must taunt this dove, for she hath lost
The Eagle Otho to beat off assault?
Fie! fie! But I will be her guard myself;
I' the Emperor's name. I here demand
Herself, and all her sisterhood. She false!

Gersa. Peace! peace, old man! I cannot think she is.

Ethelbert. Whom I have known from her first infancy.
Baptized her in the bosom of the Church,
Watched her as anxious husbandmen the grain,
From the first shoot till the unripe mid-May,
Then to the tender ear of her June days,
Which, lifting sweet abroad its timid green,
Is blighted by the touch of calumny!
You cannot credit such a monstrous tale?

Gersa. I cannot. Take her. Fair Erminia,
I follow you to Friedburg,—is't not so?

Erminia. Aye, so we purpose.

Ethelbert.   Daughter, do you so?
How's this? I marvel! Yet you look not mad.

Erminia. I have good news to tell you, Ethelbert.

Gersa. Ho! ho, there! Guards!
Your blessing, father! Sweet Erminia,
Believe me, I am well nigh sure—

Erminia.   Farewell!
Short time will show.   [*Enter Chiefs.*
          Yes, father Ethelbert,
I have news precious as we pass along.

Ethelbert. Dear daughter, you shall guide me.

Erminia.   To no ill.

Gersa. Command an escort to the Friedburg lines.
          [*Exeunt Chiefs.*
Pray let me lead. Fair lady, forget not
Gersa, how he believed you innocent.
I follow you to Friedburg with all speed.

          [*Exeunt.*

ACT III

SCENE I.—*The Country*.

Enter ALBERT

Albert. O that the earth were empty, as when Cain
Had no perplexity to hide his head !
Or that the sword of some brave enemy
Had put a sudden stop to my hot breath,
And hurled me down the illimitable gulf
Of times past, unremembered !   Better so
Than thus fast-limed in a cursèd snare,—
The white limbs of a wanton.   This the end
Of an aspiring life !   My boyhood past
In feud with wolves and bears, when no eye saw
The solitary warfare, fought for love
Of honour 'mid the growling wilderness ;
My sturdier youth, maturing to the sword,
Won by the syren-trumpets, and the ring
Of shields upon the pavement, when bright-mailed
Henry the Fowler passed the streets of Prague.
Was't to this end I louted and became
The menial of Mars, and held a spear,
Swayed by command, as corn is by the wind ?
Is it for this, I now am lifted up
By Europe's thronèd Emperor, to see
My honour be my executioner,—
My love of fame, my prided honesty,
Put to the torture for confessional ?
Then the damned crime of blurting to the world
A woman's secret !—though a fiend she be,
Too tender of my ignominious life ;
But then to wrong the generous Emperor
In such a searching point, were to give up
My soul for foot-ball at hell's holiday !
I must confess,—and cut my throat,—to-day ?
To-morrow ?   Ho ! some wine !

Enter SIGIFRED

Sigifred. A fine humour——
Albert. Who goes there ?   Count Sigifred ?   Ha ! ha !

Sigifred. What, man, do you mistake the hollow sky
For a thronged tavern, and these stubbed trees
For old serge hangings,—me, your humble friend,
For a poor waiter? Why, man, how you stare!
What gipsies have you been carousing with?
No, no more wine: methinks you've had enough.

Albert. You well may laugh and banter. What a fool
An injury may make of a staid man!
You shall know all anon.

Sigifred.   Some tavern brawl?

Albert. 'Twas with some people out of common reach;
Revenge is difficult.

Sigifred.   I am your friend;
We meet again to-day, and can confer
Upon it. For the present I'm in haste.

Albert. Whither?

Sigifred.   To fetch King Gersa to the feast.
The Emperor on this marriage is so hot,
Pray heaven it end not in apoplexy!
The very porters, as I passed the doors,
Heard his loud laugh, and answered in full choir.
I marvel, Albert, you delay so long
From these bright revelries; go, show yourself,
You may be made a duke.

Albert.   Ay, very like.
Pray, what day has his Highness fixed upon?

Sigifred. For what?

Albert. The marriage. What else can I mean?

Sigifred. To-day. O, I forgot, you could not know;
The news is scarce a minute old with me.

Albert. Married to-day! To-day! You did not say so?

Sigifred. Now, while I speak to you, their comely heads
Are bowed before the mitre.

Albert.   O! monstrous!

Sigifred. What is this?

Albert   Nothing, Sigifred. Farewell!
We'll meet upon our subject. Farewell, Count!
                                                    [*Exit.*

Sigifred. To this clear-headed Albert? He brain-turned!
'Tis as portentous as a meteor.
                                                    [*Exit.*

SCENE II.—*An Apartment in the Castle.*

Enter, as from the Marriage, OTHO, LUDOLPH, AURANTHE,
  CONRAD, *Nobles, Knights, Ladies, &c.   Music.*

Otho. Now, Ludolph! Now, Auranthe! Daughter fair!
What can I find to grace your nuptial day
More than my love, and these wide realms in fee!
  Ludolph. I have too much.
  Auranthe.   And I, my liege, by far.
  Ludolph. Auranthe! I have! O, my bride, my love!
Not all the gaze upon us can restrain
My eyes, too long poor exiles from thy face,
From adoration, and my foolish tongue
From uttering soft responses to the love
I see in thy mute beauty beaming forth!
Fair creature, bless me with a single word!
All mine!
  Auranthe. Spare, spare me, my lord; I swoon else.
  Ludolph. Soft beauty! by to-morrow I should die,
Wert thou not mine.   [*They talk apart.*
  1st Lady. How deep she has bewitched him!
  1st Knight. Ask you for her recipe for love philtres.
  2nd Lady. They hold the Emperor in admiration.
  Otho. If ever king was happy that am I!
What are the cities 'yond the Alps to me,
The provinces about the Danube's mouth,
The promise of fair sail beyond the Rhone;
Or routing out of Hyperborean hordes,
To these fair children, stars of a new age?
Unless perchance I might rejoice to win
This little ball of earth, and chuck it them
To play with!
  Auranthe.   Nay, my lord, I do not know——
  Ludolph. Let me not famish.
  Otho (*to Conrad*).   Good Franconia,
You heard what oath I sware, as the sun rose,
That unless Heaven would send me back my son,
My Arab,—no soft music should enrich
The cool wine, kissed off with a soldier's smack;

Now all my empire, bartered for one feast,
Seems poverty.

    Conrad.   Upon the neighbour plain
The heralds have prepared a royal lists ;
Your knights, found war-proof in the bloody field,
Speed to the game.

    Otho.   Well, Ludolph, what say you ?

    Ludolph. My lord !

    Otho.   A tourney ?

    Conrad.   Or, if 't please you best——

    Ludolph. I want no more !

    1st Lady.   He soars !

    2nd Lady.   Past all reason.

    Ludolph. Though heaven's choir
Should in a vast circumference descend
And sing for my delight, I'd stop my ears !
Though bright Apollo's car stood burning here,
And he put out an arm to bid me mount,
His touch an immortality, not I !
This earth, this palace, this room, Auranthe !

    Otho. This is a little painful ; just too much.
Conrad, if he flames longer in this wise
I shall believe in wizard-woven loves
And old romances ; but I'll break the spell.
Ludolph !

    Conrad. He'll be calm, anon.

    Ludolph.   You called ?
Yes, yes, yes, I offend. You must forgive me ;
Not being quite recovered from the stun
Of your large bounties. A tourney, is it not ?

                         [*A senet heard faintly.*

    Conrad. The trumpets reach us.

    Ethelbert (*without*).   On your peril, sirs,
Detain us !

    1st Voice (*without*). Let not the abbot pass.

    2nd Voice (*without*).   No !
On your lives !

    1st Voice (*without*). Holy father, you must not.

    Ethelbert (*without*). Otho !

    Otho.   Who calls on Otho ?

    Ethelbert (*without*).   Ethelbert !

    Otho. Let him come in.

Enter ETHELBERT, *leading in* ERMINIA

                              Thou cursed abbot, why
Hast brought pollution to our holy rites?
Hast thou no fear of hangman, or the faggot?
   Ludolph. What portent—what strange prodigy is this?
   Conrad. Away!
   Ethelbert.   You, Duke?
   Erminia.   Albert has surely failed me!
Look at the Emperor's brow upon me bent!
   Ethelbert. A sad delay!
   Conrad.   Away, thou guilty thing!
   Ethelbert. You again, Duke? Justice, most noble Otho!
You—go to your sister there, and plot again,
A quick plot, swift as thought to save your heads;
For lo! the toils are spread around your den,
The world is all agape to see dragged forth
Two ugly monsters.
   Ludolph.   What means he, my lord?
   Conrad. I cannot guess.
   Ethelbert.   Best ask your lady sister
Whether the riddle puzzles her beyond
The power of utterance.
   Conrad.   Foul barbarian, cease;
The Princess faints!
   Ludolph.   Stab him! O, sweetest wife!
               [*Attendants bear off* AURANTHE.

   Erminia. Alas!
   Ethelbert. Your wife?
   Ludolph.   Ay, Satan! does that yerk ye?
   Ethelbert. Wife! so soon!
   Ludolph.   Ay, wife! Oh, impudence!
Thou bitter mischief! Venomous bad priest!
How dar'st thou lift those beetle brows at me—
Me—the prince Ludolph, in this presence here,
Upon my marriage-day, and scandalise
My joys with such opprobrious surprise?
Wife! Why dost linger on that syllable,
As if it were some demon's name pronounced
To summon harmful lightning, and make yawn
The sleepy thunder? Hast no sense of fear?
No ounce of man in thy mortality?

Tremble ! for, at my nod, the sharpened axe
Will make thy bold tongue quiver to the roots,
Those grey lids wink, and thou not know it, monk !

Ethelbert. O, poor deceivèd Prince ! I pity thee !
Great Otho ! I claim justice——

Ludolph.   Thou shalt have 't !
Thine arms from forth a pulpit of hot fire
Shall sprawl distracted ? O that that dull cowl
Were some most sensitive portion of thy life,
That I might give it to my hounds to tear !
Thy girdle some fine zealous-painèd nerve
To girth thy saddle ! And those devil's beads
Each one a life, that I might every day
Crush one with Vulcan's hammer !

Otho.   Peace, my son ;
You far outstrip my spleen in this affair.
Let us be calm, and hear the abbot's plea
For this intrusion.

Ludolph.   I am silent, sire.

Otho. Conrad, see all depart not wanted here.

[*Exeunt Knights, Ladies, &c.*

Ludolph, be calm. Ethelbert, peace awhile.
This mystery demands an audience
Of a just judge, and that will Otho be.

Ludolph. Why has he time to breathe another word ?

Otho. Ludolph, old Ethelbert, be sure, comes not
To beard us for no cause ; he's not the man
To cry himself up an ambassador
Without credentials.

Ludolph.   I'll chain up myself.

Otho. Old abbot, stand here forth. Lady Erminia,
Sit. And now, abbot ! what have you to say ?
Our ear is open. First we here denounce
Hard penalties against thee, if 't be found
The cause for which you have disturbed us here,
Making our bright hours muddy, be a thing
Of little moment.

Ethelbert.   See this innocent !
Otho ! thou father of the people called,
Is her life nothing ? Her fair honour nothing ?
Her tears from matins until even-song
Nothing ? Her burst heart nothing ? Emperor !

Is this your gentle niece—the simplest flower
Of the world's herbal—this fair lily blanched
Still with the dews of piety, this meek lady
Here sitting like an angel newly-shent,
Who veils its snowy wings and grows all pale,—
Is she nothing?

    Otho.   What more to the purpose, abbot?
    Ludolph. Whither is he winding?
    Conrad.   No clue yet!
    Ethelbert. You have heard, my liege, and so, no doubt,
    all here,
Foul, poisonous, malignant whisperings;
Nay open speech, rude mockery grown common,
Against the spotless nature and clear fame
Of the princess Erminia, your niece.
I have intruded here thus suddenly,
Because I hold those base weeds, with tight hand,
Which now disfigure her fair growing stem,
Waiting but for your sign to pull them up
By the dark roots, and leave her palpable,
To all men's sight, a lady innocent.
The ignominy of that whispered tale
About a midnight gallant seen to climb
A window to her chamber neighboured near,
I will from her turn off, and put the load
On the right shoulders; on that wretch's head,
Who, by close stratagems, did save herself,
Chiefly by shifting to this lady's room
A rope-ladder for false witness.

    Ludolph.   Most atrocious!
    Otho. Ethelbert, proceed.
    Ethelbert.   With sad lips I shall:
For, in the healing of one wound, I fear
To make a greater. His young highness here
To-day was married.
    Ludolph.   Good.
    Ethelbert.   Would it were good!
Yet why do I delay to spread abroad
The names of those two vipers, from whose jaw
A deadly breath went forth to taint and blast
This guileless lady?
    Otho.   Abbot, speak their names.

Ethelbert. A minute first. It cannot be—but may
I ask, great judge, if you to-day have put
A letter by unread?

    Otho.   Does't end in this?

    Conrad. Out with their names!

    Ethelbert.   Bold sinner, say you so?

    Ludolph. Out, hideous monk!

    Otho.   Confess, or by the wheel——

    Ethelbert. My evidence cannot be far away;
And, though it never come, be on my head
The crime of passing an attaint upon
The slanderers of this virgin——

    Ludolph.   Speak aloud!

    Ethelbert. Auranthe, and her brother there!

    Conrad. Amaze!

    Ludolph.   Throw them from the windows!

    Otho. Do what you will!

    Ludolph.   What shall I do with them?
Something of quick dispatch, for should she hear,
My soft Auranthe, her sweet mercy would
Prevail against my fury. Damned priest!
What swift death wilt thou die? As to the lady,
I touch her not.

    Ethelbert.   Illustrious Otho, stay!
An ample store of misery thou hast;
Choke not the granary of thy noble mind
With more bad bitter grain, too difficult
A cud for the repentance of a man
Grey-growing. To thee only I appeal,
Not to thy noble son, whose yeasting youth
Will clear itself, and crystal turn again.
A young man's heart, by Heaven's blessing, is
A wide world, where a thousand new-born hopes
Empurple fresh the melancholy blood:
But an old man's is narrow, tenantless
Of hopes, and stuffed with many memories,
Which being pleasant, ease the heavy pulse—
Painful, clog up and stagnate. Weigh this matter
Even as a miser balances his coin;
And, in the name of mercy, give command
That your Knight Albert be brought here before you.
He will expound this riddle; he will show

A noon-day proof of bad Auranthe's guilt.

 Otho. Let Albert straight be summoned.

         [*Exit one of the Nobles.*

 Ludolph.   Impossible!

I cannot doubt—I will not—no—to doubt

Is to be ashes!—withered up to death!

 Otho. My gentle Ludolph, harbour not a fear;

You do yourself much wrong.

 Ludolph.   O, wretched dolt!

Now, when my foot is almost on thy neck,

Wilt thou infuriate me? Proof! Thou fool!

Why wilt thou tease impossibility

With such a thick-skulled persevering suit?

Fanatic obstinacy! Prodigy!

Monster of folly! Ghost of a turned brain!

You puzzle me,—you haunt me, when I dream

Of you my brain will split! Bold sorcerer!

Juggler! May I come near you? On my soul

I know not whether to pity, curse, or laugh.

Enter ALBERT *and the Nobleman*

Here, Albert, this old phantom wants a proof!

Give him his proof! A camel's load of proofs!

 Otho. Albert, I speak to you as to a man

Whose words once uttered pass like current gold;

And therefore fit to calmly put a close

To this brief tempest. Do you stand possessed

Of any proof against the honourableness

Of Lady Auranthe, our new-spousèd daughter?

 Albert. You chill me with astonishment. How's this?

My liege, what proof should I have 'gainst a fame

Impossible of slur?   [OTHO *rises.*

 Erminia.   O, wickedness!

 Ethelbert. Deluded monarch, 'tis a cruel lie.

 Otho. Peace, rebel-priest!

 Conrad.   Insult beyond credence!

 Erminia. Almost a dream!

 Ludolph.   We have awaked from!

A foolish dream that from my brow hath wrung

A wrathful dew. O, folly! why did I

So act the lion with this silly gnat?

Let them depart. Lady Erminia!

I ever grieved for you, as who did not?
But now you have, with such a brazen front,
So most maliciously, so madly, striven
To dazzle the soft moon, when tenderest clouds
Should be unlooped around to curtain her,
I leave you to the desert of the world
Almost with pleasure.   Let them be set free
For me !   I take no personal revenge
More than against a nightmare, which a man
Forgets in the new dawn.   [*Exit* LUDOLPH.
   Otho. Still in extremes !   No, they must not be loose.
   Ethelbert. Albert, I must suspect thee of a crime
So fiendish——
   Otho.   Fear'st thou not my fury, monk?
Conrad, be they in your safe custody
Till we determine some fit punishment.
It is so mad a deed, I must reflect
And question them in private ; for perhaps,
By patient scrutiny, we may discover
Whether they merit death, or should be placed
In case of the physicians.
       [*Exeunt* OTHO *and Nobles*, ALBERT *following.*
   Conrad. My guards, ho !
   Erminia.   •   Albert, wilt thou follow there?
Wilt thou creep dastardly behind his back,
And shrink away from a weak woman's eye?
Turn, thou court-Janus ! thou forget'st thyself ;
Here is the duke, waiting with open arms

Enter Guards

To thank thee ; here congratulate each other ;
Wring hands ; embrace ; and swear how lucky 'twas
That I, by happy chance, hit the right man
Of all the world to trust in.
   Albert.   Trust ! to me !
   Conrad (*aside*). He is the sole one in this mystery.
   Erminia. Well, I give up, and save my prayers for
     Heaven !
You, who could do this deed, would ne'er relent,
Though, at my words, the hollow prison-vaults
Would groan for pity.
   Conrad.   Manacle them both !

Ethelbert. I know it—it must be—I see it all!
Albert, thou art the minion!
   Erminia.   Ah! too plain——
   Conrad. Silence! Gag up their mouth! I cannot bear
More of this brawling. That the Emperor
Had placed you in some other custody!
Bring them away.   *[Exeunt all but* ALBERT.
   Albert. Though my name perish from the book of honour,
Almost before the recent ink is dry,
And be no more remembered after death
Than any drummer's in the muster-roll!
Yet shall I season high my sudden fall
With triumph o'er that evil-witted duke!
He shall feel what it is to have the hand
Of a man drowning, on his hateful throat.

Enter GERSA *and* SIGIFRED

   Gersa. What discord is at ferment in this house?
   Sigifred. We are without conjecture; not a soul
We met could answer any certainty.
   Gersa. Young Ludolph, like a fiery arrow, shot
By us.
   Sigifred. The Emperor, with crossed arms, in thought.
   Gersa. In one room music, in another sadness,
Perplexity everywhere!
   Albert.   A trifle more!
Follow; your presences will much avail
To tune our jarred spirits. I'll explain.

                              [Exeunt

ACT IV

SCENE I.—AURANTHE'S *Apartment.*

AURANTHE *and* CONRAD *discovered*

   Conrad. Well, well, I know what ugly jeopardy
We are caged in; you need not pester that
Into my ears. Pr'ythee, let me be spared
A foolish tongue, that I may bethink me
Of remedies with some deliberation.

You cannot doubt but 'tis in Albert's power
To crush or save us?
 Auranthe.   No, I cannot doubt.
He has, assure yourself, by some strange means,
My secret; which I ever hid from him,
Knowing his mawkish honesty.
 Conrad.   Cursed slave!
 Auranthe. Ay, I could almost curse him now myself.
Wretched impediment! Evil genius!
A glue upon my wings, that cannot spread,
When they should span the provinces! A snake,
A scorpion, sprawling on the first gold step,
Conducting to the throne high canopied.
 Conrad. You would not hear my counsel, when his life
Might have been trodden out, all sure and hushed;
Now the dull animal forsooth must be
Entreated, managed! When can you contrive
The interview he demands?
 Auranthe.   As speedily
It must be done as my bribed woman can
Unseen conduct him to me; but I fear
'Twill be impossible, while the broad day
Comes through the panes with persecuting glare.
Methinks, if 't now were night I could intrigue
With darkness, bring the stars to second me,
And settle all this trouble.
 Conrad.   Nonsense! Child!
See him immediately; why not now?
 Auranthe. Do you forget that even the senseless door-
   posts
Are on the watch and gape through all the house?
How many whisperers there are about,
Hungry for evidence to ruin me,—
Men I have spurned, and women I have taunted?
Besides, the foolish prince sends, minute whiles,
His pages—so they tell me—to inquire
After my health, entreating, if I please,
To see me.
 Conrad. Well, suppose this Albert here;
What is your power with him?
 Auranthe.   He should be
My echo, my taught parrot! but I fear

He will be cur enough to bark at me;
Have his own say; read me some silly creed
'Bout shame and pity.

 Conrad.   What will you do then?

 Auranthe. What I shall do, I know not: what I would
Cannot be done; for see, this chamber-floor
Will not yield to the pick-axe and the spade,—
Here is no quiet depth of hollow ground.

 Conrad. Sister, you have grown sensible and wise,
Seconding, ere I speak it, what is now,
I hope, resolved between us.

 Auranthe.   Say, what is 't?

 Conrad. You need not be his sexton, too: a man
May carry that with him shall make him die
Elsewhere,—give that to him; pretend the while
You will to-morrow succumb to his wishes,
Be what they may, and send him from the Castle
On some fool's errand; let his latest groan
Frighten the wolves!

 Auranthe.   Alas! he must not die!

 Conrad. Would you were both hearsed up in stifling
  lead!
Detested——

 Auranthe. Conrad, hold! I would not bear
The little thunder of your fretful tongue,
Tho' I alone were taken in these toils,
And you could free me; but remember, sir,
You live alone in my security:
So keep your wits at work, for your own sake,
Not mine, and be more mannerly.

 Conrad.   Thou wasp!
If my domains were emptied of these folk,
And I had thee to starve——

 Auranthe.   O, marvellous!
But, Conrad, now be gone; the host is looked for;
Cringe to the Emperor, entertain the lords.
And, do ye mind, above all things, proclaim
My sickness, with a brother's saddened eye,
Condoling with Prince Ludolph. In fit time
Return to me.

 Conrad. I leave you to your thoughts.

               [Exit.

Auranthe (sola). Down, down, proud temper! down,
    Auranthe's pride!
Why do I anger him when I should kneel?
Conrad! Albert! help! help! What can I do?
O, wretched woman! lost, wrecked, swallowed up,
Accursèd, blasted! O, thou golden Crown,
Orbing along the serene firmament
Of a wide empire, like a glowing moon;
And thou, bright sceptre! lustrous in my eyes
There—as the fabled fair Hesperian tree,
Bearing a fruit more precious! graceful thing,
Delicate, godlike, magic! must I leave
Thee to melt in the visionary air,
Ere, by one grasp, this common hand is made
Imperial? I do not know the time
When I have wept for sorrow; but methinks
I could now sit upon the ground, and shed
Tears, tears of misery. O, the heavy day!
How shall I bear my life till Albert comes?
Ludolph! Erminia! Proofs! O heavy day!
Bring me some mourning weeds, that I may 'tire
Myself as fits one wailing her own death:
Cut off these curls, and brand this lily hand,
And throw these jewels from my loathing sight,—
Fetch me a missal, and a string of beads,—
A cup of bittered water, and a crust,—
I will confess, O, holy Abbot!—How!
What is this? Auranthe! thou fool, dolt,
Whimpering idiot! up! up! and quell!
I am safe! Coward! why am I in fear?
Albert! he cannot stickle, chew the cud
In such a fine extreme,—impossible!
Who knocks?   *[Goes to the door, listens, and opens it*

Enter ALBERT

Albert, I have been waiting for you here
With such an aching heart, such swooning throbs
On my poor brain, such cruel, cruel sorrow,
That I should claim your pity! Art not well?
    Albert. Yes, lady, well.
    Auranthe.   You look not so, alas!
But pale, as if you brought some heavy news.

Albert. You know full well what makes me look so pale.

Auranthe. No! Do I? Surely I am still to learn
Some horror; all I know, this present, is
I am near hustled to a dangerous gulf,
Which you can save me from,—and therefore safe,
So trusting in thy love; that should not make
Thee pale, my Albert.

Albert.   It doth make me freeze.

Auranthe. Why should it love?

Albert.   You should not ask me that,
But make your own heart monitor, and save
Me the great pain of telling. You must know.

Auranthe. Something has vext you, Albert. There are
    times
When simplest things put on a sombre cast;
A melancholy mood will haunt a man,
Until most easy matters take the shape
Of unachievable tasks; small rivulets
Then seem impassable.

Albert.   Do not cheat yourself
With hope that gloss of words or suppliant action,
Or tears, or ravings, or self-threatened death,
Can alter my resolve.

Auranthe.   You make me tremble,
Not so much at your threats, as at your voice,
Untuned, and harsh, and barren of all love.

Albert. You suffocate me! Stop this devil's parley,
And listen to me; know me once for all.

Auranthe. I thought I did. Alas! I am deceived.

Albert. You are not deceived. You took me for
A man detesting all inhuman crime;
And therefore kept from me your demon's plot
Against Erminia. Silent? Be so still;
For ever! Speak no more; but hear my words,
Thy fate. Your safety I have bought to-day
By blazoning a lie, which in the dawn
I'll expiate with truth.

Auranthe.   O cruel traitor!

Albert. For I would not set eyes upon thy shame;
I would not see thee dragged to death by the hair,
Penanced, and taunted on a scaffolding!
To-night, upon the skirts of the blind wood

That blackens northward of these horrid towers,
I wait for you with horses. Choose your fate.
Farewell!

   Auranthe. Albert, you jest; I'm sure you must.
You, an ambitious Soldier! I, a Queen,
One who could say,—Here, rule these Provinces!
Take tribute from these cities for thyself!
Empty these armouries, these treasuries,
Muster thy warlike thousands at a nod!
Go! conquer Italy!

   Albert.   Auranthe, you have made
The whole world chaff to me. Your doom is fixed.

   Auranthe. Out, villain! dastard!

   Albert.   Look there to the door!
Who is it?

   Auranthe. Conrad, traitor!

   Albert.   Let him in.

Enter CONRAD

Do not affect amazement, hypocrite,
At seeing me in this chamber.

   Conrad.   Auranthe?

   Albert. Talk not with eyes, but speak your curses out
Against me, who would sooner crush and grind
A brace of toads, than league with them t' oppress
An innocent lady, gull an Emperor,
More generous to me than autumn sun
To ripening harvests.

   Auranthe.   No more insult, sir!

   Albert. Ay, clutch your scabbard: but, for prudence sake,
Draw not the sword; 'twould make an uproar, Duke,
You would not hear the end of. At nightfall
Your lady sister, if I guess aright,
Will leave this busy castle. You had best
Take farewell too of worldly vanities.

   Conrad. Vassal!

   Albert. To-morrow, when the Emperor sends
For loving Conrad, see you fawn on him.
Good even!

   Auranthe. You'll be seen!

   Albert.   See the coast clear then.

   Auranthe (*as he goes*). Remorseless Albert!

Cruel, cruel, wretch !   [*She lets him out.*

    Conrad. So we must lick the dust ?

    Auranthe.   I follow him.

    Conrad. How ?   Where ?   The plan of your escape ?

    Auranthe.   He waits

For me with horses by the forest-side,

Northward.

    Conrad. Good, good ! he dies.   You go, say you ?

    Auranthe. Perforce.

    Conrad. Be speedy, darkness !   Till that comes,

Fiends keep you company !   [*Exit.*

    Auranthe.   And you ! and you !

And all men !   Vanish !

            [*Retires to an inner apartment.*

SCENE II.—*An Apartment in the Castle.*

Enter LUDOLPH *and* Page

    Page. Still very sick, my lord ; but now I went,

And there her women, in a mournful throng,

Stood in the passage whispering ; if any

Moved 'twas with careful steps, and hushed as death.

They bade me stop.

    Ludolph.   Good fellow, once again

Make soft inquiry ; pr'ythee, be not stayed

By any hindrance, but with gentlest force

Break through her weeping servants, till thou com'st

E'en to her chamber-door, and there, fair boy,—

If with thy mother's milk thou hast sucked in

Any divine eloquence,—woo her ears

With plaints for me, more tender than the voice

Of dying Echo, echoed.

    Page.   Kindest master !

To know thee sad thus, will unloose my tongue

In mournful syllables.   Let but my words reach

Her ears, and she shall take them coupled with

Moans from my heart, and sighs not counterfeit.

May I speed better !   [*Exit Page*

    Ludolph (solus). Auranthe !   My life !

Long have I loved thee, yet till now not loved :

Remembering, as I do, hard-hearted times

When I had heard e'en of thy death perhaps,
And—thoughtless!—suffered thee to pass alone
Into Elysium!—now I follow thee,
A substance or a shadow, wheresoe'er
Thou leadest me—whether thy white feet press,
With pleasant weight, the amorous-aching earth,
Or thro' the air thou pioneerest me,
A shade!   Yet sadly I predestinate!
O, unbenignest Love, why wilt thou let
Darkness steal out upon the sleepy world
So wearily, as if Night's chariot wheels
Were clogged in some thick cloud?   O, changeful Love,
Let not her steeds with drowsy-footed pace
Pass the high stars, before sweet embassage
Comes from the pillowed beauty of that fair
Completion of all-delicate Nature's wit!
Pout her faint lips anew with rubious health;
And, with thine infant fingers, lift the fringe
Of her sick eyelids; that those eyes may glow
With wooing light upon me ere the morn
Peers with disrelish, grey, barren, and cold!

Enter GERSA *and Courtiers*

Otho calls me his Lion,—should I blush
To be so tamed? so——
   Gersa.   Do me the courtesy,
Gentlemen, to pass on.
   1st Knight.   We are your servants.
                          [*Exeunt Courtiers.*
   Ludolph. It seems then, sir, you have found out the man
You would confer with;—me?
   Gersa.   If I break not
Too much upon your thoughtful mood, I will
Claim a brief while your patience.
   Ludolph.   For what cause
Soe'er, I shall be honoured.
   Gersa.   I not less.
   Ludolph. What may it be?   No trifle can take place
Of such deliberate prologue, serious 'haviour.
But, be it what it may, I cannot fail
To listen with no common interest;
For though so new your presence is to me,

Otho the Great

I have a soldier's friendship for your fame.
Please you explain.

    Gersa.   As thus :—for, pardon me,
I cannot, in plain terms, grossly assault
A noble nature ; and would faintly sketch
What your quick apprehension will fill up ;
So finely I esteem you.

    Ludolph.   I attend.

    Gersa. Your generous father, most illustrious Otho,
Sits in the banquet-room among his chiefs ;
His wine is bitter, for you are not there ;
His eyes are fixed still on the open doors,
And ev'ry passer in he frowns upon,
Seeing no Ludolph comes.

    Ludolph.   I do neglect.

    Gersa. And for your absence may I guess the cause?

    Ludolph. Stay there ! No—guess? More princely you
    must be
Than to make guesses at me. 'Tis enough.
I'm sorry I can hear no more.

    Gersa.   And I
As grieved to force it on you so abrupt ;
Yet, one day, you must know a grief, whose sting
Will sharpen more the longer 'tis concealed.

    Ludolph. Say it at once, sir ! Dead—dead?—is she
    dead?

    Gersa. Mine is a cruel task : she is not dead,
And would, for your sake, she were innocent.

    Ludolph. Hungarian ! thou amazest me beyond
All scope of thought, convulsest my heart's blood
To deadly churning ! Gersa, you are young,
As I am ; let me observe you, face to face ;
Not grey-browed like the poisonous Ethelbert,
No rheumèd eyes, no furrowing of age,
No wrinkles, where all vices nestle in
Like crannied vermin,—no ! but fresh, and young,
And hopeful-featured. Ha ! by heaven, you weep !
Tears, human tears ! Do you repent you then
Of a cursed torturer's office? Why shouldst join—
Tell me,—the league of devils? Confess—confess—
The lie !

    Gersa. Lie !—but begone all ceremonious points

Of honour battailous ! I could not turn
My wrath against thee for the orbêd world.

    Ludolph. Your wrath, weak boy ?   Tremble at mine, unless
Retraction follow close upon the heels
Of that late 'stounding insult !   Why, has my sword
Not done already a sheer judgment on thee ?
Despair, or eat thy words !   Why, thou wast nigh
Whimpering away my reason !   Hark ye, sir,
It is no secret, that Erminia,
Erminia, sir, was hidden in your tent,—
O, blessed asylum ! comfortable home !
Begone ! I pity thee ; thou art a gull,
Erminia's last new puppet !

    Gersa.   Furious fire !
Thou mak'st me boil as hot as thou canst flame !
And in thy teeth I give thee back the lie !
Thou liest !   Thou, Auranthe's fool !   A wittol !

    Ludolph. Look ; look at this bright sword ;
There is no part of it, to the very hilt,
But shall indulge itself about thine heart !
Draw ! but remember thou must cower thy plumes,
As yesterday the Arab made thee stoop.

    Gersa. Patience ! Not here ; I would not spill thy blood
Here, underneath this roof where Otho breathes,—
Thy father,—almost mine,

    Ludolph.   O, faltering coward !

Enter PAGE

Stay, stay ; here is one I have half a word with.
Well ?   What ails thee, child ?

    Page.   My lord
    Ludolph.   What wouldst say ?
    Page. They are fled !
    Ludolph.   They !   Who ?
    Page.   When anxiously
I hastened back, your grieving messenger,
I found the stairs all dark, the lamps extinct,
And not a foot or whisper to be heard.
I thought her dead, and on the lowest step
Sat listening ; when presently came by
Two muffled up,—one sighing heavily,
The other cursing low, whose voice I knew

For the Duke Conrad's.   Close I followed them
Thro' the dark ways they chose to the open air,
And, as I followed, heard my lady speak.

   Ludolph. Thy life answers the truth!

   Page.   The chamber's empty!

   Ludolph. As I will be of mercy!   So, at last,
This nail is in my temples!

   Gersa.   Be calm in this.

   Ludolph. I am.

   Gersa.   And Albert, too, has disappeared;
Ere I met you, I sought him everywhere;
You would not hearken.

   Ludolph.   Which way went they, boy?

   Gersa. I'll hunt with you.

   Ludolph.   No, no, no.   My senses are
Still whole.   I have survived.   My arm is strong—
My appetite sharp—for revenge!   I'll no sharer
In my feast; my injury is all my own,
And so is my revenge, my lawful chattels!
Terrier, ferret them out!   Burn—burn the witch .
Trace me their footsteps!   Away!

                              [Exeunt.

ACT V

Scene I.—*A part of the Forest.*

Enter Conrad *and* Auranthe

   Auranthe. Go no further; not a step more.   Thou art
A master-plague in the midst of miseries.
Go,—I fear thee!   I tremble, every limb,
Who never shook before.   There's moody death
In thy resolvèd looks!   Yes, I could kneel
To pray thee far away!   Conrad, go! go!—
There! yonder, underneath the boughs I see
Our horses!

   Conrad. Ay, and the man.

   Auranthe.   Yes, he is there!
Go, go,—no blood! no blood!—go, gentle Conrad!

   Conrad. Farewell!

   Auranthe. Farewell!   For this Heaven pardon you!

                            [Exit Auranthe.

Conrad. If he survive one hour, then may I die
In unimagined tortures, or breathe through
A long life in the foulest sink o' the world!
He dies! 'Tis well she do not advertise
The caitiff of the cold steel at his back.   [*Exit* CONRAD.

Enter LUDOLPH *and Page*

Ludolph. Missed the way, boy? Say not that on your
  peril!
Page. Indeed, indeed, I cannot trace them further.
Ludolph. Must I stop here? Here solitary die
Stifled beneath the thick oppressive shade
Of these dull boughs—this even of dark thickets—
Silent,—without revenge?—pshaw! bitter end,—
A bitter death—a suffocating death,—
A gnawing—silent—deadly, quiet death!
Escaped?—fled?—vanished? melted into air?
She's gone! I cannot clutch her! no revenge!
A muffled death, ensnared in horrid silence!
Sucked to my grave amid a dreamy calm!
O, where is that illustrious noise of war,
To smother up this sound of labouring breath,
This rustle of the trees!

      [AURANTHE *shrieks at a distance.*
Page.   My lord, a noise!
This way—hark!
Ludolph.   Yes, yes! A hope! A music!
A glorious clamour! How I live again!   [*Exeunt*

SCENE II.—*Another part of the Forest.*

Enter ALBERT (*wounded*)

Albert. Oh! for enough life to support me on
To Otho's feet!

Enter LUDOLPH

Ludolph.   Thrice villainous, stay there!
Tell me where that detested woman is,
Or this is through thee!
Albert.   My good Prince, with me
The sword has done its worst; not without worst

Done to another,—Conrad has it home !
I see you know it all !
    Ludolph.   Where is his sister ?

Enter AURANTHE

    Auranthe. Albert !
    Ludolph. Ha ! There ! there ! He is the paramour !—
There—hug him—dying ! O, thou innocence,
Shrine him and comfort him at his last gasp ;
Kiss down his eyelids ! Was he not thy love ?
Wilt thou forsake him at his latest hour ?
Keep fearful and aloof from his last gaze,
His most uneasy moments, when cold death
Stands with the door ajar to let him in ?
    Albert. O that that door with hollow slam would close
Upon me sudden ! for I cannot meet,
In all the unknown chambers of the dead,
Such horrors !
    Ludolph.   Auranthe ! what can he mean ?
What horrors ? Is it not a joyous time ?
Am I not married to a paragon
"Of personal beauty and untainted soul" ?
A blushing fair-eyed purity ? A sylph,
Whose snowy timid hand has never sinned
Beyond a flower plucked, white as itself ?
Albert, you do insult my bride—your mistress—
To talk of horrors on our wedding-night !
    Albert. Alas ! poor Prince, I would you knew my heart !
'Tis not so guilty——
    Ludolph.   Hear ! he pleads not guilty !
You are not ? or, if so, what matters it ?
You have escaped me, free as the dusk air,
Hid in the forest, safe from my revenge ;
I cannot catch you ! You should laugh at me,
Poor cheated Ludolph ! Make the forest hiss
With jeers at me ! You tremble—faint at once,
You will come to again. O cockatrice,
I have you ! Whither wander those fair eyes
To entice the devil to your help, that he
May change you to a spider, so to crawl
Into some cranny to escape my wrath ?
    Albert. Sometimes the counsel of a dying man

Doth operate quietly when his breath is gone:
Disjoin those hands—part—part—do not destroy
Each other—forget her!—Our miseries
Are equal shared, and mercy is——

Ludolph. A boon
When one can compass it. Auranthe, try
Your oratory; your breath is not so hitched.
Ay, stare for help! [ALBERT *dies.*
There goes a spotted soul
Howling in vain along the hollow night!
Hear him! He calls you—sweet Auranthe, come!

Auranthe. Kill me!

Ludolph. No! What? Upon our marriage night?
The earth would shudder at so foul a deed!
A fair bride! A sweet bride! An innocent bride!
No! we must revel it, as 'tis in use
In times of delicate brilliant ceremony:
Come, let me lead you to our halls again!
Nay, linger not; make no resistance, sweet;—
Will you? Ah, wretch, thou canst not, for I have
The strength of twenty lions 'gainst a lamb!
Now—one adieu for Albert! Come away! [*Exeunt.*

SCENE III.—*An inner Court of the Castle.*

Enter SIGIFRED, GONFRID, *and* THEODORE, *meeting*

1st Knight. Was ever such a night?

Sigifred. What horrors more?
Things unbelieved one hour, so strange they are,
The next hour stamps with credit.

1st Knight. Your last news?

Gonfrid. After the page's story of the death
Of Albert and Duke Conrad?

Sigifred. And the return
Of Ludolph with the Princess.

Gonfrid. No more, save
Prince Gersa's freeing Abbot Ethelbert,
And the sweet lady, fair Erminia,
From prison.

1st Knight. Where are they now? Hast yet heard?

Gonfrid. With the sad Emperor they are closeted;

I saw the three pass slowly up the stairs,
The lady weeping, the old abbot cowled.

Sigifred. What next?

1st Knight. I hate to think on 't.

Gonfrid. 'Tis with fate.

1st Knight. One while these proud towers are hushed as
death.

Gonfrid. The next our poor Prince fills the arched rooms
With ghastly ravings.

Sigifred. I do fear his brain.

Gonfrid. I will see more. Bear you so stout a heart?

[*Exeunt into the Castle.*

SCENE IV.—*A Cabinet, opening towards a Terrace.*

OTHO, ERMINIA, ETHELBERT, *and a Physician, discovered*

Otho. O, my poor boy! My son! My son! My
Ludolph!
Have ye no comfort for me, ye physicians
Of the weak body and soul?

Ethelbert. 'Tis not in medicine,
Either of heaven or earth, to cure, unless
Fit time be chosen to administer.

Otho. A kind forbearance, holy abbot. Come,
Erminia; here, sit by me, gentle girl;
Give me thy hand; hast thou forgiven me?

Erminia. Would I were with the saints to pray for you!

Otho. Why will ye keep me from my darling child?

Physician. Forgive me, but he must not see thy face.

Otho. Is then a father's countenance a Gorgon?
Hath it not comfort in it? Would it not
Console my poor boy, cheer him, heal his spirits?
Let me embrace him; let me speak to him;
I will! Who hinders me? Who's Emperor?

Physician. You may not, Sire; 'twould overwhelm him
quite,
He is so full of grief and passionate wrath;
Too heavy a sigh would kill him, or do worse.
He must be saved by fine contrivances;
And, most especially, we must keep clear
Out of his sight a father whom he loves;

His heart is full, it can contain no more.
And do its ruddy office.

    Ethelbert.   Sage advice ;
We must endeavour how to ease and slacken
The tight-wound energies of his despair,
Not make them tenser.

    Otho.   Enough ! I hear, I hear.
Yet you were about to advise more,—I listen.

    Ethelbert. This learned doctor will agree with me,
That not in the smallest point should he be thwarted,
Or gainsaid by one word ; his very motions,
Nods, becks, and hints, should be obeyed with care,
Even on the moment ; so his troubled mind
May cure itself.

    Physician.   There are no other means.

    Otho. Open the door ; let's hear if all is quiet.

    Physician. Beseech you, Sire, forbear.

    Erminia.   Do, do.

    Otho.   I command !
Open it straight :—hush !—quiet !—my lost boy !
My miserable child !

    Ludolph (*indistinctly without*). Fill, fill my goblet,—
    here's a health !

    Erminia.   O, close the door !

    Otho. Let, let me hear his voice ; this cannot last ;
And fain would I catch up his dying words,
Though my own knell they be ! This cannot last !
O let me catch his voice—for lo ! I hear
A whisper in this silence that he's dead !
It is so ! Gersa ?

Enter GERSA

    Physician.   Say, how fares the Prince ?

    Gersa. More calm ; his features are less wild and flushed ;
Once he complained of weariness.

    Physician.   Indeed !
'Tis good,—'tis good ; let him but fall asleep,
That saves him.

    Otho.   Gersa, watch him like a child ;
Ward him from harm,—and bring me better news !

    Physician. Humour him to the height. I fear to go ;
For should he catch a glimpse of my dull garb,

It might affright him, fill him with suspicion
That we believe him sick, which must not be.
  Gersa. I will invent what soothing means I can.

                                          [*Exit* Gersa.

  Physician. This should cheer up your Highness;
    weariness
Is a good symptom, and most favourable;
It gives me pleasant hopes.   Please you, walk forth
Upon the terrace; the refreshing air
Will blow one half of your sad doubts away.

                                          [*Exeunt.*

Scene. V.—*A Banqueting Hall, brilliantly illuminated, and
  set forth with all costly magnificence, with Supper-tables
  laden with Services of Gold and Silver.   A door in the
  back scene, guarded by two Soldiers.   Lords, Ladies,
  Knights, Gentlemen, &c., whispering sadly, and ranging
  themselves; part entering and part discovered.*

  1st Knight. Grievously are we tantalised, one and all;
Swayed here and there, commanded to and fro,
As though we were the shadows of a sleep,
And linked to a dreaming fancy.   What do we hear?
  Gonfrid. I am no seer; you know we must obey
The Prince from A to Z, though it should be
To set the place in flames.   I pray, hast heard
Where the most wicked Princess is?
  1st Knight.   There, sir,
In the next room; have you remarked those two
Stout soldiers posted at the door?
  Gonfrid.   For what?
                                          [*They whisper.*

  1st Lady. How ghast a train!
  2nd Lady. Sure this should be some splendid burial.
  1st Lady. What fearful whispering!   See, see,—Gersa
    there!

                        Enter Gersa

  Gersa. Put on your brightest looks; smile if you can;
Behave as all were happy; keep your eyes
From the least watch upon him; if he speaks
To any one, answer, collectedly,

Without surprise, his questions, howe'er strange.
Do this to the utmost,—though, alas! with me
The remedy grows hopeless! Here he comes,—
Observe what I have said,—show no surprise.

Enter LUDOLPH, *followed by* SIGIFRED *and Page*

Ludolph. A splendid company! rare beauties here!
I should have Orphean lips, and Plato's fancy,
Amphion's utterance, tonèd with his lyre,
Or the deep key of Jove's sonorous mouth,
To give fit salutation. Methought I heard,
As I came in, some whispers,—what of that?
'Tis natural men should whisper; at the kiss
Of Psyche given by Love, there was a buzz
Among the gods!—and silence is as natural.
These draperies are fine, and being a mortal,
I should desire no better; yet, in truth,
There must be some superior costliness
Some wider-domèd high magnificence!
I would have, as a mortal I may not,
Hangings of heaven's clouds, purple and gold,
Slung from the spheres; gauzes of silver mist,
Looped up with cords of twisted wreathèd light,
And tasselled round with weeping meteors!
These pendent lamps and chandeliers are bright
As earthly fires from dull dross can be cleansed;
Yet could my eyes drink up intenser beams
Undazzled;—this is darkness,—when I close
These lids, I see far fiercer brilliances,—
Skies full of splendid moons, and shooting stars,
And spouting exhalations, diamond fires,
And panting fountains quivering with deep glows.
Yes—this is dark—is it not dark?
      Sigifred.   My lord,
'Tis late; the lights of festival are ever
Quenched in the morn.
      Ludolph.   'Tis not to-morrow then?
      Sigifred. 'Tis early dawn.
      Gersa.   Indeed full time we slept;
Say you so, Prince?
      Ludolph.   I say I quarrelled with you;

We did not tilt each other,—that's a blessing,—
Good gods! no innocent blood upon my head!
  Sigifred. Retire, Gersa!
  Ludolph.   There should be three more here:
For two of them, they stay away perhaps,
Being gloomy-minded, haters of fair revels,—
They know their own thoughts best.
                             As for the third,
Deep blue eyes, semi-shaded in white lids,
Finished with lashes fine for more soft shade,
Completed by her twin-arched ebon-brows;
White temples, of exactest elegance,
Of even mould, felicitous and smooth;
Cheeks fashioned tenderly on either side,
So perfect, so divine, that our poor eyes
Are dazzled with the sweet proportioning,
And wonder that 'tis so,—the magic chance!
Her nostrils, small, fragrant, fairy-delicate;
Her lips—I swear no human bones e'er wore
So taking a disguise;—you shall behold her!
We'll have her presently; ay, you shall see her,
And wonder at her, friends, she is so fair;
She is the world's chief jewel, and, by heaven!
She's mine by right of marriage!—she is mine!
Patience, good people, in fit time I send
A summoner,—she will obey my call,
Being a wife most mild and dutiful.
First I would hear what music is prepared
To herald and receive her; let me hear!
  Sigifred. Bid the musicians soothe him tenderly.
                    [A soft strain of Music.
  Ludolph. Ye have none better? No, I am content:
'Tis a rich sobbing melody, with reliefs
Full and majestic; it is well enough,
And will be sweeter, when ye see her pace
Sweeping into this presence, glistened o'er
With emptied caskets, and her train upheld
By ladies habited in robes of lawn,
Sprinkled with golden crescents, others bright
In silks, with spangles showered, and bowed to
By Duchesses and pearlèd Margravines!
Sad! that the fairest creature of the earth—

I pray you mind me not—'tis sad, I say,
That the extremest beauty of the world
Should so entrench herself away from me,
Behind a barrier of engendered guilt!

    2nd Lady. Ah! what a moan!
    1st Knight.   Most piteous indeed!
    Ludolph. She shall be brought before this company,
And then—then—
    1st Lady. He muses.
    Gersa.   O, Fortune! where will this end?
    Sigifred. I guess his purpose! Indeed he must not have
That pestilence brought in,—that cannot be,
There we must stop him.
    Gersa.   I am lost! Hush, hush!
He is about to rave again.
    Ludolph. A barrier of guilt! I was the fool,
She was the cheater! Who's the cheater now,
And who the fool? The entrapped, the cagèd fool,
The bird-limed raven? She shall croak to death
Secure! Methinks I have her in my fist,
To crush her with my heel! Wait, wait! I marvel
My father keeps away. Good friend—ah! Sigifred?
Do bring him to me,—and Erminia,
I fain would see before I sleep—and Ethelbert,
That he may bless me, as I know he will,
Though I have cursed him.
    Sigifred.   Rather suffer me
To lead you to them.
    Ludolph.   No, excuse me,—no!
The day is not quite done. Go, bring them hither.
                     [*Exit* SIGIFRED.
Certes, a father's smile should, like sunlight,
Slant on my sheavèd harvest of ripe bliss.
Besides, I thirst to pledge my lovely bride
In a deep goblet; let me see—what wine?
The strong Iberian juice or mellow Greek?
Or pale Calabrian? Or the Tuscan grape?
Or of old Ætna's pulpy wine-presses,
Black stained with the fat vintage, as it were
The purple slaughter-house, where Bacchus' self
Pricked his own swollen veins! Where is my page?
    Page. Here, here!

Ludolph. Be ready to obey me; anon thou shalt
Bear a soft message for me; for the hour
Draws near when I must make a winding up
Of bridal mysteries—a fine-spun vengeance!
Carve it on my tomb, that, when I rest beneath,
Men shall confess, this Prince was gulled and cheated,
But from the ashes of disgrace he rose
More than a fiery dragon, and did burn
His ignominy up in purging fires!
Did I not send, sir, but a moment past,
For my father?
    Gersa.   You did.
    Ludolph.   Perhaps 'twould be
Much better he came not.
    Gersa.   He enters now!

    Enter OTHO, ERMINIA, ETHELBERT, SIGIFRED, *and*
                  Physician

    Ludolph. Oh! thou good man, against whose sacred
           head
I was a mad conspirator, chiefly too
For the sake of my fair newly wedded wife,
Now to be punished!—do not look so sad!
Those charitable eyes will thaw my heart,
Those tears will wash away a just resolve,
A verdict ten times sworn! Awake—awake—
Put on a judge's brow, and use a tongue
Made iron-stern by habit! Thou shalt see
A deed to be applauded, 'scribed in gold!
Join a loud voice to mine, and so denounce
What I alone will execute!
    Otho.   Dear son,
What is it? By your father's love, I sue
That it be nothing merciless!
    Ludolph.   To that demon?
Not so! No! She is in temple-stall,
Being garnished for the sacrifice, and I,
The Priest of Justice, will immolate her
Upon the altar of wrath! She stings me through!—
Even as the worm doth feed upon the nut,
So she, a scorpion, preys upon my brain!
I feel her gnawing here! Let her but vanish

   M

Then, father, I will lead your legions forth,
Compact in steelèd squares and spearèd files,
And bid our trumpets speak a fell rebuke
To nations drowsed in peace!

   Otho.   To-morrow, son,
Be your word law; forget to-day——

   Ludolph.   I will,
When I have finished it! Now,—now, I'm pight,
Tight-footed for the deed!

   Erminia.   Alas! Alas!

   Ludolph. What angel's voice is that? Erminia.
Ah! gentlest creature, whose sweet innocence
Was almost murdered; I am penitent.
Wilt thou forgive me? And thou, holy man,
Good Ethelbert, shall I die in peace with you?

   Erminia. Die, my lord?

   Ludolph.   I feel it possible.

   Otho.   Physician?

   Physician. I fear he is past my skill.

   Otho.   Not so!

   Ludolph. I see it—I see it—I have been wandering!
Half mad—not right here—I forget my purpose.
Bestir—bestir—Auranthe! Ha! ha! ha!
Youngster! page! go bid them drag her to me!
Obey! This shall finish it!   [*Draws a dagger.*

   Otho.   Oh, my son! my son!

   Sigifred. This must not be—stop there!

   Ludolph.   Am I obeyed?
A little talk with her—no harm—haste! haste!

                            [*Exit Page.*

Set her before me—never fear I can strike.

   Several Voices. My lord! My lord!

   Gersa.   Good Prince!

   Ludolph. Why do ye trouble me? out—out—away!
There she is! take that! and that! no, no,
That's not well done—where is she?

*The Doors open. Enter Page. Several Women are seen
    grouped about* AURANTHE *in the inner room.*

   Page. Alas! My lord, my lord! they cannot move her!
Her arms are stiff—her fingers clenched and cold.

Ludolph. She's dead!

> [*Staggers and falls into their arms.*

Ethelbert. Take away the dagger.

Gersa.   Softly; so!

Otho. Thank God for that!

Sigifred.   It could not harm him now.

Gersa, No!—brief be his anguish!

Ludolph. She's gone! I am content. Nobles, good
    night!
We are all weary—faint—set ope the doors—
I will to bed! To-morrow——   [*Dies.*

THE CURTAIN FALLS

THE CAP AND BELLS

OR, THE JEALOUSIES

A FAERY TALE.   UNFINISHED

In midmost Ind, beside Hydaspes cool,
There stood, or hovered, tremulous in the air,
A faery city, 'neath the potent rule
Of Emperor Elfinan; famed ev'rywhere
For love of mortal women, maidens fair,
Whose lips were solid, whose soft hands were made
Of a fit mould and beauty, ripe and rare,
To pamper his slight wooing, warm yet staid:
He loved girls smooth as shades, but hated a mere shade.

This was a crime forbidden by the law;
And all the priesthood of his city wept,
For ruin and dismay they well foresaw
If impious prince no bound or limit kept,
And faery Zendervester overstept;
They wept, he sinned, and still he would sin on,
They dreamt of sin, and he sinned while they slept;
In vain the pulpit thundered at the throne,
Caricature was vain, and vain the tart lampoon.

Which seeing, his high court of parliament
Laid a remonstrance at his Highness' feet,
Praying his royal senses to content
Themselves with what in faery land was sweet,
Befitting best that shade with shade should meet:
Whereat, to calm their fears, he promised soon
From mortal tempters all to make retreat,—
Aye, even on the first of the new moon
An immaterial wife to espouse as heaven's boon.

Meantime he sent a fluttering embassy
To Pigmio, of Imaus sovereign,
To half beg, and half demand, respectfully,

The hand of his fair daughter Bellanaine ;
An audience had, and speeching done, they gain
Their point, and bring the weeping bride away ;
Whom, with but one attendant, safely lain
Upon their wings, they bore in bright array,
While little harps were touched by many a lyric fay.

As in old pictures tender cherubim
A child's soul thro' the sapphired canvas bear,
So, thro' a real heaven, on they swim
With the sweet princess on her plumaged lair,
Speed giving to the winds her lustrous hair ;
And so she journeyed, sleeping or awake,
Save when, for healthful exercise and air
She chose to *promener à l'aile* or take
A pigeon's somerset, for sport or change's sake

"Dear Princess, do not whisper me so loud,"
Quoth Coralline, nurse and confidant.
"Do not you see there, lurking in a cloud,
Close at your back, that sly old Crafticant ?
He hears a whisper plainer than a rant :
Dry up your tears, and do not look so blue ;
He's Elfinan's great state-spy militant,
His running, lying, flying footman too,—
Dear mistress, let him have no handle against you !

"Show him a mouse's tail, and he will guess,
With metaphysic swiftness, at the mouse ;
Show him a garden, and with speed no less
He'll surmise sagely of a dwelling-house,
And plot, in the same minute, how to chouse
The owner out of it ; show him a——" " Peace !
Peace ! nor contrive thy mistress' ire to rouse !"
Returned the Princess, "my tongue shall not cease
Till from this hated match I get a free release.

"Ah, beauteous mortal !" "Hush !" quoth Coralline,
"Really you must not talk of him, indeed."
"You hush !" replied the mistress with a shine
Of anger in her eyes, enough to breed
In stouter hearts than nurse's fear and dread :

'Twas not the glance itself made Nursey flinch,
But of its threat she took the utmost heed;
Not liking in her heart an hour-long pinch,
Or a sharp needle run into her back an inch.

So she was silenced, and fair Bellanaine,
Writhing her little body with ennui,
Continued to lament and to complain,
That Fate, cross-purposing, should let her be
Ravished away far from her dear countree;
That all her feelings should be set at nought,
In trumping up this match so hastily,
With lowland blood; and lowland blood she thought
Poison, as every staunch true-born Imaian ought.

Sorely she grieved, and wetted three or four
White Provence rose-leaves with her faery tears,
But not for this cause;—alas! she had more
Bad reasons for her sorrow, as appears
In the famed memoirs of a thousand years,
Written by Crafticant, and published
By Parpaglion and Co., (those sly compeers
Who raked up ev'ry fact against the dead,)
In Scarab Street, Panthea, at the Jubal's Head.

Where, after a long hypercritic howl
Against the vicious manners of the age,
He goes on to expose with heart and soul,
What vice in this or that year was the rage,
Backbiting all the world in ev'ry page;
With special strictures on the horrid crime,
(Sectioned and subsectioned with learning sage),
Of faeries stooping on their wings sublime
To kiss a mortal's lips, when such were in their prime.

Turn to the copious index, you will find
Somewhere in the column, headed letter B,
The name of Bellanaine, if you're not blind;
Then pray refer to the text, and you will see
An article made up of calumny
Against this highland princess, rating her
For giving way, so over fashionably,
To this new-fangled vice, which seems a burr
Stuck in his moral throat no coughing e'er could stir.

There he says plainly that she loved a man!
That she around him fluttered, flirted, toyed,
Before her marriage with great Elfinan;
That after marriage, too, she never joyed
In husband's company, but still employed
Her wits to 'scape away to Angle-land;
Where lived the youth, who worried and annoyed
Her tender heart, and its warm ardours fanned
To such a dreadful blaze her side would scorch her hand.

But let us leave this idle tittle-tattle
To waiting-maids and bedroom coteries,
Nor till fit time against her fame wage battle.
Poor Elfinan is very ill at case;
Let us resume his subject if you please;
For it may comfort and console him much
To rhyme and syllable his miseries;
Poor Elfinan! whose cruel fate was such,
He sat and cursed a bride he knew he could not touch.

Soon as (according to his promises)
The bridal embassy had taken wing,
And vanished, bird-like, o'er the suburb trees,
The Emperor, empierced with the sharp sting
Of love, retired, vexèd and murmuring
Like any drone shut from the fair bee-queen,
Into his cabinet, and there did fling
His limbs upon a sofa, full of spleen,
And damned his House of Commons, in complete chagrin

"I'll trounce some of the members," cried the Prince,
"I'll put a mark against some rebel names,
I'll make the Opposition-benches wince,
I'll show them very soon, to all their shames,
What 'tis to smother up a Prince's flames.
That ministers should join in it, I own,
Surprises me!—they too at these high games!
Am I an Emperor? Do I wear a crown?
Imperial Elfinan, go hang thyself or drown!

"I'll trounce 'em!—there's the square-cut chancellor,
His son shall never touch that bishopric;
And for the nephew of old Palfior,

I'll show him that his speeches made me sick,
And give the colonelcy to Phalaric;
The tiptoe marquis, moral and gallant,
Shall lodge in shabby taverns upon tick;
And for the Speaker's second cousin's aunt,
She sha'n't be maid of honour,—by heaven that she sha'n't!

"I'll shirk the Duke of A.; I'll cut his brother ·
I'll give no garter to his eldest son;
I won't speak to his sister or his mother.
The Viscount B. shall live at cut-and-run;
But how in the world can I contrive to stun
That fellow's voice, which plagues me worse than any,
That stubborn fool, that impudent state-dun,
Who sets down ev'ry sovereign as a zany,—
That vulgar commoner, Esquire Biancopany?

"Monstrous affair! Pshaw! pah! what ugly minx
Will they fetch from Imaus for my bride?
Alas! my wearied heart within me sinks,
To think that I must be so near allied
To a cold dullard fay,—ah, woe betide!
Ah, fairest of all human loveliness!
Sweet Bertha! what crime can it be to glide
About the fragrant plaitings of thy dress,
Or kiss thine eyes, or count thy locks, tress after tress?"

So said, one minute's while his eyes remained
Half lidded, piteous, languid, innocent;
But, in a wink, their splendour they regained,
Sparkling revenge with amorous fury blent.
Love thwarted in bad temper oft has vent:
He rose, he stampt his foot, he rang the bell,
And ordered some death-warrants to be sent
For signature:—somewhere the tempest fell,
As many a poor fellow does not live to tell.

"At the same time, Eban,"—(this was his page,
A fay of colour, slave from top to toe,
Sent as a present, while yet under age,
From the Viceroy of Zanguebar,—wise, slow
His speech, his only words were "Yes," and "No,"

But swift of look and foot and wing was he,)—
"At the same time, Eban, this instant go
To Hum the soothsayer, whose name I see
Among the fresh arrivals in our empery.

"Bring Hum to me.   But stay—here, take my ring,
The pledge of favour, that he not suspect
Any foul play, or awkward murdering,
Tho' I have bowstrung many of his sect;
Throw in a hint, that if he should neglect
One hour the next shall see him in my grasp,
And the next after that shall see him necked
Or swallowed by my hunger-starved asp,—
And mention ('tis as well) the torture of the wasp."

These orders given, the Prince, in half a pet,
Let o'er the silk his propping elbow slide,
Caught up his little legs, and, in a fret,
Fell on the sofa on his royal side.
The slave retreated backwards, humble-eyed,
And with a slave-like silence closed the door,
And to old Hum thro' street and alley hied;
He "knew the city," as we say, of yore,
And for short cuts and turns, was nobody knew more.

It was the time when wholesale dealers close
Their shutters with a moody sense of wealth,
But retail dealers, diligent, let loose
The gas (objected to on score of health),
Conveyed in little soldered pipes by stealth,
And make it flare in many a brilliant form,
That all the powers of darkness it repell'th,
Which to the oil-trade doth great scaith and harm,
And supersedeth quite the use of the glow-worm.

Eban, untempted by the pastrycooks,
(Of pastry he got store within the palace,)
With hasty steps, wrapped cloak, and solemn looks,
Incognito upon his errand sallies,
His smelling-bottle ready for the alleys;
He passed the hurdygurdies with disdain,
Vowing he'd have them sent on board the galleys;
Just as he made his vow it 'gan to rain,
Therefore he called a coach, and bade it drive amain.

" I'll pull the string," said he, and further said,
" Polluted jarvey ! Ah, thou filthy hack !
Whose springs of life are all dried up and dead,
Whose linsey-woolsey lining hangs all slack,
Whose rug is straw, whose wholeness is a crack ;
And evermore thy steps go clatter-clitter ;
Whose glass once up can never be got back,
Who prov'st, with jolting arguments and bitter,
That 'tis of modern use to travel in a litter.

" Thou inconvenience ! thou hungry crop
For all corn ! thou snail-creeper to and fro,
Who, while thou goest, ever seem'st to stop,
And fiddle-faddle standest while you go ;
I' the morning, freighted with a weight of woe,
Unto some lazar-house thou journeyest,
And in the evening tak'st a double row
Of dowdies, for some dance or party drest,
Besides the goods meanwhile thou movest east and west.

" By thy ungallant bearing and sad mien,
An inch appears the utmost thou couldst budge ;
Yet at the slightest nod, or hint, or sign,
Round to the curb-stone patient dost thou trudge,
Schooled in a beckon, learnèd in a nudge,
A dull-eyed Argus watching for a fare ;
Quiet and plodding, thou dost bear no grudge
To whisking tilburies or phaetons rare,
Curricles, or mail-coaches, swift beyond compare.'

Philosophizing thus, he pulled the check
And bade the coachman wheel to such a street,
Who, turning much his body, more his neck,
Louted full low, and hoarsely did him greet :
" Certes, monsieur were best take to his feet,
Seeing his servant can no further drive
For press of coaches, that to-night here meet,
Many as bees about a straw-capped hive,
When first for April honey into faint flowers they dive."

Eban then paid his fare, and tiptoe went
To Hum's hotel ; and, as he on did pass
With head inclined, each dusky lineament
Showed in the pearl-paved street, as in a glass ;

His purple vest, that ever peeping was
Rich from the fluttering crimson of his cloak,
His silvery trousers, and his silken sash,
Tied in a burnished knot, their semblance took
Upon the mirrored walls, wherever he might look.

He smiled at self, and, smiling, showed his teeth
And seeing his white teeth, he smiled the more ;
Lifted his eye-brows, spurned the path beneath,
Showed teeth again, and smiled as heretofore,
Until he knocked at the magician's door ;
Where, till the porter answered, might be seen,
In the clear panel more he could adore,—
His turban wreathed of gold, and white, and green,
Mustachios, ear-ring, nose-ring, and his sabre keen.

"Does not your master give a rout to-night?"
Quoth the dark page.   "Oh, no !" returned the Swiss,
"Next door but one to us, upon the right,
The *Magazin des Modes* now open is
Against the Emperor's wedding ;—and, sir, this
My master finds a monstrous horrid bore ;
As he retired, an hour ago I wis,
With his best beard and brimstone, to explore
And cast a quiet figure in his second floor.

"Gad ! he's obliged to stick to business !
For chalk, I hear, stands at a pretty price ;
And as for aqua vitæ—there's a mess !
The *dentes sapientiæ* of mice,
Our barber tells me too, are on the rise,—
Tinder's a lighter article,—nitre pure
Goes off like lightning,—grains of Paradise
At an enormous figure !—stars not sure !—
Zodiac will not move without a slight douceur !

"Venus won't stir a peg without a fee,
And master is too partial, *entre nous*,
To——"   "Hush—hush !" cried Eban, "sure that is he
Coming downstairs,—by St. Bartholomew !
As backwards as he can,—is 't something new ?

Or is 't his custom, in the name of fun?"
"He always comes down backward, with one shoe"—
Returned the porter—"off, and one shoe on,
Like, saving shoe for sock or stocking, my man John!"

It was indeed the great Magician,
Feeling, with careful toe, for every stair,
And retrograding careful as he can,
Backwards and downwards from his own two pair:
"Salpietro!" exclaimed Hum, "is the dog there?
He's always in my way upon the mat!"
"He's in the kitchen, or the Lord knows where,"—
Replied the Swiss,—"the nasty, whelping brat!"
"Don't beat him!" returned Hum, and on the floor came
        pat.

Then facing right about, he saw the page,
And said: "Don't tell me what you want, Eban;
The Emperor is now in a huge rage,—
'Tis nine to one he'll give you the rattan!
Let us away!" Away together ran
The plain-dressed sage and spangled blackamoor,
Nor rested till they stood to cool, and fan,
And breathe themselves at th' Emperor's chamber door,
When Eban thought he heard a soft imperial snore.

"I thought you guessed, foretold, or prophesied,
That 's Majesty was in a raving fit?"
"He dreams," said Hum, "or I have ever lied,
That he is tearing you, sir, bit by bit."
"He's not asleep, and you have little wit,"
Replied the page; "that little buzzing noise,
Whate'er your palmistry may make of it,
Comes from a plaything of the Emperor's choice,
From a Man-Tiger-Organ, prettiest of his toys."

Eban then ushered in the learnèd seer:
Elfinan's back was turned, but, ne'ertheless,
Both, prostrate on the carpet, ear by ear,
Crept silently, and waited in distress,
Knowing the Emperor's moody bitterness;
Eban especially, who on the floor 'gan

Tremble and quake to death,—he fearèd less
A dose of senna-tea or nightmare Gorgon
Than the Emperor when he play'd on his Man-Tiger-
    Organ.

They kissed nine times the carpet's velvet face
Of glossy silk, soft, smooth, and meadow-green,
Where the close eye in deep rich fur might trace
A silver tissue, scantly to be seen,
As daisies lurked in June grass, buds in green ;
Sudden the music ceased, sudden the hand
Of majesty, by dint of passion keen,
Doubled into a common fist, went grand,
And knocked down three cut glasses and his best inkstand.

Then turning round, he saw those trembling two :
" Eban," said he, " as slaves should taste the fruits
Of diligence, I shall remember you
To-morrow, or next day, as time suits,
In a finger conversation with my mutes,—
Begone !—for you, Chaldean ! here remain ;
Fear not, quake not, and as good wine recruits
A conjurer's spirits, what cup will you drain ?
Sherry in silver, hock in gold, or glassed champagne ?

" Commander of the Faithful ! " answered Hum,
" In preference to these, I'll merely taste
A thimble-full of old Jamaica rum."
" A simple boon ! " said Elfinan ; " thou mayst
Have Nantz, with which my morning-coffee's laced."
" I'll have a glass of Nantz, then,"—said the seer,—
" Made racy—(sure my boldness is misplaced !)—
With the third part—(yet that is drinking dear !)—
Of the least drop of *crême de citron*, crystal clear."

" I pledge you, Hum ! and pledge my dearest love,
My Bertha ! "   " Bertha ! Bertha ! " cried the sage
" I know a many Berthas ! "   " Mine's above
All Berthas ! " sighed the Emperor.   " I engage,"
Said Hum, "in duty, and in vassalage,
To mention all the Berthas in the earth ;—

There's Bertha Watson,—and Miss Bertha Page,—
This famed for languid eyes, and that for mirth,—
There's Bertha Blount of York,—and Bertha Knox of
    Perth."

"You seem to know "—"I do know," answered Hum,
"Your Majesty's in love with some fine girl
Named Bertha ; but her surname will not come,
Without a little conjuring." "'Tis Pearl,
'Tis Bertha Pearl ! What makes my brains so whirl ?
And she is softer, fairer than her name !"
"Where does she live ?" asked Hum. "Her fair locks
    curl
So brightly, they put all our fays to shame !—
Live ?—O ! at Canterbury, with her old grand-dame."

"Good ! good !" cried Hum, "I've known her from a
    child !
She is a changeling of my management ;
She was born at midnight in an Indian wild ;
Her mother's screams with the striped tigers' blent,
While the torch-bearing slaves a halloo sent
Into the jungles ; and her palanquin,
Rested amid the desert's dreariment,
Shook with her agony, till fair were seen
The little Bertha's eyes ope on the stars serene."

"I can't say," said the monarch ; "that may be,
Just as it happened, true or else a bam !
Drink up your brandy, and sit down by me,
Feel, feel my pulse—how much in love I am !
And if your science is not all a sham
Tell me some means to get the lady here,"
"Upon my honour !" said the son of Cham,
"She is my dainty changeling, near and dear,
Although her story sounds at first a little queer."

"Convey her to me, Hum, or by my crown,
My sceptre, and my cross-surmounted globe,
I'll knock you "—"Does your majesty mean—*down* ?
No, no, you never could my feelings probe
To such a depth !" The Emperor took his robe,

And wept upon its purple palatine,
While Hum continued, shamming half a sob,—
"In Canterbury doth your lady shine?
But let me cool your brandy with a little wine."

Whereat a narrow Flemish glass he took,
That since belonged to Admiral De Witt,
Admired it with a connoisseuring look,
And with the ripest claret crownèd it;
And, ere the lively bead could burst and flit,
He turned it quickly, nimbly upside down,
His mouth being held conveniently fit
To catch the treasure: "Best in all the town!"
He said, smacked his moist lips, and gave a pleasant frown.

"Ah! good my Prince, weep not!" And then again
He filled a bumper. "Great Sire, do not weep!
Your pulse is shocking, but I'll ease your pain."
"Fetch me that ottoman, and prithee keep
Your voice low," said the Emperor; "and steep
Some lady's-fingers nice in Candy wine;
And prithee, Hum, behind the screen do peep
For the rose-water vase, magician mine!
And sponge my forehead,—so my love doth make me pine.

"Ah, cursèd Bellanaine!" "Don't think of her,"
Rejoined the Mago, "but on Bertha muse;
For, by my choicest best barometer,
You shall not throttled be in marriage noose;
I've said it, Sire; you only have to choose—
Bertha or Bellanaine." So saying, he drew
From the left pocket of his threadbare hose
A sampler, hoarded slyly, good as new,
Holding it by his thumb and finger full in view.

"Sire, this is Bertha Pearl's neat handy-work;
Her *name*, see here, *Midsummer, ninety-one*."
Elfinan snatched it with a sudden jerk,
And wept as if he never would have done,
Honouring with royal tears the poor homespun;
Whereon were broidered tigers with black eyes,
And long-tailed pheasants, and a rising sun,
Plenty of posies, great stags, butterflies
Bigger than stags,—a moon,—with other mysteries.

The monarch handled o'er and o'er again
These day-school hieroglyphics with a sigh;
Somewhat in sadness, but pleased in the main
Till this oracular couplet met his eye
Astounded: *Cupid, I do thee defy!*
It was too much. He shrunk back in his chair,
Grew pale as death, and fainted—very nigh.
"Pho! nonsense!" exclaimed Hum, "now don't despair:
She does not mean it, really. Cheer up, hearty—there!

"And listen to my words. You say you won't,
On any terms, marry Miss Bellanaine;
It goes against your conscience—good! Well, don't.
You say you love a mortal. I would fain
Persuade your honour's highness to refrain
From peccadilloes. But, Sire, as I say,
What good would that do? And, to be more plain,
You would do me a mischief some odd day,
Cut off my ears and hands, or head, too, by my fay!

"Besides, manners forbid that I should pass any
Vile strictures on the conduct of a prince
Who should indulge his genius, if he has any,
Not, like a subject, foolish matters mince.
Now I think on 't, perhaps I could convince
Your Majesty there is no crime at all
In loving pretty little Bertha, since
She's very delicate,—not over tall,—
A fairy's hand, and in the waist why—very small."

"Ring the repeater, gentle Hum!" " 'Tis five,"
Said gentle Hum; "the nights draw in apace;
The little birds, I hear, are all alive;
I see the dawning touched upon your face;
Shall I put out the candles, please your Grace?"
"Do put them out, and, without more ado,
Tell me how I may that sweet girl embrace,—
How you can bring her to me." "That's for you,
Great Emperor! to adventure, like a lover true."

"I fetch her?"—"Yes, an't like your Majesty;
And as she would be frightened wide awake

To travel such a distance through the sky,
Use of some soft manœuvre you must make,
For your convenience and her dear nerves' sake;
Nice way would be to bring her in a swoon,
Anon, I'll tell what course were best to take;
You must away this morning."   "Hum! so soon?"
"Sire, you must be in Kent by twelve o'clock at noon."

At this great Cæsar started on his feet,
Lifted his wings, and stood attentive-wise.
"Those wings to Canterbury you must beat,
If you hold Bertha as a worthy prize.
Look in the Almanack—*Moore* never lies—
April the twenty-fourth,—this coming day,
Now breathing its new bloom upon the skies,
Will end in St. Mark's Eve;—you must away,
For on that eve alone can you the maid convey."

Then the magician solemnly 'gan to frown,
So that his frost-white eyebrows, beetling low,
Shaded his deep green eyes and wrinkles brown
Plaited upon his furnace-scorchèd brow:
Forth from his hood that hung his neck below,
He lifted a bright casket of pure gold,
Touched a spring-lock, and there in wool or snow,
Charmed into ever freezing, lay an old
And legend-leavèd book, mysterious to behold.

"Take this same book,—it will not bite you, Sire;
There, put it underneath your royal arm;
Though it's a pretty weight it will not tire.
But rather on your journey keep you warm:
This is the magic, this the potent charm,
That shall drive Bertha to a fainting fit!
When the time comes don't feel the least alarm,
But lift her from the ground, and swiftly flit
Back to your palace.   .   .   .

"What shall I do with that same book?"   "Why, merely
Lay it on Bertha's table, close beside
Her work-box, and 'twill help your purpose dearly;
I say no more."   "Or good or ill betide,

Through the wide air to Kent this morn I glide!"
Exclaimed the Emperor.   "When I return,
Ask what you will,—I'll give you my new bride!
And take some more wine, Hum;—O heavens! I burn
To be upon the wing!   Now, now that minx I spurn!"

"Leave her to me," rejoined the magian:
"But how shall I account, illustrious fay!
For thine imperial absence?   Pho! I can
Say you are very sick, and bar the way
To your so loving courtiers for one day;
If either of their two archbishops' graces
Should talk of extreme unction, I shall say
You do not like cold pig with Latin phrases,
Which never should be used but in alarming cases."

"Open the window, Hum!   I'm ready now!
"Zooks!" exclaimed Hum, as up the sash he drew,
"Behold your Majesty, upon the brow
Of yonder hill, what crowds of people!"   "Where?"
The monster's always after something new,"
Returned his Highness, "they are piping hot
To see my pigsney Bellanaine.   Hum! do
Tighten my belt a little,—so, so,—not
Too tight,—the book!—my wand!—so, nothing is forgot."

"Wounds! how they shout!" said Hum, "and there,—
          see, see!
Th' ambassador's returned from Pigmio!
The morning's very fine,—uncommonly!
See, past the skirts of yon white cloud they go,
Tingeing it with soft crimsons!   Now below
Those sable-pointed heads of firs and pines
They dip, move on, and with them moves a glow
Along the forest side!   Now amber lines
Reach the hill top, and now throughout the valley shines."

"Why, Hum, you're getting quite poetical!
Those *nows* you managed in a special style."
"If ever you have leisure, Sire, you shall
See scraps of mine will make it worth your while,
Tit-bits for Phœbus!—yes, you well may smile.

Hark! hark! the bells!"   "A little further yet,
Good Hum, and let me view this mighty coil."
Then the great Emperor full graceful set
His elbow for a prop, and snuffed his mignonette.

The morn is full of holiday; loud bells
With rival clamours ring from every spire;
Cunningly-stationed music dies and swells
In echoing places; when the winds respire,
Light flags stream out like gauzy tongues of fire;
A metropolitan murmur, lifeful, warm,
Comes from the northern suburbs; rich attire
Freckles with red and gold the moving swarm;
While here and there clear trumpets blow a keen alarm.

And now the fairy escort was seen clear,
Like the old pageant of Aurora's train,
Above a pearl-built minster, hovering near;
First wily Crafticant, the chamberlain,
Balanced upon his grey-grown pinions twain,
His slender wand officially revealed;
Then black gnomes scattering sixpences like rain;
Then pages three and three; and next, slave-held,
The Imaian 'scutcheon bright,—one mouse in argent field.

Gentlemen pensioners next; and after them,
A troop of wingèd Janizaries flew;
Then slaves, as presents bearing many a gem;
Then twelve physicians fluttering two and two;
And next a chaplain in a cassock new;
Then Lords in waiting; then (what head not reels
For pleasure?)—the fair Princess in full view,
Borne upon wings,—and very pleased she feels
To have such splendour dance attendance at her heels.

For there was more magnificence behind:
She waved her handerchief.   "Ah, very grand!"
Cried Elfinan, and closed the window-blind;
"And, Hum, we must not shilly-shally stand,—
Adieu! adieu!   I'm off for Angle-land!
I say, old Hocus, have you such a thing
About you,—feel your pockets, I command,—

I want, this instant, an invisible ring,—
Thank you, old mummy!—now securely I take wing."

Then Elfinan swift vaulted from the floor,
And lighted graceful on the window-sill;
Under one arm the magic book he bore,
The other he could wave about at will;
Pale was his face, he still looked very ill:
He bowed at Bellanaine, and said—"Poor Bell!
Farewell! farewell! and if for ever! still
For ever fare thee well!"—and then he fell
A laughing!—snapped his fingers!—shame it is to tell!

"By 'r Lady! he is gone!" cries Hum, "and I—
(I own it)—have made too free with his wine;
Old Crafticant will smoke me.   By-the-bye!
This room is full of jewels as a mine.
Dear valuable creatures, how ye shine!
Sometime to-day I must contrive a minute,
If Mercury propitiously incline,
To examine his scrutoire, and see what's in it,
For of superfluous diamonds I as well may thin it.

"The Emperor's horrid bad; yes, that's my cue!"
Some histories say that this was Hum's last speech;
That, being fuddled, he went reeling through
The corridor, and scarce upright could reach
The stair-head; that being glutted as a leech,
And used, as we ourselves have just now said,
To manage stairs reversely, like a peach
Too ripe, he fell, being puzzled in his head
With liquor and the staircase: verdict—*found stone dead*.

This is a falsehood Crafticanto treats;
And as his style is of strange elegance,
Gentle and tender, full of soft conceits,
(Much like our Boswell's), we will take a glance
At his sweet prose, and, if we can, make dance
His woven periods into careless rhyme;
O, little faery Pegasus! rear—prance—
Trot round the quarto—ordinary time!
March, little Pegasus, with pawing hoof sublime!

Well, let us see,—*tenth book and chapter nine*,—
Thus Crafticant pursues his diary :—
"'Twas twelve o'clock at night, the weather fine,
Latitude thirty-six ; our scouts descry
A flight of starlings making rapidly
Towards Thibet.   Mem. :—birds fly in the night ;
From twelve to half-past—wings not fit to fly
For a thick fog—The Princess sulky quite ;
Called for an extra shawl, and gave her nurse a bite.

"Five minutes before one—brought down a moth
With my new double-barrel—stewed the thighs
And made a very tolerable broth—
Princess turned dainty, to our great surprise,
Altered her mind, and thought it very nice :
Seeing her pleasant, tried her with a pun,
She frowned ; a monstrous owl across us flies
About this time,—a sad old figure of fun ;
Bad omen—this new match can't be a happy one.

"From two to half-past, dusky way we made,
Above the plains of Gobi,—desert, bleak ;
Beheld afar off, in the hooded shade
Of darkness, a great mountain (strange to speak),
Spitting, from forth its sulphur-baken peak,
A fan-shaped burst of blood-red, arrowy fire,
Turbaned with smoke, which still away did reek,
Solid and black from that eternal pyre,
Upon the laden winds that scantly could respire.

"Just upon three o'clock a falling star
Created an alarm among our troop,
Killed a man-cook, a page, and broke a jar,
A tureen, and three dishes, at one swoop,
Then passing by the Princess, singed her hoop :
Could not conceive what Coralline was at,
She clapped her hands three times and cried out
      'Whoop,'
Some strange Imaian custom.   A large bat
Came sudden 'fore my face, and brushed against my hat.

"Five minutes thirteen seconds after three,
Far in the west a mighty fire broke out,

Conjectured, on the instant, it might be,
　The city of Balk—'twas Balk beyond all doubt :
A griffin, wheeling here and there about,
　Kept reconnoitring us—doubled our guard—
Lighted our torches, and kept up a shout,
　Till he sheered off—the Princess very scared—
And many on their marrowbones for death prepared.

"At half-past three arose the cheerful moon—
　Bivouacked for four minutes on a cloud—
Where from the earth we heard a lively tune
　Of tambourines and pipes, serene and loud,
　While on a flowery lawn a brilliant crowd
Cinque-parted danced, some half-asleep reposed
　Beneath the green-faned cedars, some did shroud
In silken tents, and 'mid light fragrance dozed,
Or on the open turf their soothèd eyelids closed.

"Dropped my gold watch, and killed a kettledrum—
　It went for apoplexy—foolish folks !—
Left it to pay the piper—a good sum—
　(I've got a conscience, maugre people's jokes)
　To scrape a little favour ; 'gan to coax
Her Highness' pug-dog—got a sharp rebuff—
　She wished a game at whist—make three revokes—
Turned from myself, her partner, in a huff ;
His Majesty will know her temper time enough.

"She cried for chess—I played a game with her—
　Castled her King with such a vixen look,
It bodes ill to his Majesty—(refer
　To the second chapter of my fortieth book,
　And see what hoity-toity airs she took).
At half-past four the morn essayed to beam—
　Saluted, as we passed, an early rook—
The Princess fell asleep, and, in her dream,
Talked of one Master Hubert, deep in her esteem.

"About this time,—making delightful way,—
　Shed a quill-feather from my larboard wing—
Wished, trusted, hoped 'twas no sign of decay—
　Thank Heaven, I'm hearty yet !—'twas no such thing :—
　At five the golden light began to spring,
With fiery shudder through the bloomèd east ;

At six we heard Panthea's churches ring—
The city all his unhived swarms had cast,
To watch our grand approach, and hail us as we passed.

" As flowers turn their faces to the sun,
So on our flight with hungry eyes they gaze,
And, as we shaped our course, this, that way run,
With mad-cap pleasure, or hand-clasped amaze ;
Sweet in the air a mild-toned music plays,
And progresses through its own labyrinth ;
Buds gathered from the green spring's middle-days,
They scattered,—daisy, primrose, hyacinth,—
Or round white columns wreathed from capital to plinth.

" Onward we floated o'er the panting streets,
That seemed throughout with upheld faces paved ;
Look where we will, our bird's-eye vision meets
Legions of holiday ; bright standards waved,
And fluttering ensigns emulously craved
Our minute's glance ; a busy thunderous roar,
From square to square, among the buildings raved,
As when the sea, at flow, gluts up once more
The craggy hollowness of a wild reefèd shore.

" And ' Bellanaine for ever ! ' shouted they ;
While that fair Princess, from her wingèd chair,
Bowed low with high demeanour, and, to pay
Their new-blown loyalty with guerdon fair,
Still emptied, at meet distance, here and there,
A plenty horn of jewels. And here I
(Who wish to give the devil her due) declare
Against that ugly piece of calumny,
Which calls them Highland pebble-stones, not worth a fly

" Still ' Bellanaine ! ' they shouted, while we glide
'Slant to a light Ionic portico,
The city's delicacy, and the pride
Of our Imperial Basilic ; a row
Of lords and ladies, on each hand, make show
Submissive of knee-bent obeisance,
All down the steps ; and as we entered, lo !
The strangest sight, the most unlooked-for chance—
All things turned topsy-turvy in a devil's dance.

"'Stead of his anxious Majesty and court
At the open doors, with wide saluting eyes,
Congées and scrape graces of every sort,
And all the smooth routine of gallantries,
Was seen, to our immoderate surprise,
A motley crowd thick gathered in the hall,
Lords, scullions, deputy-scullions, with wild cries
Stunning the vestibule from wall to wall,
Where the Chief Justice on his knees and hands doth crawl.

" Counts of the palace, and the state purveyor
Of moth's down, to make soft the royal beds,
The Common Council and my fool Lord Mayor
Marching a-row, each other slipshod treads ;
Powdered bag-wigs and ruffy-tuffy heads
Of cinder wenches meet and soil each other ;
Toe crushed with heel ill-natured fighting breeds,
Frill-rumpling elbows brew up many a bother,
And fists in the short ribs keep up the yell and pother.

" A Poet, mounted on the Court-Clown's back,
Rode to the Princess swift with spurring heels,
And close into her face, with rhyming clack,
Began a Prothalamion ;—she reels,
She falls, she faints ! while laughter peals
Over her woman's weakness.   'Where,' cried I,
'Where is his Majesty ?'   No person feels
Inclined to answer ; wherefore instantly
I plunged into the crowd to find him or to die.

" Jostling my way I gained the stairs, and ran
To the first landing, where, incredible !
I met, far gone in liquor, Hum,"——
                                        So far so well,—
For we have proved the Mago never fell
Down stairs on Crafticanto's evidence ;
And therefore duly shall proceed to tell,
Plain in our own original mood and tense,
The sequel of this day, though labour 'tis immense !

.   .   .   .

NO MORE WAS WRITTEN

KING STEPHEN

ACT I

SCENE I.—*Field of Battle.*

Alarum. Enter King STEPHEN, KNIGHTS, *and Soldiers*

Stephen. If shame can on a soldier's vein-swoll'n front
Spread deeper crimson than the battle's toil,
Blush in your casing helmets ! for see, see !
Yonder my chivalry, my pride of war,
Wrenched with an iron hand from firm array,
Are routed loose about the plashy meads,
Of honour forfeit.   O that my known voice
Could reach your dastard ears, and fright you more !
Fly, cowards, fly !   Gloucester is at your backs !
Throw your slack bridles o'er the flurried manes,
Ply well the rowel with faint trembling heels,
Scampering to death at last !

    1st Knight.   The enemy
Bears his flaunt standard close upon their rear.

    2nd Knight. Sure of a bloody prey, seeing the fens
Will swamp them girth-deep.

    Stephen.   Over head and ears.
No matter !   'Tis a gallant enemy ;
How like a comet he goes streaming on.
But we must plague him in the flank,—hey, friends ?
We are well breathed—follow !

Enter Earl BALDWIN *and Soldiers, as defeated*

    Stephen.   De Redvers !
What is the monstrous bugbear that can fright
Baldwin ?

    Baldwin. No scarecrow, but the fortunate star
Of boisterous Chester, whose fell truncheon now
Points level to the goal of victory.

This way he comes, and if you would maintain
Your person unaffronted by vile odds,
Take horse, my Lord.
    Stephen.   And which way spur for life?
Now I thank heaven I am in the toils,
That soldiers may bear witness how my arm
Can burst the meshes. Not the eagle more
Loves to beat up against a tyrannous blast,
Than I to meet the torrent of my foes.
This is a brag—be 't so,—but if I fall,
Carve it upon my 'scutcheoned sepulchre.
On, fellow soldiers! Earl of Redvers, back!
Not twenty Earls of Chester shall brow-beat
The diadem.   [*Exeunt. Alarum.*

SCENE II.—*Another part of the Field.*

Trumpets sounding a Victory. *Enter* GLOUCESTER,
KNIGHTS, *and Forces*

    Gloucester. Now may we lift our bruisèd visors up
And take the flattering freshness of the air,
While the wild din of battle dies away
Into times past, yet to be echoed sure——
In the silent pages of our chroniclers.
    1*st Knight.* Will Stephen's death be marked there, my
        good Lord,
Or that we give him lodging in yon towers?
    Gloucester. Fain would I know the great usurper's fate.

Enter two CAPTAINS *severally*

    1*st Captain.* My Lord!
    2*nd Captain.* Most noble Earl!
    1*st Captain.* The King——
    2*nd Captain.*   The Empress greets——
    Gloucester. What of the King?
    1*st Captain.*   He sole and lone maintains
A hopeless bustle 'mid our swarming arms,
And with a nimble savageness attacks,
Escapes, makes fiercer onset, then anew
Eludes death, giving death to most that dare

Trespass within the circuit of his sword!
He must by this have fallen. Baldwin is taken;
And for the Duke of Bretagne, like a stag
He flies, for the Welsh beagles to hunt down.
God save the Empress!

Gloucester.　　　　　　Now our dreaded Queen:
What message from her Highness?

2nd Captain.　　　　　　Royal Maud
From the thronged towers of Lincoln hath looked down,
Like Pallas from the walls of Ilion,
And seen her enemies havocked at her feet.
She greets most noble Gloucester from her heart,
Entreating him, his captains, and brave knights,
To grace a banquet. The high city gates
Are envious which shall see your triumph pass;
The streets are full of music.

Enter 2ND KNIGHT

Gloucester.　　　　　　Whence come you?

2nd Knight. From Stephen, my good Prince—Stephen!
　　　　Stephen!

Gloucester. Why do you make such echoing of his name?

2nd Knight. Because I think, my Lord, he is no man,
But a fierce demon, 'nointed safe from wounds,
And misbaptizèd with a Christian name.

Gloucester. A mighty soldier!—Does he still hold out?

2nd Knight. He shames our victory. His valour still
Keeps elbow-room amid our eager swords,
And holds our bladed falchions all aloof.
His gleaming battle-axe, being slaughter-sick,
Smote on the morion of a Flemish knight,
Broke short in his hand; upon the which he flung
The heft away with such a vengeful force
It paunched the Earl of Chester's horse, who then
Spleen-hearted came in full career at him.

Gloucester. Did no one take him at a vantage then?

2nd Knight. Three then with tiger leap upon him flew,
Whom with his sword swift drawn and nimbly held,
He stung away again, and stood to breathe,
Smiling. Anon upon him rushed once more
A throng of foes, and in this renewed strife,
My sword met his and snapped off at the hilt.

Gloucester. Come, lead me to this man—and let us move
In silence, not insulting his sad doom
With clamorous trumpets. To the Empress bear
My salutation as befits the time.

[*Exeunt* GLOUCESTER *and Forces.*

SCENE III.—*The Field of Battle. Enter* STEPHEN,
unharmed.

Stephen. Another sword! And what if I could seize
One from Bellona's gleaming armoury,
Or choose the fairest of her sheavèd spears!
Where are my enemies? Here, close at hand,
Here come the testy brood. O, for a sword!
I'm faint—a biting sword! A noble sword!
A hedge-stake—or a ponderous stone to hurl
With brawny vengeance, like the labourer Cain.
Come on! Farewell my kingdom, and all hail
Thou superb, plumed, and helmeted renown!
All hail! I would not truck this brilliant day
To rule in Pylos with a Nestor's beard—
Come on!

Enter DE KAIMS *and* KNIGHTS

De Kaims. Is 't madness, or a hunger after death,
That makes thee thus unarmed throw taunts at us?
Yield, Stephen, or my sword's point dips in
The gloomy current of a traitor's heart.

Stephen. Do it, De Kaims, I will not budge an inch.

De Kaims. Yes, of thy madness thou shalt take the
meed.

Stephen. Darest thou?

De Kaims. How, dare, against a man disarmed?

Stephen. What weapons has the lion but himself?
Come not near me, De Kaims, for by the price
Of all the glory I have won this day,
Being a king, I will not yield alive
To any but the second man of the realm,
Robert of Gloucester.

De Kaims.   Thou shalt vail to me.

Stephen. Shall I, when I have sworn against it, sir?
Thou think'st it brave to take a breathing king,

That, on a court-day bowed to haughty Maud,
The awêd presence-chamber may be bold
To whisper, There's the man who took alive
Stephen—me—prisoner.   Certes, De Kaims,
The ambition is a noble one.

    De Kaims.   'Tis true.
And, Stephen, I must compass it.

    Stephen.   No, no,
Do not tempt me to throttle you on the gorge,
Or with my gauntlet crush your hollow breast,
Just when your knighthood is grown ripe and full
For lordship.

    A Soldier. Is an honest yeoman's spear
Of no use at a need?   Take that.

    Stephen.   Ah, dastard!

    De Kaims. What, you are vulnerable! my prisoner!

    Stephen. No, not yet.   I disclaim it, and demand
Death as a sovereign right unto a king
Who 'sdains to yield to any but his peer,
If not in title, yet in noble deeds,
The Earl of Gloucester.   Stab to the hilt, De Kaims,
For I will never by mean hands be led
From this so famous field.   Do you hear!   Be quick!

          [*Trumpets. Enter the Earl of* CHESTER *and
                      Knights.*

SCENE IV.—*A Presence Chamber.   Queen* MAUD *in a
    Chair of State, the Earls of* GLOUCESTER *and*
    CHESTER, *Lords, Attendants.*

    Maud. Gloucester, no more.   I will behold that
           Boulogne:
Set him before me.   Not for the poor sake
Of regal pomp and a vain-glorious hour,
As thou with wary speech, yet near enough,
Hast hinted.

    Gloucester. Faithful counsel have I given;
If wary, for your Highness' benefit.

    Maud. The Heavens forbid that I should not think so,
For by thy valour have I won this realm
Which by thy wisdom I will ever keep.

To sage advisers let me ever bend
A meek attentive ear, so that they treat
Of the wide kingdom's rule and government,
Not trenching on our actions personal.
Advised, not schooled, I would be; and henceforth
Spoken to in clear, plain, and open terms,
Not side-ways sermoned at.

 Gloucester.   Then, in plain terms,
Once more for the fallen king—

 Maud.   Your pardon, brother,
I would no more of that; for, as I said,
'Tis not for worldly pomp I wish to see
The rebel, but as dooming judge to give
A sentence something worthy of his guilt.

 Gloucester. If 't must be so, I'll bring him to your
  presence.   [*Exit* GLOUCESTER.

 Maud. A meaner summoner might do as well.
My Lord of Chester, is 't true what I hear
Of Stephen of Boulogne, our prisoner,
That he, as a fit penance for his crimes,
Eats wholesome, sweet, and palatable food
Off Gloucester's golden dishes—drinks pure wine,
Lodges soft?

 Chester. More than that, my gracious Queen,
Has angered me. The noble Earl, methinks,
Full soldier as he is, and without peer
In counsel, dreams too much among his books.
It may read well, but sure 'tis out of date
To play the Alexander with Darius.

 Maud. Truth! I think so. By Heavens, it shall not last!

 Chester. It would amaze your Highness now to mark
How Gloucester overstrains his courtesy
To that crime-loving rebel, that Boulogne——

 Maud. That ingrate!

 Chester.   For whose vast ingratitude
To our late sovereign lord, your noble sire,
The generous Earl condoles in his mishaps,
And with a sort of lackeying friendliness
Talks off the mighty frowning from his brow,
Woos him to hold a duet in a smile,
Or, if it please him, play an hour at chess——

 Maud. A perjured slave!

Chester.   And for his perjury,
Gloucester has fit rewards—nay, I believe,
He sets his bustling household's wits at work
For flatteries to ease this Stephen's hours,
And make a heaven of his purgatory;
Adorning bondage with the pleasant gloss
Of feasts and music, and all idle shows
Of indoor pageantry; while syren whispers,
Predestined for his ear, 'scape as half-checked
From lips the courtliest and the rubiest
Of all the realm, admiring of his deeds.
  Maud. A frost upon his summer!
  Chester.   A queen's nod
Can make his June December.   Here he comes.

            .   .   .   .

THE END

LETCHWORTH
THE TEMPLE PRESS
PRINTERS

EVERYMAN,
I·WILL·GO·WITH
THEE,
&·BE·THY·GVIDE
IN·THY·MOST·NEED
TO·GO·BY·THY·SIDE

2044

821
KEA

RKL
19 05